FROMMER'S
EasyGuide
TO

S0-AZG-131

LOS ANGELES & SAN DIEGO

By
Christine Delsol & Maribeth Mellin

Easy Guides are ✦ Quick To Read ✦ Light To Carry
✦ For Expert Advice ✦ In All Price Ranges

FrommerMedia LLC

JAN 2 8 2016

Published by
FROMMER MEDIA LLC

ISBN 978-1-62887-160-9 (paper), 978-1-62887-161-6 (e-book)

Editorial Director and Editor: Pauline Frommer
Production Editor: Donna Wright
Cartographer: Roberta Stockwell
Cover Designer: Howard Grossman

For information on our other products or services, see www.frommers.com.

Frommer Media LLC also publishes its books in a variety of electronic formats. Some content that appears in print may not be available in electronic formats.

Manufactured in the United States of America

5 4 3 2 1

AN IMPORTANT NOTE

The world is a dynamic place. Hotels change ownership, restaurants hike their prices, museums alter their opening hours, and busses and trains change their routings. And all of this can occur in the several months after our authors have visited, inspected, and written about, these hotels, restaurants, museums and transportation services. Though we have made valiant efforts to keep all our information fresh and up-to-date, some few changes can inevitably occur in the periods before a revised edition of this guidebook is published. So please bear with us if a tiny number of the details in this book have changed. Please also note that we have no responsibility or liability for any inaccuracy or errors or omissions, or for inconvenience, loss, damage, or expenses suffered by anyone as a result of assertions in this guide.

CONTENTS

ABOUT THE AUTHORS

Christine Delsol became immersed in Southern California culture at a tender age during summers with her Los Angeles cousins and has spent an inordinate portion of her adult life traveling I-5 between her Northern California home and L.A. She has spent most of her career in newspapers, including 8 years as a travel editor at the *San Francisco Chronicle*. She has won an Associated Press writing award, two Lowell Thomas awards from the American Society of Travel Writers, and Mazatlán's Golden Deer Award. She is the author of *Pauline Frommer's Guide to Cancún & the Yucatán* and co-author of *Frommer's Mexico* and *Frommer's Cancún & the Yucatán*. She still writes frequently for the *Chronicle's* travel section and contributes monthly travel columns on California and Mexico to its website, SFGate.com. She lives in the San Francisco Bay Area with her husband and has an absurdly well-traveled 27-year-old daughter.

Maribeth Mellin is an award-winning journalist and photographer based in San Diego, CA. She has been awarded the prestigious Pluma de Plata, Mexico's highest award for travel writing. In addition, her articles on medical, social, and legal issues have garnered numerous awards. Mellin has authored several travel books and her articles and photos have appeared in the *U-T San Diego, Los Angeles Times, Dallas Morning News, Endless Vacation Magazine, the San Francisco Chronicle,* and other publications. She also has contributed to multiple websites including Concierge.com and TravelCNN.com. When not traveling the globe, she enjoys time at home with her husband near the beach in San Diego.

ABOUT THE FROMMER TRAVEL GUIDES

For most of the past 50 years, Frommer's has been the leading series of travel guides in North America, accounting for as many as 24% of all guidebooks sold. I think I know why.

Though we hope our books are entertaining, we nevertheless deal with travel in a serious fashion. Our guidebooks have never looked on such journeys as a mere recreation, but as a far more important human function, a time of learning and introspection, an essential part of a civilized life. We stress the culture, lifestyle, history, and beliefs of the destinations we cover, and urge our readers to seek out people and new ideas as the chief rewards of travel.

We have never shied from controversy. We have, from the beginning, encouraged our authors to be intensely judgmental, critical—both pro and con—in their comments, and wholly independent. Our only clients are our readers, and we have triggered the ire of countless prominent sorts, from a tourist newspaper we called "practically worthless" (it unsuccessfully sued us) to the many rip-offs we've condemned.

And because we believe that travel should be available to everyone regardless of their incomes, we have always been cost-conscious at every level of expenditure. Though we have broadened our recommendations beyond the budget category, we insist that every lodging we include be sensibly priced. We use every form of media to assist our readers, and are particularly proud of our feisty daily website, the award-winning Frommers.com.

I have high hopes for the future of Frommer's. May these guidebooks, in all the years ahead, continue to reflect the joy of travel and the freedom that travel represents. May they always pursue a cost-conscious path, so that people of all incomes can enjoy the rewards of travel. And may they create, for both the traveler and the persons among whom we travel, a community of friends, where all human beings live in harmony and peace.

Arthur Frommer

THE BEST OF LOS ANGELES & SAN DIEGO

Angelenos know L.A. will never have the sophistication of Paris or the historical riches of Rome, but they lay claim to one of the most entertaining cities in the United States, if not the world. It really is warm and sunny most days of the year, movie stars actually do live and dine among regular folk, and you can't swing a smartphone without hitting an in-line skater at the beach.

San Diegans boast about their climate as well, but turn their backs on big-city woes. Blue skies are the norm and although traffic has increased, it's still possible to drive several miles without coming to a car-clogging halt. Laid back, mellow, and chill to the max, San Diegans surf before work, swim toward sunsets, and enjoy Shakespeare and Santana under moonlit skies.

The choices for adventure, amusement, and illumination are endless. We've highlighted our favorites here to help guide you to the ultimate L.A. and San Diego experiences.

THE best OF LOS ANGELES

The Best Only-in-L.A. Experiences

- **Cruising the Coast:** Driving along the sunny coastline with your hair blowing in the warm wind is the quintessential Southern California experience—one that never loses its appeal, even for locals. See chapter 4 for ideas.
- **Basking at the Beach:** While you're tanning, you can watch a volleyball tournament at Hermosa Beach, take surf lessons at Manhattan Beach, or gawk at the world's vainest weightlifters pumping iron at Venice's Muscle Beach. See chapter 4.
- **Cruising Sunset Boulevard:** Yes, cruising is inevitably a major part of your stay, and this one provides a cross-section of everything L.A.: legendary clubs, studios, and hotels recognizable from movies and TV. You end up at Malibu's fabled beaches, where those classy "Baywatch" episodes were filmed. See p. 90.

o **Taking a Gourmet Picnic to the Hollywood Bowl:** A picnic laid out under the stars, a bottle of wine, and music from the Los Angeles Philharmonic or a national touring act, all played out in front of the majestic white Frank Lloyd Wright–designed band shell. Ah! . . . See p. 129.

o **Embarrassing Yourself on Ocean Front Walk:** Yes, you can station yourself at an outdoor cafe to observe the human carnival that defines Venice Beach from a safe distance, but you can't say you've "been there, done that" until you rent skates and see if you can hold your own with the tan and trim locals.

o **Dinner and a Movie at the Cemetery:** Take a picnic basket to the **Hollywood Forever Cemetery** (p. 132) for a summer Saturday evening of classic cinema projected onto the mausoleum wall. The actors you're watching just might be lying at rest not far from where you're sitting. See p. 88.

o **Touring the Walt Disney Concert Hall:** This stunning feat of art and architecture is the crown jewel of a continually revitalizing Downtown. Architect Frank Gehry's curvaceous stainless-steel exterior, rivaling his Guggenheim masterpiece in Spain, houses one of the world's most acoustically perfect concert halls. See p. 101.

o **Auditioning to be a Game Show Contestant:** Bring your bubbliest personality, and you, too, might win fame and fortune on "Jeopardy," "The Price Is Right," or "Wheel of Fortune." (Set up the audition before you arrive in L.A.) See p. 112.

The Best Hotels

o **Best Seaside Grande Dame:** Staying at the impeccably restored **Casa del Mar,** built as an exclusive beach club in 1926, is reminiscent of touring a European palace. It's one of Santa Monica's only hotels right on the beach—panoramic ocean views in every room—in the middle of, yet insulated from, all the action. See p. 33.

o **Best Attitude-Free Beverly Hills Hideaway:** Small, discreet **L'Ermitage** has Hollywood stars streaming in through its private underground entrance, and movie execs making deals in the lobby's curtained nooks, but every guest is a VIP at this bastion of luxury. See p. 40.

o **Best Art Deco Masterpiece:** Rising 15 stories above Sunset Boulevard, the **Sunset Tower** is this former luxury apartment building captures the elegance of a more glamorous era that saw Hollywood royalty and reclusive Howard Hughes as tenants. See p. 50.

o **Best Arts & Crafts Retreat:** A soothing peaceful environment, with a Japanese garden inspired by the hotel's sumptuous Craftsman-era design, make **The Ambrose** in Santa Monica is a welcome escape from the fast-paced L.A. scene. The included parking, breakfast, bicycles, and car service in a London taxi are additional stress-fighters. See p. 37.

o **Best New England-Style B&B:** Ideal for couples or travelers needing a breather, the **Inn at Playa del Rey** delivers the slower pace and personal attention that only a bed-and-breakfast can. Just 10 minutes from LAX but a world away from L.A., it offers a one-of-a-kind natural setting within a bird preserve and luxury comforts—including view suites with a two-sided fireplace a jacuzzi for two. See p. 38.

o **Best Cheap Hollywood Digs:** Fashioned from a 1920s boarding house that sheltered many a Hollywood star early in their careers, the friendly **Orange Drive Hostel** is within steps of the Dolby Theatre and a block from Hollywood Boulevard, the Chinese Theatre, and the Walk of Fame. With period furniture, abundant windows, and Craftsman architectural details, it feels more like a B&B. See p. 51.

o **Best Old Hollywood Revival:** Shingled bungalows developed by Charlie Chaplin in the 1920s as hideaway for himself and his industry pals have been restored with impeccable period detail for duty as large, very private accommodations. With no front desk or restaurant, **The Charlie** is less like a hotel than a vacation home. Bungalows—all but one studio offering a full kitchen and private patio—are named after the stars known to have stayed or played in them. See p. 48.

o **Best Family-Friendly Resort:** The amenities at **Terranea Resort,** a sprawling, Mediterranean-style oceanfront resort in Rancho Palos Verdes, are unequaled in Los Angeles. It boasts huge rooms, six restaurants, a nine-hole golf course, multiple water sports, spa, and a water play area and kids club. See p. 36.

The Best Food

o **Best Modern Tapas:** Spanish celebrity chef José Andrés put L.A. on the dining map with his contrasting traditional and contemporary takes on tapas at **The Bazaar by José Andrés** in the glitzy-glam SLS Hotel in Beverly Hills. Innovative cocktails like margaritas with salt "air" are a revelation. See p. 60.

o **Best Steakhouse:** Every dish is extraordinary at Wolfgang Puck's **Cut**—from the Wagyu beef (American and Japanese) to the buttery marrow to the creamed spinach. See p. 63.

o **Best Celebrity Spotting:** Sigh. The staff won't treat YOU like a celebrity if you aren't one, but **The Ivy** (p. 67) is a mecca for boldfaced names. You're near guaranteed to spot a Julia Roberts, or at least a Goldie Hawn, over your meal. And if you can ignore the snooty service, you'll find the Italian fare here is quite delish.

o **Most Romantic Restaurant:** A French/Mediterranean charmer, **The Little Door** is hidden behind, well, a little door, on the edge of West Hollywood. Sit at the shaded patio amid the cascading bougainvillea while sipping champagne and savoring filo-wrapped pork, and you'd swear you're in Provence. See p. 67.

o **Best Museum Restaurant:** Ensconced in the Los Angeles County Museum of Art, **Ray's & Stark Bar** is hands down L.A.'s best museum restaurant/bar. The patio is adjacent to the famous lamppost installation, and the seasonal, Mediterranean-style food is top-notch. Even the cocktails are seasonal. See p. 94.

o **Best Rustic Restaurant:** A drive high into the hills above Malibu takes you to **Saddle Peak Lodge,** a timber-and-stone former hunting lodge adorned with Teddy-era antiques, a crackling fireplace, and antlers mounted on the wall. Where else can you dine on grilled elk tenderloin by candlelight? See p. 57.

o **Best Seafood:** By establishing itself as one of L.A.'s best seafood restaurants, **Water Grill** bolstered Downtown's bid to be taken seriously as a dining destination. See p. 73.

The Best Free Things to Do

o **Mulholland Drive:** Ride along the top of the mountain ridge that divides the Los Angeles basin and San Fernando Valley, passing homes with million-dollar views and stopping at pullouts to see the city splayed out at your feet. It's achingly romantic at night, when the lights twinkle below. See p. 92.

o **Evening Jazz Performances:** The Los Angeles County Museum of Art offers free jazz concerts every Friday evening April through November. It's the perfect coda to a satisfying day of art appreciation. See p. 135.

o **Free Museum Admission Days:** Nearly all of L.A.'s art galleries and museums are open free to the public one day of the week or month, and several never charge admission at all. See p. 103.

o **Hollywood Bowl Rehearsals:** It's not widely known, but the L.A. Philharmonic's morning rehearsals are open to the public most Tuesday and Thursday mornings in summer, at no charge. Bring coffee and doughnuts and enjoy. See p. 129.

o **Pay Respects at Cemeteries to the Stars:** Spend some downtime with Humphrey Bogart, Clark Gable, Marilyn Monroe, and all their famous pals at L.A.'s most enduring celebrity hangouts. Six public cemeteries showcase the final curtain calls of dozens of stars, from Rudolph Valentino and Al Jolson to Michael Jackson and Elizabeth Taylor. See p. 88.

o **Watching a Sitcom Taping:** Tickets are yours for the asking, and as an audience member you have a chance to wander the soundstage, marvel at the cheesy three-wall sets that look so real on TV, and witness the bloopers that never make it to broadcast (and are often far more entertaining than the script). See p. 111.

THE best OF SAN DIEGO

The Best Authentic Experiences

o **Lingering in Balboa Park:** San Diego's pride and joy never ceases to delight locals, who gather here for celebrations, picnics, exercise, and immersion in the arts. Nights are magical, with lights glowing on El Prado, blues drifting from a street musician's sax, and museums holding concerts, lectures, and parties. See p. 214.

o **Seeing the City from on High:** Bird's eye views of San Diego are different wherever you perch. In daylight, from cliff tops at **Cabrillo National Monument** (p. 228) the panorama takes in Navy bases, San Diego Bay, downtown, Coronado, and the horizon south to Mexico. At night, watch jetliners descend to the airport, seemingly skimming downtown's sparkling skyline from **Bertrand's at Mr. A's** (p. 200). **Mt. Soledad** (p. 232) offers the ultimate view of the coastline.

o **Catching the Perfect Sunset:** There's good reason for the name—**Sunset Cliffs** (p. 240) faces the horizon's ever-changing palette without obstructions. Bring a towel or beach chair and linger as vibrant colors streak the darkening sky.

o **Wiggling Your Toes in the Sand:** Seriously, how could you not spend time on the beach? Choose **Coronado Beach, La Jolla Shores,** or **Pacific Beach** for the wholesome family experience; **Mission Beach** for wild, rowdy partying; or **Ocean Beach** for laid-back funk and awesome surf. See beaches p. 240–241.

o **Conquering a New Sport:** Try balancing on a surfboard or paddleboard, kayaking amid seals, catching a sea bass, or captaining a Catamaran. See p. 238.

o **Applauding Under the Stars:** Absorb the bard's language during the **Globe's** (p. 252) outdoor summer Shakespeare festival, hum with the symphony during the **Summer Pops** (p. 252), or catch a concert by the bay at **Humphrey's** (p 253).

The Best Hotels

- **Crystal Pier Hotel:** Waves swish against pilings beneath cozy cottages at this quint-essential beach retreat perfect for families, romantics, and recluses. See p. 189.
- **Hotel del Coronado:** If I win the lottery, I'll give everyone I love at least one night in a balcony suite at this Victorian sandcastle. It's that special. See p. 195.
- **Lafayette Hotel:** Bypass downtown's chic hip hotels for this retro old-timer, where neighborhood artists and musicians gather for Sunday pool parties and live music plays outside and in. See p. 185.
- **La Valencia Hotel:** Step into La Jolla's blushing pink grande dame for a flash of the past, when guests wore seersucker suits and fancy dresses while sipping martinis in the sea-facing sale. Though the dress code is far more casual, the glamour remains. See p. 192.
- **Paradise Point Resort & Spa:** Families return annually to this sprawling tropical resort on Mission Bay. See p. 188.

The Best Food

- **Addison:** Dress to impress fellow diners, including international celebs and politi-cos, at the aptly named Grand Del Mar with acclaimed chef William Bradley's exquisite contemporary French cuisine. See p. 259.
- **George's at the Cove:** Choose between gourmet Californian in the serene dining room or casual bistro fare with jaw-dropping views of the cove on the terrace at this La Jolla institution. See p. 208.
- **Filippi's:** Join local multi-generational families joshing around and laughing over hearty pizzas and pastas—the kids will feel right at home. See p. 199.
- **Market:** Farm forays spark the chef's fertile imagination for inspired seasonal menus. Servers nail each description and expertly pair dishes with craft cocktails; you'll feel right at home in jeans or a suit. See p. 199.
- **Nine-Ten:** Jamaican jerk pork belly might seem odd on an "evolving California cuisine" menu, but Jason Knibb's take on tradition paired with Rachel King's deca-dent desserts delight discerning gourmands. See p. 209.

The Best Family Experiences

- **Balboa Park:** How could anyone grow bored in Balboa Park with the zoo, IMAX theater, museums featuring trains, planes, dinosaurs, playgrounds, carousel, and miniature train ride, as diversions? See p. 214.
- **San Diego Zoo:** You could return several times and still not see everything at this world-famous zoo. See p. 221.
- **Birch Aquarium at Scripps:** Learn about sea creatures at this excellent aquarium with more than 60 marine-life tanks (including a giant kelp forest), hands-on tide pool, and jaw-dropping ocean views. See p. 232.
- **Belmont Park:** It's not Coney Island, but this small amusement area keeps kids busy with rides, carny games, and wave machines. See p. 228.
- **Mission Bay:** Bring along a kite or Frisbee, rent a bike or skates, or simply slide and swing at this playground for all. See p. 240.
- **Animal Attractions:** With a lineup like the San Diego Zoo (p. 221), the San Diego Zoo Safari Park (p. 264), and SeaWorld (p. 230), it's easy to put together a memo-rable, animal-centric holiday.

SAN DIEGO'S best OUTDOOR EXPERIENCES

o **Catch Some Air:** Join an expert flyer on a ganglier at Torrey Pines Gliderport, and soar like a bird, no experience necessary. Sound terrifying? Watching is nearly as much fun. See p. 231.

o **Take a Hike:** Poised on a majestic cliff overlooking the Pacific, **The Torrey Pines State Reserve** protects the rarest pine tree in North America and has short trails that immerse hikers in a delicate and beautiful coastal environment. See p. 234.

o **Paddling with the Fishes:** The calm surfaces and clear waters of the San Diego–La Jolla Underwater Park are the ultimate spot for kayaking, snorkeling, or scuba diving. This ecological reserve features sea caves and vibrant marine life, including California's state fish, the electric-orange garibaldi. See p. 241.

o **Witnessing the Desert's Spring Fling:** Anza-Borrego Desert State Park's sandy brown landscape bursts into color in spring when a kaleidoscopic carpet of blooms blankets the desert floor. The 90-mile scenic drive through the mountains and down to the desert floor takes about 2 hours. See p. 266.

o **Cruising San Diego Bay:** Whether it's a weekend-brunch sightseeing tour, a chartered sailboat excursion, or just a water-taxi ride to Coronado, don't miss an opportunity to spend some time on San Diego Bay. Spanish conquistador Sebastian Vizcaino described it in 1602 as a "port which must be the best to be found in all the South Sea." See p. 256.

SUGGESTED ITINERARIES

L os Angeles alone covers so much territory and so many sights you can easily become overwhelmed. Add San Diego to the mix and decision-making just might take all the fun out of vacationing. But we've tried to make it easier to plan your trip by creating itineraries to ensure you get to see and do what matters most in what inevitably will be too short a visit. You'll likely find other things you want to do or see as you read about each city; use our itineraries as a base for your adventures. For longer visits, build on these using the suggestions in the following chapters.

ICONIC LOS ANGELES IN 1 DAY

I'll refrain from yelling "What were you thinking?" and just say that L.A. in a day requires an early start, stamina, and (you'll hear this a lot) a car. Using Sunset Boulevard and Pacific Coast Highway (PCH) as your main arteries between several L.A. icons gives you a broad overview of the L.A. microcosm (and often rivals the freeways for speed). ***Start:*** *E. Observatory Road off N. Vermont Canyon Road.*

---

1 Griffith Observatory ★★

Get to this longtime landmark on the south slope of Mount Hollywood when it opens. In addition to panoramic city and mountain views, you'll see the largest image of the universe ever produced, and peer at heavenly bodies through massive telescopes, day or night. See p. 88.

Return to N. Vermont Canyon Road, continue when it becomes N. Vermont Avenue, turn right on Los Feliz Boulevard, then left on N. Western to:

2 Sunset Boulevard & the Sunset Strip ★★★

Starting at the Saharan Motor Hotel, this is a crash course in what western L.A. is all about, in roughly an hour's drive (not including the detour you're going to take). The legendary boulevard takes you from kinda-seedy Hollywood to flamboyant West Hollywood, past Beverly Hills mansions and through tony Westside, Brentwood, and Pacific Palisades, where you'll catch PCH. See p. 90.

When you reach Sepulveda Boulevard (just before I-405/San Diego Fwy.) turn right and follow it to Getty Center Drive and the:

3 J. Paul Getty Museum at the Getty Center ★★★

Perched on a slope of the Santa Monica Mountains and swathed in Italian travertine marble, the Getty Center is remarkable, from its stunning postmodern design and enormous art collection (including van Gogh's "Irises") to its gorgeous landscaped gardens and postcard views of Los Angeles and the Pacific. Admission is free (though parking is not). See p. 83.

4 Lunch at Getty Center's Garden Terrace Cafe ☕ ★

One of several dining options at the Getty Center, the Garden Terrace Cafe serves lunch in a beautiful outdoor setting overlooking the Central Garden. You can also pick up a picnic lunch on the Plaza Level and head down to the flower-filled picnic area.

Backtrack to Sunset Boulevard and continue west; in Pacific Palisades, turn left on Temescal Canyon Road to Pacific Coast Highway and drive south along the ocean to:

5 Venice Beach's Ocean Front Walk ★★★

This crazy, pseudo-bohemian scene is a surreal assemblage of wild-eyed skaters, street performers, musclemen, apocalyptic evangelists, break dancers, stoned drummers, and schlock shops—a daily carnival that could only have developed in L.A. If you're feeling adventurous, rent some in-line skates and take your chances among the locals. Cap the day with a kingly sausage at Jody Maroni's (p. 60) on the beach, or venture inland to Joe's Restaurant (p. 58) for a more traditional meal.

ICONIC LOS ANGELES IN 2 DAYS

Your second day focuses on classic and backwoods Hollywood. You'll need advance reservations for the studio tour and the Hollywood Bowl (order a picnic dinner at least day ahead as well). **Start:** *Melrose Avenue between N. Gower and Van Ness.*

1 Paramount Pictures ★★★

Begin the day with a visit to the only major studio left in Hollywood. These hallowed grounds ooze filmmaking history, from the first "Cinderella" movie (a silent starring Mary Pickford) to the "Godfather" films, "Serpico," "Chinatown," and other movies from its 1960s and '70s heyday. What you'll see on the 2-hour behind-the-scenes tour depends on what's being filmed that day. See p. 112.

Right behind Paramount Pictures on Santa Monica Boulevard is the main entrance to:

2 Hollywood Forever Cemetery ★★★

The "resting place of Hollywood immortals" is the friendliest of several cemeteries where celebrities remain forever at rest. Pick up a map of the stars' burial sites and roam the meticulously manicured grounds to pay respects to Rudolph Valentino, Peter Lorre, Jayne Mansfield, and many more—all under a splendid view of the Hollywood sign. See p. 132.

Drive west on Santa Monica Boulevard and turn right on Vine Street to:

3 The Hungry Cat ★★ ☕

Have a leisurely lunch at one of the most straightforward, and affordable, of L.A.'s new breed of seafood restaurants, focused on inventive but accessible fish preparations. A chicken sandwich and a burger are available for non-fish eaters. See p. 69.

Continue north on Vine Street, turn left on Franklin, north onto N. Highland; veer left onto N. Cahuenga and turn left on Cahuenga Access Road, then left again onto:

4 Mulholland Drive ★★

This winding, scenic road, dotted with palatial homes of people who make way too much money, follows Hollywood Hills' peaks and canyons. It offers amazing views of L.A. and the San Fernando Valley, but the real surprise is how much natural beauty this urban behemoth contains. Two fantastic view overlooks appear within the first several miles; continue as far as time allows before returning to your starting point. See p. 92.

When you return to Cahuenga, head south on I-405, and just a few miles down the freeway on your right side is the exit for the:

5 Hollywood Bowl ★★★

Pick up your picnic dinner (ordered the previous day) and join in one of L.A.'s grandest traditions: dining on the lawn while watching a live performance by the L.A. Philharmonic or a variety of other performances under the stars on a warm night. See p. 129.

ICONIC LOS ANGELES IN 3 DAYS

Architectural landmarks from the 19th, 20th, and 21st centuries and a wealth of museums are the focus here, along with an optional spin through Hollywood's most famous tourist attractions to close out the day. ***Start:*** *S. Grand Avenue at 1st Street.*

1 Walt Disney Concert Hall ★★★

The strikingly beautiful Walt Disney Concert Hall is a masterpiece of design by renowned architect Frank Gehry. Even if you don't have the slightest interest in architecture, your first sight of the impossibly curvaceous stainless-steel exterior will rock you. Get there by 10am to take the excellent 45-minute self-guided audio tour, narrated by actor John Lithgow (check the website first for days when tours are unavailable). See p. 101.

Leave your car at the concert hall and walk east on W. 2nd Street for 3 blocks, turn right to W. 3rd Street and the:

2 Bradbury Building ★★

L.A.'s oldest commercial building, a National Historic Landmark built in 1893, is a wonder of Victorian architecture. Behind its stolid Romanesque exterior is a marvelous light-flooded courtyard, open cage elevators, marble stairs, and wrought-iron railings, beloved of photographers and filmmakers. It has been featured in "Blade Runner," "DOA," "Chinatown," "(500) Days of Summer," and many other movies, as well as countless TV shows and music videos. Roam at will through the ground-floor corridor and staircase landings that are open to the public. See p. 96.

Continue on Broadway to E. 5th Street, turn right and walk 3½ blocks to:

3 Cafe Pinot 🍽

Celebrity chef Joachim Splichal's Patina in the Disney Concert Hall is open only for dinner, but this less formal restaurant serves his California/French cuisine in the garden of the

Los Angeles Itineraries

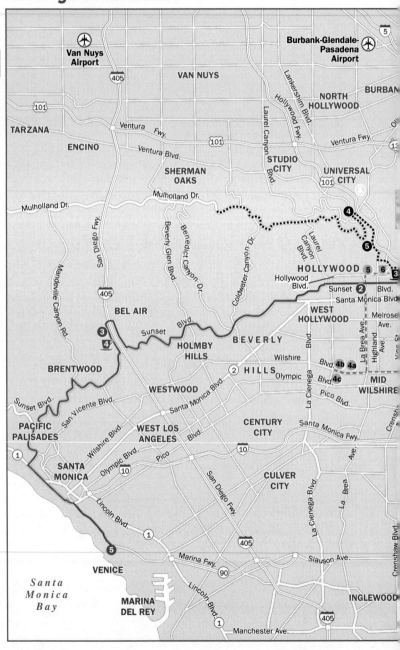

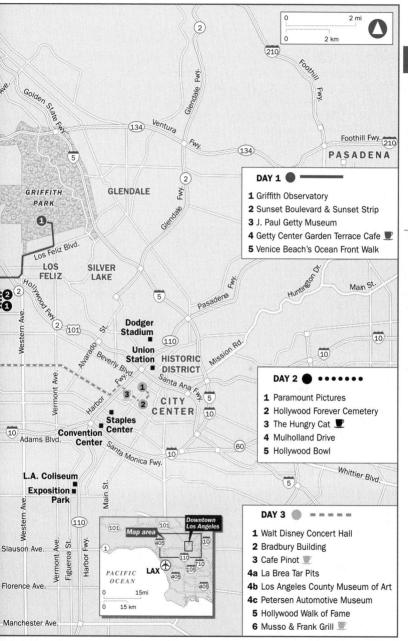

DAY 1 ●━━━━

1 Griffith Observatory
2 Sunset Boulevard & Sunset Strip
3 J. Paul Getty Museum
4 Getty Center Garden Terrace Cafe ☕
5 Venice Beach's Ocean Front Walk

DAY 2 ● ● ● ● ● ● ●

1 Paramount Pictures
2 Hollywood Forever Cemetery
3 The Hungry Cat ☕
4 Mulholland Drive
5 Hollywood Bowl

DAY 3 ● ▬ ▬ ▬ ▬

1 Walt Disney Concert Hall
2 Bradbury Building
3 Cafe Pinot ☕
4a La Brea Tar Pits
4b Los Angeles County Museum of Art
4c Petersen Automotive Museum
5 Hollywood Walk of Fame
6 Musso & Frank Grill ☕

splendid 1926 L.A. Central Library. The walk will give you a glimpse of the rapidly revitalizing neighborhood. See p. 73.

Backtrack on E. 5th Street about 200 feet and turn left through Hope Place to reach S. Hope Street, and continue to The Walt Disney Concert Hall to pick up your car. Turn right on S. Grand Avenue, right again on Wilshire Boulevard and drive 6 miles to:

4 Museum Row

Several museums vie for your attention in these few blocks of L.A.'s Miracle Mile: **La Brea Tar Pits and Page Museum ★★** (p. 93), the gooey asphalt swamp that has been spitting out Ice Age fossils ever since excavation began in 1906; **The Los Angeles County Museum of Art ★★★** (p. 93), with seven buildings of masterpieces from ancient times through the present; and the **Petersen Automotive Museum ★★** (p. 96), which puts L.A.'s infatuation with the automobile into historic perspective. If you choose LACMA, figure on the whole afternoon; you could probably fit the other two in, especially if you forgo the **Walk of Fame,** below. See p. 89.

Drive west on Wilshire Boulevard to S. Fairfax Ave and turn right. Continue 2½ miles to Hollywood Boulevard and the:

5 Hollywood Walk of Fame ★

Starting at the west end of the world's most famous sidewalk, begin by comparing your hands and feet to the imprints left by Humphrey Bogart or Marilyn Monroe at the entrance court to Grauman's Chinese Theatre **★★** (now actually TCL, but no one knows or cares). More than 2,400 celebrities been honored here, but you won't recognize half the names. You can buy a map listing every star's address, or get the "Walk of Fame" app for your smartphone. See p. 89.

Between N. Las Palmas and N. Cherokee avenues, stop for dinner or continue farther on the Walk of Fame and then return to:

6 Musso & Frank Grill 🍽 ★

Hollywood's oldest restaurant and a paragon of Hollywood's halcyon-era grills is part restaurant, part history museum. This was practically a second home to Faulkner, Hemingway, and Orson Welles, among others. Top off one of their grilled meat specialties with martinis that still set the standard. See p. 69.

LOS ANGELES FOR FAMILIES IN 3 DAYS

The trick to traveling with children is providing enough stimulation to fend off revolt, without packing in so much as to trigger a meltdown. You also don't want to bore adults to tears; fortunately, that's not a problem with most of L.A.'s kid-friendly attractions. Buy Disneyland and Universal Studios Hollywood tickets online in advance, preferably including a Front of Line Pass at the latter, which will save you hours in line. See "Especially for Kids" in chapter 4 (p. 110) for more ideas.

Day 1: The Happiest Place on Earth

Though somewhat overshadowed by Orlando's bigger, newer Disney World, Disneyland (p. 142) is more intimate, easier to navigate, and endowed with the personal stamp of Walt Disney (he and his wife, Lillian, lived above the firehouse on Main Street while Disneyland was built). With all the rides, character meet-and-greets, parades, and other attractions, this is a minimum of one full day. See chapter 5 for ideas on organizing your visit.

Day 2: Kid-Cool Culture & a Beach Treat

Avoid uttering the word "museum," and you can delight children while expanding their horizons at any number of educational L.A. attractions. For a small sampling, start in Downtown's Exposition Park at the California Science Center (p. 98), which fascinates kids with the retired space shuttle Endeavour, a 50-foot animatronic woman and countless hands-on exhibits that teach (sshhh) them about science. Then head to Hollywood to Pink's to be part of a bona fide cultural icon by noshing the lowly hot dog in one of more than 20 variations. Now you're ready for La Brea Tar Pits (p. 93), where the "eewww" factor reels kids in, and the cool dinosaurs at the adjoining Page Museum seal the deal. Finish out the day at the Santa Monica Pier (p. 82), where diversions include a carousel, an arcade, a Ferris wheel, and a small aquarium. Or . . . just give the kids a pail and shovel and let them loose on the beach.

Day 3: Star Tours

Start the day when Universal Studios Hollywood (p. 103) opens. Kids love the sets from "How the Grinch Stole Christmas," "King Kong," "Despicable Me," and "Shrek" attractions, and exciting "Revenge of the Mummy," "Jurassic Park," and other rides. After a full day, head south on U.S. 101 to Hollywood for Italian food at Miceli's (p. 76), where wait staff belting out opera and show tunes create a boisterous atmosphere. Check www.walkoffame.com to find your children's favorites first, then make your way on Hollywood Boulevard to find the stars on the Walk of Fame (p. 89). Stop at Grauman's Chinese Theatre (p. 87) to compare hands and feet (and a few other body parts) with the prints of Hollywood stars, including R2D2.

LOS ANGELES & SAN DIEGO IN 5 DAYS

You can combine Los Angeles and San Diego in a single vacation if you don't try to see absolutely everything. You'll have more fun and get a better feel for each city if you choose a few iconic sights and activities. We suggest you begin your trip in Los Angeles, the bigger, busier city, and end in more mellow San Diego.

Days 1 & 2: Los Angeles

Follow the "Iconic Los Angeles" itineraries for Days 1 and 2.

Day 3: Los Angeles to San Diego

Point your compass south on PCH to survey the 42-mile coastline south of Los Angeles. The drive presents one classic Southern California beach town after another, from Huntington Beach, the official "Surf City, USA," to moneyed but mellow Newport Beach, to artsy Laguna Beach. A short detour inland at Dana Point will take you to Mission San Juan Capistrano and its loyal swallows. PCH merges with I-5 at Doheny State Beach, but you can stay to the right and follow the Coast Highway to picturesque, low-key San Clemente (where the road becomes El Camino Real) and join I-5 south of town. Give yourself at least 3 hours for the entire drive to San Diego, but allow plenty of time to stop and wiggle your toes in the sand and explore beguiling town centers. See p. 153.

I-5 travels through the Marine Corps Base Camp Pendleton, which covers 125,000 acres, including the longest section of undeveloped coastline in Southern California. You might spot helicopters hovering over the ocean or trucks kicking up sand inland as the troops practice manuevers. The base's coastline ends at **Oceanside,** the northernmost coastal city in San Diego County.

Ruby's Diner 🍵 ★

Escape from the car in Oceanside and stretch your legs while strolling above the surf to the end of the Oceanside Pier and Ruby's Diner (1 Oceanside Pier; www.rubys.com; ☎ **760/433-7829**). The menu's packed with comfort foods from burgers to turkey pot pie, plus breakfast is served all day. Save room for a classic shake.

PCH resumes skirting the coast at Oceanside and runs south to La Jolla, paralleling I-5. You can catch glimpses of the ocean and coastal towns from the freeway or continue your leisurely drive. Classy Carlsbad's small downtown leads to two long state beaches, which give way to funky Encinitas and stylish Solana Beach. Both roads pass through estuaries as they approach the Del Mar Racetrack & Fairgrounds. Check the sky to the east when you reach this point—you might spot colorful hot air balloons floating over the valleys. Tudor-style Del Mar comes next, followed by Torrey Pines State Beach backed by the steep cliffs at Torrey Pines State Reserve. You could continue along PCH from here through La Jolla and the more urban beach cities, but the road gets mighty crowded and complicated. Better to veer on to I-5 for the rest of your drive.

Days 4 & 5: San Diego

Follow the Iconic San Diego itineraries for Days 1 and 2.

ICONIC SAN DIEGO IN 1 DAY

If you have only one day in San Diego, stick to these three key areas offering an overview of the area's attributes.

---

1 Balboa Park ★★★

For complete immersion in nature, culture, and history, you can't beat this sprawling park. Enter the park via the Cabrillo Bridge, official entryway to the 1915–16 Panama-California Exposition. Wander along the pedestrian El Prado past ornate, century-old Spanish Colonial buildings housing fine museums; see p. 214 to choose which ones to visit. Step into the fragrant **Botanical Building** for a fern-shaded break from the sun. See p. 216.

Lunch in the Park 🍵

Enter the gracious 1915 House of Hospitality for a relaxing lunch on the patio at El Prado. See p. 201.

2 The Embarcadero ★

After lunch, head downtown to the **Embarcadero** along the San Diego Bay waterfront. Start at the Beaux-Arts **San Diego County Administration Building** (corner of Grape St. and N. Harbor Dr.), veering into **Waterfront Park.** Continuing along the Embarcadero, you'll pass the *Star of India's* tall masts at the **Maritime Museum.** See p. 224, the **USS** *Midway* aircraft carrier museum.

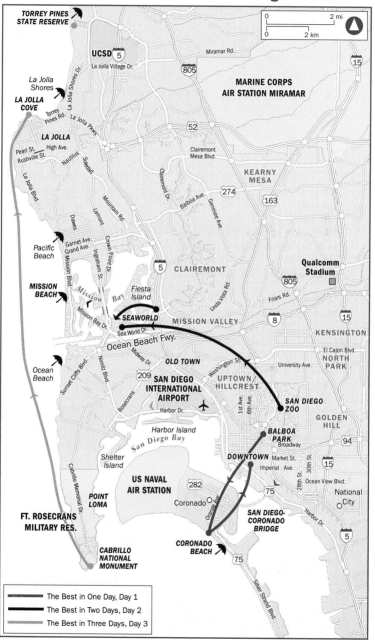

San Diego Itineraries

TORREY PINES
STATE RESERVE

UCSD 5
La Jolla Village Dr.

Miramar Rd.

La Jolla
Shores

LA JOLLA
COVE

MARINE CORPS
AIR STATION MIRAMAR

LA JOLLA

Pearl St. High Ave.
Rushville St.
Nautilus

Clairemont
Mesa Blvd.

KEARNY
MESA

Pacific
Beach

Garnet Ave.
Grand Ave.

MISSION
BEACH

Fiesta
Island

SEAWORLD

MISSION VALLEY

KENSINGTON

Ocean
Beach

Ocean Beach Fwy.

OLD TOWN

SAN DIEGO
INTERNATIONAL
AIRPORT

UPTOWN
HILLCREST

El Cajon Blvd.
University Ave.

NORTH
PARK

Harbor Dr.

SAN DIEGO
ZOO

GOLDEN
HILL

Harbor Island

San Diego Bay

Shelter
Island

BALBOA
PARK
Broadway

DOWNTOWN Market St.
Imperial Ave.

Ocean View Blvd.

National
City

US NAVAL
AIR STATION

Coronado

SAN DIEGO-
CORONADO
BRIDGE

POINT
LOMA

FT. ROSECRANS
MILITARY RES.

CORONADO
BEACH

CABRILLO
NATIONAL
MONUMENT

Qualcomm
Stadium

The Best in One Day, Day 1
The Best in Two Days, Day 2
The Best in Three Days, Day 3

3 Hotel del Coronado & Coronado Beach ★★★

Board the Coronado ferry at Broadway Pier in late afternoon. If you're feeling energetic, rent a bike at the Ferry Landing and cruise along broad streets to the beach. If not, take the Coronado Shuttle. Kick off your shoes and walk along the sand to "the Del." (p. 195), a frothy Victorian landmark. Stroll through the elegant lobby (with shoes on, please) and boutiques in the underground tunnels.

4 The Gaslamp Quarter ★★

Ride the ferry downtown as the sunset casts a golden glow over the skyline. Finish the day in the historic **Gaslamp Quarter** choosing from dozens of restaurants before claiming a rooftop seat at **Altitude** (p. 254). Should you need one more adventure before bedtime, check out the comedy scene at **Tipsy Crow** (p. 255).

ICONIC SAN DIEGO IN 2 DAYS

Visit the critters and take in the beach scene on your second San Diego day.

1 Head to the San Diego Zoo ★★★

You'll get a healthy dose of animals at the **San Diego Zoo** (p. 221). Begin with the bus tram and end with aerial tram for a complete overview. *Tip:* Skip the sandals and wear comfy walking shoes.

2 Mission Bay Park ★★★ & Mission Beach ★★

Now there's time to play or take a siesta on the beach. Mission Bay (p. 228) is best for biking, skating, and boating. Mission Beach (p. 240) has unparalleled people-watching along the boardwalk, plus rides and games at **Belmont Park** (p. 228). Stay until sunset and ride the Giant Dipper coaster for postcard-perfect sunset views.

Festive Dining ☕

Continue the family fun with mariachis and giant margaritas at **Casa Guadalajara** (see p. 205) in Old Town.

ICONIC SAN DIEGO IN 3 DAYS

It's time to take in San Diego from above at Cabrillo National Monument and sample the high life in classy La Jolla. You'll need a rental car for the day to cruise along some of San Diego's most scenic coastline.

1 Cabrillo National Monument ★★★

You've seen Point Loma framing the north end of San Diego from the Coronado ferry, the zoo's aerial tram, and downtown's Embarcadero. Now look down on them all from 422 feet above the water line at this pocket of urban wilderness. In winter, you might spot gray whales; dolphins appear year round.

Fish Two Ways

Order lunch amid the crowd around the fresh fish display at **Point Loma Seafoods** (see p. 207), carry your tray to tables beside the sportfishing marina, and watch anglers unloading the freshest possible catch of the day.

2 La Jolla ★★★

Continue the seaside theme at **La Jolla Cove** (p. 241). If the tide is low, carefully clamber around the tide pools beside the cove to spot delicate white anemones and scuttling hermit crabs. Listen for the sounds of barking as you follow the path southwest along **Scripps Park** (p. 231) to the **Children's Pool** (p. 241), where harbor seals have taken over the sand. Walk a block inland to Prospect Street and browse through boutiques before a fab dinner in one of La Jolla's finest restaurants.

SAN DIEGO FOR FAMILIES IN 3 DAYS

Choose a hotel in one of the beach areas or, if watching your budget, one with a pool in Mission Valley. Every neighborhood has at least one park or playground where kids can let loose, and spend as much time as possible at the beach.

Day 1: Museums & a Beach

Give the kids pool time before heading to Balboa Park around 9:30am. Stroll the Prado sans crowds, and arrive at the **Reuben H. Fleet Science Center** (p. 218) to play with the science gadgets and catch the first IMAX movie. With a museum for just about every interest (including trains and planes), a large playground, and several lawns where play is encouraged, the park should fill 3 hours or more. After all that culture, head to Ocean Beach for fab burgers and shakes (nobody can drink a whole one) at **Hodad's** (5010 Newport Ave.; ✆ **619/ 224-4623;** daily 11am–10pm). Walk 1 block to the beach and play for the rest of the day.

Day 2: Animal Parks & Museums

Head to the **San Diego Zoo** (p. 221): it amuses all ages, eats up at least four hours, and allows same day re-entry. Afterwards, head downtown for a pizza, Greek salad, or taco at cafes near the carousel at **Seaport Village** (p. 246), then cross **Harbor Drive** to the **New Children's Museum** (p. 224). Toddlers are happiest here; older kids prefer the **USS Midway Museum's** (p. 225) cockpits and flight simulators. Continue along the **Embarcadero** (p. 177) to Waterside Park and let the kids play while you renergize.

Day 3: On & About the Water

Don't even try to hold back squeals and shouts when spotting a spouting leviathan during a **whale-watching boat tour** (p. 237), or catching a sea bass on a **fishing trip** (p. 243). For tamer boat trips, consider the **Coronado Ferry** (p. 176) or a **harbor cruise** (p. 256). The important thing is getting on the water at least once. Drive to La Jolla's **Birch Aquarium** (p. 232) and carefully scoop sea urchins and starfish from tide pools before scrambling about the rocks at **La Jolla Cove** (p. 241) and spotting harbor seal at the **Children's Pool.** Grab a table on the patio at **Sammy's Woodfired Pizza** (702 Pearl St., La Jolla; ✆ **858/156-5222;** Mon–Thurs 11:30am–9pm, Fri–Sat 11:30am–10pm, Sun 11:30am–9:30pm) for dinner.

LOS ANGELES ESSENTIALS

by Christine Delsol

Los Angeles is the second-largest city in the nation, and unlike most other major U.S. cities, it came of age with the automobile. That, combined with the vast valley it occupies, has created an endless thicket of freeways, shifting neighborhood boundaries and punishing distances that can be confounding for a visitor. This chapter will help you navigate and find places to stay and dine.

GETTING THERE

By Air

Of the five L.A.-area airports, most visitors fly into **Los Angeles International Airport** (www.lawa.org/lax; ✆ 310/646-5252), or LAX. The world's sixth-largest airport in number of passengers carried, it lies oceanside between Marina del Rey and Manhattan Beach, within minutes of Santa Monica and nearby beaches, and about a half-hour from Downtown, Hollywood, and the Westside (depending, as always, on traffic). Free **shuttle buses** connect the nine terminals. Travelers with disabilities may request special accessible minibuses when they check in.

A free 24-hour **Cell Phone Waiting Lot** at the corner of 96th Street and Vicksburg Avenue is for drivers picking up passengers. Map, parking, shuttle-van, weather, and other information about LAX is online at **www. lawa.org/lax.** All car-rental agencies are within a few minutes' drive in the surrounding neighborhood; each provides a complimentary airport shuttle.

For some travelers, one of the smaller airports might be more convenient than LAX. The small **Bob Hope Airport** (BUR; 2627 N. Hollywood Way, Burbank; www.bobhopeairport.com; ✆ 818/840-8840) is best if you're headed for Hollywood or the valleys, and it's even closer to Downtown L.A. than LAX is. It also has good links to Las Vegas and other Southwestern cities. **Long Beach Municipal Airport** (LGB; 4100 Donald Douglas Drive, Long Beach; www.lgb.org; ✆ 562/570-2600), south of LAX, avoids L.A. if you're visiting Long Beach or northern Orange County. **John Wayne Airport** (SNA; 18601 Airport Way, Santa Ana; www.ocair.com ✆ 949/252-5200) is closest to Disneyland and Knott's Berry Farm. **Ontario International Airport** (ONT; 1923 E. Avion St., Ontario; www. lawa.org/ont; ✆ 909/937-2700) is best for those bound for San Bernardino, Riverside, and other inland communities, but it's convenient if you're heading to Palm Springs or Pasadena.

By Car

Several major highways lead to Los Angeles: I-5 from the north and south; I-10 heading west from Florida; and scenic U.S. 101, which follows the western seaboard from the Oregon state line.

From the north, southbound I-5 enters Los Angeles County (and its traffic) just north of the San Fernando Valley. To reach L.A.'s Westside and beaches, take I-405 south; to get to Hollywood, take California 170 south to U.S. 101 south (the Hollywood Freeway). I-5 travels along Downtown's eastern edge and into Orange County.

If entering L.A. via the **scenic coastal route** from the north, take U.S. 101 to I-405 or I-5, or stay on U.S. 101, following the directions above.

From the east, I-10 cuts through Downtown and ends at the beach. For Orange County, take California 57 south. If you're heading to the Westside, take I-405 north. To get to the beaches, take California 1 (Pacific Coast Highway, or PCH) north or south, depending on your destination.

From the south, heading north on I-5, take I-405 when it splits off to the west to reach the Westside and beach communities. Stay on I-5 to Downtown and Hollywood.

By Bus

Greyhound (www.greyhound.com; © **800/231-2222** or 214/849-8100), runs comfortable express buses to Los Angeles from San Francisco, Las Vegas, San Diego, and Phoenix. **MegaBus** (www.megabus.com) operates a similar service from the San Francisco Bay Area and Las Vegas. See the chapter 9 for details.

By Train

Amtrak (www.amtrak.com; © **800/872-7245**) serves Los Angeles' Union Station from hundreds of U.S. cities. See chapter 9 for details.

By Cruise Ship

About a million visitors enter Los Angeles through the **World Cruise Center,** also known as the San Pedro Terminal, at the **Port of Los Angeles.** See chapter 9.

ARRIVING

Getting into Town from the Airport (LAX)
BY CAR

To reach **Santa Monica** and other northern beach communities, exit the airport, take Sepulveda Boulevard north to Lincoln Boulevard (California 1), which connects to the Pacific Coast Highway (PCH) in Santa Monica. You *can* take I-405 north, but you'll be sorry—that stretch of freeway is always heavily congested.

To reach **Redondo, Hermosa, Manhattan,** and the other southern beach towns, take Sepulveda Boulevard south and follow signs to California 1 (PCH) south.

To reach **Beverly Hills** or **Hollywood,** exit the airport via Century Boulevard and take I-405 north (expect heavy traffic) to Santa Monica Boulevard east. If you use the carpool lane (two or more passengers) on I-405, move to a normal lane at least one to two exits before the one you need, or you may be trapped.

To reach **Downtown** or **Pasadena,** exit the airport, take Sepulveda Boulevard south, then take I-105 east to I-110 north.

One of the city's busiest interchanges is from the Santa Monica Freeway (I-10) to the San Diego Freeway (I-405) on the way to LAX—this beastly bottleneck has caused many a missed flight. If you're heading to LAX, the scenic route may prove to be the fastest. From I-10 west-bound, exit south to La Brea Avenue. Go right on Stocker Street, then left on La Cienega Boulevard. Veer right on La Tijera Boulevard and left on Airport Boulevard, then follow the signs. You can use this trick from West Hollywood and Beverly Hills as well—simply take La Cienega south, continuing as above. If you're driving a rental car from Santa Monica or Venice Beach, take Lincoln Boulevard south to a left on Manchester Boulevard to a right on Airport Boulevard; follow the signs for rental car return.

BY CAR SERVICE

For about the same price you would pay for a taxi, you can hire a convenient and comfortable personal car service. **M and M Car Service** (www.mandmcarservice.com; ✆ **310/738-9898** for same-day service or 310/285-0193 for reservations) is friendly and reliable, with rates starting at $50 (gratuity not included) for service to LAX from Santa Monica, and slightly more for LAX pickup.

BY SHUTTLE

Many city hotels provide free shuttles for guests; ask when you make reservations. **SuperShuttle** (www.supershuttle.com; ✆ **800/258-3826** or 310/782-6600) offers regularly scheduled minivans from LAX to any location in the city, as does **Prime Time Shuttle** (www.primetimeshuttle.com; ✆ **800/733-8267** or 310/536-7922). Fares range from about $15 to $35 per person, depending on your destination. Reservations aren't needed when you arrive, but are required for a return to the airport. (A cab will probably be cheaper and more convenient for a group of three or more.)

BY METRO RAIL

Budget-minded travelers can take L.A.'s Metro Rail service (a combination of light rail and subway trains) from LAX to many destinations for less than $3 (the combined fare and purchase of a reloadable farecard called "TAP")—but be prepared to spend an hour or so in transit. The airport's free "G" shuttle takes you to the Aviation/LAX light-rail station on the Green Line, four stops north of Redondo Beach. Traveling six stops east connects with the Blue Line, which heads south to Long Beach and north to Downtown; further connections lead to Hollywood and Universal City (Red Line) or Pasadena (Gold Line). Ask your hotel for the closest station. Metro Rail operates from 4am to midnight. Check the **Los Angeles County Metropolitan Transit Authority (Metro)** website at www.metro.net for details or call ✆ **323/466-3876.**

BY PUBLIC BUS

Metro's **FlyAway** express buses, which have free Wi-Fi and reclining seats and allow one carry-on and up to three pieces of luggage per passenger, offer the easiest and quickest public transit from LAX to some destinations. Buses to Union Station and central locations in Van Nuys (San Fernando Valley), Westwood (UCLA), Hollywood and Santa Monica pick up passengers on each terminal's lower level; look for a green "Flyaway, Long-Distance Buses and Vans" sign. One-way fare is $8 for all destinations except Westwood, which costs $10; only debit or credit cards are accepted (no cash). Three routes have hourly departures from LAX: Westwood from 6am to 11pm, Santa Monica from 6:45am to 11:45pm, and Hollywood from 5:15am to 10:15pm; Union Station and Van Nuys have 24-hour service, roughly on the half-hour. Metro schedules on www.metro.net/flyaway list only departure times; note how long your trip takes and add in a cushion of time for the return.

If you're heading to Santa Monica and not overburdened by bags, you may take the airport's free "C" shuttle to the LAX City Bus Center, where you can board the Rapid 3 express line operated by Santa Monica's **Big Blue Bus** (www.bigbluebus.com; ℭ **310/451-5444**). Fare for the approximately half-hour ride is $2.

Local Metro buses and other regional buses also travel between LAX and many points in greater Los Angeles; a one-way Metro bus ride is $1.75 (transfer included when reloadable TAP farecard is used). See www.metro.net for the schedules.

BY TAXI

Taxis are at the arrivals level under the yellow sign outside each terminal. Ask for a list of prices to various major destinations before setting off. The flat price between LAX and Downtown L.A. is $47; expect to pay at least $53 to Hollywood and Beverly Hills, $40 to Santa Monica, and $80 to the Valley and Pasadena in light traffic, up to 20% more in heavy traffic. There's also a $4 surcharge for trips from LAX.

VISITOR INFORMATION

The **Los Angeles Convention and Visitors Bureau** (www.discoverlosangeles.com; ℭ **800/228-2452** or 213/624-7300) is the city's main source for information. In addition to maintaining an informative website, it operates two **walk-in visitor centers:** Downtown at Union Station, 800 N. Alameda St., open Monday through Friday 10am to 10 pm and Saturday through Sunday 10am to 7pm; and at the Hollywood & Highland Center, 6801 Hollywood Blvd. at Highland Avenue (ℭ **323/467-6412**).

Many communities also have their own information centers and detailed websites:

o The **Beverly Hills Visitors Center,** 9400 S. Santa Monica Blvd., Suite 102 (love beverlyhills.com; ℭ **800/345-2210** or 310/248-1015), offers maps, a store, and concierge services; it's open Monday through Friday 9am to 5pm and Satuday through Sunday 10am to 5pm.

o **The Hollywood Arts Council** (www.discoverhollywood.com; ℭ **323/462-2355**).

o The **West Hollywood Convention and Visitors Bureau,** 8687 Melrose Ave., M-38 (www.visitwesthollywood.com; ℭ **800/368-6020** or 310/289-2525), is inside the Pacific Design Center and open Monday through Friday 8:30am to 6pm.

o The **Santa Monica Convention and Visitors Bureau** (www.santamonica.com; ℭ **800/544-5319** or 310/393-7593) maintains its primary walk-in visitor center at 2427 Main St., open Monday through Friday 9am to 5pm, Saturday through Sunday 9am to 5pm.

o The **Malibu Chamber of Commerce** (www.malibu.org).

o The **Pasadena Convention and Visitors Bureau,** 300 E. Green St., (www.pasa denacal.com; ℭ **626/795-9311** or 800/307-7977), open Monday through Friday 8am to 5pm.

City Layout

Los Angeles isn't a single compact city like San Francisco, but a sprawling suburbia comprising dozens of disparate communities located on the ocean, the slopes of

website-watching: THE BEST OF L.A. ONLINE

In addition to the visitor center websites, here are some others that can help you make the most of your vacation:

- **www.la.eater.com**: Everything you wanted to know about eating in L.A., from restaurant reviews to latest trends to themed lists to gossip.
- **www.tvtickets.com**: Audiences Unlimited, Inc.'s site is your online source for free tickets to dozens of sitcoms and talk shows.
- **www.losangeles.com**: This site talks travel, arts, entertainment, contemporary culture, and politics.
- **www.festivalfinder.com** or **www.festivalusa.com**: These sites list music and other festivals in and around Los Angeles.

scrubby canyons and mountains, or the flatlands of a huge desert basin. Most visitors spend the bulk of their time either along the coastline, in Hollywood, or on the city's ever-trendy Westside.

Neighborhoods in Brief

See the "Los Angeles Neighborhoods" map on p. 24.

SANTA MONICA & THE BEACHES

These are among the premier places to book a hotel—especially during summer, when the beaches can be a good 20 degrees cooler than the rest of the city, and on sunny winter days. Fair warning: The skies may be mostly gray at times, especially in May and June. Still, the 60-mile beachfront stretching from Malibu to the Palos Verdes peninsula has milder weather and less smog than inland communities. The coastal towns each have a distinct charm, and are connected from Santa Monica south by a walk/bike path. They're listed below from north to south.

Malibu At the northern border of Los Angeles County, 25 miles from Downtown, Malibu was once a privately owned ranch—purchased in 1857 for 10¢ an acre and now the most expensive real estate in L.A. Today its 27 miles of wide beaches, beachfront cliffs, sparsely populated hills, and relative remoteness from the inner city make it popular with celebs from David Geffen to Dustin Hoffman. With ample green space and dramatic rocky outcroppings, Malibu's rural beauty is unsurpassed in L.A., and surfers flock here too for great, if crowded, waves.

Santa Monica L.A.'s premier beach community is known for its festive ocean pier, stylish oceanfront hotels, artsy atmosphere, and large population of homeless residents (an oxymoron, yes, but it fits). Shopping is king here, especially along the Third Street Promenade. With Venice Beach, it's also part of a growing young techie community dubbed "Silicon Beach."

Venice Beach Tobacco mogul Abbot Kinney set out in 1904 to transform a marsh into a resort town modeled after its Italian namesake, creating a series of narrow canals linked by bridges. This refreshingly eclectic community (officially just "Venice") was once a sketchy area, but gentrification has brought scores of great restaurants, boutiques, and rising property values as movie and pop stars move in. Though some of L.A.'s most interesting architecture lines funky Main Street, Venice Beach is best-known for Ocean Front Walk, a nonstop Mardi Gras of all manner of colorful characters.

Marina del Rey Just south of Venice, Marina del Rey is a quieter, more upscale waterside community best known for its man-made small-craft harbor, the largest of its kind in the world. Fittingly, it offers a wide variety of fishing trips, harbor tours, dinner cruises, and private charters.

Manhattan, Hermosa & Redondo beaches These laid-back, mainly residential neighborhoods have modest homes (except for oceanfront real estate), mild weather, and residents happy to have fled the L.A. hubbub. There are excellent beaches for volleyball, surfing, and tanning here, but when it comes to cultural activities, pickings can be slim. The restaurant scene, while limited, has been improving steadily, with some great bars and clubs near their respective piers.

L.A.'S WESTSIDE & BEVERLY HILLS

The **Westside,** sandwiched between West Hollywood and the coastal communities, includes some of Los Angeles' most prestigious neighborhoods, with names you're sure to recognize:

Beverly Hills Beverly Hills is an enclave of palm-lined streets, palatial homes, famous residents (Jack Nicholson, Warren Beatty and Annette Bening), and high-priced shops. A healthy mix of filthy rich, wannabes, and tourists creates a unique—and sometimes snobby-surreal—atmosphere.

Bel Air & Holmby Hills In the hills north of Westwood and west of Beverly Hills, these are old-money residential areas that are featured prominently on most maps to the stars' homes.

Brentwood Brentwood is best known as the famous backdrop to the O. J. Simpson melodrama. The neighborhood itself is generic, a relatively upscale mix of tract homes, restaurants, and strip malls. The Getty Center looms over Brentwood from its hilltop perch next to I-405.

Westwood An urban village founded in 1929 and home to the University of California at Los Angeles (UCLA), Westwood brims with student energy and a lively culinary scene.

Century City Primary draws in this compact and rather bland area, sandwiched between West Los Angeles and Beverly Hills, are the 20th Century Fox studios and Westfield Century City mall.

West Los Angeles This catch-all label generally applies to everything that isn't one of the other Westside neighborhoods. It's basically the area south of Santa Monica Boulevard, north of Venice Boulevard, east of Santa Monica and Venice, and west and south of Century City.

HOLLYWOOD & WEST HOLLYWOOD

Hollywood Though starry-eyed young hopefuls still gravitate to this historic heart of L.A.'s film industry, today's Hollywood is mostly illusion. Many movie studios have moved to more spacious homes in Burbank, the Westside, and other parts of the city. Still, visitors keep streaming in to Hollywood's landmark attractions, such as the star-studded Walk of Fame and Grauman's Chinese Theatre. The city's $1-billion, 30-year revitalization project has produced signs that Hollywood Boulevard is coming out of its long, seedy slump. Refurbished movie houses, stylish restaurants and clubs, and boutique hotels have sprung up. The Hollywood & Highland complex anchors the neighborhood, with shopping, entertainment, and a luxury hotel built around the beautiful Dolby Theatre, designed specifically to host the Academy Awards.

Scruffy, but fun, **Melrose Avenue** is the city's funkiest shopping district, catering to often-raucous youth with secondhand and avant-garde clothing shops. There are also a number of good restaurants.

The stretch of Wilshire Boulevard running through the southern part of Hollywood is known as the **Mid-Wilshire** district, or the Miracle Mile. It's lined with contemporary high-rise apartments and office buildings. The section just east of Fairfax Avenue, known as Museum Row, is home to almost a dozen museums, including the Los Angeles County Museum of Art and the La Brea Tar Pits.

Up Western Avenue in the northernmost part of Hollywood, **Griffith Park** is one of the country's largest urban parks, home to the Los Angeles Zoo, the famous Griffith Observatory, the outdoor Greek Theater, and the landmark "Hollywood" sign.

West Hollywood This key-shaped town between Beverly Hills and Hollywood houses some of the area's best restaurants, clubs, shops, and art galleries; the epicenter is at the intersection of Santa Monica and La

Los Angeles Neighborhoods

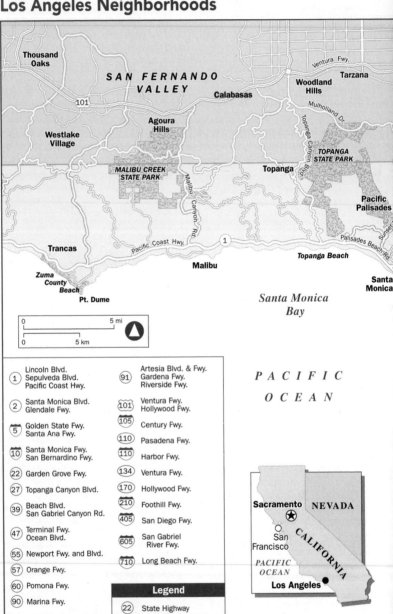

Thousand Oaks

SAN FERNANDO VALLEY

Calabasas

Ventura Fwy.

Tarzana

Woodland Hills

101

Mulholland Dr.

Agoura Hills

Westlake Village

MALIBU CREEK STATE PARK

Malibu Canyon Rd.

Topanga Canyon Blvd.

TOPANGA STATE PARK

Topanga

Pacific Palisades

Trancas

Pacific Coast Hwy.

1

Palisades Beach Rd.

Sunset

Topanga Beach

Zuma County Beach

Pt. Dume

Malibu

Santa Monica

Santa Monica Bay

0   5 mi

0   5 km

1 Lincoln Blvd.
Sepulveda Blvd.
Pacific Coast Hwy.

2 Santa Monica Blvd.
Glendale Fwy.

5 Golden State Fwy.
Santa Ana Fwy.

10 Santa Monica Fwy.
San Bernardino Fwy.

22 Garden Grove Fwy.

27 Topanga Canyon Blvd.

39 Beach Blvd.
San Gabriel Canyon Rd.

47 Terminal Fwy.
Ocean Blvd.

55 Newport Fwy. and Blvd.

57 Orange Fwy.

60 Pomona Fwy.

90 Marina Fwy.

91 Artesia Blvd. & Fwy.
Gardena Fwy.
Riverside Fwy.

101 Ventura Fwy.
Hollywood Fwy.

105 Century Fwy.

110 Pasadena Fwy.

110 Harbor Fwy.

134 Ventura Fwy.

170 Hollywood Fwy.

210 Foothill Fwy.

405 San Diego Fwy.

605 San Gabriel
River Fwy.

710 Long Beach Fwy.

PACIFIC OCEAN

Legend

22 State Highway

101 U.S. Highway

210 Interstate Highway

Sacramento

NEVADA

San Francisco

CALIFORNIA

PACIFIC OCEAN

Los Angeles

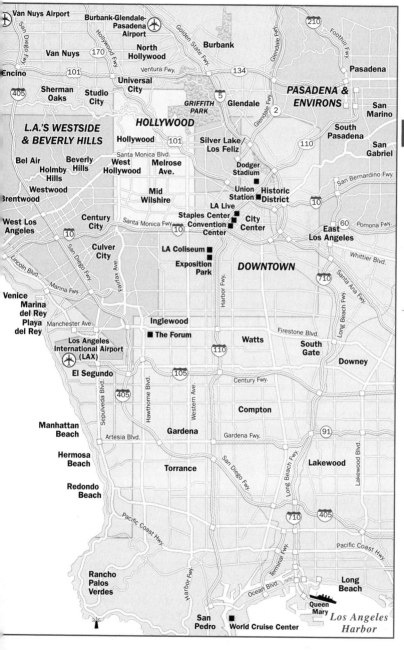

Cienega boulevards. "WeHo" is also the center of L.A.'s gay community. Highlights include the 1½ miles of Sunset Boulevard known as Sunset Strip, the chic Sunset Plaza retail strip, and the liveliest stretch of Santa Monica Boulevard.

DOWNTOWN

Despite several major cultural and entertainment centers (the Walt Disney Concert Hall, L.A. LIVE, Cathedral of Our Lady of the Angels) and a handful of trendy restaurants, Downtown L.A. isn't a tourist hub. But it's worth a look particularly for its sophisticated restaurant and a bar scene.

Easily recognized by the tight cluster of high-rise offices, the city's business center can seem eerily vacant on weekends and evenings. Outlying residential communities such as **Koreatown, Little Tokyo,** and **Chinatown,** though, are enticingly vibrant. (See "L.A.'s Ethnic Neighborhoods," p. 107.) The "Historic Core" also includes intriguing architecture such as the Bradbury Building (p. 96).

El Pueblo de Los Angeles Historic District This 44-acre ode to the city's early years is worth a visit. Chinatown is small and touristy but can be plenty of fun for souvenir hunting or traditional dim sum. **Olvera Street,** evoking the city's Mexican origins, re-creates a traditional market and includes some cultural landmarks. Little Tokyo, a genuine gathering place for the Southland's Japanese American population, is full of shops and restaurants offering authentic flair.

Silver Lake/Los Feliz These residential neighborhoods northwest of Downtown brim with arty, multicultural areas with unique cafes, theaters, and art galleries, as well as a popular local music scene. Its old-school architectural styles from early L.A. include

Hollywood bungalows and Spanish haciendas that silent-screen stars once called home.

Exposition Park This area southwest of Downtown is home to the Los Angeles Memorial Coliseum, the L.A. Sports Arena, the Natural History Museum, the African-American Museum, and the California Science Center. The University of Southern California (USC) is next door.

UNIVERSAL CITY

The San Fernando Valley Known locally as "the Valley," this area was popularized in the 1980s by the notorious mall-crazed "Valley Girl" stereotype. Sandwiched between the Santa Monica and San Gabriel mountain ranges, the Valley is mostly residential or commercial, and off the tourist track, except for **Universal City,** west of Griffith Park between U.S. 101 and California 134. This is home to Universal Studios Hollywood and the CityWalk shopping and entertainment complex. About the only reason to go to **Burbank,** west of these other suburbs and north of Universal City, is to see a TV shows taping at NBC or Warner Brothers Studios.

Glendale Home to Forest Lawn, the city's best cemetery for very retired movie stars.

PASADENA & ENVIRONS

Best known for the New Year's Day Tournament of Roses Parade, **Pasadena** was spared from the tear-down fervor that swept L.A. in the mid-2000s, so it has a refreshing old-time feel, with Arts and Crafts cottages and brick and stone commercial buildings that attract TV and movie productions. No longer a secret, Pasadena's "Old Town" has become a popular pedestrian shopping district. But it still radiates vintage charm, with dazzling views of the San Gabriel Mountains on non-smoggy days.

GETTING AROUND

By Car

L.A. is a sprawling, car-crazed metropolis, and you do need wheels to get around easily. (Public transportation is useful for only a limited number of attractions.) The elaborate network of freeways that knits the city's disparate parts together requires patience for dealing with the traffic. Consult a map before you hit the road and carry a sturdy map or use a GPS navigation system for problems en route (keeping in mind the hands-free driving law is strictly enforced). For a detailed view of L.A.'s freeway system, see the maps with live traffic alerts on www.go511.com or quickmap.dot.ca.gov; there's also an easy-to-read, London Tube-style version with exits marked at www.stonebrown design.com/los-angeles-freeways.html.

High-occupancy vehicle (**HOV**) lanes, restricted to vehicles carrying two or more people, can get you there faster, but be aware portions of at least two freeways (I-10 and I-110) have converted their HOV lanes to high-occupancy toll (**HOT**) lanes, which require a FasTrak transponder even for carpoolers. Ask your car-rental agency if switchable transponders come with your vehicle; if so, any tolls will be automatically billed to your account.

CAR RENTALS

Los Angeles is one of the cheapest places in America to rent a car. The major national companies usually rent economy and compact cars for about $40 per day (hybrids $80–$90) or $200-plus per week, with unlimited mileage. All the major car-rental agencies have offices at the airports and in the larger hotels; lower prices come to those who book ahead.

L.A. DRIVING TIPS

Many Southern California freeways have designated **carpool lanes,** also known as High Occupancy Vehicle (HOV) lanes or "diamond" lanes (after the large, white diamonds painted in the lane). Most require two passengers (others three), and you can't leave the HOV lane for several miles at a time, making it all too easy to miss an exit. Most on-ramps are metered during even light congestion to regulate the flow of traffic onto the freeway; cars in HOV lanes can usually pass the signal without stopping. Don't use the HOV lane illegally—fines begin around $350.

Keep in mind that pedestrians have the right of way at all times, so stop for people who have stepped off the curb. Some areas, especially Pasadena, allow pedestrians to cross not only from corner to corner but also diagonally across the intersection. See p. 269 for more tips on driving in California.

Always allow more time than you think it will actually take to get where you're going. You need time for traffic and parking. Double your margin during weekday rush hours, from 6 to 9am and 3 to 7pm. Freeways are much more crowded than you'd expect all day Saturday, especially heading toward the ocean on a sunny day.

PARKING

Explaining the parking situation in Los Angeles is like explaining the English language—there are as many exceptions as rules. In some areas, every establishment has a convenient free lot or ample street parking; other areas are pretty manageable for those with a quick eye, but in more congested parts of town (particularly around restaurants after 7pm) you might have to give in and use valet parking. Restaurants and nightclubs rarely provide valet service for free; most often they charge $6 to $15. Some areas, like Santa Monica and Beverly Hills, offer self-park lots and garages near the neighborhood action; costs range from $2 to $10. In the heart of Hollywood and on the Sunset Strip, self-park lots can run up to $20. Most hotels listed in this book offer self-parking and/or valet parking, ranging from $10 to $40 per day.

Beware of parking in residential neighborhoods. Many allow only permit parking, so you'll be ticketed and possibly towed (especially in West Hollywood and Beverly Hills).

BY PUBLIC TRANSPORTATION

There *are* visitors who successfully tour Los Angeles entirely by public transportation (I've met them both), but we can't honestly recommend it for most visitors. L.A. has grown up around—and is best traversed by—the automobile, and many areas are inaccessible without one. Still, if you're in the city for only a short time, are on a very tight budget, or don't plan to move around a lot, public transport can work.

The city's trains and buses are operated by the **Los Angeles County Metropolitan Transit Authority, or Metro** (www.metro.net; © 323/GO-METRO [466-3876]), and its brochures and schedules are available at every area visitor center.

BY BUS

Spread-out stops, sluggish service, and frequent transfers make extensive touring by bus impractical. For straight shots and short hops, and however, buses are economical and eco-friendly. I don't recommend riding buses late at night.

Basic bus fare is $1.75 for local lines, with transfers costing 50¢, if you're paying by cash; transfers are free when using a reloadable $1 TAP farecard. A Metro Day Pass, $7, gives you (and up to two kids age 4 or younger) unlimited bus and rail rides all day; they can be purchased while boarding any Metro Bus (exact change is needed) or at the self-service vending machines at Metro Rail stations.

The **Downtown Area Short Hop (DASH)** shuttle system operates buses throughout Downtown and Hollywood. Service runs every 5 to 30 minutes, depending on time of day, and costs 50¢. Contact the Department of Transportation (www.ladottransit.com; © 213/808-2273) for schedule and route information.

The **Cityline** shuttle will get you around West Hollywood on weekdays and Saturdays (9am–6pm), excepting major holidays. The free minibus runs about every half-hour from La Brea and Fountain avenues all the way to Beverly and N. San Vicente boulevards near Cedars-Sinai Hospital. For more information, go to www.weho.org/cityline or call © 800/447-2189.

BY RAIL & SUBWAY

Although no rival to New York's subway, the **MetroRail** system continues to expand, attracting more than 10 million passengers monthly—double the ridership of a decade ago. It operates daily from 4am to midnight, with extended service on Friday night into the wee hours of Saturday morning (between 2 and 3am, depending on the route.) Here's an overview of what's currently in place:

The **Metro Blue Line,** a mostly aboveground rail line, connects Downtown Los Angeles with Long Beach.

The **Metro Red Line,** L.A.'s first and busiest subway, begins at Union Station, the city's main train depot, and travels west under Wilshire Boulevard, looping north into Hollywood, Universal City, and San Fernando Valley.

The **Metro Purple Line** subway starts at Union Station, shares six stations with the Red Line Downtown, and continues to the Mid-Wilshire area.

The **Metro Green Line** connects Norwalk in eastern Los Angeles County to LAX and Redondo Beach. A connection with the Blue Line offers visitors access from LAX to Downtown L.A. or Long Beach.

The **Metro Gold Line** is a 14-mile link between Pasadena and Union Station in Downtown L.A. Stops include Old Pasadena, the Southwest Museum, and Chinatown.

The **Metro Expo Line,** an 8.6-mile segment opened in 2012, connects Culver City and the Westside with Downtown Los Angeles via Expo Park and USC.

MetroRail includes two rapid-transit bus lines. The **Metro Orange Line** uses 18 miles of dedicated bus lanes from the Red Line's North Hollywood station through the

San Fernando Valley to Chatsworth. The 26-mile **Metro Silver Line** heads west from El Monte to Union Station and then dips south to Harbor Gateway, using a combination of city streets, dedicated lanes and freeway HOT lanes.

The base Metro fare is $1.75 for all lines. A Metro Day Pass is $7; weekly passes are $25. Passes sell at Metro Customer Centers and convenience and grocery stores.

Amtrak (www.amtrakcalifornia.com; ✆ **800/872-7245** or 001/215-856-7953 outside the U.S.) runs trains along the California coast, connecting San Diego, Los Angeles, San Francisco (with bus connections for the latter), and points in between. Multiple trains run every day. One-way fares for popular segments can range from $31 (Los Angeles–Santa Barbara) to $37 (Los Angeles–San Diego) to $59 (San Francisco–Los Angeles); fares fluctuate and discounts may be available.

BY TAXI

Distances are long in Los Angeles, and cab fares are high; even a short trip can cost $20 or more. Taxis currently charge $2.85 at the flag drop, plus $2.70 per mile (except for the $47 flat-rate fare to LAX from Downtown). A $4 service charge is added to fares from LAX. An additional charge of $30¢ is added for each 37 seconds of delay, which can pile up quickly. Don't forget to add a 15% tip to all fares.

Except in the heart of Downtown, cabs will rarely pull over when hailed. Cabstands are at airports, at Downtown's Union Station, and at major hotels. To ensure a ride, order a taxi in advance from **Checker Cab** (www.ineedtaxi.com; ✆ **800/300-4007** or 213/222-3333), **L.A. Taxi** (✆ **213/627-7000**), or **United Taxi** (www.unitedtaxi.com; ✆ **800/822-8294**, text 323/207-8294). Ride-sharing services with smartphone apps such as Lyft, Uber, and Sidecar also operate in L.A.

Los Angeles Calendar of Events

JANUARY

Tournament of Roses, Pasadena. A spectacular parade marches down Colorado Boulevard, with lavish floats, music, and extraordinary equestrian entries, followed by the Rose Bowl football game. Camping out along Colorado Boulevard the night before in order to secure a good spot is a tradition of long standing. See www.tournamentofroses.com or call ✆ **626/449-4100.** January 1.

Martin Luther King, Jr., Parade, Long Beach. This parade down Martin Luther King, Jr. Avenue and Anaheim Street ends with a fest in Martin Luther King, Jr., Park. Third Monday in January.

Chinese New Year & Golden Dragon Parade, Los Angeles. Dragon dancers and martial arts masters parade through Downtown's Chinatown. Chinese opera and other events are scheduled. Info at www.lachinesechamber.org. Late January or early February.

FEBRUARY

Northern Trust Open Golf Tournament, Pacific Palisades. The PGA Tour makes its only Tinseltown appearance at the Riviera Country Club, overlooking the ocean. Expect to see stars in attendance. Visit www.northerntrustopen.com or call ✆ **800/752-OPEN** (0736). Mid-February.

MARCH

Los Angeles Marathon, Downtown. This run from Dodger Stadium to the Santa Monica Pier attracts thousands of participants, from world champs to the guy next door. It also features a 5K run/walk from Dodger Stadium the day before. Go to www.lamarathon.com. Mid-March.

California Poppy Blooming Season, Antelope Valley. Less than an hour's drive north of L.A., the hillsides of the state California Poppy Reserve blazes with brilliant reds and oranges that dazzle the senses. See www.parks.ca.gov. Mid-March to mid-May. For information on the annual **California Poppy Festival** (usually mid to late April), visit www.poppyfestival.com.

MAY

Cinco de Mayo, Los Angeles. A weeklong celebration of Mexico's victory over the French Army in 1862 celebrates Mexican culture in general. Large crowds, live music, dancing, and food amount to a citywide carnival, kicking off in late April with Fiesta Broadway (www.fiestabroadway.la), a free, 24-square-block street festival in Downtown. El Pueblo de Los Angeles State Historic Park (elpueblo.lacity.org) in Downtown also hosts festivities. Week surrounding May 5.

Venice Art Walk, Venice Beach. This annual weekend event features docent-guided tours of galleries and studios and a self-guided art walk through dozens of private home studios, coordinated by Venice Family Clinic. Visit www.theveniceartwalk.org. Second half of May.

Long Beach Lesbian & Gay Pride Parade and Festival, Shoreline Park, Long Beach. This event features rock and country music, dancing, food, and more than 100 decorated floats. Go to www.longbeachpride.com. Second half of May.

Doheny Blues Festival, Doheny State Beach, Dana Point. Great blues, rock, and soul (past acts have included Gregg Allman, Buddy Guy, and Keb' Mo') fill three stages at a grassy waterfront park. See www.dohenybluesfestival.com. Mid- to late May.

JUNE

Playboy Jazz Festival, Los Angeles. George Lopez has replaced Bill Cosby as master of ceremonies at this elite gathering of jazz musicians at the Hollywood Bowl, now presented by the Los Angeles Philharmonic. Visit www.hollywoodbowl.com/playboyjazz. Mid-June.

LA Pride, West Hollywood. One of the world's largest lesbian and gay pride festivals includes outdoor stages, dance tents, food, and general revelry leading up to the parade down Santa Monica Boulevard. Go to www.lapride.org. Early to mid-June.

Los Angeles Film Festival, Los Angeles. With more than 60,000 attending, the festival showcases more than 175 American and international indies, short films, and music videos during the 10-day event. See www.lafilmfest.com. Mid to late June.

Mariachi USA Festival, Los Angeles. The Hollywood Bowl's family-oriented celebration of Mexican culture and tradition is one of the world's largest mariachi festivals. Visit www.mariachiusa.com or call ✆ **800/MARIACHI** (627-4224) or 323/850-2000. Mid- to late June.

JULY

Lotus Festival, Echo Park. Celebrants gather to witness the spectacular blooms of Echo Lake's floating lotus grove. Festivities take an Asian and South Pacific islands theme, including tropical music, ethnic foods, exotic birds, and a sale of lotus-inspired arts and crafts. Admission is free. Go to www.facebook.com/lalotusfestival. Second weekend of July.

US Open of Surfing, Huntington Beach. World-class surfers competing off long stretches of beautiful beach—plus extreme sports like BMX biking and skateboarding—attract more than 500,000 people. See www.surfcityusa.com. Late July or early August.

Festival of Arts & Pageant of the Masters, Laguna Beach. This 70-year tradition revolves around a performance-art production in which actors re-create famous old-masters paintings. Festivities include live music, crafts sales, art demonstrations, workshops, and the grass-roots Sawdust Festival. Visit www.foapom.com. July through August.

AUGUST

Nisei Week Japanese Festival, Los Angeles. A weeklong celebration of Japanese culture and heritage—L.A.'s oldest ethnic festival—is held in Little Tokyo. Festivities include parades, food, taiko drum performances, arts, and arts and crafts. Visit www.niseiweek.org. Mid-August.

SEPTEMBER

Los Angeles County Fair, Pomona. Horse racing, arts, agricultural displays, celeb entertainment, and carnival rides are among the attractions at one of the largest county fairs in the world, held at the Los Angeles County Fair and Exposition Center. Visit www.lacountyfair.com. Throughout September.

Long Beach Blues Festival, Long Beach. Great performances by blues legends such as Etta James, Drive John, and the Allman

Brothers have made this don't-miss event for lovers of the blues. Go to www.jazzandblues. org. Labor Day weekend.

Sunset Strip Music Festival, West Hollywood. Two outdoor stages and landmark clubs such as Whiskey a Go Go showcase contemporary rock, metal, and electronic music from dozens of acts. Past awards have gone to Jane's Addiction, Ozzy Osbourne, and Joan Jett. The 2-day event includes an all-ages Sunset Boulevard street festival. Go to www.sunsetstripmusicfestival.com. Late September.

Simon Rodia Watts Towers Jazz Festival, Los Angeles. A tribute to the roots of jazz in gospel and blues also celebrates avant-garde and Latin jazz. See www.wattstowers. org. Late September.

OCTOBER

Catalina Island JazzTrax Festival, Catalina Island. Contemporary jazz greats play at Avalon's legendary Casino Ballroom. This enormously popular festival takes place over two consecutive weekends. See www.jazztrax.com for advance ticket sales and a schedule of performers. Mid-October.

Hollywood Film Festival, Hollywood. More than 50 films from the U.S. and abroad are screened, with celebrities in abundance. Visit www.hollywoodfilmfestival.com. Mid-October.

West Hollywood Halloween Costume Carnaval, West Hollywood. One of the world's largest Halloween parties draws more than 500,000 people, many dressed in outlandish drag couture. See www.visitwesthollywood. com/halloween-carnaval. October 31.

NOVEMBER

American Indian Arts Marketplace, Autry National Center. This showcase of Native American arts and culture includes traditional dances, music, and arts and crafts, as well as a chance to sample Native American foods. See www.theautry.org/marketplace. Early November.

AFI Fest, Los Angeles. The biggest names in the international film world gather to see new films from around the globe, hosted by the American Film Institute. Visit www.afi. com. Early November.

Doo Dah Parade, Pasadena. Participants in this outrageous spoof of the Rose Parade have included the Briefcase Precision Drill Team and a kazoo-playing marching band. Visit www.pasadenadoodahparade.info. Mid- to late November.

Hollywood Christmas Parade, Hollywood. Star-studded parade marches through the heart of Hollywood. Go to www.the hollywoodchristmasparade.com. Sunday after Thanksgiving.

DECEMBER

Christmas Boat Parade of Lights. Sailors festoon their crafts with colorful lights, and several harbors hold nighttime parades. Participants range from tiny dinghies with a single strand of lights to showy yachts with elaborate nativity scenes; Huntington Harbor includes tours of boat and house decorations. **Channel Island Harbor** (Ventura), www. channelislandharbor.org; **Marina Del Rey,** www.mdrboatparade.org; **Huntington Harbor,** www.cruiseoflights.org. Mid-December.

[FastFACTS] LOS ANGELES

Area Codes   L.A. has eight area codes. **213,** covers just the Downtown business area. When calling western L.A. and the beach communities, you'll usually use the **310** or **424** area codes. Other areas of L.A. use **323, 562, 818, 747,** and **626.** Call ✆ **411** for directory assistance.

Doctors & Dentists
For a doctor referral, contact the Los Angeles County Medical Association (www.lacmanet.org; ✆ 213/683-9900). For dental referrals, contact the Los Angeles Dental Society (www.ladental.com; ✆ **213/380-7669**).

Disabled travelers
Los Angeles' spirit of tolerance and diversity makes it a welcoming place for travelers with disabilities. The LA Tourism and Convention Board

lists accessible attractions and city services at www.discoverlosangeles.com/blog/los-angeles-disabled-visitors.

Embassies & Consulates All embassies are located in the nation's capital, Washington, D.C. The following countries are among those with consulates in Los Angeles (closed on public holidays):

Australia: 2029 Century Park East, Suite 3150, Los Angeles. www.losangeles.consulate.gov.au; ✆ **310/229-2300.** Monday through Friday 9am to 5pm.

Canada: 550 South Hope St., 9th floor, Los Angeles. www.losangeles.gc.ca; ✆ **213/346-2700.** Monday through Friday 8:30am to 4:30pm.

New Zealand: 2425 Olympic Blvd., Suite 600E, Santa Monica. www.nzcgla.com; ✆ **310/566-6555.** Monday through Friday 8:30am to 4:30pm.

United Kingdom: 2029 Century Park East, Suite 1350, Los Angeles. www.gov.uk/government/world/usa; ✆ **310/789-0031.** Monday through Friday 9am to 4pm.

Emergencies Call ✆ **911** to report a fire, call the police, or get an ambulance anywhere in the United States. This is a toll-free call.

Health People with respiratory problems should keep in mind that L.A.'s air quality can be poor, particularly in the valleys in the mid- to late summer (too many cars, too little wind). When air quality is worst, warnings air on local TV and radio stations urging people to avoid outdoor activities. Visit the website aqmd.enviroflash.info for smog level advisories.

L.A. averages 320 sunny days a year—be sure to wear long-sleeved shirts and wide-brim hats in midday and use sunscreen with an SPF rating of at least 30.

Hospitals Centrally located **Cedars-Sinai Medical Center,** 8700 Beverly Blvd., Los Angeles (www.cedars-sinai.edu; ✆ **310/423-3277**), has a 24-hour emergency room staffed by some of the country's finest doctors. Near the Convention Center in Downtown, **California Hospital Medical Center,** 1401 South Grand Ave. (www.chmcla.org; ✆ **213/748-2411**), has a 24/7 emergency room and is a certified primary stroke center. **Good Samaritan Hospital** (goodsam.org; ✆ **213/977-2121**), affiliated with USC, is also conveniently located, at 1225 Wilshire Blvd., Los Angeles; its 24-hour emergency room is among the busiest in the region.

LGBT Travelers When **West Hollywood,** or WeHo, was incorporated in 1984, it elected a lesbian mayor and a predominantly gay city council. It has the largest concentration of gay- and lesbian-oriented businesses and services; Santa Monica, Venice, Silver Lake, Long Beach, and Studio City are other lesbian and gay enclaves.

Many gay-oriented publications provide information and up-to-date listings, including **Frontiers** (www.frontiersla.com), a Southern California–based biweekly, and **Metro Source** magazine (www.metrosource.com), a New York and L.A.-based monthly. They are available at most newsstands citywide. **Ragemonthly.com** also contains a comprehensive calendar of LGBT events in Southern California.

Pets If you're traveling with your pet, be aware that animals are restricted from most public beaches and some state parks or areas within the parks, such as backcountry trails. The city of Los Angeles, which has strict leash laws and stiff fines for failing to pick up waste, operates nine dog parks (two off-leash); www.laparks.org/info/dogparks.htm has addresses and hours.

WHERE TO STAY

Santa Monica & the Beaches

EXPENSIVE

Beach House Hotel Hermosa Beach ★★ Staying at this luxurious hotel, tucked between Redondo Beach and Manhattan Beach, is more like visiting a wealthy friend's beach house in Newport (R.I., not CA). The breezy the split-level studio suites are individually owned and outfitted to meet every need, including a kitchenette, gas fireplace, oversized bathrooms and furnished patios or balconies. It stands on The Strand, a popular 26-mile paved coastal path, and one of Southern California's most popular beaches is right across the walk, so summer can get chaotic. Calm reigns behind the inn's double-paned windows and solid, insulated walls, spring for a second- or third-story room just for privacy's sake. Most studios overlook the beach, and room rates rise in proportion to the amount of water in your window view. You're steps away from the Huntington Beach Pier and the town's nightlife—the Comedy & Magic Club (p. 131), where Jay Leno holds forth on a regular basis, is just 4 blocks away.

1300 The Strand (reached from Beach Dr. btw. 13th and 14th sts.), Hermosa Beach. www.beach-house.com. ℂ **888/895-4559** or 310/374-3001. 96 units. $249–$809 double. Rates include continental breakfast. Valet parking $25. **Amenities:** Room service, spa, kitchenettes, free Wi-Fi.

Casa del Mar ★★★
One of Santa Monica's only hotels right on the beach, this 1926 former Italian Renaissance Revival beachclub has a whiff of a European palace about it. The property was converted into an opulent hotel by the owners of adjacent Shutters on the Beach (p. 36) in 1999, and they did not skimp on the luxurious linens or Italian marble. The enormous lobby's plush yet casual living-room style furniture sets the mood, carried out in guest rooms with solid European-style wooden four-poster beds and armoires set off by sea green and ocean blue walls and textiles. Most have sea views, abundantly displayed through floor-to-ceiling windows. **Catch Restaurant,** with small plates and ocean-inspired entrees, and **Terrazza,** a cafe and lounge that replaced the Veranda lobby lounge in summer 2014, take full advantage of the views of the ocean and Santa Monica Pier. The valet parking fee is onerous, but the hotel dropped its Wi-Fi charge in 2013.

1910 Ocean Way (next to the Santa Monica Pier), Santa Monica. www.hotelcasadelmar.com. ℂ **800/898-6999** or 310/581-5533. 129 units. $383–$695 double; from $940 suite. Valet parking $34. Pets accepted ($15/night per pet; limit 2). **Amenities:** 2 oceanfront restaurants; lobby lounge for cocktails and light fare; concierge; health club w/spa services; heated outdoor pool; room service, free Wi-Fi.

Huntley Santa Monica Beach ★
The grand 18-story facade and somewhat lower prices than charged by its coastal kin are alluring, but know going in that this might be the least beachy hotel within view of an ocean. The former apartment building's transformation into a boutique hotel—though it's really too big to qualify—went for high impact in the splashy lobby, most strikingly with a back-lit wall of lacquered piranhas. Guest rooms are more subdued, with neutral hues and a modern version of traditional furnishings; though not especially luxurious, they are pleasant and comfortable. Sun-worshippers should know there's no pool (or much outdoor space), and reaching the beach so enticingly viewed through the 9th- through 17th-floor windows requires a trek. The clientele tilts heavily toward business travelers and hipsters looking for shopping ops. But the hotel's crown jewel, the shiny, 18th-floor **Penthouse** restaurant and bar, serves up a transcendent view of the city skyline and a high possibility of celebrity-spotting success along with its genuinely excellent contemporary American cuisine.

1111 2nd St. (Wilshire Blvd. and California Ave.), Santa Monica. www.thehuntleyhotel.com. ℂ **310/394-5454.** 209 units. $279–$579 double; from $450 suite. Valet parking $37. **Amenities:** Restaurant/bar; lobby cafe; concierge; fitness center; room service; business center; Wi-Fi ($10/day).

Malibu Beach Inn ★★
What if, instead of braving choppy waters and fighting off seasickness, you could go whale-watching without ever leaving your cloud-like bed? That's how it's done at this inn on "Billionaire's Beach," between Santa Monica

Santa Monica Hotels & Restaurants

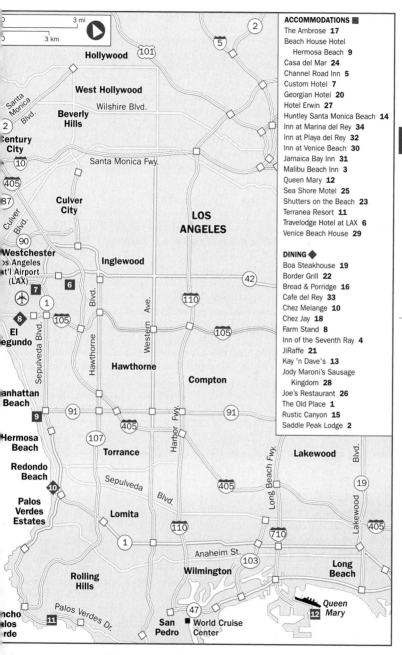

ACCOMMODATIONS ■

The Ambrose **17**
Beach House Hotel
    Hermosa Beach **9**
Casa del Mar **24**
Channel Road Inn **5**
Custom Hotel **7**
Georgian Hotel **20**
Hotel Erwin **27**
Huntley Santa Monica Beach **14**
Inn at Marina del Rey **34**
Inn at Playa del Rey **32**
Inn at Venice Beach **30**
Jamaica Bay Inn **31**
Malibu Beach Inn **3**
Queen Mary **12**
Sea Shore Motel **25**
Shutters on the Beach **23**
Terranea Resort **11**
Travelodge Hotel at LAX **6**
Venice Beach House **29**

DINING ◆

Boa Steakhouse **19**
Border Grill **22**
Bread & Porridge **16**
Cafe del Rey **33**
Chez Melange **10**
Chez Jay **18**
Farm Stand **8**
Inn of the Seventh Ray **4**
JiRaffe **21**
Kay 'n Dave's **13**
Jody Maroni's Sausage
    Kingdom **28**
Joe's Restaurant **26**
The Old Place **1**
Rustic Canyon **15**
Saddle Peak Lodge **2**

and Santa Barbara. Its uncluttered, contemporary design is perfect for a setting that produces perfect sunsets, and the service is spot-on but unpretentious, as befits a beach house. All rooms have full or partial ocean views; the King Corner Room (really a studio) hits the sweet spot between space, view, and price, with the bed facing double glass doors opening onto a Pacific panorama. For a change of scenery, you can gorge on ocean views from the warmth of the Lobby Lounge's fireplace. In August 2014, the hotel instituted Mixology Fridays, adding a different trio of specialty cocktails each week—a Classic, a Creation and an Original—to its regular cocktail menu. If you can bestir yourself, it's a short walk to Malibu Pier and Malibu Lagoon State Beach; Pepperdine University, Getty Villa, and the new Anthony C. Beilenson Interagency Visitor in the Santa Monica Mountains are a short drive away.

22878 Pacific Coast Hwy. (slightly north of Sweetwater Canyon Rd.), Malibu. www.malibubeachinn.com. ⓒ **310/456-6444.** 47 units. From $243–$825 double; from $725 suite. Valet parking $27. **Amenities:** Restaurant; lobby lounge; spa; concierge; private beach; room service; business center; free Wi-Fi.

Shutters on the Beach ★★★

This shingled gray and white confection has a small edge over its sibling Casa del Mar, with balconies on every guest room (the two are the only Santa Monica hotels opening directly onto the beach). Rates escalate with the extent of the ocean view, from no view in the least expensive rooms on up through seven levels plus three levels of suites. The interiors designed by Michael Smith, known for his work in the Obama White House, produced large, airy rooms in blues and whites that call to mind an oceanside mansion in the Hamptons. The decor is chic and homey at the same time, with throws draped casually over chairs upholstered in plaids and stripes. Some have fireplaces or whirlpool tubs, and all have operable floor-to ceiling windows. It's a short, pleasant walk along the beach to the Santa Monica Pier, but there's plenty to keep you at the hotel—including a pop-up beach bar (PUBB), that opened in summer 2014. *Tip:* The hotel, though adult-oriented, does tend to fill up with kids in the summer. If you're sensitive to rollicking children, best to plan a visit before Memorial Day or after Labor Day.

1 Pico Blvd. (at Appian Way), Santa Monica. www.shuttersonthebeach.com. ⓒ **800/334-9000** or 310/458-0030. 198 units. $495–$995 double; from $1,245 suite. Valet parking $34. Pets accepted ($125 per stay). **Amenities:** Restaurant; cafe; lobby lounge; babysitting; concierge; health club and spa; Jacuzzi; outdoor pool; room service; sauna; beach-equipment rentals (seasonal); free Wi-Fi.

Terranea Resort ★★★

This sprawling, Mediterranean-style luxury resort rose in 2009 on the peninsula occupied until 1987 by the old Marineland of the Pacific park. Its magnitude and amenities are unequaled in Los Angeles. Commanding 102 acres of hilly coastline, only one-quarter occupied by the resort, its greatest amenities are fresh air and open space. Terranea is not a base for seeing the L.A. sights, which are an hour away; it's a place to settle in, relax, and revel in natural beauty. The experience doesn't come cheap, so make the most of it. Snorkeling, kayaking, golf, spa treatments, yoga classes, and hiking trails with signs that clue you in to the local ecology are all at your disposal, though the rocky beach isn't suited for swimming. This is the kid-friendliest resort in L.A., with a Splash Zone play area and a kids club. The smallest guest room is 450 square feet; suites, casitas, bungalows, and villas go up from there. All have patios or balconies, and transcendent ocean views. Of its six restaurants, the seasonal California cuisine at **mar'sel** is the current foodie favorite, but the more casual **Nelson's** boasts the best view, rivaled by the wrap-around balcony at the **Lobby Bar.**

100 Terranea Way Dr. (off Palos Verdes Dr. South), Rancho Palos Verdes. www.terranea.com. ⓒ **866/802-8000** or 310/265-2800. 582 units. $350–$690 double; from $715 suite. Valet parking

$35; self-parking $25. Pets accepted ($125 per stay). **Amenities:** 6 restaurants; 2 bars; concierge; business center; 9-hole golf course; health club and spa; Jacuzzi; 3 outdoor heated pools; room service; extensive recreational equipment rentals. Wi-Fi (included in the $25 resort fee).

MODERATE

The Ambrose ★★ Located in a residential neighborhood, this is a nest for the traveler who values peace and quiet above proximity to the beach. Its Arts and Crafts design brings the Asian influences of that movement to the forefront in its serene Japanese garden with reading nooks, a koi pond, fountains, and artwork. The hotel's efforts to recycle or compost 75% of its waste, and its use of locally grown organic foods and environmentally sensitive cleaning products, earned it a LEED "green" certification. (Hybrid cars get preferential parking here.) But it's the included amenities that win guests over: underground parking, breakfast, bicycles, and shuttle service around Santa Monica in an adorable, biodiesel-fueled London taxi. Guest rooms are luxuriously furnished in keeping with the Arts and Crafts theme, with solid, dark wood furniture and textiles in rich, earthy colors.

1255 20th St. (at Arizona Ave.), Santa Monica. www.ambrosehotel.com. ✆ **877/262-7673** or 310/315-1555. 77 units. $279–$429 double. Rates include continental breakfast. Free parking. **Amenities:** Exercise room; room service; free local shuttle; free Wi-Fi.

Channel Road Inn ★★ This rare West Coast example of a shingled Colonial Revival house, built in 1910, is tucked into woodsy Santa Monica Canyon, north of the city limits. It was restored and opened as a B&B in 1989, and it is simply gorgeous. The gracious living room, where afternoon tea, wine and hors d'oeuvres are served, is dominated by an enormous Batchelder tile fireplace, and sets the tone with white wicker armchairs and blue upholstery contrasting with the dark wood built-in shelves and trim. The 15 airy, individually decorated rooms come in an array of layouts with varying combinations of four-poster beds, fireplaces or whirlpool tubs; all but the "Cozy Queen" offer ample space. A few rooms offer peeks at the ocean, .2 mile away, but the garden views are equally enticing. The grounds include a quiet rose garden and a private hillside hot tub. The inn provides bicycles, beach chairs, and towels for beach forays.

219 W. Channel Rd. (west of East Rustic Rd./Channel Lane), Santa Monica. www.channelroadinn. com ✆ **310/459-1920.** 15 units. $185–$365 double; from $275 suite. $25 for extra guest. Rates include full breakfast and afternoon tea, wine, and hors d'oeuvres. Free parking. One room accepts pets ($65). **Amenities:** Concierge; Jacuzzi; bicycles; free Wi-Fi.

Georgian Hotel ★★ A pristine Art Deco masterpiece, this eight-story ocean-view (but not quite beachfront) hotel became one of Santa Monica's first "skyscrapers" upon opening in 1933. It was a favorite haunt for the movie industry elite, and Bugsy Siegel was rumored to have been the man behind the basement speakeasy that now serves as meeting and event space. The bright, meticulously restored lobby oozes classic Hollywood atmosphere, and the delightful veranda with teak furniture overlooking the ocean remains from those storied days. Guest rooms in peachy-buttery-coffee hues are outfitted with 1930s-style furnishings and Art Deco fixtures, and stocked with luxury amenities. Most have at least a partial ocean view, but you'll need to be above the third floor for full-on panoramas. There's no pool or spa, and the beach is a 5-minute walk down the bluff and across a footbridge over PCH—a little shorter than at some of its blufftop neighbors. *Tip:* Rooms facing the ocean are smallish and get some noise from Ocean Avenue; request a room on the north side for water views sans noise.

1415 Ocean Ave. (btw. Santa Monica Blvd. and Broadway), Santa Monica. www.georgianhotel.com. ✆ **800/538-8147** or 310/395-9945. 84 units. $255–$299 double; from $355 suite. Valet parking $24. Pets accepted ($150 per stay). **Amenities:** Restaurant/lobby bar; concierge; gym; room service; free Wi-Fi.

Hotel Erwin ★   This colorful, ever-so-Venice Beach hotel sits 2 blocks inland from Ocean Front Walk's surreal and sometimes seedy carnival, and conveniently near the hip, Abbot Kinney shopping corridor. New carpets in beachy colors enhance the spacious guest rooms' post-modern vibe, while surfboards and a mural by L.A. tattoo/ graffiti artist Norm bring public areas into sync with the outer edges of Southern California culture. (Guest rooms are a bit more subdued.) A new locavore restaurant and bar, **Barlo Kitchen & Cocktails,** replaced Hash. Summer 2014 brought menu makeovers: The weekend Barlo Brunch Club made its debut, presenting a vintage cartoon display to go with the vintage cereal buffet and classic brunch items tweaked Southern California-style, such as chorizo omelets and duck-and-bacon sausage; the rooftop **High Lounge,** famous for its 360-degree views, added small plates inspired by street food from throughout the world. The Erwin is just far enough from the beach to comfort families and seekers of respite from the hijinks, yet close enough to take in the show by small doses. If you'd rather your beach time not include street performers, tattoo artists, skaters, and assorted hangers-on, look elsewhere.

1697 Pacific Ave. (at 17th Ave.), Venice. www.hotelerwin.com. ✆ **800/786-7789** or 310/452-1111. 119 units. $229–$399 double; from $269 suite. Valet parking $32. **Amenities:** Restaurant; rooftop lounge; free pass to local fitness centers; room service; free Wi-Fi.

Inn at Playa del Rey ★★★   This charming New England-style B&B is better for winding down than for sightseeing. Not only is it about a half-hour drive from L.A.s' major sights (yet less than 10 minutes from LAX), it deserves your full attention—and you deserve its soothing ways. The inn stands at the edge of the Ballona Wetlands, a bird sanctuary separating Playa del Rey from Ballona Creek and Marina del Rey just beyond. White linens and slipcovers, along with fresh breezes admitted by the many large windows, create a bright, airy environment. Guest rooms range from standard queens to a grand suite and offer various combinations of marina or sanctuary views, fireplaces, Jacuzzi tubs, and sun-soaked decks. You can walk to the beach at the end of the street or check out a bicycle and follow the nearby 30-mile-long coastal path. *Fun fact:* The old horse ring slowly being reclaimed by the wetlands just beneath the inn's windows was used by Elizabeth Taylor while filming "National Velvet."

435 Culver Blvd. (1.1 mi. west of Lincoln Blvd.,/Hwy. 1), Playa del Rey. www.innatplayadelrey.com. ✆ **310/574-1920.** 21 units. $205–$385 double; from $335 suite. Rates include full breakfast and afternoon wine and cheese. Free parking. From Lincoln Blvd./Hwy. 1, turn west on W. Jefferson Blvd., which becomes Culver. **Amenities:** Bikes; Jacuzzi; business center; free Wi-Fi.

Inn at Venice Beach ★   I prefer this calm, sleek hotel to those on Ocean Front Walk; the beachfront scene can morph from fun to tiresome after an hour or so. (If you relish being in the midst of the human carnival, you might like the comparable but somewhat more expensive **Venice on the Beach**). The quiet (for Venice) residential location, abutting Marina del Rey, puts you within an easy walk of the beach but provides respite when you need it. Spacious guest rooms are predominantly white (bedding, walls, furniture), set off by dark carpeting and one tomato-colored accent wall; upper-level rooms have open-beam ceilings, and most have balconies. Mini-fridges in every room are a nice perk. All look down on the cobblestone courtyard where continental breakfast is served in good weather. Staff will loan you beach towels, and you can rent bikes and in-line skates nearby.

327 Washington Blvd., Venice. www.innatvenicebeach.com. © **800/828-0688** or 310/821-2557. 43 units. $170–$289 double; from $204 suite. Rates include continental breakfast. Parking $14. **Amenities:** Exercise room; business center; free Wi-Fi.

Jamaica Bay Inn ★★   This 4-year-old inn doesn't look like anything special from the street, but once on the property you do get a whiff of the West Indies as the name promises. Palm trees, sloping lawns, and the adjacent Mother's Beach enhance the illusion, while public spaces (with louvered windows) and balconied guest rooms do their part with rattan furnishings and warm colors. In 2012, the original Vu restaurant was replaced with the indoor/outdoor **Beachside Restaurant & Bar,** whose seasonal menu is very popular. Keep in mind this is not an ocean beach but a harbor, so don't plan to play tag with the waves or go bodysurfing. You probably won't much enjoy swimming in the less-than-crystalline water, either (the hotel pool is a better choice). But clean, soft sand, playground equipment, and shallow water make it a good, safe place for kids to play and wade. I consider Jamaica Bay the best place to stay on this beach—independently owned, more affordable than the Ritz down the road, and more personal than the Marriott.

4175 Admiralty Way (at Palawan Way), Marina Del Rey. www.jamaicabayinn.com. © **888/823-5333** or 310/823-5333. 111 units. $190–$254 double; from $259 suite. Extra guest $15. Valet parking $24; self-parking $16. **Amenities:** Jacuzzi; outdoor pool; gym; business center; room service; free Wi-Fi.

INEXPENSIVE

Inn at Marina del Rey ★★   Behind the blocky, featureless motel facade beats the heart of a boutique hotel. The pleasant surprise begins at check-in; from the front desk to the housekeeping crew, every member of the staff makes it abundantly clear that your happiness is top priority. Comfortable, modern guest rooms provide ample space and plenty of extras—refrigerator, microwave, a small but serviceable work desk with an extra outlet on the lamp. The tiny pool, with a built-in spa tub, is well-maintained, and towels are provided; there's also a small but well-equipped gym. The drawback? It's a mile to the beach, not a particularly pleasant walk along the busy boulevard. Renting a bike is a reasonable option, not only for the beach but for exploring the canals, parks, and marina (ask the front desk for help and directions to the nearby bike path). Venice's Abbot Kinney, currently one of L.A.'s hottest shopping districts, is right around the corner. Rates are low for this area to begin with, but the free parking, Wi-Fi, and expanded continental breakfast make it a genuine bargain.

737 W. Washington Blvd. (.1 mi. west of Abbot Kinney), Marina del Rey. www.pacificahotels.com/innatmarinadelrey. © **800/821-8277** or 310/821-4455. 68 units. $128–$259; suites from $259. Rates include continental breakfast. Free covered parking. **Amenities:** Outdoor heated pool; exercise room; spa tub; laundry facilities; business center; free Wi-Fi.

Sea Shore Motel ★   A little of the old Route 66 lives in this small roadside motel plunked in the middle of Santa Monica's trendy Main Street dining and shopping strip. Just 2 blocks from the beachfront biking path, it might be the best bargain going for beach-lovers who don't have to see water right outside their window. The staff is unfailingly friendly and helpful. Despite the nondescript exterior, rooms offer 27-inch flat-screen HDTVs, terra-cotta tile floors, granite counters, and refrigerators; coffeemakers, tea kettles, microwaves, toasters, and beach gear are available for the asking. The rooftop deck is prime territory at sunset. Spacious suites for as many as six people are an especially good deal, and they book well in advance.

2637 Main St. (btw. Ocean Park Blvd. and Hill St.), Santa Monica. www.seashoremotel.com. © **310/392-2787.** 25 units. $125–$175 double; suites from $180. Extra person $10. Children 11 and under stay free in parent's room. Free parking. Pets accepted Nov–Feb only ($10/night). **Amenities:** Cafe; free Wi-Fi.

FOR TRAVELERS on the fly:
HOTELS NEAR LAX

Though hardly a beach destination, LAX is also in the coastal zone, as any driver who has tunneled under the belly of an enormous jet taxiing over the Pacific Coast Highway can attest. Area accommodations are less thrilling, a collection of chain hotels whose highest and best use is to provide a roof, bed, and shower for passengers arriving late, departing early, or in transit.

The best of the lot is the glam **Custom Hotel** (8639 Lincoln Blvd.; www.jdvhotels.com; ✆ **877/287-8601** or 310/645-0400; $79–$189 double), with chic and spacious rooms, two gyms and a near-nightly party at its fire-pit lit outdoor pool.

Travelodge Hotel at LAX (5547 W. Century Blvd. at Aviation Blvd.; www.travelodgelax.com; ✆ **800/421-3939** or 310/649-4000; $75–$168 double), a few blocks farther way, is utterly nondescript but has a nice pool in a tropical garden, and it adjoins a 24-hour Denny's. It offers a day use rate for travelers waiting through layovers and flight delays ($60, 9am–8pm), and accepts pets ($20). Free shuttle service requires guests to call after picking up their luggage.

Venice Beach House ★★ Built while Venice's founder, Abbot Kinney, was dredging canals and building boardwalks and piers, this two-story, National Register-listed Craftsman home is draped in ivy as if trying to ward off the cacophany of Ocean Front Walk 1 block away. For legions of repeat guests, history and character trump sound-proofing and constant refurbs. As one of Venice's first mansions, it was plenty luxurious for 1911. Retaining the dark wood, lattice-framed portico and other Craftsman hallmarks, it's palpably lived in, as antique furnishings, shelves of vintage books and faded Oriental rugs attest. The least expensive rooms share a bathroom with his-and-her clawfoot tubs; "deluxe suites" are large rooms with a sitting area and private bath. Of these, the Aimee MacPherson has a separate entrance, while the bright, airy James Peasgood has a cathedral ceiling and double-size Jacuzzi. The "super deluxe" Venice Pier is a true suite with a fireplace and separate sitting room.

15 30th Ave. (at Speedway, 1 block west of Pacific Ave.), Venice. www.venicebeachhouse.com. ✆ **310/823-1966.** 9 units, 5 with private bathroom. $150–$170 double with shared bathroom; $210–$305 double with private bathroom; suite $355–$375. Extra person $20. Rates include expanded continental breakfast. Parking $14/day. **Amenities:** Free Wi-Fi.

L.A.'s Westside & Beverly Hills
EXPENSIVE

L'Ermitage ★★★ Tucked away in a leafy residential Beverly Hills neighborhood—built as a condominium complex in the 1970s—this small, discreet hotel has a European feel that sets it apart from its luxury counterparts. Its private underground VIP entrance has made it a favorite hideaway for famous guests, Michael Jackson and Elizabeth Taylor among them, while recovering from plastic surgery or escaping paparazzi. Movie execs hammer out deals in the lobby's curtained nooks, and autographed scripts adorn the walls: "Jaws," "Glory," "Groundhog Day," "The Wedding." Yet everyone is treated as the most important guest here. What matters are the huge (650 square feet minimum) rooms, primarily white with warm wood tones, with their balconies, walk-in closets, and separate soaking tubs in the large bathrooms. And the lovely 24-hour rooftop pool with 360-degree views. The nightly handwritten notes with the weather forecast. Sunday brunch in the verdant garden. And a dozen other small touches that make this top choice in Beverly Hills. The hotel began a rolling update of all the rooms in 2014 that is scheduled for completion in early 2015.

9291 Burton Way (btw. Foothill Rd. and N. Maple Dr.), Beverly Hills. www.viceroyhotelsandresorts. com/en/beverlyhills. © **877/235-7582** or 310/278-3344. 117 units. $339–$699 double; suites from $798. Extra person $35. Valet parking $35. Pets up to 40 lb. accepted ($35/night). **Amenities:** Restaurant; lounge; 24-hr. room service; 24-hr. pool; spa/fitness center; in-room business centers; car service within 3 mi.; free Wi-Fi.

Montage Beverly Hills ★★★ Presiding over the tony Golden Triangle shopping district, Montage Laguna Beach oozes elegance. It would be hard to find fault with the flawless service, impeccably manicured courtyard, and extensive spa that shares the rooftop with a casual restaurant and mosaic-tiled pool graced by sweeping views of the Hollywood Hills. The contemporary rendition of Spanish Colonial Revival style—crown moldings, wood furniture, potted trees, marble and mosaic tile bathrooms—was inspired by Hollywood's golden age estates. Warm, inviting rooms have balconies or patios and ample work desks; some have fireplaces. In addition to **Scarpetta**'s Italian fare and the **Rooftop Grill,** afternoon tea is served in the lobby. For something completely different, check out the two-bedroom Film Noir suite (starting at $1,914), unveiled in late 2013. As part of the city's centennial celebration, it was designed with 1940s-style wallpaper, furniture, and period Lalique accessories. It has its own special room service menu of popular dishes from that period, and the minibar sports a "Press for Champagne" button to summon a tuxedo-clad butler. *Tip:* This is one of the most heavily discounted Beverly Hills luxury hotels on aggregator sites.

225 N. Canon Dr. (btw. Wilshire Blvd. and N. Dayton Way), Beverly Hills. www.montagebeverlyhills. com. © **888/860-0788** or 310/499-4199. 201 units. $344–$1,275 double; from $620 suite. Parking $40. Pets allowed ($30 daily). **Amenities:** 2 restaurants; cafe; bar; concierge; spa; fitness center; rooftop heated pool; room service; business center; free Wi-Fi.

The Mosaic Hotel Beverly Hills ★★ This small hotel in a modest four-story building occupies its own niche, providing more personal service than nearby luxury mega-resorts but more features than the small boutique hotels, including a heated pool and car service for shopping trips and other nearby explorations. The lobby introduces the mosaic theme in its gold, brown and white tile accents. The designers made the most of the limited space by allowing traffic flow from check-in directly to the bar and **Hush,** the hotel's California-cuisine restaurant, where the mosaic theme reappears. Guest rooms are more subdued, all muted earth tones with the subtlest of patterns in the carpet. Standard rooms are small but not cramped, and they pack a lot of luxury per square foot: Frette linens and robes, Bose stereo system, down blankets, body pillows, Bulgari bath products, rain showerheads, and large work desks. For stays of more than a night or two, though, it's worth upgrading to a roomier corner room.

125 Spalding Dr. (btw. Wilshire and Charleville blvds.), Beverly Hills. www.mosaichotel.com. © **800/463-4466** or 310/278-0303. 49 units. $277–$558 double; suites from $404. Valet and self parking $30. Dogs under 35 lb. accepted ($100 per stay). **Amenities:** Restaurant; bar; 24-hr. exercise room; heated outdoor pool; sauna; room service; business center; car service within 3 mi.; free Wi-Fi.

MODERATE

Crescent Hotel ★★ At the edge of Beverly Hills' shopping district, this elegantly quirky hotel was built in 1927 to house starlets of the silent and early "talkies" era. The hotel has restored not only the period's Art Deco detail—the entry stairs and front desk are a showpiece—but its spirit. Hallways serve as galleries for vintage Hollywood photographs and works by contemporary artists (including drummer Mick Fleetwood—who would have guessed he was a butterfly guy?). Turkish cotton linens, heavenly mattresses, floor-to-ceiling drapes, and spa robes are sheer luxury. The gregarious staff will produce toothpaste if you forgot it and even press your clothes before you go out, for no additional charge. In late 2012, the entrance moved to the side street to improve traffic flow and create space for a tiled, tented terrace that serves as the excellent restaurant and lounge. The classy restaurant/lounge space has a wonderful speakeasy atmosphere, especially on live music nights (Mondays and Wednesdays). *Tip:* The two "Itty Bitty Rooms," an incredible deal at $99, can't be booked online; management prefers to rent them to repeat guests who understand how truly itty bitty—though comfortable and stylish—they are. But if you're traveling solo and don't plan to spend much time in your room, give them a call.

403 N. Crescent Dr. (btw. Santa Monica Blvd. and Brighton Way), Beverly Hills. www.crescentbh. com. ✆ **310/247-0505.** 35 units. $99 single; $182–$276 double. Check website for advance purchase and last-minute rates. Rates include continental breakfast. Valet parking $28. Entrance is around the corner on Brighton Way. Pets under 25 lb. accepted ($100 per stay; 50% refundable). **Amenities:** Restaurant; lounge; library; day pass to nearby fitness club; 24-hr. room service; refrigerators (on request); free Wi-Fi.

Élan Hotel ★★★

Just a block from Beverly Center and a mile from Farmers Market and The Grove, the Élan is ideal for visitors who want to save their money for shopping—or who just want a convenient, affordable base to explore both Beverly Hills and West Hollywood. The hotel retained some details from the original facade of a 1969 retirement home while turning it into a sophisticated, contemporary boutique hotel. It doesn't compete with the big luxury hotels on features—there's no pool, fitness center or restaurant—but guests will hardly notice the difference while they're in the sleek lobby and stylish, impeccable rooms decorated in warm earth tones during a 2014 update. Standard rooms are on the small side, but high ceilings and well-placed custom furniture compensate admirably. The beds, made up with goose-down comforters and soft cotton linens, are firm; guests preferring softer beds can request a pillow-top cover. Cotton robes, plush towels, mini-fridges, and Wolfgang Puck Coffee also add a touch of luxury. Best of all, nothing is too much to ask of the kind and helpful staff.

8435 Beverly Blvd. (at N. Croft Ave., east of La Cienega Blvd.), Los Angeles. www.elanhotel.com. ✆ **866/203-2212** or 323/658-6663. 49 units. $153–$249 double; suites from $234. Rates include continental breakfast and evening wine and cheese reception. Valet parking $24 plus tax. **Amenities:** Room service; mini-fridge; free computer work stations in lobby; free Wi-Fi.

Farmer's Daughter ★★

Before central L.A. had The Grove, before Third Street had trendy boutiques, Fairfax Avenue had the Farmer's Daughter, a modest motel across from CBS Studios that prospered from a steady stream of "The Price is Right" contestants. Contestants still come, but a 2003 makeover transformed the motel into a kitschy-cool "design hotel," perfectly located for shoppers and sightseers. It's easy to miss the sign; just pull in when you see the giant blue gingham picnic tablecloth forming the facade's top two stories. Lobby walls look like barn siding, the pool is lined by an armada of oversized rubber ducks, and rooms sport rooster-print wallpaper, denim bedspreads, gingham curtains, and a milking stool for the easy chair's footrest. None of which distracts from cushy amenities such as a large work desk, an iPod docking station, C. O. Bigelow toiletries, and a rain showerhead. Everything seems a little brighter since 2014's guest-room refresh. New, luxurious Robin Rooms depart from the rustic theme to emphasize art and technology, providing commissioned artworks, a curated book collection, custom furniture, USB charging stations, and alarm clocks and mirrors with Bluetooth speakers. The restaurant, **TART,** remodeled in late 2013, puts its own stamp on traditional comfort food and delivers speedy room service. (But don't miss the venerable Farmers Market across the street.) *Tip:* Look into the racy No Tell Room for a special couple's getaway.

115 S. Fairfax Ave. (btw. W. 3rd and W. 1st sts., south of Beverly Dr.), Los Angeles. www.farmers daughterhotel.com. ✆ **800/334-1658** or 323/937-3930. 66 units. $179–$408 double; from $260 Robin Room; from $229 suite. Valet parking $24 plus tax. **Amenities:** Restaurant; bar; room service; gift shop; morning coffee and tea service; outdoor pool; bicycles; library; free Wi-Fi.

Hotel Angeleno Los Angeles ★

This hotel was created from one of the round Holiday Inn towers that proliferated in the 1960s and '70s, looking outdated as soon as they went up. But they did have an incredible view from every room, and this one, rising 17 stories over I-405, was reincarnated in 2006 as a design-conscious modern hotel. The triangular rooms are attractive, if not memorable, and have small balconies. Top-notch service lifts the Angeleno above the ordinary, as do luxurious extras such as 37-inch HDTVs, pillowtop mattresses, silky Italian linens, ergonomic desks, and of course, those views. Double-paned glass combats noise from the nation's busiest freeway, but light sleepers should ask for a room on the Church Lane side (rooms 01–08 on each floor). The rooftop **West** restaurant and cocktail lounge serves seasonal California fare, but the view is why you want to go. Dinner is pricey, so consider having lunch or a cocktail here and making other dinner plans. The immediate area has little to offer a tourist, but the hotel's free shuttle will take you to the Getty Center, UCLA, and Westwood—or to any other destination within 3 miles.

170 N. Church Lane (at intersection of Sunset Blvd. and I-405), Los Angeles. www.hotelangeleno. com. ✆ **310/476-6411.** 209 units. $179–$323 double; from $269 suite. Rates include evening wine reception. Free valet parking. **Amenities:** Rooftop restaurant/lounge; lobby cafe; concierge; business center; fitness center; heated outdoor pool; 24-hr. room service; refrigerator and microwave (on request); free shuttle within 3 mi.; free Wi-Fi.

Luxe Hotel Sunset Boulevard ★★

Far removed from the action in Santa Monica and Hollywood, this low-rise luxury resort hotel is spread over 7 acres and offers numerous amenities comparable to a five-star hotel. The hotel is split between the main building (lobby, restaurant, some rooms) and an uphill building (more rooms, pool, fitness center, spa, tennis court). It's a bit of a hike, but a shuttle is available. Enormous guest rooms—522 square feet minimum—are tasteful, if a bit staid, in restful shades of beige and brown. Less than half come with balconies, but they are distributed through all price levels. Beds have comfy pillowtop mattresses, down duvets and silky Italian linens, and all rooms include flat-screen TVs, iPod docking stations, robes, and thick cotton towels. There is no poolside cafe or bar, but room service delivers there in summer months. UCLA, Westwood, and the Getty Center are within the free shuttle's 3-mile radius.

11461 Sunset Blvd. (at N. Church Lane, just east of I-405), Los Angeles. www.luxehotels.com/ sunset. ✆ **310/476-6571.** 162 units. $215–$265 double; from $249 suite. Extra person $30. Valet parking $25. Pets under 50 lb. accepted ($150–$250 per stay). **Amenities:** Restaurant; cocktail and piano lounge; 24-hr. room service; concierge; fitness center; outdoor heated pool; spa; tennis court; business center; free shuttle within 3 mi.; free Wi-Fi.

INEXPENSIVE

Best Western Plus Carlyle Inn ★★

Less than a half-block south of the city limit, this small but well-designed inn is a terrific alternative to pricey hotels in Beverly

BUDGET watch

A longtime favorite among budget-minded travelers who want a taste of nearby Beverly Hills and West Hollywood, the **Beverly Laurel Motor Inn** embarked on a full-scale renovation in 2014 that was scheduled for completion at the end of the year. Basically a four-story motel built around a small pool, it has won travelers over with its immaculate housekeeping, low parking fee, and such extras as a mini-fridge, microwave, generous closet space, and kitchenettes in some units. The outstanding coffee shop, **Swingers,** is renowned for its burgers and malts. The hotel remains open during renovation and has been offering "secret rates" to those who call for bookings. ***Note:*** Rates for 2015 had not been set at press time. The information below was valid for 2014, but come New Year's, much of it is likely to change.

8018 Beverly Blvd. (btw. La Cienega Blvd. and Fairfax Ave.), Los Angeles. www.beverlylaurelmotorhotel.com, ✆ **855/680-3238** or 323/651-2441. $123–$195 double. 52 units. Self parking $5. Pets allowed ($50 per night). **Amenities:** Outdoor pool. Wi-Fi ($6 per day).

Hills proper, while also being convenient to UCLA, Hollywood, and many L.A. attractions. Spotless rooms are arranged around an inner courtyard, modern with a bit of a tropical vibe, furnished with chairs, lounges, and cafe tables with umbrellas. There's a hot tub on the upper-level sun deck. Rooms come with queen, king, or two double beds; kings have larger living areas and marble bathrooms, while those with two doubles are a bit tight on space. All have quality contemporary furniture, work desks, mini-fridges, as well as such upscale perks as 37-inch flat-screen TVs, bathrobes, and Keurig coffeemakers. The included hot breakfast is several notches above the norm, and the thoughtful staff is a font of information. ***Tip:*** The No. 7 bus stops around the corner on W. Pico Boulevard and goes straight to Santa Monica Pier.

1119 S. Robertson Blvd. (btw. Pico and Olympic blvds.), Los Angeles. www.carlyle-inn.com. ✆ **800/322-7595** or 310/275-4445. 32 units. $139–$239 double. Rates include buffet breakfast. Parking $16. **Amenities:** Exercise room; Jacuzzi; business center; free Wi-Fi.

Hollywood & West Hollywood

EXPENSIVE

London West Hollywood ★★★ In the early 1980s, before West Hollywood became a city, hotel impresario Severyn Ashkenazy (the Mondrian, L'Ermitage) ran afoul of county height limits when building his new Le Bel Age, just south of the Sunset Strip, and he was forced to leave the 10th floor undeveloped. Bel Age's successor, the all-suites London West Hollywood, inherited that empty floor. New owners in 2013 obtained city permission to turn the languishing space into the hotel's grandest suites yet. The London was already a paragon of luxury, with a glam marble lobby, a rooftop pool area styled as an English garden, and a restaurant by celebrity chef Gordon Ramsay. Sleek, retro-styled suites—the smallest is 725 square feet—feature textured walls, embossed-leather furniture, and roomy bathrooms with sunken tubs. Most have balconies, while ground-floor suites have full patios (but not much of a view). The service is impeccable without being stuffy, and the concierge desk can pull rabbits out of hats. The new Gate Suites, unveiled in September 2014, were imagined as city flats surrounding London's Hyde Park. Each is individually designed but all feature blue-and-cream interiors, panoramic city views, oversized Waterworks "bath environments," and butler entrances or studies. Most rates are remarkably moderate for this level of luxury, though the Gate Suites raise the ceiling significantly.

1020 N. San Vicente Blvd. (south of Sunset Blvd.), West Hollywood. www.thelondonwesthollywood. com. © **866/282-4560** or 310/854-1111. 226 units. $300–$1,299. Rates include expanded continental breakfast. Valet parking $38. **Amenities:** 2 restaurants; bar; concierge; exercise room; spa; rooftop pool; room service; free Wi-Fi.

Petit Ermitage ★★

Bohemian chic—shabby chic, to some—is the trademark of this eccentric hotel, recognizable by its stained-glass entrance. Vintage furniture, a piano whimsically painted to look like a psychedelic face, faded rugs, and distressed (but working) fireplaces may seem to suggest the hotel hasn't been updated in decades, but it's all part of the design. Shabby it may be in some aspects, but it's also thoughtfully artsy, with hand-painted walls and original art from owner Stephan Ashkenazy's (son of hotelier Severen) collection of Dali, Miro, and others. Demi suites, the least expensive rooms, are large and comfortable, with a dining nook, wet bar or small kitchen, and, in some, a quaint writing desk. All suites have heavenly, custom-designed Thermopedic L'Ermitage mattresses. Set on a quiet street 3 blocks off the Sunset Strip, it offers peace in a neighborhood roiling with entertainment options. But you may need nothing more than the private rooftop club with its Butterfly Bar and garden, a sunken outdoor living room with a fireplace and couches stocked with fur throws, the Masters Lounge (a trippy version of a Victorian parlor), a heated saltwater pool, and 360-degree views of the Hollywood Hills.

8822 Cynthia St. (at Larrabee, north of Santa Monica Blvd.), West Hollywood. www.petitermitage. com. © **310/854-1114.** 80 suites. $225–$475. Valet parking $36. Pets up to 15 lb. accepted ($150 per stay). **Amenities:** Restaurant; private rooftop club w/heated saltwater pool; bar; exercise room; room service; kitchens (in some); free Wi-Fi.

The Redbury at Hollywood & Vine ★

From the four-story trompe l'oeil curtain on the tomato-red building to the movie-marquee entry to the bold (okay, garish) geometric and damask patterns on the mish-mash of quasi-Victorian, mid-century retro and modern chairs, there's not a subtle square inch in this exceedingly red boutique hotel at L.A.'s most famous intersection. Despite the danger of sensory overload, the studio, one- and two-bedroom "flats" are among the largest rooms in L.A., and all have fully stocked kitchens and combo washer/dryers. The beds have comfy pillowtop mattresses, and each unit has a private balcony or patio. Record players and an eclectic selection of vinyl 45s are a unique touch. On-site is top Mediterranean restaurant, Cleo; the Avalon nightclub is next door (miraculously, the noise doesn't seep into the hotel.)

1717 Vine St. (btw. Hollywood Blvd. and Yucca St.), Hollywood. www.theredbury.com. © **877/962-1717** or 323/962-1717. 57 units $242–$809. Valet parking $39. Metro Red Line to Hollywood/Highland. Pets less than 40 lb. allowed ($120 per stay of 7 days). **Amenities:** Restaurant; 3 bars; free passes to nearby 24 Hour Fitness; spa and pool privileges at sister property SLS; room service; car service within 3 mi.; Wi-Fi ($10/day).

Sunset Marquis Hotel & Villas ★★

A rock-star magnet since it opened in 1963, this sprawling, Mediterranean-style, all-suite hotel has gone so far as to install a state-of-the-art recording studio for such guests as Katy Perry and the Rolling Stones. Fortunately, the staff is so blasé that every guest gets the same friendly and efficient treatment; if you wind up next to members of Green Day at sexy **Bar 1200,** you'll get your drinks just as quickly as the rockers do. Across from the bar, the **Morrison Hotel Gallery** exhibits fine-art music and sports photographs from a collection that also extends throughout the hotel. Guest rooms aren't the biggest in their price

Hollywood & West Hollywood Hotels & Restaurants

ACCOMMODATIONS ■

Best Western Hollywood
  Hills Hotel **14**
Chamberlain West
  Hollywood **20**
The Charlie **24**
Èlan Hotel **31**
Le Montrose Suite Hotel **22**
Le Parc Suite Hotel **25**
London West Hollywood **21**
Magic Castle Hotel **2**
Orange Drive Hostel **3**
Petit Ermitage **23**
The Redbury **11**
Roosevelt Hotel **6**
Sunset Tower **18**
Sunset Marquis Hotel **19**

DINING ◆

Chaya Brasserie **29**
El Cholo **38**
Hatfield's **35**
Hungry Cat **12**
The Ivy **30**
Kings Road Cafe **32**
Lucques **27**
Musso & Frank Grill **9**
The Little Door **33**
Osteria Mozza **36**
Pink's Hot Dogs **34**
Petrossian **28**
Providence **37**
Roscoe's Chicken 'n'
  Waffles **15**
Toi on Sunset **1**

HOLLYWOOD HILLS

Wattles Park

WEST HOLLYWOOD

FAIRFAX

CBS Television City

Pan-Pacific Park

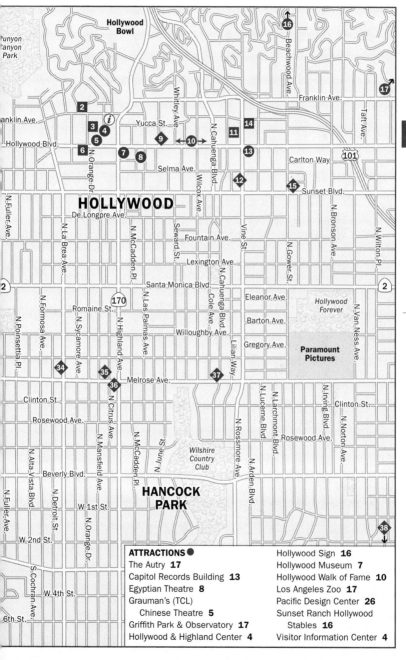

LOS ANGELES ESSENTIALS | Where to Stay

3

ATTRACTIONS ●

The Autry **17**
Capitol Records Building **13**
Egyptian Theatre **8**
Grauman's (TCL)
   Chinese Theatre **5**
Griffith Park & Observatory **17**
Hollywood & Highland Center **4**

Hollywood Sign **16**
Hollywood Museum **7**
Hollywood Walk of Fame **10**
Los Angeles Zoo **17**
Pacific Design Center **26**
Sunset Ranch Hollywood
   Stables **16**
Visitor Information Center **4**

range, but a remodel of its 101 suites, unveiled in summer 2014, brought in streamlined custom furnishings with plenty of color pop. Villas go all out with private alarm systems, butlers, and even a few baby grand pianos. The new seasonal California/Mediterranean restaurant **Cavatina** opened just in time for the 2014 Grammys. Despite being just a block from the Sunset Strip, the hotel feels tranquil, in part because of the hedges, stone pathways, and koi pond act as a buffer.

1200 Alta Loma Rd. (south of Sunset Blvd., west of N. La Cienaga Blvd.), West Hollywood. www.sunsetmarquishotel.com. C **800/858-9758** or 310/657-1333. 154 units. $270–$285 double; from $375 suite; from $465 villa. Valet parking $34. Up to 2 pets up to 10 lb. allowed ($200 per stay of up to 2 weeks). **Amenities:** Restaurant; bar; concierge; free access to Equinox across the street; Jacuzzi; 2 outdoor heated pools; room service; sauna; spa; business center; Wi-Fi ($12/day).

MODERATE

Chamberlain West Hollywood ★   The greatest asset of this modern, four-story boutique hotel, a converted apartment building, is its location on a leafy residential street 2 blocks from the Sunset Strip and Santa Monica Boulevard. A close second is its generously sized rooms, each a suite with separate living and sleeping areas. Variations on the large, gleaming lobby's geometrical black and white motif carry into guest rooms, taking on muted yellow and blue accents. All units have gas fireplaces, two HDTVs, mini-fridges, desks, and a small balcony. The gym and rooftop pool are small but adequate, and the pool has terrific city and hillside views. The Bistro restaurant is fine for a snack or a light meal, and room service will deliver to the roof (just be prepared to wait). While the Chamberlain doesn't necessarily stand out from the competition, its proximity to famous night spots such as the Whiskey A Go-Go and Viper Room make it a good mid-range choice. *Tip:* Avoid ground-floor rooms, which are dark because of the hotel's shady, downward-sloping street.

1000 Westmount Dr. (1 block west of La Cienega Blvd.), West Hollywood. www.chamberlainwesthollywood.com. C **800/201-9652** or 310/657-7400. 114 units. $200–$384 deluxe to 1-bedroom suite. Valet parking $38/$29 hybrids. Dogs up to 25 lb. allowed ($110 per stay). **Amenities:** Restaurant/bar; concierge; newly expanded fitness center; heated rooftop pool; business center; 24-hr. room service; car service within 3 mi; free Wi-Fi.

The Charlie ★★★   These shingled storybook bungalows were developed by Charlie Chaplin in the 1920s, on a farm once owned by actress Ruth Gordon's family, as a pied-à-terre for himself and a hideaway for his Hollywood friends. The restored rooms are named for stars reported to have stayed or partied in them over the years. Each is different, but all share attention to period detail, plenty of space, modern black-and-white kitchens couched in traditional style, and an abundance of natural light. Except for a single studio—considerably larger than comparably priced hotel rooms, with a full kitchen and private entry patio—all units are one- or two-bedroom suites. The Charlie is a super-private two-story cottage with an office area, patio, and two of the "Little Tramp's" canes displayed over the fireplace. The Marilyn, where the actress lived in the 1940s, is a free-standing two-bedroom with a private wrap-around patio. This is not a full-service hotel; with no front desk, fitness center or restaurant, it's more akin to a vacation rental—a sublime, atmospheric retreat swaddled in greenery, yet convenient to the diversions of West Hollywood, Beverly Hills, and Hollywood.

819 N. Sweetzer Ave. (btw. Waring and Willoughby), West Hollywood. www.thecharliehotel.com. C **323/988-9000.** 13 units. $225–$250 studio; $270-$650 suites. Extra bed $50. Free parking. Pets under 60 lb. allowed ($100 per pet for stays under 7 days). **Amenities:** Full kitchens; free Wi-Fi.

Le Montrose Suite Hotel ★★   For less than the price of most hotel rooms in the area, this all-suite hotel offers large split-level studio and one-bedroom apartments, on a quiet street only 2 blocks from the Sunset Strip. The contemporary rooms are plain but modern with plenty of comforts, from fireplaces to pillowtop mattresses to huge HDTVs and twice-daily maid service. Most rooms have balconies, and all but the lowest price categories have kitchenettes. The sedate atmosphere enhances the just-like-home feeling, though **Privato,** the restaurant (for guests only), has a lounge and wine bar if you're seeking nightlife without the full-on craziness of the Strip. The only real view is on the roof, which has a saltwater swimming pool, Jacuzzi, and tennis courts. This is a popular place for long-term stays, not only for tourists but for music and movie people who don't relish a big scene.

900 Hammond St. (btw. Cynthia St. and Phyllis Ave.), West Hollywood. www.lemontrose.com. ✆ **800/776-0666** or 310/855-1115. 133 units. $219–$539 suite. Valet parking $38. Pets up to 30 lb. accepted ($100 per stay). **Amenities:** Restaurant; bar; 2 bikes; fitness center; sauna; Jacuzzi; outdoor heated saltwater pool; room service; sauna; lighted tennis court; babysitting; laundry facilities; charging stations for electric cars; free Wi-F.

Le Parc Suite Hotel ★★ Stylish but not especially distinctive, this all-suite hotel's unusually large junior and one-bedroom units are well-endowed with living rooms, balconies, fireplaces, kitchenettes, two HD TVs, spacious bathrooms with vanities, and desks equipped with outlets. All got new carpets, paint, and earth-toned furniture in 2012. The leafy residential street is a short drive from Hollywood's attractions, Los Angeles' Museum Row and Farmers Market, and Rodeo Drive in Beverly Hills. It's close to the Pacific Design Center, so you might spot some big-name designers here, and music industry celebrities looking to stay out of the spotlight show up at times. But vacationers make up the bulk of the clientele; it's one of L.A.'s better choices for families in need of elbow room. The bistro-style **Knoll** is adequate but won't keep you from seeking out some of the area's more interesting restaurants. The rooftop lounge has a pool, tennis court, and the hotel's only skyline views.

733 N. West Knoll Dr. (btw. Melrose Ave. and Sherwood Dr.), West Hollywood. www.leparcsuites. com. ✆ **800/578-4837** or 310/855-8888. 154 units. $170–$569 junior or 1-bedroom suite. Parking $38. Pets accepted ($100 per stay). **Amenities:** Restaurant w/full bar; concierge; well-equipped gym; sauna; Jacuzzi; outdoor heated pool; room service; sauna; lighted rooftop tennis court; business center; car service within 3 mi.; free Wi-Fi.

Magic Castle Hotel ★ A block away from the stars on the Walk of Fame, this basic hotel is well-located for exploring Hollywood on a budget. The helpful, outgoing staff and free snacks around the clock go a long way toward compensating for lack of a restaurant, room service, or fitness center. Its former life as an apartment building means large rooms, generic but bright and uncluttered, and full-size kitchens. Unexpected touches of luxury include bathrobes and slippers (including kids' sizes) and pillowtop mattresses. The garden setting is an effective buffer from the never-ending traffic just beyond. *Tip:* Staying at the hotel also gets you into the members-only Magic Castle illusionist club next door.

7025 Franklin Ave. (btw. La Brea and Highland aves.), Hollywood. www.magiccastlehotel.com. ✆ **323/851-0800.** 43 units. $189–$199 double; from $228 suite. Rates include continental breakfast. Parking $11. **Amenities:** Outdoor heated pool; free use of nearby fitness center; laundry facilities; free Wi-Fi.

Roosevelt Hotel, Hollywood ★★ The last hotel left standing from Hollywood's glory days was financed in the 1920s by a group that included Mary Pickford, Douglas Fairbanks, and Louis B. Mayer. It hosted the first Academy Awards in 1929 and was Marilyn Monroe's home during her modeling days. Following its resurrection in 2005, the hot **Teddy's** nightclub made the Hollywood Roosevelt the darling of a new generation of young Hollywood hipsters. The 12-story landmark is in the midst of a rolling renovation that began in January 2014 and is scheduled for completion sometime in summer 2015. The first rooms to emerge were clad in soothing gray and white, with lots of light wood, set off by darker hardwood floors and sparing use of bright color spots. Sumptuous new bedding includes custom-made linens; bathrooms feature rain showers. They feel a little more retro, so paradoxically more contemporary, than counterparts still awaiting their makeover. Poolside cabana rooms, renovated in 2011, also have a sleek retro look. The Spanish-influenced lobby's handcrafted columns, ornate ceiling, and magnificent arches, meanwhile, have changed little. But many guests care little about any of that; they're here for the scene. Good luck trying to get into Teddy's, but other options include the late-night DJ parties at the poolside **Tropicana** bar; the clubby **Library Bar**'s craft cocktails, served omakase style; **The Spare Room,** a cocktail lounge with vintage bowling lanes; and **Beacher's Madhouse,** a racy, Vaudeville-inspired theater. In addition to **Public Kitchen & Bar,** the main restaurant, **25 Degrees** serves some of L.A.'s best burgers, 24 hours a day.

7000 Hollywood Blvd. (at N. Orange Dr.), Hollywood. www.hollywoodroosevelt.com. © **800/950-7667** or 323/466-7000. 300 units. $254–$478 double; from $314 poolside cabana rooms; from $382 suite. Valet parking $35. Metro Red Line to Hollywood/Highland. Pets allowed in some rooms ($100 per stay). **Amenities:** 2 restaurants; 5 bars; theater; concierge; executive-level rooms; exercise room; Jacuzzi; Olympic-size outdoor pool; business center; 24-hr. room service; spa; Wi-Fi ($15 per day).

Sunset Tower Hotel ★★★ Once home to Harlow, Gable, Marilyn, and even reclusive Howard Hughes, the Sunset Tower began life in 1929 as a luxury apartment building. Today, it is 15 stories of Art Deco glory rising above Sunset Boulevard. In reviving it in 2005, hotelier Jeff Klein preserved the elegance of a more glamorous era. Stars of this era flock here again today, but you'd never know it—that's the way they want it. Road-weary tourists receive the same gracious service as the biggest celeb—front desk staffers call you by name, and the **Tower Bar**'s cocktails are delivered by waiters in white jackets to the soft strains of a piano. Some competitors have larger rooms, but none more tasteful than these. Subtle art-deco accents echo the building's exterior, furnishings are gleaming wood and brass, and muted colors leave the spectacle to the floor-to-ceiling windows (south-facing rooms have fantastic city views). The hotel's **Argyle Spa** is widely considered one of Los Angeles' best. The pool is small, but it has one of the best views of any in the area, and the modern fitness room is open 24 hours.

8358 Sunset Blvd. (on the Sunset Strip, north of Fountain Ave.), West Hollywood. www.sunsettower hotel.com. © **323/654-7100.** 74 units. $245–$385 double; from $335 suite. Valet parking $36. Pets accepted ($100 per stay). **Amenities:** Restaurant; poolside grill; bar/lounge; concierge; exercise room; heated outdoor pool; room service; full-service spa; dog park; free Wi-Fi.

INEXPENSIVE

Best Western Hollywood Hills Hotel ★ This basic chain hotel has had some work done, as they say in Hollywood, and the stylish lobby is a delightful surprise after seeing the clunky (though also rehabbed), 1950s facade. The best rooms are in back, away from the traffic noise; they overlook the pool and have views of the nearby hillside. All rooms (kings or two doubles only) are contemporary and attractive, if somewhat generic, and have refrigerators and microwaves. The location, a 5-minute walk from Hollywood and Vine, is the biggest draw, and that intersection's Metro Line station allows you to visit Universal Studios sans wheels. Location probably also explains the major caveat here: Rates swing wildly, even from one weekday to the next. It's a tremendous deal if you hit it right, and laughably overpriced if you don't.

(More than $500 after taxes for a motel room, even a nice one? C'mon.) Don't book without first clicking the "dates are flexible" link and perusing the calendar, which displays daily prices.

6141 Franklin Ave. (btw. Vine and Gower sts.), Hollywood. www.hollywoodhillshotel. © **800/287-1700** or 323/464-5181. 86 units. $102–$499 double. Valet parking $15. Metro Red Line to Hollywood/Vine. Pets accepted by advance arrangement ($75/night). **Amenities:** Coffee shop; pool; free Wi-Fi.

Orange Drive Hostel ★★ If L.A.'s boutique hotels are too hard on your wallet, this boutique hostel could be the answer. Set in a mature garden, it occupies a stately 1920s manor home that later became a boarding house for some of Hollywood's biggest stars early in their careers. You're within steps of the Dolby Theatre and a block from Hollywood Boulevard, the Chinese Theatre and the Walk of Fame. It's not much farther to the Runyon Canyon Trail and its fantastic views of the Hollywood sign. Though the atmosphere is relaxed, you're surrounded by Hollywood's nightlife, restaurants, and ample transportation options that bring Universal Studios, The Grove, and Beverly Hills within easy reach. With period furniture, abundant windows, and Craftsman architectural detail, the private rooms are more akin to a B&B than a traditional hostel. Breakfast here is DIY, though, with everything except milk provided. The staff is as friendly as it is resourceful. *Tip:* Pay cash to avoid the bank credit-card fees, which are passed on to guests.

1764 N. Orange Dr. (½ block south of Franklin), Los Angeles. www.orangedrivehostel.com/ © **323/850-0350.** 12 units. $82–$94 double (shared bathroom); $92–$105 private bathroom; $38–$44 per person dorm. $50 refundable deposit ($20 for dorm room). Rates include full breakfast (DIY.) Parking $5. Metro Red Line to Hollywood/Highland. Hostel Hopper shuttle to major attractions ($20–$85 roundtrip, depending on destination). **Amenities:** Shared kitchen; common TV room; laundry facilities; barbecue grills; concierge; business center; free Wi-Fi.

Downtown
EXPENSIVE
The Ritz-Carlton Los Angeles ★★★ The legions of well-heeled travelers who
will stay *only* at the Ritz-Carlton will find luxury taken to its high-tech extreme at this one. Built next to the L.A. LIVE entertainment complex in 2010, it features such gewgaws as a mini TV built into the bathroom mirror. (Is this necessary? No. Is it cool? Very.) Guest rooms are sophisticated and supremely comfortable, while service is attentive and seemingly effortless. The rooftop pool has astounding city views, and the sparkly, 8,000-square-foot full-service spa, Downtown's first, harks back to Hollywood's glamour days. The Ritz occupies floors 22 through 26 of a hotel tower shared with sister property JW Marriott. They have separate entrances and lobbies but share access to restaurants, bars, and the spa. **WP24 by Wolfgang Puck,** serving Chinese fusion in its formal dining room on the Ritz's 24th floor, includes a large lounge and **Nest at WP24,** a restaurant within a restaurant offering Asian-inspired snacks, appetizers, and entrees in a more casual atmosphere.

900 W. Olympic Blvd. (at Georgia St.), Los Angeles. www.ritzcarlton.com. © **888/275-8063** or 213/743-8800. 123 units. $369–$569 double; from $600 suite. Valet parking $42. Metro Red or Purple Line to Civic Center/Grand Park. **Amenities:** Restaurant/lounge; concierge and club level; fitness center and spa; rooftop pool; business center; car service; room service; Wi-Fi ($13/day).

MODERATE
JW Marriott Hotel Los Angeles ★ This member of another high-end Marriott
brand occupies the first 21 floors of a tower shared with the Ritz-Carlton. The two hotels up the ante for Downtown, which had been saddled with a skimpy selection of

virtually indistinguishable business-oriented chain hotels while rapidly revitalizing on the residential, cultural, retail, and restaurant fronts. Then came L.A. LIVE; the Ritz and JW Marriott followed. The JW doesn't match the Ritz's fine-tuned, all-out luxury, but its sleek, spacious rooms—strong chocolate and orange accents spice up a predominantly white color scheme—solid contemporary furniture, and above-average amenities certainly feel luxurious. JW guests have access to the Ritz's spa and WP4 restaurant. It has its own large pool deck on the fourth floor. Among the shared restaurants and lounges located within the JW are the casual **LA Market** restaurant and the **Mixing Room,** serving intriguing specialty cocktails and new spins on classic favorites (cucumber gin martini, anyone?) along with small plates.

900 W. Olympic Blvd. (at Figueroa St.), Los Angeles. www.marriott.com. © **888/832-9136** or 213/765-8600. 878 units. From $249–$419 double; from $750 suite. Valet parking $42. Metro Red or Purple Line to Civic Center/Grand Park. **Amenities:** 2 restaurants; 2 bars; concierge; fitness center; Jacuzzi; outdoor pool; room service; business center; spa. Wi-Fi ($13–$15/day).

Los Angeles Athletic Club ★

Let's get one thing out of the way right now: Rooms in this hotel atop the old-school athletic club are dark. Walls are dark, drapes are dark, and lighting is minimal. Think of it as stepping into a work of film noir, and you'll be right at home. Which is not to say it's old-fashioned—elegant guest rooms offer custom-built furniture, pillowtop mattresses, flat-screen TVs, and refrigerators. The hotel's graceful stone and woodwork are legacies of its 1912 architecture, and the building oozes history. Charlie Chaplin lived here when he was getting started (ask for the Social Club Suite), and hallways are festooned with photos of athletes from throughout the decades. Your hotel stay confers all the perks of club membership. The dining room's excellent food is also healthy—they have a way with quinoa—and the eighth-floor snack bar is downright cheap (also healthy). In 2013, the club transformed its no-name, third-floor watering hole into **Invention,** a carefully researched shrine to pre-Prohibition cocktails. But the best perk is free rein in L.A.'s most extensive athletic facility, including its classes and personal trainers. *Tip:* The club has a dress code, which varies by location, and cell phones are not allowed in certain areas.

431 West 7th St. (at S. Olive St.), Los Angeles. www.laachotel.com. © **800/421-8777** or 213/625-2211. 72 units. $189–$319 double; suites from $349. Rates include full breakfast. Parking $20. Metro Purple, Red, Blue or Expo line to 7th St./Metro Center. **Amenities:** Restaurant; snack bar; 2 bars; full-service gym; indoor pool; babysitting; room service; business center; free Wi-Fi.

Omni Los Angeles ★

Though designed for business travelers and conventions, this 17-story tower crowning historic Bunker Hill is ideally situated for sampling Los Angeles' greatly improved cultural offerings. The Museum of Contemporary Art is right next door, and the L.A. Music Center, Walt Disney Concert Hall, and Cathedral of Our Lady of the Angels are a short walk. The two-story atrium lobby is a work of art in itself, with a sculpture by David Stromeyer and art by the likes of David Hockney and Jim Dine. Expansive guest rooms with tasteful traditional furnishings have such luxurious touches as feather and foam pillows, triple-sheeted beds, and oversized desks with desktop connections. West- and north-facing rooms have an impressive view of the Disney Concert Hall. The OmniKids program provides a "Kitchen Kids" backpack at check-in and use of a rolling backpack filled with toys, books, and games. You'll find one of Downtown's biggest disparities between weekend and weekday rates here; weekenders are sometimes more than $100 a night lower.

251 S. Olive St. (btw. 2nd and 3rd), Los Angeles. www.omnihotels.com. © **888/444-6664** or 213/ 617-3300. 453 units. $189–$609 double; from $540 suite. Valet parking $40. Pets under 25 lb. accepted ($50 per stay). Metro Red or Purple Line to Pershing Square or Civic Center/Grand Park.

Amenities: Restaurant; lounge; babysitting; children's programs; concierge; 24-hr. gym; lap pool; business center; room service; car service; Wi-Fi ($10/day; free w/Select Guest membership).

INEXPENSIVE

Figueroa Hotel ★   This unabashedly idiosyncratic standby for budget travelers is a love-it-or-hate-it kind of place. Through no doings of its own, it now stands in a rapidly gentrifying patch of Downtown, just a couple of blocks from the lofty Ritz and JW and across the street from L.A. LIVE. The 12-story, 1926 Spanish Colonial building began life as a YWCA residence, and the architecture is evident in the beamed ceilings, fans, and tile flooring in "The Fig's" lobby—which then on Moroccan chandeliers, hand-glazed walls, and Persian kilims. Comfortable but dimly lit guest rooms are equally eclectic—a little Mexican tile here, a few Oriental rugs there, wrought-iron beds everywhere. The over-the-top Moroccan Suites, at least, are focused on their theme. The kaleidoscope of styles and colors tends to distract from scuffed furniture and bald patches in rugs, which may be a deal-breaker for some but incidental to others. The hotel's style effectively filters out guests accustomed to the Ritz or even Holiday Inn; its international clientele veers toward anti-corporate types who value sensation over perfection. But the garden Verandah bar by the mosaic-tiled pool and Jacuzzi is a favorite cooling-off spot for locals and tourists alike.

939 S. Figueroa St. (at Olympic Blvd.), Los Angeles. www.figueroahotel.com. ✆ **800/421-9092** or 213/627-8971. 265 units. $149–$229 double; from $225 suite. Parking $16. Metro Red or Purple Line to 7th St/Metro Center. **Amenities:** Restaurant; bar; Jacuzzi; outdoor pool; Wi-Fi (AT&T hotspot, $5/day); free Internet computer in lobby.

Metro Plaza Hotel ★   An older but well-maintained hotel with an accommodating 24-hour front desk, this is a good budget choice for travelers arriving from Union Station (a 5-minute walk) and visiting Chinatown, Olvera Street and El Pueblo, and Little Tokyo. The Walt Disney Concert Hall and MOCA are about a mile away. You could even walk to Dodger Stadium and get there faster than driving on traffic-choked game days. Two subway lines serving Union Station greatly expand your sightseeing options. The rooms are a bit worn and the decor outdated, but they are clean, comfortable and quite spacious for L.A. Mini-fridges are a nice bonus. The huge bathrooms, which have been upgraded, have massaging spa showerheads. The complimentary continental breakfast is very basic, so if you want to fuel up for the day, ask the front desk to suggest some alternatives.

711 N. Main St. (btw. W. Cesar E. Chavez and Ord), Los Angeles. www.metroplazahoteldowntown la.com. ✆ **800/223-2223** or 213/680-0200. 80 units. $109–$129 double; suites from $139. Rates include continental breakfast. One child under 12 stays free in parent's room. Extra person $10. Parking $4. Metro Purple or Red lines to Union Station. **Amenities:** Exercise room; free Wi-Fi.

Universal City

Unless your vacation revolves around the Universal Studios Hollywood park, there isn't much reason to stay in Universal City. Pickings are relatively slim and consist mainly of chain hotels. The best of these are the moderately priced **Hilton Universal City & Towers** (www.universalcity.hilton.com; ✆ **800/ 445-8667** or 818/506-2500) and the pricier **Sheraton Universal Hotel** (www.sheraton.com/universal; ✆ **800/325-3535** or 818/980-1212).

MODERATE

The Beverly Garland ★   A mile from Universal Studios, the hotel that actress Beverly Garland (Fred MacMurray's wife on "My Three Sons") and her husband built in 1972 shed the Holiday Inn brand in November 2013 and undertook a complete redesign, including an addition of a new landscaped garden area. Garland's son, James Crank, still runs the hotel and is in charge of the multi-phase transformation of the property into a boutique hotel with a Southern California retro look. Guest rooms, with bold red accents against a black, white, and wood background, evoke the '40s just before Art Deco gave way to anonymous Modernism. Balconies in all rooms overlook the grassy grounds that provide respite from Hollywood's abundance of concrete. (Requesting a room facing Vineland Ave. will dampen the ceaseless hum of traffic from the nearby 101 freeway.) KidSuites are designed for families, with a partitioned section providing privacy for both parents and kids. The staff is congenial, and the shuttle to and from Universal Studios is free.

4222 Vineland Ave. (west of Hwy 101), North Hollywood. www.beverlygarland.com. ⓒ **800/238-3759** or 818/980-8000. 256 units. $146–$199 double. Up to 2 children 17 and under stay free in parent's room. Parking $19. Metro Red Line to Universal/Studio City. **Amenities:** Restaurant; bar; heated outdoor pool; sauna; 2 lighted tennis courts, free shuttle to Universal Studios and subway, free Wi-Fi.

Pasadena
EXPENSIVE

Langham Huntington Hotel & Spa ★★ This Spanish Mission Revival–style luxury resort was born as the Hotel Wentworth in 1907 and was soon bought by railroad magnate Henry Huntington, whose name has endured through Sheraton and Ritz-Carlton incarnations and its current union with the international Langham group. It remains proudly opulent and unabashedly traditional, even though the current hotel is a replica, built after new earthquake standards forced the original's demolition in 1988. Two historic ballrooms were preserved and restored to the new hotel, whose 23 magnificently landscaped acres feel like a European baronial estate. The public areas and grounds, including an outstanding Japanese garden, are where the hotel shines. Dinner at the steakhouse **Royce,** Sunday brunch at the poolside **Terrace,** or afternoon tea in the **Lobby Lounge** make delightful escapes from everything L.A. Another option is the new and quite modern **Chuan Spa,** unveiled in June 2014, which specializes in treatments based on traditional Chinese medicine and new high-tech skin care techniques. Despite various updates, rooms and cottages are subject to random gaps in quality, whether it be too few electrical outlets, slow-draining tubs and sinks, or ineffectual air-conditioning. Still, they are spacious, sumptuously furnished, and flooded with natural light. The occasional misstep is significant only in contrast with the illusion of perfection the place projects.

1401 S. Oak Knoll Ave. (at Huntington Circle, btw. Huntington Garden Dr. and Wentworth Ave.). www.pasadena.langhamhotels.com. ⓒ **800/591-7481** or 626/568-3900. 380 units. $200–$469 double; from $375 suite. Valet parking $25. **Amenities:** 2 restaurants; 2 bars/lounges; concierge; fitness center; Jacuzzi; heated outdoor pool; room service; full-service spa w/whirlpool, sauna, and steam room; 3 lighted tennis courts; business center; free Wi-Fi.

MODERATE

Bissell House Bed & Breakfast ★ The grand, three-story 1887 Victorian-Craftsman hybrid where the Bissell vacuum company heiress once lived on "Millionaire's Row," tucked behind hedges on Orange Grove Avenue, is now a classic B&B with a full complement of antiques and chintz. Each room has a different layout and theme. Third-floor rooms have the most space, with beds tucked into the roofline's nooks, but be aware there's no elevator. All have private bathrooms; if you're hankering for a long soak in a deep claw-foot tub, go for the Prince Albert or Morning Glory room. The Garden Room has a whirlpool tub. The English Holiday Room, name notwithstanding, includes a work desk. But my favorite is Victoria's Room, once Anna

Pasadena Hotels, Restaurants & Attractions

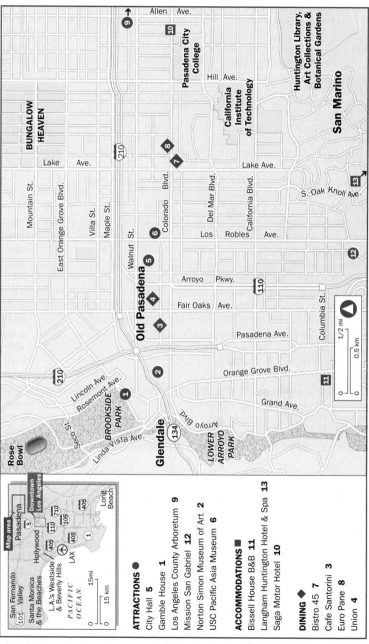

ATTRACTIONS ●
City Hall **5**
Gamble House **1**
Los Angeles County Arboretum **9**
Mission San Gabriel **12**
Norton Simon Museum of Art **2**
USC Pacific Asia Museum **6**

ACCOMMODATIONS ■
Bissell House B&B **11**
Langham Huntington Hotel & Spa **13**
Saga Motor Hotel **10**

DINING ◆
Bistro 45 **7**
Cafe Santorini **3**
Euro Pane **8**
Union **4**

Bissell's sun room, with its narrow solarium porch and writing desk overlooking the pool and gardens. Flat-screen TVs in most rooms are an incongruous but appreciated perk not found in many B&Bs, and the lush garden includes a pool, Jacuzzi, and deck. The vegetarian morning repast can be adjusted to guests' dietary needs.

201 Orange Grove Ave. (at Columbia St.), South Pasadena. www.bissellhouse.com. ⓒ **626/441-3535.** 7 units. $169–$350 double. Rates include full breakfast and afternoon tea and dessert. Free parking. **Amenities:** Jacuzzi; outdoor pool; DVD library; free Wi-Fi.

INEXPENSIVE

Saga Motor Hotel★★   Without trying to hide its heritage as a motel along the old Route 66—the huge street sign is kitschy, and the low-slung street entrance is very 1950s—this great alternative to Old Pasadena's pricey hotels has evolved beyond the basic roadside motor court. Except for the wall-mounted air-conditioning unit, the rooms' sponge-painted walls, wide-screen TVs, and upscale bathroom amenities wouldn't be out of place in a mid-range hotel. The shelf of small potted plants above the TV is a day-brightener, and the Hollywood-style bathroom light bar and floral wallpaper strip lifted an otherwise generic bathroom above the ordinary. Furnishings are simple but good, solid quality. The large central pool is surrounded by palm trees and a well-tended garden. The location, a few blocks of the Foothill (210) Freeway, couldn't be more convenient. It's a straight shot to Old Pasadena, a mile from the Huntington Library, and within a few minutes of the Rose Bowl and Gamble House.

1633 E. Colorado Blvd. (btw. Allen and Sierra Bonita aves.), Pasadena. www.thesagamotorhotel.com. ⓒ **800/793-7242** or 626/795-0431. 70 units. $85–$105 double; from $142 suite. Rates include continental breakfast. Free parking. Pets under 15 lb. allowed ($35 per stay). **Amenities:** Outdoor heated pool; free laundry facilities; mini-fridge; business center; free Wi-Fi.

WHERE TO DINE

Santa Monica & the Beaches

EXPENSIVE

Boa Steakhouse ★★ STEAK   Carnivores are in their element here. From the 40-day dry-aged New York strip to pasture-raised veal Delmonico to Japanese wagyu market choices, there's not a mediocre meat in the house (though I have to question whether spaghetti and meatballs is the best use for Kobe beef). You choose the rub, ranging from straightforward tri peppercorn to adventurous bacon jam, and the sauces. Sides sold separately punish the wallet, but hand-cut crispy fries and chipotle lime corn, among others, are a challenge to resist. Like the menu, the decor strays seriously from traditional steakhouse atmosphere. Gluten-free menus (which should be a natural for any steakhouse) don't subtract many items from the regular menu. *Note:* A second Boa Steakhouse is in West Hollywood's at 9200 W. Sunset Blvd. (ⓒ **310/278-2050**).

101 Santa Monica Blvd. (at Ocean Ave.), Santa Monica. www.boasteak.com. ⓒ **310/899-4466.** Reservations recommended. Main courses $28–$78. Mon–Wed noon–4:30pm and 5:30–10:30pm, Thurs noon–3pm and 5:30–11pm, Fri noon–3pm and 5:30–11:30pm, Sat noon–4:30pm and 5:30–11:30pm, Sun noon–4:30pm and 5:30–10pm. Self-parking free for lunch with validation, valet parking for dinner $7 with validation.

Cafe Del Rey ★ CALIFORNIAN   With a fantastic view of sailboats bobbing in the marina, this lively restaurant is perfect for a long, leisurely meal. The menu takes its cues from the Mediterranean's coastal towns, emphasizing simplicity and fresh, seasonal ingredients, including a raw bar. A summer menu might include free-range chicken-tomato fricassee or duck breast with harts of palm, but fish and seafood have a starring role. The chef's selection of the day's fresh catch, such as swordfish with endive, snap peas, baby carrots in sumac broth, are a good bet.

4451 Admiralty Way (btw. Lincoln and Washington blvds.), Marina del Rey. www.cafedelreymarina. com. ⒸⒸ **310/823-6395.** Reservations recommended. Main courses $20–$50. Mon–Thurs 5:30– 10pm, Fri–Sat 5:30–10:30pm, Sun 5–9:30pm. Valet parking free for lunch, $4 for dinner.

Inn of the Seventh Ray ★★ ORGANIC   This rustic spot in Topanga Canyon began life as a church and did time as a feed store, gas station, and junkyard before being renovated into one of L.A.'s most romantic restaurants. Outdoor seating overlooks a creek engulfed by vines and shrubs; indoors, a glass roof frames mountain views. The food is prepared to promote both physical and spiritual health, with seasonal organic ingredients or produce from known local farms. Meat and fish are slowcooked at 180 degrees or less to prevent oxidants from forming, and water is treated by reverse osmosis and then alkalinized to add healing properties. Don't worry; it's not hippie-trippy food. While you can get a delicious summer vegetable succotash, the menu is rife with sophisticated dishes such as Copper River salmon, achiote-flavored chicken with polenta crème fraîche, and charcoal crust filet mignon.

128 Old Topanga Canyon Rd. (Calif. 27), Topanga. www.innoftheseventhray.com. ⒸⒸ **310/455- 1311.** Reservations recommended. Main courses $20–$44. Mon–Fri 11:30am–3pm and 5:30– 10pm, Sat 10:30am–3pm and 5:30–10pm, Sun 9:30am–3pm and 5:30–10pm. Valet parking $4 or free street parking.

JiRaffe ★★ CALIFORNIAN/FRENCH   The purple Peruvian gnocchi and rock shrimp appetizer is legendary at this restaurant, which melds the region's sophistication with its relaxed beach atmosphere. In fact, the appetizers as a whole—including sweet corn *agnolotti*, black linguini, and deep-sea crab cakes with parsnip puree—very nearly upstage the main dishes. A local favorite since 1996, it occupies a bright loft space with walls of windows, 2 blocks from the beach. The best entrees are perfectly cooked barbequed wild California king salmon and caramelized pork chops with wild rice, bacon, and apple chutney. The three-course Monday night bistro menu is a bargain at $38; the regular menu is also available.

502 Santa Monica Blvd. (corner of 5th St.), Santa Monica. www.jirafferestaurant.com. ⒸⒸ **310/917- 6671.** Reservations recommended. Main courses $21–$34. Mon 5:30–9pm; Tues–Thurs 5:30– 10pm, Sat 5:30–10:30pm. Valet parking $8.

Saddle Peak Lodge ★★ AMERICAN   This old hunting lodge—a weathered old three-story timber-and-stone building high in the Malibu hills, filled with antiques, a rustic fireplace, and stuffed animal heads—is all about game, from both land and sea. The tasting menu is the only way to grasp the breadth of culinary artistry practiced here, but the signature Elk tenderloin with caramelized figs, so tender you don't need a knife, is a good way to start if you go for an entrée. A juicy Niman Ranch pork chop with bacon hash and lavender crumble, or pan-roasted Idaho rainbow trout with grilled eggplant and heirloom potatoes are other outstanding choices, and an extensive list of reasonably priced wine can complement whatever you choose. A popular Sunday brunch is served on the woodsy terrace.

419 Cold Canyon Rd. (call for directions), Calabasas/Agoura. www.saddlepeaklodge.com. ⒸⒸ **818/222-3888.** Main courses $29–$54; tasting menu $105. Wed–Fri 5–9pm; Sat 5–10pm; Sun 10:30am–2pm and 5–9pm. Valet parking $4.

MODERATE

Border Grill ★ LATIN AMERICAN   Light, healthful "modern Mexican" cuisine is the focus of this urban cantina, created by Mary Sue Milliken and Susan Feniger before they hit it big on Bravo's "Top Chef Masters" and Food Network's "Too Hot Tamales." Though it's often packed and can get noisy, this is no nachos-and-tacos quick stop, but a tribute to the complex, authentic cuisines of Mexico's Oaxaca and the Yucatán, with supporting roles by other parts of Latin America, prepared with fresh fruits, vegetables and herbs, and handmade corn masa and tortillas. In addition to quesadillas, enchiladas, and tacos like you've probably never had before, you can get a variation on the traditional Yucatecan *cochinita pibil* (pork marinated in achiote and oranges, slow-roasted in banana leaves), *pescado Veracruzano* (pan-seared sustainable fresh fish in tomato, kalamata olive, jalapeño, wine and garlic broth) and, just for good measure, a chile relleno burger.

1445 4th St. (btw. Broadway and Santa Monica Blvd.), Santa Monica. www.bordergrill.com. ℭ **310/451-1655.** Reservations recommended. Main courses $16–$36. Mon–Thurs 11:30am–10pm; Fri 11:30am–11pm; Sat–Sun 10am–10pm. Metered parking on street, parking lots.

Chez Jay's ★ Cleverly disguised as dive bar (which it partly is), this is a nugget of history on a multimillion-dollar plot of land near the Santa Monica Pier. The creaky classic was opened by the late Jay "Peanuts" Fiondella, an old-timer who staunchly refused to sell to developers. Marlon Brando, Frank Sinatra, Peter Sellers, Kevin Spacey, Madonna, George Clooney have all been regulars. The popular rumor is that astronaut Alan Shepard took a peanut from Jay's to the moon and back, then a mischievous Steve McQueen tried to eat it. Of course, there's a jukebox in the corner, a marlin mounted on the wall, peanut shells on the floor, and well-worn red vinyl booths. They serve a great steak, and the bar is just the type where you'd expect to find Brando or Sinatra. On the waterfront, look for the neon sign and the wooden door with a little porthole on the east side of Ocean Avenue, a half-block south of the pier.

1657 Ocean Ave. (btw. Olympic Blvd. and Colorado Ave.). www.chezjays.com ℭ **310/395-1741.** Main courses $11–$30. Mon–Fri 11:45am–2pm and 5:30–9:30pm; Sat–Sun 5:30–9:30pm. Metered street parking.

Chez Melange ★★ NEW AMERICAN/FUSION Chez Melange lives up to its name in style as well as cuisine; part bistro, part tapas bar, part gastropub, and part cocktail lounge, it draws three generations of regulars to Redondo's "Hollywood Riviera." The delightful "Toasties" change often, usually involving artisan bread, garlic and extraordinary cheese. You'll find some unexpected combinations on the menu, such as Maine lobster with black bean sauce and Chinese sausage. Don't be timid here; just go for it and thank me later. The impressive wine list has a fine selection of wines by the glass. Under the same roof, Bouzy gastropub offers more casual fare, and the Bar Comida's eclectic small plates lineup changes every night.

1611 S. Catalina Ave. (1 block east of Esplanade, at Ave. I), Redondo Beach. www.chezmelange. com. ℭ **310/540-1222.** Reservations recommended. Main courses $13–$29. Mon–Thurs 5:30–9:30pm; Fri–Sat 5:30–10pm; Sun 9:30am–2pm and 5:30–9pm. Valet $4; free self-parking in underground garage.

Joe's Restaurant ★★ CALIFORNIAN Ensconced in a tiny (but remodeled) storefront on Venice Beach's main shopping strip is a true L.A. bargain. The best tables are tucked away on the trellised outdoor patio, but no matter where you sit, you'll enjoy the prices as much as the varied upscale fare such as crispy, anise-flavored sweetbreads, rock shrimp-filled zucchini flowers, and roasted king salmon. The set three-course lunch is a great deal, and brunch is among the best in town, with a wide variety of choices such as a green chili and turkey chorizo breakfast burrito, pan-seared salmon with curried carrot puree and crispy Swiss chard, or red wine–braised short rib hash with roasted red potatoes and fried eggs.

1023 Abbot Kinney Blvd., Venice. www.joesrestaurant.com. ℂ **310/399-5811.** Main courses $14–$32; prix fixe lunch $19. Tues–Thurs noon–2:30pm and 6–10pm; Fri noon–2:30pm and 6–11pm; Sat 11am–2:30pm and 6–11pm; Sun 11am–2:30pm and 6–10pm. Free street parking; valet parking $6.

Malibu Farm Pier Cafe ★★ AMERICAN

Taking over a long-empty, state-owned space at the end of the renovated Malibu Pier in summer 2013, the Malibu Farm Pier Cafe has won locals over with fresh, organic fare sourced mainly from the owner's and other local farms. The menu emphasizes vegetables and grains, simple preparations, and restrained use of sauces; each day's menu is brief but, in rotating with seasonal availability, has a wide range, from crab cakes to portobello burgers to minted lamb. And with its spot over the water, it has ocean views in every direction.

23000 Pacific Coast Hwy. (5.8 mi north of Topanga Canyon Blvd.), Malibu. www.malibu-farm.com. ℂ **310/456-1112.** Main courses: breakfast and lunch $9–$25, dinner $18–$32. Mon–Tues 9am–3pm; Wed–Sun 9am–3pm and 5–9:30pm. Free street parking, nearby pay lots.

Old Place ★★ NEW AMERICAN

Back in the early 20th century, before the Santa Monica Mountains sprouted ultra-private movie stars' woodsy spreads, this rustic little wooden building was a (very) small-town post office and general store. Now that it's a restaurant, it can handle the demand for its five booths and three tables only by limiting seatings to three times: 5, 6:30, and 8:30pm (you can also eat at the bar, first-come, first-served). The planning, and driving, required is rewarded by an unfailingly excellent meal in a bucolic setting. The brief but frequently changing menu features large portions of hearty updated classics such as beef stew and oak-grilled chicken-chanterelle potpie, as well as an oak-grilled fresh fish of the day from the Channel Islands. It all comes on mismatched tableware and with occasional shortages of certain menu items (the kitchen doesn't have a freezer) later in the evening—a good thing to keep in mind when choosing a reservation time.

29983 Mulholland Hwy., Cornell/Agoura Hills. www.oldplacecornell.com. ℂ **818/706-9001.** Main courses $14–$20. Thurs–Fri 4–10pm; Sat–Sun 9am–10pm. Closed Mon–Wed. Free parking.

Rustic Canyon Wine Bar & Seasonal Kitchen ★★ CALIFORNIAN

Serving simply prepared dishes inspired by the sustainable bounty from local farmers, ranchers, and fishermen, this restaurant grew out of the monthly dinners its founder once held in his home. Small but comfortable, it manages a few tables in the bar area. Chef Jeremy Fox, who garnered a Michelin star while working in the Napa Valley, plates the food with sharing in mind. Appetizers, such as grilled "brown turkey" figs with homemade ricotta and corn polenta croutons or duck rillettes with gherkins, peach preserves and black garlic, far outnumber the main courses (pork with polenta and caper salsa verde, roasted half chicken with roasted savoy cabbage and king trumpet mushrooms)—maximizing the variety of tastes you can experience in one meal.

1119 Wilshire Blvd. (btw. 11th and 12th sts.), Santa Monica. www.rusticcanyonwinebar.com. ℂ **310/393-7050.** Reservations recommended. Main courses $15–$39. Sun–Thurs 5:30–10:30pm; Fri–Sat 5:30–11pm. Valet parking $8.

INEXPENSIVE

Bread & Porridge ★ AMERICAN

Though this venerable neighborhood cafe, with fruit-crate labels adorning the walls and tabletops, has expanded its menu and hours, and added beer and wine, breakfast and lunch are still its stock in trade. You can get all the standards—pancakes, French toast, omelets, scrambles—as well as a breakfast quesadilla or burrito. Gourmet breakfast sausages are the menus' stars, ranging from maple breakfast and mild chicken apple sausages to classic pork links and spicy

Cajun andouille. A vast variety of big salads shares the bill with pastas, hearty sandwiches, and a few beef and chicken plates, including burgers, for other meals, no matter what time of day you want to eat them. Prices that once were flat-out bargains have crept up but are still reasonable by Santa Monica standards.

2315 Wilshire Blvd. (3 blocks west of 26th St.), Santa Monica. www.breadandporridge.com. ✆ **310/453-4941.** Main courses $7–$17. Mon–Fri 7am–7pm. Metered street parking.

Farm Stand ★★ MEDITERRANEAN/TURKISH   An unassuming restaurant on El Segundo's old-timey Main Street, the Farm Stand channels its devotion to health-promoting and sustainable foods into dishes based on Mediterranean and Middle Eastern cuisine—and takes great care that those values stay behind the curtain when the food appears on your plate. The menu, adorned by a confetti of colored symbols denoting dairy-free, vegan, vegetarian, gluten-free, and non-GMO dishes, includes daily specials ranging from lasagna to filet mignon kabobs to wild mahi mahi. The regular menu is impressive in its variety, from the starters to the pastas and stews—the walnut pomegranate stew is surprising and delicious—to fire-roasted, free-range Cornish hen and barbecued wagyu beef short ribs.

422 Main St. (at Pine Ave.), El Segundo. www.farmstand.us. ✆ 310/640-3276. Main courses $10–$23. Mon–Fri 11am–10pm; Sat–Sun 10am–10pm. Street parking.

Jody Maroni's Sausage Kingdom ★★ GRILL   The same family has sold wieners on Venice Beach since 1976, and now offers 17 varieties. We won't say "healthy," but these "lesser-evil" sausages are homemade from fresh meat, produce and spices; naturally low in sodium and fat; and in most cases free of preservatives or MSG. All the traditional sausages are there, but you owe it to yourself to try the smoky Polish pork (made with dark beer), tequila chicken (jalapeños, corn, and lime), or pomegranate chicken (fresh basil and cardamom). And don't miss the chili cheese fries. Other locations include Universal CityWalk (✆ 818/622-5639) and LAX Terminal 6 (✆ 310/646-3472). *Note:* Though hot dogs appear on the menu, do not mistake this for a hot dog stand. They are as mediocre as the sausages are sublime.

2011 Ocean Front Walk (north of Venice Blvd.), Venice. www.jodymaroni.com. ✆ **310/822-5639.** Sandwiches $5–$9. Daily 8am–6:30pm (varies seasonally, and closes when it rains).

Kay 'n Dave's Cantina ★ BREAKFAST/MEXICAN   A longtime local breakfast favorite, serving not only fluffy French toast and omelets but killer breakfast burritos and *chilaquiles* (Mexico's morning staple), Kay 'n Dave's is known chiefly for big portions of affordable, lard-free Mexican food. The Oaxaca-born chef goes beyond the familiar with dishes such as *molcajete* (a slow-cooked stew) and *clayuda* (a kind of "pizza" with a large tortilla base), then mixes things up with such creations as portabella mushroom quesadilla and salmon and spinach enchiladas. Kids are in their element here with their own menu and plenty of crayon artwork.

262 26th St. (south of San Vicente Blvd.), Brentwood. kayndaves.com. ✆ **310/260-1355.** Main courses $8–$22. Mon–Thurs 11am–9pm; Fri 11am–9:30pm; Sat 9am–9:30pm; Sun 9am–9pm. Metered street parking.

L.A.'s Westside & Beverly Hills
EXPENSIVE

The Bazaar by José Andrés ★★★ SPANISH/TAPAS   The hottest dining room in L.A. is SAAM, the restaurant-within-a-restaurant at The Bazaar, a playground where

kid-friendly RESTAURANTS

Café Pinot (p. 73), an upscale offshoot of chic Patina, is unexpectedly adept at catering to kids' tastes, and those 10 and under order anything from the menu for free.

On the other end of the scale, **Pink's Hot Dogs** (p. 70) in Hollywood proudly embraces the humble frank by preparing it in dozens of variations.

Start your day at the Mexican mini-chain **Kay 'n Dave's Cantina** (p. 60) with five kinds of fluffy pancakes, a killer breakfast burrito, enchiladas, fajitas, and more—all lard-free; every table sports a kids' menu and crayons.

Miceli's (p. 76) in Universal City, is a cavernous Italian restaurant whose waitstaff belts out show tunes or opera favorites. Kids love the boisterous atmosphere.

celebrity chef José Andrés (PBS' "Made in Spain") unleashes his avant-garde Spanish cuisine in the splashy SLS Hotel. In one cavernous open space, disparate lounge spaces are fashioned as a piazza, each with its own playful ambience—bullfighter pictures and the open kitchen in Rojo, glossy pink walls in Patisserie, the uncluttered Blanca, and the cool, moody Bar Centro. You can order a variety of impeccable tapas, such as garlic shrimp, chicken-béchamel fritters or ceviche and avocado roll, in any of these. But it's the small molecular-gastronomy bites dispensed in SAAM that inspire people to swoon. In the quiet, intimate room, which seats only 40, Andrés unveils 22 tiny courses. These may include a cocktail served with lotus root chips, liquid black spherified olives, a tiny carrot fritter, jicama-wrapped guacamole, or a chicken wing with a dab of buffalo sauce, ranch dressing, and a bit of celery artfully arranged on top—no two presentations are alike. Safe to say it's nothing you've experienced before. Even cocktails get the molecular treatment: Margaritas come with salt "air," and slushy caipirinhas are made at your table with liquid nitrogen.

465 S. La Cienega Blvd. (in SLS Hotel), Beverly Hills. www.thebazaar.com. © **310/246-5555.** Reservations required. Tapas $9–$19. SAAM tasting menu (food only) $150 per person. Mon–Wed 6–9:45pm; Thurs–Fri 6–10:45pm; Sat 5:30–10:45pm. Valet parking $14.

Craft Los Angeles ★★★ NEW AMERICAN   Everything is served family style, meant for sharing, at the second (after New York's Craft Restaurant) of celebrity chef Tom Colicchio's now-burgeoning empire. His farm-to-table concept embodies simplicity, relying on superb ingredients and stellar execution rather than a flurry of complex ingredients. Craft's greatest strength is its top-quality, expertly cooked meats, guaranteed antibiotic-free, such as velvety roasted lamb sirloin and incomparable braised short ribs—but earthy ricotta cavatelli and wild mushroom pasta, and sides such as roasted baby eggplant, easily hold their own. The concept of simplicity reaches its greatest heights in the salads; the lightly dressed red Russian kale with pecans and Asian pear is sublime.

10100 Constellation Blvd. (btw. Ave. of the Stars and Century Park E), Century City. www.craft restaurant.com. © **310/279-4180.** Reservations recommended. Main courses $21–$46. Mon–Fri 11:30am–2:30pm and 6–10pm; Sat 6–10pm. Valet $8; self-parking free with validation after 5pm Mon–Fri and all day Sat–Sun.

Hotels & Restaurants in Beverly Hills & the Westside

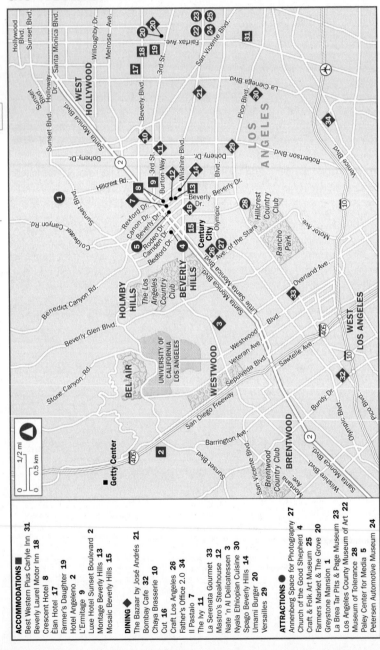

Cut ★★ STEAK   The praise is as high as the prices at this stylish modern steak-house, designed as one big open space with leather booths and wooden tables. A haven for Hollywood's power elite, it serves L.A.'s most expensive steak—a 6-ounce filet that fetches $120 and northward, depending on market prices. This is also the place to find American *and* Japanese Wagyu beef as well as Illinois and Nebraska corn-fed beef, all grilled and then finished under a superheated broiler. Side dishes are similarly extraordinary, from creamed spinach topped with an organic fried egg to mac and cheese made with Cavatappi pasta and Quebec cheddar. Exotic starters include Kerala soft-shell crab with green tomato chutney and bone marrow flan. And, of course, imported caviar. If dinner costing the equivalent of a weekend getaway is out of reach, **Sidebar** across the hall offers haute pub grub—Wagyu beef sliders, tempura onion rings with paprika-saffron aioli—with some of the same rarefied atmosphere.

9500 Wilshire Blvd. (in the Beverly Wilshire Hotel), Beverly Hills. www.wolfgangpuck.com. © **310/276-8500.** Reservations required. Main courses $50–$120 and up. Mon–Thurs 6–10pm; Fri 6–11pm; Sat 5:30–11pm. Valet parking $14 with validation.

Mastro's Steakhouse ★★★ STEAK/SEAFOOD   Pass on the somber, clubby first-floor dining room and slip into a black leather booth upstairs, where the piano bar is, in this classic and quite opulent steakhouse. Ahi tuna tartare or oysters Rockefeller are fitting starts to an 18-oz. bone-in fillet or Chef's Cut rib-eye chop, cooked to perfection and served on sizzling 400°F (204°C) plates. Either will easily feed three people, especially if you add some classic creamed or sauteed spinach and lyonnaise potatoes. A simple lemoncello, mango, and raspberry ice cream is the perfect finish, but a variety of dessert wines, ports, and cordials, and expertly mixed cocktails, also stand ready to serve if you can't manage another bite.

46 N. Canon Dr. (btw. Dayton Way and Wilshire Blvd.), Beverly Hills. www.mastrosrestaurants.com. © **310/888-8782.** Reservations recommended. Main courses $26–$84. Restaurant Sun–Thurs 5–11pm, Fri–Sat 5pm–midnight. Lounge daily 4:30pm–1am. Valet parking $9.

Matsuhisa ★ JAPANESE/PERUVIAN   The far from obvious but deliciously creative marriage of Japanese ingredients with South American salsas and spices is a result of chef/owner Nobuyuki Matsuhisa's arrival in Los Angeles following a stint in Peru in 1987, and the resulting cuisine in this landmark restaurant still captivates. (His introduction of yellowtail sashimi with jalapeños was a game-changer in the U.S.) More than two-dozen species of sushi lead the extensive menu, as well as a dozen sushi rolls and another two dozen vegetable and fish tempura options. Hot and cold special dishes showcase Matsuhisa's mastery in such creations as Peruvian-style sashimi, king crab with ginger salsa, and lamb chops with miso anticucho sauce. Sadly, the small, crowded dining room is dim and lacks privacy—big names are whisked through to private rooms—and it suffers in comparison to newer restaurants charging similar prices. *Note:* An outpost of Matsuhisa's successful Nobu chain, geared toward a younger crowd, is a mile up the street, 903 N. La Cienega Blvd. (© **310/657-5711**).

129 N. La Cienega Blvd. (north of Wilshire Blvd.), Beverly Hills. www.nobumatsuhisa.com. © **310/659-9639.** Reservations required. Main courses $19–$32 or market price; sushi $6–$14 per order; full *omakase* dinner from $100. Mon–Fri 11:45am–2:15pm and 5:45–10:15pm; Sat–Sun 5:45–10:15pm. Valet parking $7.

Spago Beverly Hills ★★★ CALIFORNIAN   After 30 years at the top of the heap, Wolfgang Puck—arguably the first celebrity chef—revamped not only his home restaurant but the entire menu in late 2012. The now contemporary space includes a massive glass wall revealing thousands of wine bottles, a glassed-in patio with twinkly lights and a retractable roof, and an open kitchen. Simpler preparations have an Asian edge, a focus on market-driven local ingredients, more small dishes for sharing, and a new, eight-course farm-to-table menu—all while adhering to a European-style attention to service and refinement of details such as Limoges dinnerware. You can still get a tried-and-true dry-aged steak with Bordelaise, but other options include grilled rack of lamb with falafel macaroons and harissa pepper aioli or even spherified basil "caviar." The 30,000-bottle wine collection, of course, survived the revamp. The rejuvenated Spago still sets the standard.

176 N. Canon Dr. (north of Wilshire Blvd.), Beverly Hills. www.wolfgangpuck.com. ℂ **310/385-0880.** Reservations required. Jacket advised for men. Main courses $18–$95, tasting menu $145. Mon 6–10pm; Tues–Fri noon–2:30pm and 6–10-pm; Sat 5:30–10:30pm, Sun 5:30–10pm. Valet parking $9.

MODERATE

Bombay Café ★★ INDIAN   Its standard cafe-type tables and chairs might not look the part, but this friendly spot offers a novel-length menu of savory curries, kormas, and tandoori. Flavors are taken from spicy South Indian street food and aren't overly Americanized for timid palates, though some dishes are mellower than others. Ask the knowledgeable staff for guidance if that's a concern. The tandoori is where Bombay Cafe really shines; Boti Kabobs of marinated lamb and Chicken Tikka with ginger, cilantro, garlic, and chile are outstanding. It doesn't slouch in the vegetarian arena, either. Try the Thali, which lets you choose two from a pleasing variety of entrees. I'm partial to Eggplant Bharta, a puree of tandoor-charred eggplant with tomatoes and spices, and Gobi Sabzi, cauliflower sauteed with green chilies and spices.

12021 W. Pico Blvd. (North of I-5, btw. S. Bundy Dr. and S. Westgate Ave.), Los Angeles. www.bombaycafe-la.com. ℂ **310/473-3388.** Reservations recommended for dinner. Main courses $8–$20. Mon–Thurs 11:30am–3pm and 5–10pm; Fri–Sat 11:30am–3pm and 5–11pm; Sun 5–10:30pm. Free parking lot.

Chaya Brasserie ★ FRENCH/JAPANESE   Reliably good, French-influenced Asian fusion cuisine, unpretentious surroundings, and an assemblage of entertainment industry stars have made this bistro one of L.A.'s hottest dining destinations since 1986. The tasting menu, available on request, is the best way to sample the sushi, pasta, meat, and seafood here, but the *a la carte* menu is full of gems such as grilled stuffed branzino with lemon artichoke salsa and duck breast with asparagus and caramelized bamboo shoots. Lightly salted black angus beef filet comes with a subtle bone marrow jus and wasabi potato puree. The best tables on warm afternoons and evenings are on the terrace, but the stage-lit interior can be sensuous in spite of the cacophony of voices, dishes, and soundtrack music. *Note:* Sister locations can be found Downtown at City National Plaza (525 S. Flower St.; ℂ **213/236-9577**) and in Venice (110 Navy St.; ℂ **310/396-1179**).

8741 Alden Dr. (east of Robertson Blvd.), Los Angeles. www.thechaya.com. ℂ **310/859-8833.** Reservations recommended. Main courses dinner $13–$39, Mon–Fri 11:30am–2:30pm; Sat 5:30–10pm; Sun 5–9pm. Valet parking $7; limited metered street parking.

Father's Office 2.0 ★★   If you can tolerate a few quirks, everything you'd want in a place for an after-work drink and a bite is yours in this younger but considerably larger sibling of the popular Santa Monica gastropub (1018 Montana Ave., ℂ **310/736-2224**). The signature burger, reputed to be the best in town, is topped with blue cheese, arugula, and caramelized onions—very good indeed, but "the best" might be a stretch. The kitchen has a no-catsup policy (you can bring your own) and a no-substitutions policy . . . perhaps to match its no-reservations policy. The variety of seasonally rotating microbrews and draft Belgian beer, or a glass of wine, should soothe ruffled feathers. Unlike the Santa Monica location, artisan cocktails are available here (but don't bother ordering a Cosmopolitan; they just won't do it).

3229 Helms Ave. (btw. Venice and W. Washington blvds.), Los Angeles. www.fathersoffice.com. ✆ **310/736-2224.** Main courses $11–$21. Mon–Thurs 5–11pm; Fri–Sat noon–midnight; Sun noon–10pm. Street parking.

Il Pastaio ★ NORTHERN ITALIAN   Aficionados of this affordable trattoria in Beverly Hills' shopping district can be found taking a breather from work or shopping, meeting friends over wine and pasta, all day long. Brothers/chefs/owners Celestino and Giacomino Drago, scions of a prominent local restaurateur family, struck gold with that formula, and the small restaurant nearly always has a waiting list. The menu, built around an extensive pasta and risotto list (all made by hand), excels at the small stuff, such as crispy *arancini,* addictive breaded rice cones filled with mozzarella and peas, then fried crispy brown; and *arrabbiata,* penne pasta in a fantastic spicy tomato-and-garlic sauce that can be embellished with shrimp or chicken for an extra charge.

400 N. Canon Dr. (at Brighton Way), Beverly Hills. www.giacominodrago.com ✆ **310/205-5444.** Main courses $13–$35. Mon–Thurs 11:30am–11pm; Fri–Sat 11:30am–midnight; Sun 11:30am–10pm. Valet parking $8.

Versailles ★ CARIBBEAN/CUBAN   Succulent roasted garlic chicken and waiters in white shirts and black bow ties are the trademarks of this Havana-style restaurant where dim lighting, Formica tables, and a deafening noise level nearly qualify it as a dive. The menu is a crash course in Cuban cooking, from the national dish, *ropa vieja* (finely shredded flank steak in a tomato and wine sauce), to fried whole red snapper. Other top picks are *bistec de pollo,* chicken pounded thin, grilled and topped with onions and lime, and *vaca frita,* slightly crispy grilled skirt steak served with onions and that famous garlic sauce. Black beans, rice, and often fried plantains accompany just about every dish. There's often a wait for a seat.

1415 S. La Cienega Blvd. (south of Pico Blvd.), Los Angeles. www.versaillescuban.com. ✆ **310/289-0392.** Main courses $12–$30. Sun–Thurs 11am–10pm; Fri–Sat 11am–11pm. Free parking.

I'll Take the Fifth . . . Taste

Since opening on La Brea in 2009, **Umami Burger** (www.umamiburger. com)—named after the fifth taste profile, savory or "umami"—is nearing the status of a cult classic. That location closed even as newer, bigger ones were being built, spreading the gospel of the coarse-ground, loosely packed burger seasoned with a soy-based sauce and spices including dried porcini mushrooms and fish. While the original burger remains the most popular, there are many variations, and each location has its own signature burger. You can find them at The Grove (189 The Grove Drive; ✆ **323/954-8626**); in Hollywood (1520 N. Cahuenga Blvd.; ✆ **323/469-3100**); Downtown (852 S. Broadway; ✆ **213/413-8626**); in the Arts District (738 E. 3rd St.; ✆ **323/263-8626**); in Los Feliz (4655 Hollywood Blvd.; ✆ **323/669-3922**); and Santa Monica, LAX, Studio City, and Burbank.

INEXPENSIVE

La Serenata Gourmet ★★ MEXICAN An enthusiastically welcomed Westside branch of the award-winning La Serenata de Girabaldi in Boyle heights, this Mexican food joint is casual and fun. More importantly, it prepares authentic dishes with quality ingredients (homemade tortillas and desserts, no lard) that could pass for home cooking in different parts of Mexico. They've nailed the *cochinita pibil,* a Yucatecan pork specialty; melt-in-your-mouth pork medallions in a chunky *molcajete* sauce with jalapeños, and Mexican sea bass in your choice of sauces (try the avocado) are two more of many standouts, along with many of the bocaditos (small bites). Be forewarned: This place is packed during prime lunch and dinner hours.

10924 W. Pico Blvd. (at Westwood Blvd.), West L.A. www.laserenataonline.com. © **310/441-9667.** Main courses $6–$22. Mon–Fri 11am–3pm and 5–10pm; Sat 11am–11pm; Sun 10am–10pm. Metered street parking.

Nate 'n Al Delicatessen ★ DELI/BREAKFAST Run by the same family since 1945 in the middle of Beverly Hills' "Golden Triangle," this L.A. original is famous for its spicy hot dogs and its unique double-baked rye bread (crisp on the outside, soft on the inside). The operating principle seems to be "if it ain't broke, don't fix it" where the Naugahyde-booth interior is concerned, but food mavens will appreciate the certified Angus beef that goes into the corned beef, brisket, short ribs and burgers, and the wild smoked salmon. This is an under-the-radar celebrity favorite, but the mother-hen waitresses don't seem to notice whether you're a big name or a just a tourist hungering for chopped liver, potato pancakes, and borscht.

414 N. Beverly Dr. (btw. S. Santa Monica Blvd. and Brighton Way), Beverly Hills. www.natenal.com. © **310/274-0101.** Main courses $9–$22. Daily 7am–9pm. Parking in public lot next door.

Nyala Ethiopian Cuisine ★ ETHIOPIAN This festive, art-filled eatery is the largest and most popular of numerous Ethiopian restaurants populating a 2-block stretch of Fairfax. Earth tones, tribal art, and African music foster a mellow mood where an ethnically mixed crowd scoops up colorful, complex stews *(wots),* chopped salads, and vegetables in a variety of savory sauces in excellent *injera,* the thick, sour, pizza-sized bread that also serves as plate and utensils. In addition to hearty stewed chicken and lamb, a wide range of vegetarian dishes (lentils, split peas, collard greens) come with their own distinctive marinades. For first-timers especially, the weekday lunch buffet is a great way to delve into this enticing cuisine (it's also a bargain). A smooth honey wine, or an African beer, complete the exotic journey.

1076 S. Fairfax Ave. (south of Olympic Blvd.), Los Angeles. www.nyala-la.com. © **323/936-5918.** Reservations recommended. Main courses $7–$12. Mon–Sat 11:30am–10:30pm; Sun noon–10pm. Metered street parking.

Hollywood & West Hollywood
EXPENSIVE

Hatfield's ★★★ NEW AMERICAN The signature "Croque Madame" appetizer, updated with yellowtail sashimi, prosciutto, and a quail egg on grilled brioche, might be all you need to send you off happy into the night at this sophisticated but utterly unpretentious restaurant. Yet the entrees, simple at their core, reach ambrosial heights with savvy tweaks like lamb, crusted with date and mint, or dry-aged New York steak, pan-roasted with salsify root and puree. Seasonal prix-fixe menus, a jaw-dropping deal in the L.A. restaurant universe, reach farther: sauteed Monterey Bay squid or pan-roasted

THE ivy LEAGUE

The Ivy ★★ AMERICAN   Unlike many of L.A.'s known celebrity hangouts, this place won't make you feel like a star if you are cheeky enough to breach its rose-festooned portals. The Ivy has a definite caste system, but those willing play the untouchable are rewarded by food that approaches perfection, served in a setting brimming with chintz and Wedgewood. You'll pay dearly for the privilege of tucking into such dishes as fresh lobster pizza, grilled fresh vegetable salad, or wagyu New York steak, but you'll probably remember it as one of the better meals you've ever had. A very good fried chicken with grilled corn, fresh wild swordfish tacos and a grass-fed beef burger with Niman Ranch bacon and imported brie come at the most down-to-earth prices; you could also get away with just one of the tasty starters, which include plump, crispy crab cakes and a fresh wild calamari skillet. **Tip:** Most of the incognito celebs sit on the elevated brick patio by the sidewalk; if star-gazing is your main goal, try just strolling casually by before you open your wallet.

113 N. Robertson Blvd. (btw. Beverly Blvd. and Alden Dr.), West Hollywood. www.theivyrestaurants.com. ✆ **310/274-8303.** Reservations recommended. Main courses $24–$98. Daily 10am–10pm. Valet parking $7.

duck breast, for example, or ricotta agnolotti with butternut squash and Parmesan on the vegetarian menu. The pillowy sugar and spice beignets and the crème fraîche cheesecake with hazelnut shortbread are two standouts on a tantalizing dessert menu.

6703 Melrose Ave. (at N. Citrus Ave.), Los Angeles. www.hatfieldsrestaurant.com. ✆ **323/935-2977.** Reservations recommended. Main courses $36–$38; seasonal prix fixe $59–$72. Tues–Thurs 6–10pm; Fri 6–10:30pm; Sat 5:30–10:30pm; Sun 5:30–9:30pm. Valet parking $7.

The Little Door ★★ FRENCH/MEDITERRANEAN   A lush courtyard with a tiled fountain and koi pond, low lighting (and noise level), and rustic Mediterranean cuisine make this hidden, converted-cottage one of L.A.'s most romantic restaurants. Stepping through that unobtrusive (and unsigned) wooden door seems to drop you into a European estate from an earlier era to feast on duck liver, black truffle and port wine mousse, followed rosemary mustard-crusted rack of lamb in Madeira and smoked garlic jus in one of four dining areas (if you can't get the courtyard, try for the quiet back room by the fireplace). Another fantastic dish is the Couscous Royale with lamb stew, chicken, and sausage. Know going in that it's expensive, and some of the servers have perfected that famous French condescension. But when everything comes together on a warm summer night, there's no better place for romance.

8164 W. 3rd St. (btw. Crescent Heights and La Jolla sts.), Los Angeles. www.thelittledoor.com. ✆ **323/951-1210.** Reservations recommended. Main courses $28–$54. Sun–Thurs 6–10pm; Fri–Sat 6–11pm. Valet parking $7; free parking on street after 8pm.

Lucques ★★ FRENCH/MEDITERRANEAN   Named for a type of French olive, this rustic bistro was a hit with food-obsessed locals from the day it opened in 1998. A quietly sophisticated atmosphere prevails in the old brick building—originally silent film star Harold Lloyd's carriage house—while bold flavors and fresh farm produce rule the kitchen. The brief menu rotates quickly in response to what's best in the markets and always displays rigorous attention to detail. Sweet corn soup with charred jalapeño and *queso fresco,* and fried soft-shell crab with mizuna, avocado, and scallions

Hallelujah!: A Brunch Worth Singing About

For more than a decade, the Gospel Brunch at the **House of Blues** (8430 Sunset Blvd., West Hollywood; www. hob.com; © **323/848-5113**) has been a Sunday tradition, feeding both body and soul with inspiring gospel performances and heaping plates of all-you-can-eat Southern home cookin', including breakfast favorites and a carving station. Every week different regional and local gospel groups perform uplifting and energetic music that invariably gets the crowd on its feet and raising the roof. Seatings are every Sunday at 10am and 1pm. Tickets are $55 for adults, $46 for seniors and $31 for kids.

are fantastic starters, while market fish with saffron couscous and vegetables with *crème fraîche,* or Niman Ranch steak with potato-tomato gratin, are good picks if they are available. The Sunday three-course prix-fixe dinner is a bargain at $55.

8474 Melrose Ave. (east of La Cienega Blvd.), West Hollywood. www.lucques.com. © **323/655-6277.** Reservations recommended. Main courses $27–$48. Mon 6–10pm; Tues–Thurs noon–2:30pm and 6–10pm; Fri–Sat noon–2:30pm and 6–10:30pm; Sun 5–10pm. Valet parking $6; metered street parking.

Osteria Mozza ★★ ITALIAN   The standard-bearer for elegant Italian cuisine, prepared from the freshest ingredients, is celebrity chef Nancy Silverton's flagship in an airy, congenial space with indoor/outdoor seating, a free-standing mozzarella bar, and a full bar along the wall. It's equally suited to a special occasion or an after-work plate of burrata (ricotta and egg ravioli and gnocchi with duck ragu are other great choices). Though you can't predict exactly what will be on the menu on any given day, second courses may range from pancetta-wrapped grilled quail to porcini-rubbed rib-eye and pan-roasted pork loin. Reservations are taken a month in advance, but the two bars, which take walk-ins, are among the best seats in the house. *Note:* Silverton's smaller and somewhat less expensive—but exceedingly trendy—**Pizzeria Mozza** is just behind Osteria at 641 N. Highland Ave. (© **323/297-0101**).

6602 Melrose Ave. (at N. Highland Ave.), West Hollywood. www.mozza-la.com. © **323/297-0100.** Reservations recommended. Main courses $20–$38. Mon–Fri 5:30–11pm; Sat 5–11pm; Sun 5–10pm. Valet parking $10.

Providence ★ MODERN AMERICAN/SEAFOOD   Daily trips to the fish market determine the menu at L.A.'s preeminent seafood restaurant. Its understated decadence is best experienced when you're in a mood to relax, as busy periods can produce 20-minute gaps between courses. Small bites display exquisite detail, such as a nasturtium leaf fashioned into a taco holding raw scallops and puffed rice. Main courses allow the wild flavors to prevail, relegating sauces to a supporting role. Some recent standouts: wild Quinault River King Salmon with red cabbage, bacon, Tahitian squash and pecan, and Sonoma-bred duck breast with smoky eggplant puree, chanterelles, and fig. There can be inconsistencies, especially in the texture of the scallops, but the sea urchins here can convert even the most rabid uni hater.

5955 Melrose Ave. (at N. Cahuenga Blvd.), Los Angeles. www.providencela.com. © **323/460-4170.** Reservations recommended. Main courses $45–$49. Mon–Thurs 6–10pm; Fri noon–2:30pm and 6–10pm; Sat 5:30–10pm; Sun 5:30–9pm. Valet parking $7; street parking.

MODERATE

Hungry Cat ★★ SEAFOOD   The original of a three-restaurant franchise is jimmied into a notch between buildings and parking decks near the back entrance of the strange Sunset + Vine complex, and it's worth seeking out. Within the modest if colorful surroundings, decadence meets whimsy in the fresh-fruit cocktails (try the kumquatini when in season), towers of seafood, whole Santa Barbara sea urchins, and spicy lamb sausage paired with Manila clams. The token meat dish is the pug burger, a perfectly charred ball of ground beef with blue cheese, bacon, avocado, and fried egg. Brunch (Saturdays and Sundays) is an event, dominated by a crudo bar redolent with lemon, lime, sake, and chili.

1535 N. Vine St. (at Sunset, near back entrance of Sunset + Vine complex), Hollywood. www.the hungrycat.com ℂ **323/462-2155.** Main courses $10–$32. Mon–Wed noon–3pm and 5:30–10pm; Thurs noon–3pm and 5:30–11pm; Fri noon–3pm and 5:30–11pm; Sat 11am–3pm and 5:30–11pm; Sun 11am–3pm and 5–10pm. Parking garage at Sunset + Vine complex (entrance on Morningstar Court).

Musso & Frank Grill ★ AMERICAN/CONTINENTAL   The classic Old Hollywood grill room lives on in Hollywood's oldest restaurant, in business since 1919. Its cachet comes from having been the haunt of Rudolph Valentino, Charlie Chaplin, and Raymond Chandler. Bogart would toss back a few with Bacall or Dashielle Hammet here; Faulkner and Hemingway worked on their screenplays. Musso & Frank is still known for its bone-dry martinis, delivered to leather booths by red-coated waiters. The old-school menu—veal scaloppini Marsala, roast lamb with mint jelly, broiled lobster—is overshadowed by the legend, but its grilled meats are still among the best to be found. *Tip:* Time-trippers can sit at the counter for the full M&F effect, or request table no. 1 in the west room, which was Charlie Chaplin's regular spot.

6667 Hollywood Blvd. (at Cherokee Ave.), Hollywood. www.mussoandfrank.com ℂ **323/467-7788.** Reservations recommended. Main courses $15–$49. Tues–Sat 11am–11pm. Parking $10.

Petrossian ★★ FRENCH   If a few days of big, brassy L.A. have you longing for the refinement of Paris, hie thee to quietly sophisticated Petrossian, the restaurant offshoot of the West Coast outpost of the New York-by-way-of-France caviar shop. Leather-covered walls, abstract paintings and vintage photos create a very Left Bank ambience, and you can talk over a meal without getting hoarse trying to outdo thumping house music. Their impeccable fish roe, naturally, appears in many of the best dishes, such as the deceptively simple Egg Royale, a soft scrambled egg served in a hollowed-out eggshell with vodka whipped cream and a dollop of caviar, or the smoked trout with asparagus, lemon, crème fraîche, and rainbow trout roe. But caviar certainly is not a requirement; the roast chicken with eggplant, currants, capers, and piquillo peppers is every bit as lively, and there's a fairly straightforward New York steak (although it doesn't rise to the level of most other dishes). The wonder is that Petrossian isn't more expensive than it is.

321 N. Robertson Blvd. (at Rosewood Ave., 1 block north of Beverly Blvd.), West Hollywood. www. petrossian.com. ℂ **310/271-6300.** Main courses $14–$40; tasting menu $75. Mon–Fri 11am–10pm; Sat 10am–10pm; Sun 10am–4pm. Metered street parking (free after 6pm).

INEXPENSIVE

El Cholo ★★ MEXICAN   Chiles rellenos are my benchmark for measuring the worth of a Mexican restaurant, and El Cholo's plump, greaseless version is among the best I've had this side of the border. Since the original restaurant opened as the Sonora Cafe in 1923, it has served authentic Mexican food while incorporating and sometimes creating a close, but more healthful, relative of Tex-Mex (Cal-Mex?). The now-ubiquitous combination plate and the delightful mess we know as nachos originated here. Now surrounded by Koreatown, the festive pink hacienda has served generations of Angelenos; Gary Cooper and Bing Crosby were among its early regulars, and Jack Nicholson still lusts after its cheese enchiladas. Though blue corn chicken enchiladas and vegetable fajitas came into being to satisfy changing tastes, original 1923 recipes such as traditional *albondigas* (meatballs) and delectable green corn tamales, available only from May to October, still grace the menu. Newer branches are Downtown (1037 S. Flower St., across from Staples Center; ℂ 213/746-7750) and in Santa Monica (1025 Wilshire Blvd., at 11th St.; ℂ 310/899-1106).

1121 S. Western Ave. (south of Olympic Blvd., btw. W. 11th St. and Harrington Ave.), Los Angeles. www.elcholo.com ℂ **323/734-2773**. Reservations suggested. Main courses $9–$18. Mon–Thurs 11am–10pm; Fri–Sat 11am–11pm; Sun 11am–9pm. Valet parking $5.

Kings Road Cafe ★ AMERICAN   This cafe is a throwback to the pre-Starbucks era, when "coffeehouse" meant a European-style neighborhood hangout grinding beans from local roasters in San Francisco's North Beach—which is exactly what inspired King's Road. This being L.A., the bowl-size cups of stellar coffee come with sunny sidewalk tables, and the occasional celebrity sighting. It's an all-day go-to place, starting with fluffy French toast and gourmet omelets in the morning and large portions of fresh, healthful, inexpensive pizza, pasta, panini, tacos, and quesadillas all day. You'll almost certainly have to wait if you want an outside table, so plan on browsing the huge magazine stand or the cafe's bakery next door.

8361 Beverly Blvd. (at Kings Rd.), Los Angeles. www.kingsroadcafe.com. ℂ **323/655-9044**. Reservations not accepted. Main courses $9–$17; breakfast $8–$14. Daily 6am–6pm. Metered street parking.

Roscoe's House of Chicken 'n' Waffles ★ BREAKFAST/SOUTHERN   President Obama ordered the No. 9 Country Boy here during his 2011 fundraising trip, and that was all it took for L.A. to embrace the unholy-sounding combination of chicken and waffles. Yes, they are served together as well as separately. (Think about it, though—how different is that from eating sweet corn bread with fried chicken?) Founded by a Harlem native in 1975, this soul food restaurant is the place to revel in

---

In the Pink

I wouldn't normally recommend a hot dog stand (no really, I mean it), but **Pink's Hot Dogs** ★ is a true L.A. icon. It started in 1939 with the late Paul and Betty Pink's used hot dog cart and now serves more than 2,000 dogs a day from its permanent stand. Two dozen variations, range from stubby Polish dogs to fat, foot-long jalapeño dogs; the truly adventurous can try Jaws, carrying a burger, a Polish dog, and bacon in one bun. Betty's recipe for the fiery chili slathered on more than half the hot dogs is still a closely guarded secret. Even the most health-conscious local is a slave to these hot dogs, and you'll encounter a cross-section of Los Angeles while waiting in the inevitable line. You'll find them at 709 N. La Brea Ave., at Melrose, West Hollywood (www.pinkshollywood.com ℂ 323/931-4223).

Southern fried chicken smothered in gravy and onions, homemade corn bread, red beans and rice, and sweet-potato pie. They also serve a variety of breakfast combos. This place is deep into don't-knock-it-until-you've-tried-it territory.

1514 N. Gower St. (at Sunset Blvd.), Los Angeles. www.roscoeschickenandwaffles.com. ☎ **323/466-7453.** Main courses $6–$14. Mon–Thurs 7am–8pm; Fri–Sat 8am–8pm; Sun 8am–4pm. Metered street parking, pay lots, valet on weekends.

Toi on Sunset ★ THAI   One of a handful of places that stay open past 2am, Toi's location in the heart of Hollywood's cluster of music stores is no accident. Toi styles itself as a rock-'n'-roll restaurant, with rock photos, posters, and artifacts covering nearly every square inch of the interior. Its random arrangement of industrial-grade tables and chairs, in a space that feels rather like a garage, flies in the face of the simple, hushed environment of the typical Thai restaurant. But they're serious about the food: flavors meld perfectly in the creamy yellow curry; the peanut sauce that accompanies satay or crispy-soft tofu triangles is thicker and more, well, peanut-y, than average. The house specialty, chicken curry somen, a spicy green curry with fresh mint served over Japanese rice noodles, is good, and their special brown rice, darker and chewier than most, is worth the extra dollar. Portions are huge. *Note:* Though the restaurant is open until 4am, alcohol is served only until midnight.

7505½ Sunset Blvd. (at N. Gardner St.), West Hollywood. www.toirockinthaifood.com. ☎ **323/874-8062.** Reservations accepted only for parties of 6 or more. Main courses $8–$19. Daily 11am–4am.

Downtown
EXPENSIVE

Drago Centro ★★ ITALIAN   On the ground floor of the City National Bank building, a mixture of local dishes and old flavors made with fresh, top-quality ingredients, in a sleek, updated version of traditional white-tablecloth surroundings, attracts a steady stream of business people on expense accounts, with a goodly contingent of locals celebrating special occasions or stopping in for a drink. The menu draws from various regions of Italy and gives them a contemporary spin—goat cheese ravioli in a silky saffron cream sauce with poppy seeds, roasted salmon with fennel aioli, and olive oil foam are cooked to perfection and served with unerring efficiency. The bar, which turns out an impressive lineup of unique cocktails, has its own innovative menu of small plates and thin-crust pizzas. Get a look at the custom-designed glass wine room and the exhibition kitchen occupying a former bank vault (used only for private parties).

525 S. Flower St. (at W. 5th St.), Los Angeles. www.dragocentro.com. ☎ **213/228-8998.** Reservations recommended. Main courses $17–$39; tasting menu $55. Mon–Fri 11:30am–2:30pm and 5–10pm; Sat–Sun 5–10pm. Valet parking $5 up to 3 hr. until 5pm; 4 hr. free after 5pm, $7 flat-rate after 3 hr. Purple or Red Line to 7th St./Metro Center.

Patina ★★ CALIFORNIAN/FRENCH   One of more than 50 varied restaurants in arts-oriented neighborhoods on both coasts from restaurateur Nick Valenti and celebrity Chef Joachim Splichal, the flagship Patina's second incarnation holds down a corner of the Walt Disney Concert Hall. French and California cuisine are woven into something new, producing a constantly changing menu featuring Splichal's signature wild game dishes, such as Scottish wood pigeon with yams, celeriac, and pear. The wine list garnered Wine Spectator's 2014 Grand Award. A paleo menu recently made its debut, but vegetarian dishes are also available, both in the tasting menu and the

Downtown Hotels & Restaurants

Exposition Park

University of
Southern California

Exposition Blvd.

ACCOMMODATIONS ■

Figueroa Hotel **12**
Los Angeles Athletic Club **14**
JW Marriott **13**
Metro Plaza Hotel **3**
Omni Hotel **7**
Ritz-Carlton **13**

DINING ◆

Cafe Pinot **9**
Church & State **16**
Cole's **15**
Drago Centro **8**
Forage **1**
Langer's Deli **6**
The Original Pantry **11**
Patina **5**
Philippe the Original **2**
Traxx **4**
Water Grill **10**

regular fare. Caviar, steaks, and exotic cheeses appear on carts after concerts end, but if you want a quiet, intimate dinner, book at the beginning of a performance.

141 S. Grand Ave. (btw 1st and 2nd sts.), Los Angeles. www.patinagroup.com. ℂ **213/972-3331.** Reservations recommended. Main courses $38–$65; tasting menu $90 (vegetarian)–$120. Tues–Sun 5–9:30pm; (on L.A. Philharmonic concert nights, last seating is 30 min. after the concert ends). Closed Mon. Valet parking $8 with validation until 8pm, free after 8pm. Metro Purple or Red Line to Civic Center/Grand Park.

Water Grill ★★ SEAFOOD   Since reopening after renovation in early 2012 with a new menu and a new chef, Water Grill has become less of an innovative concept restaurant and more of a traditional seafood house. This doesn't please all fans of what was anointed L.A.'s best seafood restaurant, but I think it should well suit the average diner just wants some good fish. The elegant dining room, with its crenellated ceiling, marble walls, and leather seats, has been modernized but remains in step with the 1922 landmark building it occupies. An extensive raw bar with at least 10 kinds of oysters is its big selling point, but the menu, while more straightforward than in its earlier days, shows some imagination. The fritto misto appetizer is a pleasing medley of wild calamari, Mexican bay scallops, white shrimp, a variety of fish and vegetables. Farmed Ecuadorian shrimp is served with grits and merguez sausage ragout; house-made squid ink pasta comes with charcoal-grilled calamari and salsa verde. Simple, but not predictable. *Note:* A second location of Water Grill opened in Santa Monica at the end of 2013 at 1401 Ocean Ave. (at Santa Monica Blvd.; ℂ **310/394-5669**).

544 S. Grand Ave. (btw. W. 5th and W. 6th sts.), Downtown. www.watergrill.com ℂ **213/891-0900.** Reservations recommended. Main courses $27–$46. Mon–Thurs 11:30am–10pm; Fri 11:30am–11pm; Sat 5–11pm; Sun 4–10pm. Valet parking $5 up to 2 hr.; $8 more than 2 hr. Metro Red or Purple Line to Pershing Square.

MODERATE

Café Pinot ★ CALIFORNIAN/FRENCH   Also from celebrity chef Joachim Splichal, this one is tucked into the garden of the L.A. Public Library and has glass walls to take advantage of the leafy setting. It's more casual, less expensive, and more kid-friendly than Patina but also serves contemporary California-French dishes, based on farmers market finds and the kitchen's huge rotisserie. Otherwise impeccable service can falter during the crowded lunchtime, and flavors don't always pop; the yellow corn and bay scallop risotto with grilled baby corn is a reliable choice. The best tables are on the shady patio; the best meals are from the rotisserie—chicken with whole-grain mustard juice is always a good bet. A happy hour menu kicks in after 2:30pm weekdays and 5pm Saturday, with small plates as well as lower-priced drinks.

700 W. 5th St. (btw. Grand and Flower sts. next to L.A. Public Library), Los Angeles. www.patina group.com. ✆ **213/239-6500.** Reservations recommended. Main courses $27–$30. Mon–Tues 11:30am–2:30pm and 5–9pm; Wed–Thurs 11:30am–2:30pm and 5–9:30pm; Fri 11:30am–2:30pm and 5–10pm; Sat 5–10pm; Sun 4:30–9pm. Lunch parking at the adjacent library $6 for 2 hr. with validation; dinner valet at the restaurant $7.

Church & State ★★ FRENCH BISTRO   This hip restaurant on the ground floor of the Biscuit Lofts was turning out classic bistro fare like garlicky escargot capped with puff pastry, duck and pork charcuterie, and roasted bone marrow long before the recently sketchy industrial zone morphed into the trendy Arts District. The 2014 arrival of Chef Tony Esnault, a Loire Valley native and protégé of Alain Ducasse, brought a lighter touch to the rustic fare in dishes such as Tagine de Légumes (quinoa, eggplant, and other vegetables with spicy harissa sauce) and peach, brie, and onion tarts, but he also executes a mean rack of lamb, with bulgur and ratatouille. The all-French wine list is exceptional, and the high, exposed loft ceiling, brick walls, open kitchen, and chalkboards with menus scribbled in French make you think you took a wrong turn and landed in Paris.

1850 Industrial St. (at Matteo St.), Los Angeles. www.churchandstatebistro.com.✆ **213/405-1434.** Reservations recommended. Main courses $19–$38. Lunch Mon–Fri 11:30am–2:30pm. Dinner Mon–Thurs 6–10pm; Fri 6–11pm; Sat 5:30–11pm; Sun 5:30–9pm. Metered street parking (free after 6pm) and nearby lots.

Forage ★★ CALIFORNIAN   Leave it to the gentrifying but still bohemian neighborhood of Silver Lake to host a restaurant whose mission is to bring top-quality seasonal fare to the masses, at affordable prices. Whether it's chicken fried rice with broccoli, shallot and scrambled egg, or grilled rib-eye steak, the food fairly glistens in the counter case where you order from a blackboard. The menu isn't large on any given day, but it changes daily so you won't likely get bored with the offerings. The outstanding pork belly sandwich with cabbage and jalapeño slaw and creamy aioli, fortunately, is one of the more enduring items. Intriguing side dishes tend to be more produce than meat, and vary more with the season. Don't write off the Petaluma free range rotisserie chicken as "just chicken"—it is truly exceptional.

3823 W. Sunset Blvd., (btw. Hyperion Ave. and Lucille Ave.), Los Angeles/Silver Lake. www.foragela. com. ✆ **323/663-6885.** Main courses $11–$18. Tues–Sat 11:30am–3pm and 5:30–9:30pm. Metered street parking.

The Original Pantry ★ AMERICAN/BREAKFAST   This comfort-food palace celebrated its 90th birthday in 2014 with its linoleum floors, Formica tables, schoolhouse lamps, and old-school menu securely in place. It's open around the clock and serves steak, chops, and all-American desserts, but its bread and butter, so to speak, is all-hours breakfast—a boon to visitors headed to the nearby L.A. Convention Center and clubbers seeking sustenance in the wee hours. Known primarily for its generous, if not gluttonous, portions, it offers everything from eggs, potatoes, toast and coffee to an enormous slab of sweet cured ham steak, eggs, and home fries; no frou-frou omelets or scrambles here. No menus, either, except for the wall-mounted chalkboards. And

L.A. live

The massive L.A. Live complex helped to transform the culinary near-wasteland that was Downtown L.A. into a place where you might actually want to have lunch or dinner. Carnivores are in luck; two of the standouts are **Fleming's Steakhouse and Wine Bar** (www.flemingssteakhouse.com; ☎ 213/745-9911) and **Lawry's Carvery** (www.lawrysonline.com; ☎ 213/222-221). Two local restaurants have expanded here: **The Farm of Beverly Hills** (www.thefarmofbeverlyhills.com; ☎ 213/747-4555) offering comfort food and sandwiches made with seasonal ingredients, and the South Coast steak and seafood restaurant **Rock'N Fish** (www.rocknfishlalive.com; ☎ 213/748-4020). **Wolfgang Puck Bar & Grill** (www.wolfgangpuck.com; ☎ 213/748-9700) showcases the celebrity chef's simpler side, though it has some competition from craft beer specialist **Yard House** (www.yardhouse.com; ☎ 213/745-9273). 2014 brought the sports bar/burger joint **Tom's Urban** (www.tomsurban.com; ☎ 213/746-8667) and its siblings **Live Basil Pizza** and **Smashburger.**

none of those new-fangled credit cards; cash or checks only, please. Lines get pretty long at certain times of day, but service is lightning fast and friendly.

877 S. Figueroa St. (at 9th St.), Los Angeles. www.pantrycafe.com. ☎ **213/972-9279.** Breakfast $5–$16; lunch and dinner $10–$29. No credit cards. Daily 24 hr. Free parking across the street with validation. Metro Red or Purple Line to 7th St./Metro Center.

Traxx ★ CALIFORNIAN Since Union Station opened in 1939, its passenger concourse has always had a restaurant, but this is the first to rise to the level of its grand Art Deco-Spanish Colonial surroundings. Dinner regulars go straight to the lovely, lantern-lit garden patio in back, but the cosmopolitan interior echoes the architecture, elegant enough for an intimate dinner while also suiting the commuter. The brief menu of small and large plates changes frequently; perennials include the signature Louisiana lump crab cakes with chipotle remoulade and the thick, moist, house-cured pork loin chop, served with Mission figs and sauteed garlic spinach. Terrific green chile pozole, served as a side for dinner, appears as a main course for lunch.

800 N. Alameda St. (at Cesar E. Chavez Ave., in Union Station), Los Angeles. www.traxxrestaurant.com. ☎ **213/625-1999.** Reservations recommended for dinner. Main courses $14–$26. Mon–Thurs 11:30am–2:30pm and 5–9pm; Fri 11:30am–2:30pm and 5–9:30pm; Sat 5–9:30pm. Free valet parking; self-parking 2 hr. at lunch and 3 hr. at dinner free with validation. Metro Red, Purple, Silver or Gold lines to Union Station.

INEXPENSIVE

Langer's Deli ★★ BREAKFAST/DELI This old-school Jewish deli, standing across the street from MacArthur Park, is quintessential Los Angeles, yet it gives New York a run for its money where the matter of the world's best hot pastrami sandwich is concerned. Langer's famous No. 19—the most-requested sandwich since the 1950s—piles lean, spicy meat on crispy rye with Swiss cheese, coleslaw, and Russian-style dressing. Langer's has been assuaging transplanted New Yorkers' homesick pangs with matzo-ball soup, fresh chopped liver, patty melts, hot sandwiches, cold fish plates—all the deli essentials—since 1947, and the rest of the population can only say "thank you." Big bonus: If you phone in your order and tell them when you plan to pick it up, they'll bring it to the curb and wait for you, with change at the ready.

704 S. Alvarado St. (at W. 7th St.), Los Angeles. www.langersdeli.com. ℂ **213/483-8050.** Main courses $7–$27. Mon–Sat 8am–4pm. Free 1-hr. parking with validation (at 7th and Westlake). Metro Red or Purple line to Westlake/MacArthur Park.

Universal City

More than three-dozen dining options beckon at Universal Studios Hollywood, including chains like Bubba Gump Shrimp Co., Bucca di Beppo, and Saddle Ranch in Universal CityWalk. For a respite from the frenzied theme-park atmosphere, these San Fernando Valley restaurants are within easy driving distance.

MODERATE

Casa Vega ★ MEXICAN   Even in the midst of the entertainment industry, there aren't many places where you can walk in at 1am and grab some dinner. This is one of the few, a '50s-style dive in an adobe-style building with red Naugahyde booths and year-round Christmas lights that's been the local favorite since 1956. It's still run by the founding family. The margaritas are strong and cheap, the chips are fresh and hot, the salsa is spicy, and all dinners come with the restaurant's signature chopped taco salad. In addition to all the usual suspects, the extensive menu includes a few Mexican favorites and regional dishes (sopes, molcajete, Sonora tacos) that don't often find their way onto U.S. menus. Tables on the patio are perfect for warm nights, and are quieter than the dim indoor dining room. On weekends, the wait for a table can be long.

13301 Ventura Blvd. (at Fulton Ave.), Sherman Oaks. www.casavega.com. ℂ **818/788-4868.** Reservations not accepted. Main courses $14–$23. Daily 11:30am–2am. Metered street parking; valet parking $4; self-parking free for lunch.

Miceli's ★ TRADITIONAL ITALIAN   To enjoy this traditional, Sicilian-style restaurant, you need to know what you're in for: all the typical Italian fare, a rollicking repertory of show tunes, opera, and old standards, and Chianti-bottle decor that just misses being over the top. The food is decent; they do best with the sauteed mushroom appetizer, the bruchetta, the lasagna, and eggplant and Italian sausage *cacciatores*. The singing is top-notch; if you have to wait tables while waiting to be discovered, this is the place do it. It is loud, though, and performing sometimes takes precedence over serving. It's a great place for kids (and conveniently located next to Universal Studios), but your only chance of a romantic evening is the private mezzanine table, reached by a spiral staircase that carries you above the activity. It books well in advance.

3655 Cahuenga Blvd. (east of Lankershim Blvd. south of Hollywood Fwy) Universal City. www.micelisrestaurant.com. ℂ **323/851-3344.** Main courses $12–$20; pizza $13–$24. Sun–Thurs 11:30am–10pm; Fri–Sat 11:30am–11pm. Valet parking, tips only. Metro Red Line to Universal/Studio City.

INEXPENSIVE

Du-par's Restaurant & Bakery ★ TRADITIONAL AMERICAN/BREAKFAST
If a hankering for buttermilk pancakes strikes late at night, this branch of the original Farmers Market coffee shop stands ready to provide. The pancakes just happen to be the best in the city. This L.A. classic has been slinging hash since 1938 and has a loyal clientele of old-timers who grew up with the place, show business types who would just as soon not see or be seen, and a younger crowd that appreciates its low prices. Though it's open around the clock and has very good sandwiches and comfort-food entrees, breakfast is really the thing here, at any hour. The French toast is eggy and

crispy around the edge, the omelets are fluffy, the banana muffins bulge with chunks of banana, and the orange juice is hand-squeezed. And then you have to face the pies. Glistening, ambrosial, freshly made pies that beckon from the glass case you try to leave. You will give in, and you'll be glad you did. *Tip:* Night owls can take advantage of the "beat the clock" specials from 4am to 6am.

12036 Ventura Blvd. (1 block east of Laurel Canyon Blvd.), Studio City. www.du-pars.com. © **818/766-4437.** $8–$17. Daily 24 hr. Free parking.

Pasadena
EXPENSIVE
Bistro 45 ★★ NEW AMERICAN/FRENCH Ensconced in a graceful Art Deco building, a sleek dining room filled with soft light creates the perfect atmosphere for award-winning New American cuisine with a French twist and an occasional tinge of the Pacific Rim, such as duck with tamari-ginger sauce. The seasonal menu changes frequently, but signature dishes include braised beef short ribs and osso bucco, which is all too rare in contemporary restaurants. The oven-fried chicken is exceptionally juicy. In addition to a comprehensive wine and beer list, including microbrews, the owner hosts wine dinners. I'd suggest planning ahead to take half your dinner home to leave room for one of the dizzying array of desserts. The signature chocolate soup is incredibly rich, but the cheesecake crepe with strawberries and the apple tart with crème fraîche ice cream and caramel are equally tempting.

45 S. Mentor Ave. (btw. E. Colorado Blvd. and E. Green St.), Pasadena. www.bistro45.com. © **626/795-2478.** Reservations recommended. Main courses $14–$40. Tues–Thurs 5–9pm; Fri 11am–2pm and 5–10pm; Sat 5–10pm; Sun 5–8:30pm. Valet parking $5.

MODERATE
Cafe Santorini ★★ MEDITERRANEAN Excellent food at an affordable price is the payoff at this hidden restaurant in the heart of bustling Old Pasadena, but the lovely second-floor space in a historic brick building doesn't hurt, either. A flower-bedecked patio looks out over the plaza below, at a safe remove from the clamor. The flavors owe more to Greece than anywhere else—*mezze* (Mediterranean appetizers) like hummus and pita, baba ghanoush and pita, baked baby eggplant, and entrees such as kebabs, *souvlaki,* and a grilled vegetable platter—but it ranges farther afield in dishes like manila clams, red curry risotto with seafood and a variety of pastas. When you're in the mood for a fine meal but not for the rarefied atmosphere or high prices of a fine-dining restaurant, this is the place.

64 W. Union St. (main entrance at the shopping plaza at the corner of Fair Oaks Ave. and Colorado Blvd.), Pasadena. www.cafesantorini.com. © **626/564-4200.** Reservations recommended on weekends. Main courses $12–$26. Mon–Thurs 11am–10pm; Fri–Sat 11am–midnight; Sun 11am–10pm. Valet parking $7 with validation; nearby garages 90 minutes free. Metro Gold Line to Memorial Park.

Union ★★★ CALIFORNIAN/ITALIAN This newcomer (as of March 2014) is a departure for lovely but staid Old Pasadena, one of the most restaurant-saturated neighborhoods in the region, if not the country. The wheat stalks in place of flowers on the tables and the shelves of pickles lining the walls (Chef Bruce Kalman is a well-known vendor at farmers markets) are early clues that you are in the realm of house-cured duck prosciutto, free-range eggs, and meals served on wood slabs. The inspiration is Italian, but the spirit is Californian; witness the spaghetti *alla chitarra,* with the pasta shaped into a tight cylinder capped with a roasted hot chile. There are more appetizers than entrees, and nothing on the brief menu is exactly what you expect—wild king salmon here comes with bean puree, pickled green almonds, and salsa verde—but it mostly turns out to be exactly what you want.

37 E Union St. (btw Fair Oaks and N. Raymond Ave.), Pasadena. www.unionpasadena.com. *C* **626/795-5841.** Main courses $12–24. Mon–Fri 5–11pm; Sat 4–11pm; Sun 4–10pm. Metered street parking; several nearby public parking garages, 90 minutes free, then $2/hr. Metro Gold Line to Memorial Park.

INEXPENSIVE

Euro Pane ★★ BAKERY/CAFE   For a tiny bakery too far from busy Old Town to get any spillover foot traffic, Euro Pane does a brisk business every day of the week. Locals from around the up-and-coming Lake Avenue shopping district keep it busy churning out fresh blueberry brioche, bread pudding, custard tarts, and other pastries—even the plain croissants are a decadent treat. The small sandwich menu packs a big wallop. The egg salad is legendary, but such fillings as tomato and feta, red pepper and goat cheese, and salmon stand proud alongside the classics. All are enclosed in your choice of oven-fresh sweet or savory breads, from baguettes and ciabatta to olive and rosemary currant. There are only a few seats, and presentation isn't much of a priority here, but you won't care after one bite. And you can always take it to go, along with a supply of breads and pastries for the pantry.

950 E. Colorado Blvd. (at Mentor Ave), Pasadena. *C* **626/577-1828.** Pastries and sandwiches $3–$10. Mon–Sat 7am–5:30pm; Sun 7am–3pm. Free street parking. Metro Gold Line to Lake.

EXPLORING LOS ANGELES

by Christine Delsol

The problem is not finding something to do in Los Angeles, it's how to narrow down the choices. Beaches, museums, parks, architectural masterpieces, historical sites, amusement parks, movie and TV studios . . . they're all here. And then there's nightlife and and world-class shopping. No matter how long you're staying, you can't do it all. You need a plan.

Keep in mind that this is a huge city where getting from one side to to the other can easily take an hour, *if* you're lucky with traffic and parking. The best strategy is to plot your excursions by neighborhood, even if it means picking up and moving to a different hotel once or twice during your stay, because every hour you don't spend on the freeway is an hour to enjoy what L.A. has to offer. Our recommended attractions are organized to help you do that. And the much-malaigned public transportation system, especially the Metro Line, actually can spare you some frustrating road time in attraction-packed areas like Hollywood and Downtown.

LOS ANGELES ATTRACTIONS
Santa Monica & the Beaches

Annenberg Community Beach House ★★ HISTORIC HOME/ BEACH   The Annenberg Community Beach House at Santa Monica State Beach is a great place for families to relax and play. Built in the '20s for Marion Davies, actress and mistress of William Hearst, this mansion was a hot spot for A-list celebs until its 2009 renovation into a public beach house. It offers a pool, guesthouse, recreation and family fitness classes, a gym, docent tours, volleyball and tennis courts (by reservation), beach rentals (chairs, balls, boogie boards, and so on), a nice cafe, and access to the wide beaches of Santa Monica.

415 Pacific Coast Hwy. (1½ mi. north of Santa Monica Boulevard), Santa Monica. beachhouse.smgov.net. ⓒ **310/458-4904.** Free admission. Daily 8:30am–5:30pm. Parking $3/hr., $12/day Apr–Oct, $18/day Nov–Mar.

Camera Obscura ★   The Camera Obscura (Latin for "dark room") is, well, a dark room that's round and has a white circular table in the middle. Turn the old ship's wheel, which turns the overhead periscope thingy, and a reverse projection of the park, ocean, and avenue is reflected onto the table (with any luck, that's not your car getting a parking ticket). It's an ancient invention that offers a few minutes of amusement in a modern world. To

Santa Monica & the Beaches Attractions

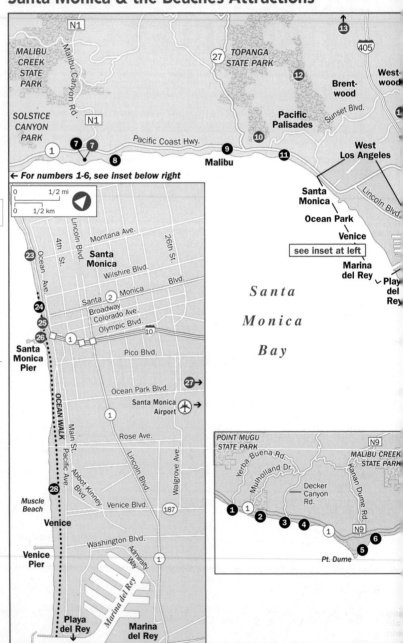

For numbers 1–6, see inset below right

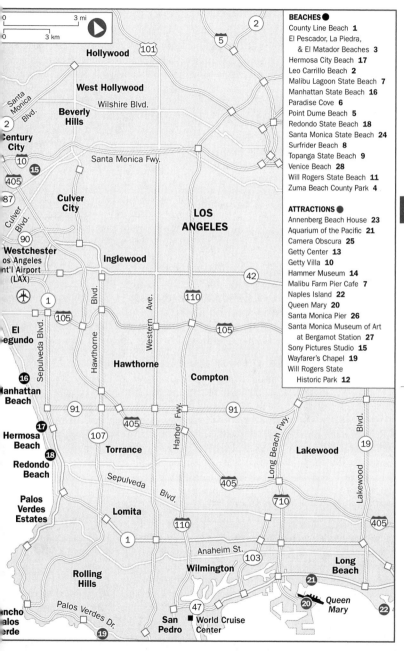

BEACHES ●
County Line Beach **1**
El Pescador, La Piedra,
   & El Matador Beaches **3**
Hermosa City Beach **17**
Leo Carrillo Beach **2**
Malibu Lagoon State Beach **7**
Manhattan State Beach **16**
Paradise Cove **6**
Point Dume Beach **5**
Redondo State Beach **18**
Santa Monica State Beach **24**
Surfrider Beach **8**
Topanga State Beach **9**
Venice Beach **28**
Will Rogers State Beach **11**
Zuma Beach County Park **4**

ATTRACTIONS ●
Annenberg Beach House **23**
Aquarium of the Pacific **21**
Camera Obscura **25**
Getty Center **13**
Getty Villa **10**
Hammer Museum **14**
Malibu Farm Pier Cafe **7**
Naples Island **22**
Queen Mary **20**
Santa Monica Pier **26**
Santa Monica Museum of Art
   at Bergamot Station **27**
Sony Pictures Studio **15**
Wayfarer's Chapel **19**
Will Rogers State
   Historic Park **12**

4

see it, go into the Senior Center where it is, hand over your driver's license, and get the key. The whole experience is a bit surreal, but fun (and free).

1450 Ocean Ave. (btw. Broadway and Santa Monica Blvd.), Santa Monica. ✆ **310/458-8644.** Mon–Thurs 9am–2pm, Sat 11am–4pm.

Ocean Front Walk ★★★ ICON   Still one of the world's most engaging bohemian locales, Venice was developed at the turn of the last century, inspired by its Italian namesake. Authentic gondolas plied miles of inland waterways lined with rococo palaces. It was the 1950s stomping ground of Jack Kerouac, Allen Ginsberg, William S. Burroughs, and other Beats; in the 1960s, it was the epicenter of L.A.'s hippie scene. It's not an exaggeration to say that no visit to L.A. would be complete without a stroll along the famous paved beach path, a surreal assemblage of every L.A. stereotype—and then some. Among stalls selling cheap sunglasses, Mexican blankets, and medical marijuana swirls a carnival of humanity that includes bikini-clad in-line skaters, tattooed bikers, tanned hunks pumping iron at Muscle Beach, panhandling vets, and hordes of tourists and gawkers. Daily performance art includes mimes, break dancers, stoned drummers, chain-saw jugglers, talking parrots, and the occasional apocalyptic evangelist. *Tip:* Pay the $4 to $15 fee for a secured lot, hide your valuables, and walk to the beach—car break-ins aren't uncommon.

Venice Beach btw. Venice Blvd. and Rose Ave., Venice.

> ### Airport or Spaceport?
>
> On your way in or out of LAX, take a moment to admire the droid-like Control Tower and UFO-shaped Theme Building. The main control tower is the newer of the two, designed to evoke a stylized Southern California palm tree. You can stop at the Theme Building to survey the view from the observation deck.

Santa Monica Museum of Art at Bergamot Station ★★ ART MUSEUM This small, friendly museum, anchoring an art and cultural center on a onetime 19th-century Red Line trolley stop, is Santa Monica's artistic epicenter. As Southern California's only museum without its own collection, it hosts intriguing and sometimes unexpected shows of contemporary local, national, and international artists, such as "Robert Swain: The Form of Color" and "Citizen Culture: Artists and Architects Shape Policy" in 2014. Visitors can park in one free lot and browse inventive installations in more than 40 galleries in the Bergamot Station complex.

2525 Michigan Ave. (off Cloverfield Blvd. south of Olympic), Santa Monica. www.smmoa.org. ✆ **310/586-6488.** $5 adults, $3 artists, students, and seniors. Tue–Sat 11am–6pm; closed Sun–Mon and legal holidays; closed btw. exhibitions. Free parking.

Santa Monica Pier ★★ LANDMARK/AMUSEMENT PARK/AQUARIUM   About a mile up the Ocean Front Walk from Venice, and making for a great round-trip stroll, the famous Santa Monica Pier was built in 1908 for passenger and cargo ships. The wooden wharf does a pretty good job of recapturing the halcyon days of yesteryear; it's also the official West Coast end of historic **Route 66.**

Diversions include seafood restaurants and snack shacks; a touristy Mexican cantina; a gaily-colored 1920s indoor wooden carousel (which Paul Newman operated in The Sting); an aquarium filled with sharks, rays, octopus, eels, and other local sea life; and a trapeze school that offers lessons. The original Muscle Beach is also just south of the pier. Free summer Twilight Dance Series concerts range from big band to Miami-style Latin. Halfway down the pier, **Pacific Park** (www.pacpark.com; ✆ 310/

260-8744), hearkens back to Pacific Ocean Park, granddaddy of the dozens of seaside amusement parks that dotted California's coast in the 19th century. This updated version has a solar-powered Ferris wheel, a vintage roller coaster, and 10 other rides, plus a high-tech arcade. Anglers still head to the end to of the pier to fish, nostalgia buffs to view the photographic display of the pier's history, and everyone head here to take in perfect panoramic views of the bay and mountains.

1116 4th St., Santa Monica (at end of Colorado Ave. off Appian Way). www.santamonicapier.org. © **310/458-8900.** Daily 24 hr. (check with individual businesses for their hours). Parking on pier deck and beachfront $6–$8; limited short-term parking also available; prepaid parking available online.

Wayfarers Chapel ★ CHURCH/ARCHITECTURE   Constructed on a broad cliff overlooking Pacific waves, this stunning church was designed by Lloyd Wright, son of celebrated architect Frank Lloyd Wright. Known locally as the "glass church," Wayfarers is like one huge window, framed in redwood and native stone. It was built as a memorial to Emanuel Swedenborg, an 18th-century Swedish philosopher who claimed to have visions of spirits and heavenly hosts. Rare plants, some native to Israel, surround the building. Free escorted tours are available by advance arrangement.

5755 Palos Verdes Dr. S., Rancho Palos Verdes. www.wayfarerschapel.org. © **310/377-1650.** Daily 9am–5pm. Free parking.

L.A.'s Westside & Beverly Hills

Annenberg Space for Photography ★★ ART MUSEUM/ARCHITECTURE
Though its claim to fame is as L.A.'s first cultural venue devoted specifically to photography, the Annenberg incorporates myriad artistic pursuits; summer 2014 brought Photosynthesis, a festival that placed country musicians on stage with prominent photographers telling stories behind their projected images—a corollary to its "Country: Portraits of an American Sound" exhibition. The building is an architectural feat inspired by a camera, with a circular digital gallery within a square building whose ceiling takes on the whirligig curves of a camera lens. Digital photography projected on 7-by14-foot screens, such as its pioneering "Digital Darkroom" exhibition, enjoys equal stature with traditional photography, as in its retrospective of National Geographic photos for the magazine's 125th anniversary. *Note:* Self-parking in the underground garage at Century Park, a block away, is $3.50 for 3 hours with validation Tuesday through Friday until 4:30pm, $1 flat rate weekdays after 4:30pm and all day weekends.

2000 Ave. of the Stars (btw. Constellation and W. Olympic), Century City. www.annenbergspacefor photography.org. © **213/403-3000.** Free admission. Wed, Fri–Sun 11am–6pm (digital programming ends at 5pm on Thurs).

Church of the Good Shepherd ★ ARCHITECTURE/HISTORIC SITE   Built in 1924, this is Beverly Hills's oldest house of worship. The relatively small church (seating 600) is in the Spanish Colonial Revival style, and its two striking steeples and lovely exterior are noticeable from any direction. In 1950 Elizabeth Taylor and her first husband, Nicky Hilton, were married here. The funerals of Alfred Hitchcock, Gary Cooper, Eva Gabor, and Frank Sinatra were held here as well.

505 N. Bedford Dr. (at Park Way), Beverly Hills. www.goodshepherdbeverlyhills.org. © **310/285-5425.** No extrance fee.

The Getty Center Los Angeles ★★★ ART MUSEUM/ARCHITECTURE   A work of art inside and out, this primary campus of the renowned J. Paul Getty Museum ("The Getty") in Brentwood features European and American art from the Middle Ages to the present. The Richard Meier-designed museum complex alone—a riot of

DAREDEVIL'S PARADISE: magic mountain

SIX FLAGS CALIFORNIA (MAGIC MOUNTAIN AND HURRICANE HARBOR ★ With 17 of the world's best/fastest/longest roller coasters, this thrill-a-minute amusement park, just beyond the San Fernando Valley, is enormously popular with teens and young adults, while Bugs Bunny World, remodeled and bolstered by a new Speedy Gonzales kiddie coaster in 2014, dishes out excitement for kids up to 48 inches tall.

The massive wooden coaster Colossus, which reigned supreme for 36 years, has been retired to make way for its successor, **Twisted Colossus,** scheduled to debut in spring 2015. Billed as the world's longest hybrid coaster, it will hurtle over the iconic wooden structure on new, high-tech steel track to produce higher speeds, overbanked turns and inversions never before possible on a wooden rig. I'll always love the smooth rush of the steel **Viper's** plunges and loops, and the record-breaking 0-to-100mph-in-7-seconds acceleration (in reverse!) of **Superman: Escape From Krypton,** but more recent coasters earn their superlatives: **Tatsu,** billed as the world's tallest, fastest, longest flying roller coaster (ridden face down); **Full Throttle,** the tallest, fastest looping coaster. The floorless **Batman the Ride** sends you through loops, inverted rolls and corkscrews with your feet dangling helplessly; **Scream,** with neither floor below nor track overhead, creates a reasonable facsimile of of real flight as you hurtle through loops, twists and precipitous drops.

I rate this the best park in the West for roller-coaster addicts (its other thrill rides are pretty average) but it's not the most comfortable—especially if you're accustomed to Disneyland. Lines are long, there's little shade, food and drink choices are limited, and frankly, it could use some of those kids roaming the grounds with a broom and dustpan. My advice: Arrive as soon as the park opens to get in a few rides before crowds and heat ramp up, take a siesta, and return in late afternoon to enjoy the evening. If at all possible, plan your visit while school is in session. If you're stuck with prime time, consider buying a Flash Pass. They're expensive ($80–$140), but it could double your ride count, making cost per ride a wash at worst.

The **Hurricane Harbor** water park is right next door. (Don't try to visit both in one day, or you won't get your money's worth at either.) Distinct areas have themes like a tropical lagoon or an African river. Primary activities are swimming, going down 20-plus water slides, rafting, and lounging; many areas are designed for the little ones.

Tip: Save up to $25 per ticket by buying tickets through the park's website.

Magic Mountain Pkwy. (off I-5, 35 mi. north of Los Angeles or Santa Monica), Valencia. www.sixflags.com/magic mountain. ✆ **661/255-4100** or 818/367-5965. $70 adults, $45 children under 48 inches tall, free ages 2 and under. Open daily March to Labor Day, weekends and holidays the rest of the year. Hurricane Harbor: $33 adults, $25 children under 48 in., free ages 2 and under. Open daily mid-June to Labor Day and weekends May and Sept; closed October through April. Both parks open at 10:30am and close between 6pm and midnight. Prices and hours are subject to change, so call to confirm. Self-parking $20, valet $35.

shapes and angles clad in white Italian travertine marble, poised on the edge of the Santa Monica Mountains and commanding panoramic views (of Los Angeles, the San Gabriel Mountains, and the Pacific)—will amaze even those who never pass through doors. A winding .75-mile ascent from the parking lot via an electric tram literally glides on air to what appears as a Xanadu in the sky. The ever-evolving Central Garden, with 500 species of plants lining walkways that wend their way to a central pool supporting a floating maze of azaleas, could have lured Louis IV from the Palace of Versailles. The Fran and Ray Stark Sculpture Garden, a collection of 28 contemporary sculptures by Elisabeth Frink, Joan Miró, Isamu Noguchi and other 20th-century greats, is a relatively recent addition to the grounds; Henry Moore's "Seated Woman" and Roy Lichtenstein's "Three Brushstrokes," among other sculptures, pop up elsewhere on the estate.

But enter the museum doors you must, in order to see the vast collection of Impressionist paintings—including a rare early Edouard Manet pastel, "Portrait of Julien de la Rochenoire," acquired and exhibited for the first time in June 2014—as well as gilded French furniture, decorative arts and contemporary photography. The trove within the galleries include van Gogh's "Irises," painted in an asylum in the last year of his life. (It's almost as famous for having cost nearly $54 million as for its artistic significance.) The galleries have programmable window louvers, which display works in the natural light in which they were created.

For help taking it all in, stop at the GettyGuide Desk in the Entrance Hall and pick up a free iPod touch loaded with a multimedia tour to follow at your own pace. (Art, architecture and garden tours led by humans are also available). In addition to snack carts and two cafes, the Getty's informal yet elegant full-service restaurant serves lunch (Tues–Sat), dinner (Sat), and Sunday brunch in full view of those astounding views. Reservations are recommended, though walk-ins are accepted if space is available.

Tip: Don't leave the kids at home just because you're going to an art museum. The Getty offers inspiring children's programs, including a family room filled with hands-on activities; drop-in art labs; Saturday family festivals; and garden concerts for kids.

1200 Getty Center Dr. (reached from N. Sepulveda Dr., 1.4 mi. north of Sunset Blvd.). www.getty. edu. © **310/440-7300** or 310/440-6810 (for restaurant reservations). Free admission. Tues–Thurs 10am–5:30pm; Sat 10am–9pm; Sun 10am–5:30pm. Open Fri until 9pm btw. Memorial Day and Labor Day. Closed Mondays and major holidays. Admission free (no reservations required); parking $15 ($10 after 5pm for evening programs and on Sat).

The Getty Villa Malibu ★★ ART MUSEUM/ARCHITECTURE
The other campus of the J. Paul Getty Museum is the famous oil tycoon's former home, built in 1974 on the edge of a Malibu bluff with dazzling ocean views. Modeled after the Villa dei Papiri in Herculaneum, Italy, a first-century Roman country house buried by the eruption of Mount Vesuvius, it's a fitting home for the collection of Greek, Roman, and Etruscan artifacts. More than 1,200 works, dating from 6500 B.C. to A.D. 400, occupy 23 galleries arranged by theme (Gods and Goddesses, Monsters and Minor Dieties . . .), while six more galleries host changing exhibitions. Displays range from everyday items such as coins and jewelry to modern interactive exhibits illustrating key moments in ancient Mediterranean history.

To fully appreciate the remarkable collection, pick up the multimedia GettyGuide on the first floor. Highlights include "Statue of a Victorious Youth," a large-scale bronze discovered in an Adriatic shipwreck that is kept in a climate-controlled room to preserve the metal (it's one of the few surviving life-size Greek bronzes), and a beautiful 450-seat open-air theater where visitors can take a break. Among the museum's related performances, lectures and other activities, the classical outdoor theater presents either a Greek comedy or tragedy every September. The Villa's education team keeps kids engaged with art-related activities such as making a mosaic with an artist in a hands-on space called the Family Forum.

17985 Pacific Coast Hwy. (1 mi. north of Sunset Blvd., via Getty Villa Dr.), Pacific Palisades. www. getty.edu. © **310/440-7300.** Free admission, but advance tickets required. Wed–Mon 10am–5pm. Open Sat until 9pm btw. Memorial day and Labor Day. Closed Tues and major holidays. Parking $15 ($10 for evening programs).

If you've seen 2013's "Star Trek Into Darkness," you've seen Greystone Mansion, but you might not recognize the Royal Children's Hospital as the opulent, 55-room Tudor Revival mansion with English gardens built on a slope overlooking Beverly Hills by oil tycoon Edward Doheny in 1928. Dozens of TV episodes, movies ("Spiderman," "X-Men," "Ghostbusters," "War and Remembrance"), commercials, and music videos are filmed annually in what is now the 19-acre Greystone Park. A self-guided tour takes you through the Formal Gardens, Mansion Gardens, and Lower Ground Estate. Picnickers are welcome in designated areas. 905 Loma Vista Dr., just off Doheny Road. www.greystonemansion.org. ✆ **310/285-6830.** Free admission. Daily 10am to 6pm during Pacific Daylight Time, to 5pm in winter. Free parking.

Hammer Museum ★ ART MUSEUM   Former Occidental Petroleum chairman/ CEO Armand Hammer's frankly unfocused personal collection of traditional western European and Anglo-American art is the linchpin of UCLA's two-story, Carrara marble museum, but the daring and sometimes controversial visiting exhibits generate the buzz, such as the provocative "Tea and Morphine: Women in Paris 1880 to 1914" in 2014. Its biennial "Made in L.A." exhibition presents a wide variety of new and experimental art in a space run by local artists. There's no reason not to look in on whatever show is up during your visit, since the museum dropped the admission fee in 2014 to prompt more frequent visits. (Some special exhibitions may still charge a fee.)

10899 Wilshire Blvd. (at Westwood Blvd.), Westwood. www.hammer.ucla.edu. ✆ **310/443-7000.** Free admission. Tues–Fri 11am–8pm; Sat–Sun 11am–5pm. Closed Jan 1, July 4, Thanksgiving, and Christmas. Parking $3 for 1st 3 hr. with validation; $3 flat rate Sat–Sun and after 6pm weekdays.

Museum of Tolerance ★ MUSEUM   It's understandable that a museum created by the institute founded by legendary Nazi hunter Simon Wiesenthal, with the mission of exposing bigotry and fostering tolerance, leans heavily on the Holocaust. The message behind the exhibition telling Anne Frank's story through rare artifacts, documents, dramatizations and an interactive lab, seems more relevant with every passing day. Still, this is not a Jewish museum; other exhibits that engage hearts and minds have included "The Point of View Diner," focusing on bullying, and the video-wall drama "Ain't You Gotta Right?" on America's civil rights struggle. Small wonder its millions of visitors have included the Dalai Lama and Jordan's King Hussein.

9786 W. Pico Blvd. (at Roxbury Dr.), Los Angeles. www.museumoftolerance.com. ✆ **310/553-8403.** Admission $16 adults, $13 seniors 62 and over, $12 students with ID and children 5–18, free for kids under 5. Advance purchase recommended; photo ID required for admission. Mon–Wed 10am–6:30pm; Thurs 10am–9:30pm; Fri–Sun (Apr–Oct) 10am–6:30pm; Fri–Sun (Nov–Mar) 10am–3:30pm; closed Sat and many Jewish and secular holidays (see schedule on website). Free underground parking.

Pacific Design Center ★ ARCHITECTURE   The bold architecture and overwhelming scale of the Pacific Design Center, created by Argentine architect Cesar Pelli, aroused controversy when it was erected in 1975. Sheathed in gently curving cobalt-blue glass, the six-story building houses more than 750,000–square–feet of wholesale interior-design showrooms and is known to locals as "the Blue Whale." In 1988 a second box-like structure, dressed in equally dramatic Kelly green, was added and the design center was surrounded by a protected outdoor plaza. The long-delayed

4

Los Angeles Attractions

EXPLORING LOS ANGELES

Red Building towers finally opened in 2013. Visitors are welcome during regular business hours and one designated Saturday each month (except June-August). Two casual Wolfgang Puck restaurants, Red 7 and Spectra, are located here.

8687 Melrose Ave. (at San Vicente Blvd.), West Hollywood. www.pacificdesigncenter.com. ☏ **310/657-0800.** Mon–Fri 9am–5pm; select Sat 10am–4pm. Parking varies; daily max typically $14.

The Paley Center for Media ★★ MUSEUM   Whether you want to relive television's Golden Age, study the media's impact on American culture or wallow in a cherished guilty pleasure, I dare you to get out of this place in under five hours, so be there when it opens. The heart of the center is a collection of 150,000 (and growing) television and radio programs and commercials—the TV pilot programs that never aired are a special treat—that you can check out and view in a private cubicle. Giggle at Orson Welles's "War of the Worlds" UFO hoax (1938), view Elvis' truncated gyrations on the "Ed Sullivan Show" (1956), sneer at Nixon's resignation speech (1974), or just look for that episode of "Castle" that you missed. If all those options are too much to contemplate, try the Weekend Screenings, which take such varied themes as the 75th anniversary of Batman's first appearance and fashions from the "Mad Men" era. In September, the center holds PaleyFestPreviews, showing pilot episodes of new shows before they air and hosting panel discussions with their stars and producers.

465 N. Beverly Dr. (at Santa Monica Blvd.), Beverly Hills. www.paleycenter.org. ☏ **310/786-1091.** Suggested contribution $10 adults, $8 students, and seniors, $5 children 13 and under. Wed–Sun noon–5pm. Closed Jan 1, July 4, Thanksgiving, and Christmas. Free parking.

Skirball Cultural Center ★ MUSEUM/ARCHITECTURE   This remarkable museum is just a fraction of this institution's efforts to make connections between Jewish heritage and American democratic values. Music, theater, comedy, film, libraries, and family and literary programs are all brought to bear in inspiring people of all cultures who share a history of pursuing the American dream. Tucked into the Santa Monica Mountains uphill from the Getty Center, the curvy campus is defined by alternating bands of gray concrete and pink granite; Israeli architect Moshe Safdie completed the fourth and final phase in fall 2013. The permanent exhibition, "Visions and Values: Jewish Life from Antiquity to America," chronicles 4,000 years of the Jewish experience, while the child-oriented "Noah's Ark" sends families on a virtual journey in a ceiling-high ark full of life-sized animals made of recycled materials.

2701 N. Sepulveda Blvd. (at Mulholland Dr.), Los Angeles. www.skirball.org. ☏ **310/440-4500.** Admission $10 adults, $7 students and seniors 65 and over, $5 children 2–12, free for kids 1 and under; free for everyone Thurs. Tues–Fri noon–5pm; Sat–Sun 10am–5pm. Closed many Jewish and secular holidays; see website for schedule. Free parking ($10 for Sunset Concerts, cash only). From I-405, exit at Skirball Center Dr./Mulholland Dr.

Hollywood & West Hollywood
ICONIC HOLLYWOOD

Grauman's Chinese Theatre ★★ LANDMARK/HISTORIC SITE   Millions of visitors flock to this outlandishly ornate movie palace's famous entry court, where Elizabeth Taylor, Paul Newman, Humphrey Bogart, Frank Sinatra, Marilyn Monroe, and about 160 other movie stars set their signatures and hand-/footprints in concrete. Betty Grable's shapely leg; the hoofprints of Gene Autry's horse, Champion; Jimmy Durante's and Bob Hope's famous noses; Whoopi Goldberg's dreadlocks; and George Burns's cigar are also captured in cement. The theater was opened in 1927 by impresario Sid Grauman, a brilliant promoter credited with originating the paparazzi-packed movie "premiere." It was designed to impress: Original Chinese heavenly doves top

stargazing: IT WAS A WONDERFUL LIFE

The Tinseltown stars that every visitor hopes to spot have an annoying habit of hiding out or blending in. Here we present the only places where you're always guaranteed to get within 6 feet of a celebrity. These cemeteries are the final homes of the rich and famous, listed in the order of their friendliness to stargazers. (If you're looking for someone in particular, visit www.findagrave.com.)

Hollywood Forever ★★★ (formerly Hollywood Memorial Park), 6000 Santa Monica Blvd., Hollywood (www.hollywood forever.com; © 323/469-1181). Weathered Victorian and Art Deco memorials add to the decaying charm, and a terrific view of the HOLLYWOOD sign over graves of many of Hollywood's founders seems especially fitting. The most notable tenant is Rudolph Valentino, who rests in an interior crypt. Outside are Tyrone Power, Jr.; Douglas Fairbanks, Sr.; Cecil B. DeMille, Hearst mistress Marion Davies, and John Huston. (Jayne Mansfield has a headstone here but is buried in Pennsylvania with her family). Best epitaph ever: Mel Blanc's "That's all, Folks." Maps are available at the entrance.

Holy Cross Cemetery ★★ 5835 W. Slauson Ave., Culver City (www.holy crossmortuary.com; © 310/836-5500). Within mere feet of each other lie Bing Crosby, Bela Lugosi (buried in his Dracula cape), and Sharon Tate; not far away are Rita Hayworth and Jimmy Durante. Also here are "Tin Man" Jack Haley and "Scarecrow" Ray Bolger, Mary Astor, John Ford, and Gloria Morgan Vanderbilt. More recent arrivals include John Candy and Mickey Rooney. The cemetery hands out maps to the stars' graves.

Hillside Memorial Park ★★ 6001 W. Centinela Ave., Baldwin Hills (www.hillside memorial.org; © 800/576-1994). The front office can provide a guide to this Jewish cemetery, whose behemoth tomb of Al Jolson—a rotunda with classical columns and a cascading fountain—is an L.A. landmark, visible from I-405. Jack

---

the facade, and two of its columns once propped up a Ming dynasty temple. TCL, one of China's biggest electronics manufacturers took the theater over from Mann's in 2013, and its official name is now TCL Chinese Theatre—but it will foerever be Grauman's Chinese Theatre to fans of Hollywood history.

6925 Hollywood Blvd. (btw. N. Highland Ave. and N. Orange Dr.), Hollywood. www.tclchinese theatres.com. © 323/464-8111. Movie ticket prices vary, but are usually around $15–$19. Parking at Hollywood & Highland Center $2 with validation. Metro Red Line to Hollywood/Highland.

Griffith Observatory ★★ LANDMARK Made world-famous by the James Dean movie "Rebel Without a Cause," Griffith Observatory's bronze domes have been Hollywood Hills landmarks since 1935. The central dome houses the 300-seat **Samuel Oschin Planetarium,** where hourly screenings of a narrated 30-minute projection show, "Centered in the Universe," reveal stars and planets that are hidden from the naked eye by the city's ubiquitous lights and smog.

Of the observatory's 60 space-related exhibits, the highlight is "The Big Picture"—the largest astronomically accurate image ever produced. The 20×152-foot porcelain enamel dazzler, covering a part of the sky containing more than a million celestial objects, is a single image of a huge scientific data set, displayed at the resolution of the telescope and camera used to capture it.

There's also the 200-seat Leonard Nimoy Event Horizon Theater (go Spock!), a Wolfgang Puck "Café at the End of the Universe," and several telescopes for public use

Benny, Eddie Cantor, Vic Morrow, and Michael Landon also are interred here.

Westwood Village Memorial Park ★★ 1218 Glendon Ave., Westwood (www.pbwvmortuary.com; 🕐 **310/474-1579**). Smack-dab in the middle of some of L.A.'s priciest real estate, this cemetery's star of stars is the simple wall crypt (number 24) of Marilyn Monroe. Her neighbors include Truman Capote, Roy Orbison, John Cassavetes, Armand Hammer, Donna Reed, and Natalie Wood. Walter Matthau and Jack Lemmon are buried here as well, so the Odd Couple can bicker for all eternity.

Forest Lawn Glendale ★ 1712 S. Glendale Ave. (www.forestlawn.com; 🕐 **800/204-3131**). The most prominent of L.A. cemeteries likes to pretend it has no celebrities. The place is immense, full of bad art and bland flat slabs that were deemed preferable to upright tombstones and monuments. The cemetery won't tell you where any of their illustrious guests are, but . . . Walt Disney's cremated remains lie in a little garden to the left of the Freedom Mausoleum; turn around to see Errol Flynn and Spencer Tracy. In the mausoleum itself are Nat "King" Cole, Chico and Gummo Marx, and George Burns with Gracie Allen. Humphrey Bogart reposes in a columbarium near the Mystery of Life statue. Unfortunately, the eternal homes of Clark Gable, Carole Lombard, Jean Harlow, Michael Jackson, and Elizabeth Taylor are in the church-like Great Mausoleum, which is guarded against public incursion.

Forest Lawn Hollywood Hills ★ 6300 Forest Lawn Dr., Los Angeles (www.forestlawn.com; 🕐 **800/204-3131**). Though less oppressive than the Glendale branch, this one exhibits the same basic attitude. Buster Keaton lies under the right lawn, near the George Washington statue. Lucille Ball, Charles Laughton, and Liberace's not-quite-gaudy-enough tomb are in the Courts of Remembrance. Bette Davis' sarcophagus is in front of the wall, to the left of the Courts entrance. Gene Autry is also buried here, almost within earshot of the museum bearing his name.

both day and night. The observatory holds "Sunset Walk & Talk" events. Locals come to this spot on the slope of Mount Hollywood for unparalleled city views, On warm nights, with the lights twinkling below, it's one of the most romantic settings in L.A.— rivaled only by the vistas from Mulholland Drive (p. 92).

2800 E. Observatory Rd. (in Griffith Park, at the end of Vermont Ave.), Los Angeles. www.griffith observatory.org. 🕐 **213/473-0800.** Planetarium tickets $7 adults, $5 seniors 60 or older and students with ID, $3 children 5–12. Wed–Fri noon–10pm; Sat–Sun 10am–10pm. Call or check website for planetarium showtimes.

Hollywood Walk of Fame ★ ICON When Grauman's ran out of space, Hollywood devised another way to pay tribute to its royalty: embedding stars in the sidewalk on Hollywood Boulevard. More than 2,400 celebrities have been honored since 1960 on the world's most famous sidewalk. Each bronze medallion, set into the center of a terrazzo star, honors a famous television, film, radio, theater, or recording personality. (**Gene Autry,** the singing cowboy, set a record with stars in all five categories.) Although about one-third of the names are now obscure, it only enhances the pleasure of spotting such famous names as **James Dean** (1719 Vine St.), **John Lennon** (1750 Vine St.), **Marlon Brando** (1765 Vine St.), **Rudolph Valentino** (6164 Hollywood Blvd.), **Marilyn Monroe** (6744 Hollywood Blvd.), **Elvis Presley** (7080 Hollywood Blvd.)— the only star that has ever been moved—**Greta Garbo** (6901 Hollywood Blvd.), **Louis**

LEGENDARY sunset boulevard

The most famous of the city's many legendary boulevards winds dozens of miles over prime real estate as it travels from Downtown (briefly turning into Cesar Chavez Ave. btw. Spring and Figueroa sts.) to the beach, a historical and microcosmic journey that defines Los Angeles as a whole—from tacky strip malls and historic movie studios to infamous strip clubs and some of the most coveted zip codes on Earth.

Starting at the **Saharan Motor Hotel** (7212 Sunset Blvd.), of many a movie shoot, traveling west takes you past the Guitar Center's **Hollywood RockWalk,** where superstars like Chuck Berry, Little Richard, Santana, and the Van Halen brothers left handprints or signatures; the **"Riot Hyatt,"** (now the Andaz) where The Doors, Led Zeppelin, and Guns N' Roses crashed and smashed from the '60s through the '80s; and **Chateau Marmont,** where Greta Garbo lived and John Belushi died.

Now you're officially cruising the **Sunset Strip**—a 1¾-mile stretch of Sunset from Crescent Heights Boulevard to Doheny Drive. Gawk at the **Comedy Store,** where Roseanne Barr, Robin Williams, and David Letterman rose to stardom; Dan Aykroyd's ramshackle **House of Blues,** where rock stars still show up for impromptu shows; the **Sunset Tower Hotel,** where Clark Gable, Marilyn Monroe, and John Wayne once lived; the ultraexclusive **Skybar** within the Mondrian hotel; the **Viper Room,** once owned by Johnny Depp, and the site of River Phoenix's overdose in 1993; **Whisky A Go-Go,** where the Doors were once a house band; and the **Rainbow Bar & Grill,** where Jimi Hendrix, Bruce Springsteen, and Bob Marley became legends.

Beyond the Strip, you drive through the tony neighborhoods of **Beverly Hills, Bel Air, Brentwood,** and **Pacific Palisades.** By the time you've reached **Malibu** and the beach where "Baywatch" was filmed, you'll have seen a vivid cross section of the city and have a pretty good idea of what L.A. is all about.

Armstrong (7000 Hollywood Blvd.), **Barbra Streisand** (6925 Hollywood Blvd.), and **Eddie Murphy** (7000 Hollywood Blvd.).

The legendary sidewalk continually adds new names, including Raymond Chandler, Julianna Margulies, Amy Poehler, and Pharrell Williams for 2015. The public is invited to dedication ceremonies, usually attended by the honoree, which the Hollywood Chamber of Commerce announces seven to 10 days before the event.

Hollywood Blvd. btw. Gower St. and La Brea Ave., and Vine St. btw. Yucca St. and Sunset Blvd. www.walkoffame.com. ✆ **323/469-8311.** No charge to attend dedications. Metro Red Line to Hollywood/Vine or Hollywood/Highland.

Hollywood Sign ★★　These famous 50-foot-high white sheet-metal letters have come to symbolize the movie industry and the city itself. Erected on Mount Lee in 1923 to advertise real estate, it originally read HOLLYWOODLAND and was outlined by thousands of light bulbs. The LAND section was damaged by a landslide, and the entire sign fell into disrepair until the Hollywood Chamber of Commerce spearheaded a campaign to repair it. Officially completed in 1978, the 450-foot-long installation is now protected by a fence and motion detectors.

The best **views** are from down below—at the corner of Sunset Boulevard and Bronson Avenue or Hollywood and Highland—from the Griffith Observatory, or from the "'Hollywood Bowl Overlook" on Mulholland Drive (about .7 mi. southwest of

Cahuenga). To reach the sign (or at least the fence) on foot requires a moderately strenuous **hike** of several miles each way. The most popular hike is the Mount Hollywood Trail from Griffith Observatory, which does not go to the mountain crowned by the sign but delivers great views of it. Griffith's longer Canyon Boulevard Trail takes you right to the fence behind the sign on Mount Lee, passing the Bronson Caves (the Batcave of the 1960s TV show) on the way. For more information, visit www.hollywood sign.org or call Griffith Park headquarters at ☎ 323/913-4688.

OTHER HOLLYWOOD ATTRACTIONS

Autry National Center of the American West ★★ ART MUSEUM   This museum in Griffith Park was the realization of a dream for actor/singer Gene Autry, America's beloved Singing Cowboy of the mid-20th century, who founded it in 1988. Its 500,000 pieces, including the collection of the Southwest Museum of the American Indian, are inventively displayed to evoke the experiences of people who settled west of the Mississippi. In addition to the expected guns, saddlery, wagons, clothing, Indian pottery and Western art displays, special exhibitions hone in on subjects such as Hopi Katsina dolls and "Route 66: The Road and the Romance." The on-site Crossroads West Cafe provides not just moderately priced dining but a showcase for the unique cuisine of the American West. Its monthly Cowboy Lunch includes discussions with Western filmmakers and actors. Docent-led tours are available on weekends.

4700 Western Heritage Way, Griffith Park. ☎ 323/667-2000. www.autrynationalcenter.org. Admission $10 adults, $6 seniors 60 and over and students 13–18, $4 children 3–12, free for kids 2 and under; free for everyone the 2nd Tues of every month. Tues–Fri 10am–4pm (until 8pm Thurs in July and Aug.); Sat–Sun 10am–5pm. Closed Jan 1, July 4, Labor Day, Thanksgiving and the day after Thanksgiving, and Dec 24–25. Free parking.

Capitol Records Building ★ ARCHITECTURE   Opened in 1956—its first recording was "Frank Sinatra Conducts Tone Poems of Color"—this 13-story tower, just north of the legendary Hollywood and Vine intersection, is one of the city's most recognizable buildings. The world's first circular office building only coincidentally resembles a stack of 45s, despite stories that it was designed with that in mind. Nat "King" Cole, Ella Fitzgerald, and Billie Holliday are among the artists featured in the giant exterior "Hollywood Jazz" mural. Look down and you'll see the sidewalk stars of Capitol's recording artists, including each of the Beatles. Numerous gold albums are on display in the lobby. *Fun fact:* The light on the rooftop spire flashes "H-O-L-L-Y-W-O-O-D" in Morse code.

1750 Vine St. (just north of Hollywood Blvd.). ☎ 323/462-6252.

Craft and Folk Art Museum ★ ART MUSEUM   They've been exploring the cultural role of craft and folk art for more than 40 years now, and nothing pleases the stewards of this museum more than to turn the preconception of the "lowly" arts on its head. The museum seeks out artists who take traditional practices in surprising directions; two recent exhibitions were a Guatemalan sculptor's creations out of discarded sports equipment and large "shacks" made of found materials for such events as the Coachella Valley Music and Arts Festival and Burning Man. A variety of public programs lets visitors learn basic woodcarving skills (while making a set of chopsticks), join a "yarn bombing" session with local "guerrilla knitters," and participate in many other hands-on activities. The museum shop is packed with curated hand-crafted works from an international array of artisans.

5814 Wilshire Blvd. (btw. Fairfax and La Brea), Los Angeles. ☎ 323/937-4230. www.cafam.org. Admission $7 adults, $5 seniors and students, free for children 9 and under; free for everyone Sun.

ON A CLEAR DAY ... mulholland drive

It's not always easy to get a good city view in Los Angeles. Even if you find the right vantage, smog may obscure the panorama. But, as they say, on a clear day, you can see forever.

Los Angeles is the world's only major city divided by a mountain range; the road on top of this range is the famous **Mulholland Drive ★★.** It travels 21 miles along the peaks and canyons of Hollywood Hills and the Santa Monica Mountains, separating the Los Angeles basin from the San Fernando Valley. The winding road provides jaw-dropping views of the city, particularly at night, and offers many opportunities to pull over and enjoy the view from 1,400 feet. (Yes, there are celebrities up in them thar hills—Leonardo DiCaprio, Paris Hilton—but you'll never see them.)

Completed in 1924, it's named after William Mulholland, engineer of the aqueduct connecting L.A. and the Valley. You don't need to drive the whole road to get the full effect. From Cahuenga Boulevard (near the Hollywood Bowl), take the Mulholland Drive turnoff heading west. After about a mile, you'll come to a scenic view area on your left. Park at the small paved parking lot (open until sunset), ooh and aah over the view of the L.A. basin, and then drive a few miles farther west until you spot the other scenic view area (unpaved) on your right, overlooking the San Fernando Valley. The whole trip should take less than an hour.

Tip: Don't drive here after 3pm on weekdays—rush-hour traffic is beastly. Also, U.S. 101 has no Mulholland Drive exit; you have to get on at Cahuenga Boulevard.

Tues–Fri 11am–5pm; Sat–Sun noon–6pm; 6:30–9:30pm 1st Thurs of every month; closed Mon. Metered street parking or nearby public lots.

The Egyptian Theatre ★ ARCHITECTURE Conceived by impresario Sid Grauman, the grandiose Egyptian Theatre is just down the street from his Chinese Theatre but has been less altered. It was based on the then-headline-news discovery of hidden treasures in Pharaohs' tombs—hence the hieroglyphic murals and enormous scarab decoration above the stage. Hollywood's first movie premiere, "Robin Hood," starring Douglas Fairbanks, was shown here in 1922, followed by "The Ten Commandments" in 1923. The sensitively restored building now screens rare, classic, and independent films. Check the online schedule for screenings hosted by celebrity guest speakers; and historic theater tours.

6712 Hollywood Blvd. (across from Grauman's Chinee Theatre, btw. N. Las Palmas Ave. and N. McCadden Place), Hollywood. www.egyptiantheatre.com. ✆ **323/466-FILM** (466-3456). Metro Red Line to Hollywood/Highland.

Farmers Market ★★★ MARKET When it opened in 1934, the original **Farmers Market** was little more than an empty lot with wooden stands set up by farmers during the Depression. Eventually, permanent buildings grew up, including the trademark shingled 10-story clock tower. Today it's a busy, sprawling marketplace with a carnival atmosphere. About 70 restaurants, shops, and grocers cater to a mix of locals, CBS Television City workers, and busloads of tourists. Retailers sell greeting cards, kitchen implements, candles, and souvenirs, but most everyone comes for the food stands offering oysters, hot doughnuts, Cajun gumbo, fresh-squeezed orange juice, corned beef sandwiches, fresh-pressed peanut butter, and all kinds of international fast food. Don't miss **Loteria Grill,** 6627 Hollywood Blvd. (© **323/930-2211;** www. loteriagrill.com) for shredded beef tacos on handmade tortillas and cool *aguas frescas,* or **Du-par's** (© **323/933-8446**) for a slice of pie. The gumbo at the **Gumbo Pot** (© **323/933-0358**) is also very popular.

At the eastern end of the Farmer's Market, the massive **Grove** retail complex is one of L.A.'s most popular megamalls. See "Shopping Malls" (p. 123).

Intersection of 3rd St. and Fairfax Blvd. www.farmersmarketla.com. © **866/993-9211** or 323/933-9211. Mon–Fri 9am–9pm, Sat 9am–8pm, Sun 10am–7pm. Parking in lot free for 2 hr. with validation, $4 for 3rd hour, $1 each additional 15 min.

The Hollywood Museum ★ MUSEUM/ARCHITECTURE In a town where day spas are as ubiquitous as Starbuck's, it's hard to comprehend that before Hollywood "makeup king" Max Factor headquartered his cosmetic empire in this grand Art Deco building in 1935 and created the signature looks of Hollywood's most famous actresses here, women who went out to have their makeup done were considered "hussies." Now restored to its original glory, the museum re-creates the Hollywood of popular imagination. The main floor, with its vivid pink lobby, focuses on Factor's cosmetic wizardry, displaying the original makeup in glass cases and admitting visitors to the rooms where Factor turned Marilyn into a blonde and Lucy into a redhead. Props, costumes, scripts, awards and vintage posters and photos bring other aspects of Old Hollywood to life on three more floors. Head to the basement for creepy stuff like Boris Karloff's mummy and Hannibal Lecter's jail cell. The museum also has a library, a screening room, an education center and a gift shop.

1660 N. Highland Ave. (south of Hollywood Blvd.), Hollywood. www.thehollywoodmuseum.com. © **323/464-7776.** Admission/tour $15 adults, $12 seniors and students; $5 children 5 and under. Wed–Sun 10am–5pm. Discounted parking with validation at adjacent lot. Metro Red Line to Hollywood/Highland.

La Brea Tar Pits and Page Museum ★★ MUSEUM This lake of primal sludge, surrounded by a brash young city, is the most incongruous museum in Los Angeles, if not the country. The primeval pools lured nearly 400 species of thirsty mammals, birds, amphibians and fish that last roamed Earth as much as 50,000 years ago, only to trap them in asphalt seeping up from underground oil deposits. One of the world's richest excavation sites for Ice Age fossils, it has been coughing up saber-tooth cats, mastodons, camels, giant jaguars and dire wolves ever since scientists began extracting their remains in 1906. You can see the best of these next door at the **Page Museum at the La Brea Tar Pits,** boasting the world's largest and most diverse collection of Ice Age plant and animal skeletons. The Fossil Lab lets you watch scientists and hordes of volunteers work on an estimated 100,000 cleaned but uncatalogued specimens and another million or so that remain to be scrubbed. The Observation Pit, which opened in 1952 and closed in the mid-'90s, reopened in summer 2014 to allow visitors to watch extractions in progress as a stop on the new Excavator Tour (timed tickets required).

5801 Wilshire Blvd. (east of Fairfax), Los Angeles. www.tarpits.org. © **323/934-7243.** Museum admission $12 adults; $9 seniors 62 and older, students with ID, and teens 13–17; $5 kids 3–12; free for 2 and under, California teachers and military with ID; free for everyone the 1st Tues of every month except July and Aug. Daily 9:30am–5pm except Jan 1, July 4, Thanksgiving, and Christmas. Parking $9. Metro Red Line to Civic Center/Grand Park.

Los Angeles County Museum of Art (LACMA) ★★★ ART MUSEUM Celebrating its 50th anniversary on Wilshire Boulevard's Miracle Mile in 2015, LACMA has grown Topsy-like, as if mirroring the city's own crazy-quilt expansion. Its 120,000-piece permanent collection now spans seven structures on its 20-acre campus. It makes

Money-Saving Tourist Passes

If you want to cram every possible attraction into your trip, consider buying a **GO Los Angeles Card** or **Southern California CityPass.** Most people will be better served by the **GO Los Angeles Card** (www.smartdestinations.com; $\textit{\textcircled{c}}$ **866/652-3053**) for general sightseeing; it offers free or discounted admission to 36 or 37 of L.A.'s most popular attractions and activities. You can choose 1-, 2-, 3-, 5-, or 7-day increments, valid any time within a 2-week period, or create a custom card. The 3-day card, the most popular, costs $200 for adults ($150 for kids 3–12). Cards for 3, 5, and 7 days include Universal Studios Hollywood (a great bargain) but not Disneyland. The card is a good value as long as you visit one major attraction such as

a theme park, or two other attractions such as a studio tour, each day. Purchase GO Cards on their website or at the Hollywood Visitor Information Center (6801 Hollywood Blvd. at Highland Ave.; $\textit{\textcircled{c}}$ **323/467-6412;** Metro Red line to Hollywood/Highland).

The CityPass (www.citypass.com; $\textit{\textcircled{c}}$ **888/330-5008**) includes a 3-day Park Hopper ticket with Magic Morning for Disneyland and California Adventure, plus 1-day tickets to Universal Studios Hollywood and SeaWorld San Diego. The pass costs $331 for adults ($289 for kids 3–9; 2 and under free) and expires 14 days after the first use. If you use all four tickets, it will save $110 over individual, full-price admission. If you use only three, the most you'll save is about $26.

for a scattered and sometimes disorienting experience, but you'll find help from staff at every turn. The global collection dates from the ancient world to the present, with its greatest strengths in Asian, Latin American, and Islamic art. Ranking among the nation's best, its collection is replete with masterworks by the likes of Van Gogh, Rembrandt, Matisse, Degas, Monet, Picasso, O'Keefe, and Hockney. Contemporary and experimental art also are well-represented. Don't even think about trying to see it all one day, or even two.

Here's a brief rundown: On the east side of the **Grand Entrance**, fronted by the Instagram-ready "Urban Light" installation, are **The Pavilion for Japanese Art;** the **Bing Center** auditorium, theater and cafe; the **Art of the Americas Building,** whose recent shows include the work of Mexican cinematographer Gabriel Figueroa and art of the ancient Americas; the **Hammer Building,** containing the children's gallery and ancient and Korean art; and the **Ahmanson Building,** housing the bulk of the permanent collections, most notably German Expressionism, Islamic art, and Indian and Southeast Asian art. To the west are the **Broad Contemporary Art Museum (BCAM),** showing the likes of Koons, Johns, Warhol, and Lichtenstein, plus the fascinating "Metropolis II" kinetic sculpture of an imagined future city; and the **Resnick Pavilion** for diverse special exhibitions. Free docent-led tours are offered daily; check the online calendar for details.

LACMA's retro restaurant and outdoor lounge, **Ray & Stark's Bar** in the Grand Entrance, offers specialty cocktails and a Mediterranean-inspired menu prepared on a wood-fired oven and grill. It's one of L.A.'s cadre of "destination restaurants."

5905 Wilshire Blvd. (btw. Curson and Fairfax), Los Angeles. www.lacma.org. $\textit{\textcircled{c}}$ **323/857-6000.** Admission $15 adults, $10 students and seniors 62 and over, free for children 17 and under; regular exhibitions free for everyone after 5pm, all day the 2nd Tues of every month and select federal holidays. Mon–Tues and Thurs 11am–5pm; Fri 11am–8pm; Sat–Sun 10am–7pm. Closed Thanksgiving and Christmas. Parking $12; free after 7pm entry.

Los Angeles Zoo and Botanical Gardens ★★   Though it doesn't compare with the world-famous San Diego Zoo (see p. 221), L.A.'s home-grown, conservation-oriented zoo is easier to fully explore. It's also a certified botanical garden, thick with mature shade trees from around the world. New habitats resembling the animals' natural environments are light-years ahead of the cruel concrete huts of old (though you can't help feeling all the creatures would rather be in the wild).

The cuddly koalas, which made their debut in in 1982, remain one of the biggest draws among more than 1,100 animals from around the world, but the zoo's latest attraction—the final phase of a 22-year master plan that culminated in 2014—is a stunner. **Rainforest of the Americas** focuses on tapirs, the emerald tree boa, goliath bird-eating spiders and other exotic and endangered Central and South American creatures not often found in U.S.zoos; the 6-foot-long giant river otters will forever change the way you think of those adorable critters. A pair of cotton-top tamarins (small, black-faced monkeys with flowing white hair) cavorting loose in the trees add to the wilderness atmosphere.

Another standout is the **LAIR** (Living Amphibians, Insects and Reptiles), housing rare animals from from forest, mountain, and desert environments. I am in total awe of the Chinese giant salamander, the world's biggest amphibian at 6 feet long, but many of the 60 species leave a lasting impression. The **Elephants of Asia,** another great new habitat, sports so many natural features that its residents are often hidden from view.

Kids will especially enjoy the **California Condor Rescue Zone,** where they can don wings and "fly" over a valley and scale rocks as biologists do. Other kid-hip areas include the classic **Tom Maniewicz Conservation Carousel,** whose dozens of hand-carved figures of California flora and fauna represent many endangered species, the **Winnick Family Children's Zoo**'s petting area, and an exhibition animal-care center.

A "Weird and Wonderful" audio tour spotlights the zoo's most intriguing animals, such as the red-knobbed hornbill, Komodo dragon, Coquerel's sifaka, and Sichuan takin. You can also download it in English or Spanish from the zoo's website, under the "Visit" tab.

The zoo is spread over a large, hilly area that gets brutally hot in the summer, and the remaining old-style exhibits provide little shade. Wear good walking shoes and bring a hat, plenty of water, and perhaps a picnic lunch (zoo food is limited and expensive). Animals are most active in the cool of the mornings—which unfortunately is also when busloads of rambunctious school kids arrive on weekdays.

5333 Zoo Dr., Griffith Park. www.lazoo.org. Ⓒ **323/644-4200.** $19 adults, $16 seniors 62 and over, $14 children 2–12, free for kids 1 and under. Daily 10am–5pm (until 6pm July 1–Labor Day). Closed Christmas. Free parking.

Madame Tussauds Hollywood ★   In the heart of Hollywood, this is the first Madame Tussauds built from the ground up. The 44,000-square-foot, three-story building houses more than 100 lifelike celebrity wax figures created at up to $300,000 a pop. They include icons from Vivien Leigh to President Obama, from Marilyn Monroe to Johnny Depp and Lady Gaga. The wax figures are artfully displayed in 14 themed areas such as the Red Carpet, A-List Party, Spirit of Hollywood, Westerns, Sport, and Action Heroes.

6933 Hollywood Blvd. (next to the Chinese Theatre,), Hollywood. www.madametussauds.com/hollywood. Ⓒ **323/798-1670.** Admission $30 adults, $23 children 4–12, free for kids 3 and under; 30% discount available online. Metro Red Line to Hollywood/Highland.

Petersen Automotive Museum ★★ MUSEUM In a city with more freeways than most cities have boulevards, this museum—founded by the publisher of "Hot Rod" and "Motor Trend" magazines—is an important stop for a visitor who wants to truly "get" L.A., where a car is less a vehicle than a definition of one's identity. Steve McQueen's 1967 Ferrari made a guest appearance here on its way to auction in 2014, briefly sharing digs with his Jaguar in the permanent collection; could you honestly picture the "Bullitt" star in something like a Chevy? In chronicling how L.A. and the automobile grew up together, the Petersen displays only about half of its more than 300 vehicles at any time. Historic autos and motorcycles on the first-floor "Streetscape" are surrounded by period architecture, while the second floor's rotating galleries display race cars, concept cars, celebrity cars and auto design and technology. Also on the second floor, a permanent exhibition on alternative power suggests the museum, like the city, is inching away from fossil-fuel addiction. The hands-on Discovery Center on the third floor teaches basic science by explaining how a car works.

6060 Wilshire Blvd. (at Fairfax Ave.), Los Angeles. www.petersen.org. ✆ **323/930-CARS** (930-2277). Admission $15 adults, $10 seniors and students, $5 children 3–12, free for kids 2 and under. Daily 10am–6pm. Parking $10.

Downtown

Angelino Heights ★★★ ARCHITECTURE For a taste of what Downtown's Bunker Hill (a major presence in film noir classics) was like before it was bulldozed for highrises, visit this residential neighborhood, widely regarded as L.A.'s first suburb, near Echo Park. Entire streets are still filled with stately gingerbread Victorian homes and later Craftsman and Mission Revival styles, most enjoying the same beautiful views that led early L.A.'s elite to build here. The well-preserved 1300 block of Carroll Avenue boasts the highest concentration of 19th-century Victorians in the city. Don't be surprised to see a film crew scouting locations here.

Bounded by U.S. 101 to the south, Echo Park Ave. to the west, W. Sunset Blvd. to the north, Boylston St. to the east; adjacent to Echo Park and Elysian Park neighborhoods.

The Bradbury Building ★★ ARCHITECTURE This National Historic Landmark, built in 1893 and designed by George Wyman, is Los Angeles's oldest commercial building and one of the city's most revered architectural achievements. Legend has it that an inexperienced draftsman named George Wyman accepted the $125,000 commission after communicating with his dead brother through a Ouija board. Capped by a magical five-story skylight, Bradbury's five-story central courtyard combines glazed brick, ornate Mexican tile floors, rich Belgian marble, Art Nouveau grillwork, handsome oak paneling, and lacelike wrought-iron railings—it's one of the great interior spaces of the 19th century. The glass-topped atrium is often used as a movie and TV set; you may have seen it in "Chinatown" and "Blade Runner."

304 S. Broadway (at 3rd St.), Downtown. ✆ **213/626-1893.** Mon–Fri 9am–6pm; Sat–Sun 9am–5pm. Metro Red or Purple Lines to Pershing Square.

California African American Museum ★ Placing equal emphasis on history, art and African American culture, this small but wide-ranging museum's best exhibits are the temporary ones. They address sometimes surprising topics, such as the "Visibly Invisible" show exploring myths and legends surrounding albinism, which opened in summer 2014; other have included a look at the march on Washington 50 years later and self-taught black artists from the South.

600 State Dr., Exposition Park. www.caamuseum.org ✆ **213/744-7432.** Free admission. Tues–Sat 10am–5pm; Sun 11am–5pm. Closed Jan 1, Thanksgiving, and Christmas. Parking $10.

Downtown Attractions

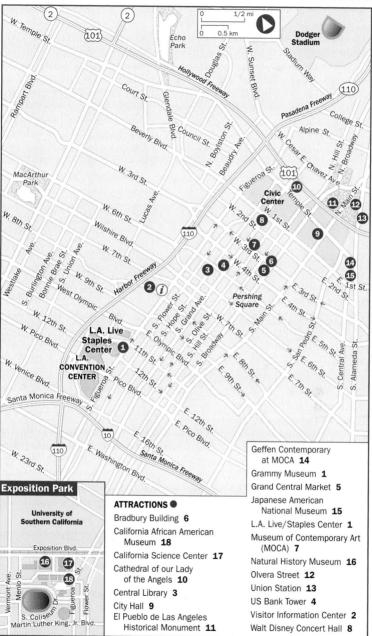

Exposition Park

University of
Southern California

Exposition Blvd.

S. Coliseum Dr.
Martin Luther King, Jr. Blvd.

Vermont Ave.
Menlo St.
Figueroa St.
Flower St.

ATTRACTIONS ●
Bradbury Building **6**
California African American
  Museum **18**
California Science Center **17**
Cathedral of our Lady
  of the Angels **10**
Central Library **3**
City Hall **9**
El Pueblo de Las Angeles
  Historical Monument **11**

Geffen Contemporary
  at MOCA **14**
Grammy Museum **1**
Grand Central Market **5**
Japanese American
  National Museum **15**
L.A. Live/Staples Center **1**
Museum of Contemporary Art
  (MOCA) **7**
Natural History Museum **16**
Olvera Street **12**
Union Station **13**
US Bank Tower **4**
Visitor Information Center **2**
Walt Disney Concert Hall **8**

California Science Center ★★★ MUSEUM   The arrival of the retired space shuttle Endeavour in late 2012 was a game-changer for this aging science museum, now Exposition Park's most popular destination. The lure of seeing a real space shuttle is near impossible to resist, and it's a monumental exhibit. Endeavor is housed in a temporary berth in the **Samuel Oschin Pavilion** while awaiting completion of a new Air and Space Center in 2017. The public can't actually board the craft, but exhibit designers thoughtfully extracted its most fascinating components for visitors' inspection: a SPACEHAB module (a "spare room" for astronauts), tires from its last mission, the galley, and—at the top of everyone's list—the Space Potty. The exhibit at the entrance details the shuttle program in California, where the orbiters were built.

Next to Endeavor, the most fascinating display is Tess, a transparent, anatomically correct, 50-foot animatronic woman in the **World of Life.** When she raises her 27-foot-long arm or stretches her 30-foot leg, her circulatory, brain, and nervous sytems light up with activity for an insider's view of the body keeping itself in balance.

Also worth seeking out is the giant Los Angeles wall map in the **Ecosystems** wing that demonstrates how a large urban area affects and manages energy, water, wildlife, smog and garbage. Museum admission is free, but some attractions, such as the High Wire Bicycle and the Motion-Based Simulator, charge $2 to $5. A seven-story IMAX theater shows films throughout the day.

700 Exposition Park Dr., Exposition Park. www.californiasciencecenter.org. © **323/724-3623** or 213/744-7400 (IMAX theater). Free admission; IMAX theater $9 adults; $6 seniors 60 and over, students 13–17, and college students with valid ID; $5 children 4–12. Multishow and group discounts available. Daily 10am–5pm. Closed Jan 1, Thanksgiving, and Christmas. Parking $10 (cash only). Metro Expo Line to Expo/Vermont.

Cathedral of Our Lady of the Angels ★ ARCHITECTURE/CHURCH   This ultracontemporary cathedral, completed in 2002, is the third-largest in the world. Designed by award-winning Spanish architect Jose Rafael Moneo, it features a 20,000-square-foot plaza with a meditation garden, more than 6,000 crypts and niches (making it the country's largest crypt mausoleum), mission-style colonnades, biblically inspired gardens, and numerous artworks by internationally acclaimed artists. While the austere, sand-colored exterior is rather uninviting (church doors don't face the street, but rather a private plaza in back, surrounded by fortresslike walls), the inside is both magnificent and serene with its soaring heights, 12,000 panes of translucent alabaster, and larger-than-life tapestries. The 25,000-pound bronze doors, created by sculptor Robert Graham, pay homage to Ghiberti's bronze baptistery door in Florence. Free self-guided tours are available, and Wednesday afternoon recitals (12:45pm; call to confirm) on the 42-ton, 6,019-pipe organ are free and open to the public.

555 W. Temple St. (at Grand Ave.), Los Angeles. www.olacathedral.org. © **213/680-5200.** Mon–Fri 6am–6pm; Sat 9am–6pm; Sun 7am–6pm. Metro Red or Purple Lineto Civic Center/Grand Park.

Charles F. Lummis House (El Alisal) and Garden ★ HISTORIC HOME/ ARCHITECTURE   El Alisal is a small, rugged, two-story "castle," built between 1889 and 1910 from large rocks and telephone poles purchased from the Santa Fe Railroad. Its creator was Charles F. Lummis, a Harvard graduate, archaeologist, and writer, who walked from Ohio to California and coined the slogan "See America First." A fan of Native American culture, Lummis popularized the concept of the "Southwest," referring to New Mexico and Arizona. He often adopted the lifestyle of the Indians, and he founded the Southwest Museum (234 Museum Dr.; theautry.org/mt-washington; © **323/667-2000**), a repository of Indian artifacts. Lummis held fabulous parties for the theatrical, political, and artistic elite, often including Will Rogers and

Theodore Roosevelt. The house's outstanding fireplace was carved by Mount Rushmore creator Gutzon Borglum.

200 E. Ave. 43, Highland Park. Los Angeles. www.socalhistory.org. © **323/460-5632.** Free admission. Fri–Sun noon–4pm.

City Hall ★ ARCHITECTURE/GOVERNMENT BUILDING

Built in 1928, the imposing, 27-story Los Angeles City Hall was the tallest building in the city for more than 30 years. Its distinctive ziggurat tower was designed to resemble the Mausoleum at Halicarnassus, one of the seven wonders of the ancient world. Featured in numerous films and television shows, it might be best known as headquarters of the "Daily Planet" in the 1950s "Superman" TV series (or from "L.A. Confidential," for a later generation). When it was built, City Hall was the sole exception to an ordinance outlawing buildings taller than 150 feet. An elevator leads to curiously underused 27th-floor Observation Deck—on the rare clear day, you can see to Mount Wilson 15 miles away. Free docent-led tours and self-guided tours are available.

200 N. Spring St. (btw. 1st and Temple sts.), Downtown. www.lacity.org/lacity. © **213/485-2121** or 213/978-1995 for tours. Mon–Fri 8am–5pm; docent tours Mon–Thurs 10am–noon. Metro Red or Purple Line to Civic Center/Grand Park.

Grammy Museum ★★ MUSEUM

The Grammys' 50-year history is just a jumping-off point for this museum anchoring the L.A. Live entertainment complex. Four floors of exhibits let visitors in on the creative and production sides of virtually every type of music—it claims more than 160 genres, from opera to polka to visual kei rock. Interactive displays let you explore differences and connections between genres, mix your own track, and compare recording technology's impact on sound quality. Depending on the rotation of temporary exhibits, you might see the latest red carpet fashions from the BET awards, Thelonius Monk's baby grand piano, or Jim Morrison's writing chair; two particularly interesting shows from 2014 were "California Dreamin': The Sounds of Laurel Canyon 1965–1977" (think The Doors, Joni Mitchell, The Mamas and the Papas) and "Pride & Joy: The Texas Blues of Stevie Ray Vaughan." Varied public events (such as evenings with recording artists) and educational programs (introduction to current DJ techniques) play as big a role as do the exhibits.

800 W. Olympic Blvd. (at Figueroa St., on L.A. LIVE campus), Los Angeles. www.grammymuseum. org. © **213/765-6800.** Admission $13 adults, $12 seniors and students, $11 children 6–17, free for kids 5 and under; $8 after 6pm when there's an evening program. Mon–Fri 11:30am–7:30pm; Sat–Sun 10am–7:30pm. Parking $5 and up. Metro Red, Purple, or Blue Line to 7th St./Metro Center.

Japanese American National Museum ★★★ MUSEUM/ARCHITECTURE

The largest U.S. museum dedicated to the Japanese experience in this country, occupying a gracefully modern pavilion by acclaimed architect Gyo Obata, displays the exquisite care and precision of a Japanese tea ceremony in both the building's design and the exhibits within. Much of the permanent collection focuses on the World War II relocation camps, enhanced by docents' stories of their own internment in those camps. Recent exhibitions have also embraced a lighter side of social consciousness, unmasking Asian stereotypes in post-war U.S. comics and hailing the Dodgers' (both Brooklyn and L.A.) contribution to civil rights by their ethnic diversity from early days. The museum store's well-chosen books, stationery, origami kits, and tea accessories make delightful gifts.

100 N. Central Ave. (at E. 1st St.), Downtown. www.janm.org. © **213/625-0414.** Admission $9 adults; $5 seniors, students and children 6–17; free for kids 5 and under; free for everyone the 3rd Thurs of every month and every Thurs after 5pm. $2 adult discount for Metro Line riders. Tue–Wed and Fri–Sun 11am–5pm; Thurs noon–8pm. Metro Gold Line to Little Tokyo/Arts District.

L.A. Central Library ★★ LIBRARY/ARCHITECTURE One of L.A.'s early architectural achievements, this is the country's third-largest library. The city rallied to save the 1926 building when arson nearly destroyed it in 1986; the triumphant restoration has returned much of its original splendor. Architect Bertram G. Goodhue employed Egyptian motifs and materials popularized by the discovery of King Tut's tomb, combining them with modern concrete blocks to great effect. Free docent-led tours are given daily and last about an hour—call ℗ **213/228-7168.** *Tip:* Parking in this area can be brutal; visit on a weekend to get a flat $1 rate with validation.

630 W. 5th St. (btw. Flower St. and Grand Ave.), Downtown. www.lapl.org/central. ℗ **213/228-7000.** Mon–Thurs 10am–8pm; Fri–Sat 10am–5:30pm; Sun 1–5pm. Validated parking at 524 S. Flower St. garage $1 1st hr., $4 2nd and 3rd hr., $3.50 per 10 min. thereafter, up to $35 maximum. $1 flat rate 3pm–library closing and on weekends. Metro Red or Purple Line to Pershing Square.

L.A. LIVE ★ CULTURAL CENTER This new entertainment center, keystone of L.A.'s Downtown gentrification project, is one of the largest and flashiest mixed-use entertainment complexes in the world, costing $2.5 billion to build and covering more than 6 city blocks (hence its nickname: Times Square West). It's anchored by the **Nokia Theatre,** the **Staples Center** (where the Lakers and Clippers play), and the **Los Angeles Convention Center,** and is crammed with a dozen chain restaurants and cafes, two huge nightclubs, a 14-screen Regal Cinema, the highly interactive **Grammy Museum,** a bowling center, **ESPN's West Coast broadcast headquarters,** and JW Marriott and Ritz-Carlton hotels (both within one 54-story tower). Whether it's worth a visit depends on your interest in mega-size sports and entertainment complexes, but I do recommend checking the website to see who's playing while you're in town.

S. Figueroa St. (btw. Venice and S. Olympic blvds.; use 800 W. Olympic Blvd. for GPS), Los Angeles. www.lalive.com. ℗ **866/548-3452** or 213/763-5483. Metro Red or Purple Lines/7th St./Metro Center.

The Museum of Contemporary Art, Los Angeles (MOCA) ★ ART MUSEUM Known for its provocative, ambitious, and sometimes difficult exhibits, MOCA is L.A.'s only museum focusing solely on art from 1940 to the present. Its 6,800-piece collection—one of the best in the country, including numerous Rothkos, Pollack's first drip painting, Johns, and dozens of other 20th century artists—as well as challenging work by emerging artists—is spread among three locations.

The imposing red sandstone **MOCA Grand Avenue** (250 S. Grand Ave. btw. W. 4th and W. Gen. Thad Kosciuszko Way; Metro Red Line to Pershing Square), the main venue, opened "Andy Warhol: Shadows," the first West Coast showing of a touring exhibition of all 102 parts of the monumental painting, in September 2014. It also houses the museum's popular restaurant, **Lemonade** (open during museum hours; ℗ **213/628-0200**). The warehouse-like **Geffen Contemporary at MOCA** in Little Tokyo (152 N. Central Ave. between E. 1st. and E. Temple; Metro Gold Line to Little Tokyo/Arts District) shows the museum's most interesting rotating exhibitions—it held the largest show of Mark Kelley's work to date in 2014. With the easiest parking of the three, it's a good place to start. **MOCA Pacific Design Center** (8687 Melrose Ave. at N. San Vicente, West Hollywood) is an earth-toned cube next to the design center that focuses on contemporary architecture and design. It also has the MOCA store.

MOCA endured six rocky years of financial problems and increasingly sparse programming before new director Philippe Vergne was lured away from New York's Dia Art Foundation in early 2014. Known for his collaborative and artist-oriented style, he has said MOCA has to be the most innovative museum in the country. He brought in

Los Angeles Attractions

EXPLORING LOS ANGELES

a new chief curator in August of 2014, but it will take time to restore the museum to its former prominence. One change he's considering is reducing admission fees.

250 S. Grand Ave. www.moca.org. © **213/626-6222.** Admission 12 adults, $7 seniors 65 and over and students, free for children 12 and under; free for everyone Thurs 5–8pm. Mon and Fri 11am–5pm; Thurs 11am–8pm; Sat–Sun 11am–6pm. MOCA Pacific Design Center: Free admission. Tues–Fri 11am–5pm; Sat–Sun 11am–6pm. All locations closed Jan 1, July 4, Thanksgiving, and Christmas. Metered street parking or $9 with validation at Walt Disney Concert Hall garage (enter Lower Grand Ave. or 2nd St.; $20 deposit upon entry, with $11 refund on exit).

Natural History Museum of Los Angeles County ★★★ MUSEUM/ARCHITECTURE

The largest natural history museum in the western United States, with more than 35 million specimens, is packed with stunning wildlife dioramas, treasures of history and edifying activities. Founded in 1913, it embarked on an ambitious retrofit and modernization in 2003. The original museum structure, fondly called the 1913 Building—a confection of Spanish Renaissance terra cotta carving, Romanesque arched windows and a traditional Beaux-Arts T-shaped layout—was restored according to the original design.

The 1913 Building's first new exhibition, **Age of Mammals,** tracing 65 million years of evolution, opened in 2010, followed in 2011 by a revamped **Dinosaur Hall** with its unique display of a baby, juvenile and adult Tyrannosaurus rex and a Triceratops never displayed before. The **Dino Lab** that let visitors watch paleontologists prepare skeletons and artifacts for the new exhibit now provides a peek at ongoing work. The museum unveiled its first permanent outdoor exhibit in 2012; the 3½-acre **Nature Gardens** feature a nature lab, a pond, a "Get Dirty Zone," an edible garden, and a pollinator garden. The transformation concluded in summer 2013, the museum's centennial year, with the unveiling of **Becoming Los Angeles,** illustrating how the city shaped and was shaped by its environment, and the **Otis Booth Pavilion,** the six-story glass cube that serves as the new home for its 63-foot whale skeleton.

The best of the beloved old favorites are still there: More dinosaurs than ever, the seasonal Insect Zoo and Butterfly Pavilion, the African animals, and ancient American art. You could easily spend the entire day here, and the new exhibits are designed for lingering. I would put the Dinosaur Hall, Nature Gardens and Becoming Los Angeles at the top of the priority list, but it depends on your interests. (The gem and mineral collection, for example, is considered one of the world's finest.)

900 Exposition Blvd. (btw. Vermont Ave. and Figueroa St.), Exposition Park. www.nhm.org. © **213/763-DINO** (763-3466). Admission $12 adults; $9 children 13–17, seniors, and students with ID; $5 children 3–12; free for kids 2 and under; free for everyone 1st Tues of month. Daily 9:30am–5pm. Closed Jan 1, July 4, Thanksgiving, and Christmas. Parking $10 and up. Metro Expo Line to Expo/Vermont.

Union Station ★★ ARCHITECTURE

Union Station, completed in 1939, is one of the finest examples of California mission-style architecture and one of the last of America's great rail stations. It was designed with the opulence and attention to detail that characterized 1930s WPA projects, such as its cathedral-like size and richly paneled ticket lobby and waiting area. Strolling through these grand historic halls, it's easy to imagine the glamorous movie stars who once boarded *The City of Los Angeles* and *The Super Chief* to journey back East during the glory days of rail travel; it's also easy to picture the many heartfelt reunions between returning soldiers and loved ones following the victorious end to World War II, in the station's heyday. Movies shot here include "Bugsy," "The Way We Were," and "Blade Runner." The latest restaurant to occupy this unusually beautiful setting is **Traxx** (p. 75).

US Bank Tower (aka Library Tower) ★ ARCHITECTURE/LANDMARK

Designed by renowned architect I. M. Pei, L.A.'s most distinctive skyscraper (it's the round one) is the tallest building between Chicago and Singapore. Built in 1989, the 73-story monolith is incorporates strong square and rectangular elements, rising from its 5th Street base in a series of overlapping spirals and cubes. The Bunker Hill Steps wrapping around the west side of the building were inspired by Rome's Spanish Steps. The Singapore investment company that bought the building in 2013 announced a year later that it would build an Empire State Building-like observation tower on the 71st floor, which has 18-foot ceilings and 360-degree views of the Los Angeles basin. It is scheduled to open in mid-2015. *Fun fact:* The glass crown at the top—illuminated at night—is the highest building helipad in the world.

633 W. 5th St. (at S. Grand Ave.), Downtown. Metro Red or Purple Line to Pershing Square.

Walt Disney Concert Hall ★★★ ARCHITECTURE

The striking Walt Disney Concert Hall is not only the new home of the Los Angeles Philharmonic, it's a key to the entire urban revitalization effort for Downtown. The Disney family insisted on the best and, with initial gift of $50 million to build a world-class performance venue, that's what they got: a masterpiece of design by world-renowned architect Frank Gehry, and acoustical quality that equals or surpasses those of the world's best concert halls. Similar to Gehry's most famous masterpiece, the Guggenheim Museum in Bilbao, the dramatic stainless-steel exterior is a series of undulating curved surfaces that form multiple glimmering facades. The 2,265-seat auditorium within is replete with curved woods and a dazzling array of organ pipes (also designed by Gehry). Joachim Splichal's Patina restaurant, the hip Concert Hall Cafe, a bookstore, and a gift shop are also inside.

The 3½-acre Concert Hall is open to the public, but to witness its full glory, do whatever it takes to attend a concert by the **Los Angeles Philharmonic** (p. 128). Also highly recommended are free audio tours, which lead visitors through the Concert Hall's history from conception to creation. The 45-minute self-guided tour is narrated by actor John Lithgow and includes interviews with Frank Gehry and former Los Angeles Philharmonic music director Esa-Pekka Salonen, among others. (Caveat: You usually won't see the auditorium—there's almost always a rehearsal in progress.) The tours are available on most non-matinee days from 10am to 2pm.

111 S. Grand Ave. (at 1st St.). www.disneyhall.com, www.laphil.com, or www.musiccenter.org. ℭ **323/850-2000** or 213/972-7211. Metro Red or Purple Line tp Civic Center/Grand Park.

Watts Towers & Art Center ★ LANDMARK/CULTURAL CENTER

Notorious as the site of 1965's deadly race riots, Watts today is a lesson in inner-city life. It's a high-density land of gray strip malls, guarded check-cashing shops, and fast-food restaurants; but it's also a community of hard-working families surviving in the middle of gangland. Although there's not much for the casual tourist here, the Watts Towers are a unique attraction, and the adjoining art gallery illustrates the fierce determination of area residents to maintain cultural integrity.

The Towers—the largest piece of folk art created by a single person—are colorful, 99-foot-tall cement and steel sculptures ornamented with mosaics of bottles, seashells, pottery, and ceramic tiles. They were completed in 1955 by Simon Rodia, an immigrant Italian tile-setter whose day job was at the legendary Malibu Potteries—could those be fragments of valuable Malibu tile encrusting the Towers? The Art Center next

free CULTURE

Almost all of L.A.'s art galleries and museums are open free of charge one day of the week or month (or both), and several charge no admission at any time. Use the following list to plan your week around the museums' free-day schedules; refer to the individual attractions listings in this chapter for more information.

Free Every Day
- J. Paul Getty Museum at the Getty Center
- The Getty Villa Malibu (advance tickets required)
- Paley Center for Media (donation suggested)
- Los Angeles County Museum of Art (*after* 5pm)
- Bergamot Arts Station & Santa Monica Museum of Art
- California African American Museum
- California Science Center
- Annenberg Space for Photography

Free Every Thursday
- Museum of Contemporary Art (MOCA), from 5 to 8pm
- Hammer Museum, from 11am to 9pm
- Japanese American National Museum, from 5 to 8pm
- Skirball Cultural Center, from noon to 9pm
- Geffen Contemporary at MOCA, from 5 to 8pm

Free Every First Tuesday
- Natural History Museum of Los Angeles County, from 9:30am to 5pm
- Page Museum at La Brea Tar Pits, from 9:30am to 5pm

Free Every First Wednesday
- Craft and Folk Art Museum, from 11am to 5pm

Free Every First Thursday
- Huntington Library, Art Collections & Botanical Gardens, from noon to 4:30pm

Free Every First Friday
- Norton Simon Museum of Art, from 6 to 9pm

Free Every Second Tuesday
- Autry National Center of the American West, from 10am to 5pm
- Los Angeles County Museum of Art, from noon to 8pm

Free Every Third Tuesday
- Los Angeles County Arboretum and Botanic Garden, from 9am to 4:30pm
- Japanese American National Museum, from 10am to 8pm

Free Every Fourth Friday
- Pacific Asia Museum, from 10am to 8pm

to these designated Cultural Landmarks has an interesting collection of ethnic musical instruments and hosts visiting art exhibits. Tours are given on request.

1727 E. 107th St., Watts. www.wattstowers.us. © **213/847-4646.** Art Center: Free admission. Wed–Sat 10am–4pm; Sun noon–4pm. Towers: Admission $7 adults, $3 seniors 55 and over and children 13–17, free for children 12 and under. Thurs–Sat 10:30am–3:30pm; Sun 12:30–3:30pm. Metro Blue Line to 103rd St./Watts Towers.

Universal City

Universal Studios Hollywood & CityWalk ★★ THEME PARK   Believing that filmmaking is an attraction unto itself, Universal Studios began offering public tours in 1964. Today Universal is not only one of the largest movie studios in the world—it's also one of the largest theme parks. By integrating shows and rides with behind-the-scenes moviemaking presentations, Universal created a whole new genre.

The main attraction continues to be the **Studio Tour,** a nearly 1-hour guided tram ride "hosted" (via video screen) by Jimmy Fallon. The wait to board might appear long, but the line moves quickly. You pass production offices on your way to the most extensive backlot reconstruction in Universal's history, including the new New York Street. Director Peter Jackson's **King Kong 360 3D,** the largest experience of its kind in the world, has joined classic stops from "War of the Worlds" and "How the Grinch Stole Christmas." In 2015, **Fast & Furious—Supercharged,** based on the blockbuster film series, will become the tour's grand finale. Along the way, the tram encounters several staged "disasters," which I won't divulge here (they're quite tame).

Other attractions are more typical high-tech theme-park fare, but all have a film or TV tie-in. The newest of these is **Despicable Me Minion Mayhem,** a 3D attraction that immerses you in the world of Gru and his mischievous minions. Unique to the park is **Super Silly Fun Land,** an interactive play area featuring an elaborate water zone (handy for cooling the kids down). **Transformers 3D: The Ride** thrusts riders into a high-octane battle between Optimus Prime and his Autobots v. Megatron.

Shrek 4D is still one of the park's best attractions, a multisensory animated show that combines 3D effects, a humorous storyline, and "surprise" special effects—the flying dragon chase is wild. **The Simpsons Ride** allows guests to join Homer, Marge, Bart, Lisa, and Maggie as they soar above the fictional "Krustyland" theme park in a "virtual roller coaster," creating the sensation of thrilling drops, turns and a 360-degree loop. **Revenge of the Mummy** is a high-tech indoor roller coaster that whips you backward and forward through a dark Egyptian tomb filled with Warrior Mummies (and ends a bit too soon). **Jurassic Park—The Ride** is also short in duration, but long on dinosaur animatronics; riders float through a world of five-story-tall T-rexes and airborne raptors on their way to a pitch-dark vertical drop and splash.

Waterworld, a fast-paced outdoor theater presentation, is far better than the film that inspired it, featuring stunts and special effects on and around a small man-made lagoon (arrive at least 15 minuntes before show time to ensure seating). Straight ahead of the park's main entrance on Main Street is the **Hollywood Ticket Office,** where you can obtain free tickets (subject to availability) for TV shows that are taping.

Lines can be brutally long; the wait for a five-minute ride is sometimes more than an hour. In summer, stifling valley heat can dog you all day. Try to avoid weekends and school holidays; if you're willing to pay extra, you can get a **"Front of Line" pass** and skip the lines, or even a VIP pass for what is essentially a private tour. You can also save time standing in line by buying and printing your tickets online. Finally, the **Southern California CityPass** (p. 94) includes admission to Universal Studios.

If you neglected to spend all your money at the park, you can drop it just ouside at **Universal CityWalk** (www.citywalkhollywood.com; ✆ **818/622-4455**). The 3-block-long pedestrian promenade is crammed with flashy name-brand stores, nightclubs (the Jon Lovitz Comedy Club, Howl at the Moon dueling piano bar, and an outpost of San Francisco's sexy Infusion Lounge), chain restaurants, a six-story 3D IMAX theater, the 18-screen **CityWalk Cinemas,** a 6,200-seat amphitheater, an indoor skydiving wind tunnel, and even a bowling alley (Take *that,* Disney!). Stop into the **Zen Zone** where you can get an inexpensive 20-minute "aqua massage." Entrance to CityWalk is free; it's open 'til 9pm weekdays and midnight Friday and Saturday.

Hollywood Fwy. (Universal Center Dr. or Lankershim Blvd. exits off 101 Hollywood Fwy.), Universal City. www.universalstudioshollywood.com. ✆ **800-UNIVERSAL** (864-8377) or 818/622-3801. One-day pass $92 adults, $84 kids ages 3–9, free for kids 2 and under. Winter 10am–6pm; summer 9am–7pm. Hours are subject to change. Self-parking $16 before 3pm, $10 after; valet and pre-ferred parking available for higher rates.

Pasadena & Environs

Note: See map on p. 55 for Pasadena attractions.

Bungalow Heaven ★★ ARCHITECTURE/LANDMARK   While the Gamble House (below) is the undisputed queen of Pasadena's (if not California's) Arts and Crafts architecture, this quiet, leafy residential neighborhood 2½ miles away became the city's first historic landmark district in 1989 on the strength of its 1,000-plus historic homes (it's since been listed on the National Register). The quaintly named neighborhood includes homes from most periods of history, but the vast majority are Craftsman bungalows, built on a more modest scale for ordinary working folk—some from kits ordered from Sears—and display the period's unique architectural hallmarks and extensive use of natural and native materials. Veritable Greene and Greene miniatures co-exist with bungalows remodeled almost beyond recognition (though more and more have been restored since the neighborhood became a landmark). Interiors are on view during the annual Bungalow Heaven house tour in April.

North of I-210 btw. Lake and Hill aves. and Washington and Orange Grove blvds. www.bungalow heaven.org. © **(626) 585-2172.**

City Hall ★★ ARCHITECTURE/GOVERNMENT BUILDING   For a quick but profound architectural fix, stroll past Pasadena's grandiose and baroque City Hall, built in 1927 from a design inspired by Italy's early Renaissance style. Its three-story rectangular base surrounds a classical colonnaded courtyard with a formal rose garden and fountain exuding Old World atmosphere. Its six-story central round tower, pierced by arches and capped by an ornate tiled dome and cupola, has been catnip to movie and TV producers, recently figuring prominently in "Parks and Recreation" and "The Big Bang Theory." The building and grounds are open to the public to stroll at will.

100 N. Garfield Ave., 2 blocks north of Colorado Blvd. Metro Gold Line to Memorial Park.

The Gamble House ★★★ ARCHITECTURE/HISTORIC HOME   The huge two-story Gamble House, built in 1908 as a California vacation home for the wealthy family of Procter & Gamble fame, is a sublime example of Arts and Crafts architecture, which rejected both the stifling Victorian architectural principles and the increasing industrialization of the period. Gamble House's interior, designed by the famous Pasadena-based Greene & Greene architectural team, abounds with intricately carved teak cornices, custom-designed furnishings, elaborate carpets, and a fantastic Tiffany glass door. Admission is by 1-hour guided tour only, departing every 20 to 30 minutes. Tickets are available at the bookstore on the day of the tour, but as tours often sell out, especially on weekends, its best to guarantee a spot by booking online in advance. *Note:* If you wear high heels, you'll have to change into slippers; no interior photography is allowed.

Additional elegant Greene & Greene creations (still private residences) around 2 blocks away along **Arroyo Terrace,** including nos. **368, 370, 400, 408, 424,** and **440.** (Walking-tour maps are available at the Gamble House bookstore.) Visitors can view the interiors only during the annual Craftsman Weekend in October.

4 Westmoreland Place (in the 300 block of N. Orange Grove Blvd.), Pasadena. www.gamblehouse. org. © **626/793-3334.** Most tours $13 adults, $10 students and seniors 65 and over, free for children 12 and under. 2pm tours are $13 and must be made at least 1 week in advance. Tours Thurs–Sun noon–3pm. Closed holidays. Bookstore Tues–Sat 10am–5pm, Sun 11:30am–5pm.

Huntington Library, Art Collections & Botanical Gardens ★★★ ART MUSEUM/ GARDEN   This magnificent, 207-acre hilltop estate is the former home to railroad magnate Henry E. Huntington (1850–1927), who amassed books as avidly as he did land. The collection includes Shakespeare first editions, Benjamin Franklin's handwritten autobiography, a 15th-century Gutenberg Bible, and the earliest manuscript of Chaucer's "Canterbury Tales" yet discovered. Rotating exhibitions show hundreds of works at a time, though some rare items are limited to visiting scholars.

The erudite tycoon also aquired a terrific collection of 18th- and 19th-century British and French art, including Gainsborough's famous "The Blue Boy" and Sir Thomas Lawrence's "Pinkie," depicting poet Elizabeth Barrett Browning's aunt as a young woman. These and other treasures are displayed in the exquisitely furnished Italianate mansion. The library's growing American art holdings, ranging from Edward Hopper to Andy Warhol, are shown in other galleries; fans of Arts and Crafts design will want to see the permanent Greene and Greene exhibition.

The splendid 120-acre **botanical gardens** feature more than 1,500 worldwide plant varieties in 15 specialized gardens. The second phase of its most recent addition opened in March 2014, making the **Liu Fang Yuan Garden of Flowing Fragrance** the largest Chinese garden outside of China, with a lake, teahouse, pavilions, and bridges interspersed with plants native to China. The **Japanese Garden** includes a traditional open-air Japanese house, koi-filled stream, and Zen garden. The **Rose Garden** cultivates 1,200 cultivars, displayed in chronological order of their breeding, There's also an exotic **Desert Garden,** tropical **Jungle Garden,** a **Children's Garden** designed for kids 2 to 7, and the glass-and-steel **Conservatory,** where visitors learn elementary botany at advanced science stations. Check "What's Blooming" on the website to see what to expect during your visit.

If the Huntington's size and wealth of activities seems overwhelming, a tour may be in order. Free, walk-in garden tours are offered daily except Tuesdays; times vary, so check at information when you arrive. Various Premier Tours (before normal public hours, $35–$38) and a private morning tour followed by English tea (minimum four people, $80 each on weekends, $75 weekdays) must be reserved in advance through the website.

1151 Oxford Rd., San Marino (near Pasadena, with easy access from Calif. 110 or I-210). www. huntington.org. ✆ **626/405-2100.** Weekday admission $20 adults, $15 seniors 65 and over, $12 students and children 12–18, $8 children 5–11, free for kids 4 and under; free for everyone 1st Thurs of every month with advance tickets. Weekend admission $23 adults, $18 seniors 65 and over, $13 students and children ages 12–18, $8 children ages 5–11, free for children 4 and under. Sept–May Mon and Wed–Fri noon–4:30pm, Sat–Sun 10:30am–4:30pm; June–Aug Wed–Mon 10:30am–4:30pm. Closed major holidays. Free parking.

Los Angeles County Arboretum and Botanic Garden ★ GARDEN/HISTORIC HOME

Tucked into the slopes of the San Gabriel Mountains, this sprawling horticultural and botanical center was once the estate of silver magnate "Lucky" Baldwin, the man who brought horse racing to Southern California. He lived on these lushly planted 127 acres overlooking the Santa Anita racetrack until 1909. Baldwin's red-and-white Queen Anne cottage starred in the opening sequence of "Fantasy Island"; the gardens are also a favorite setting for films and weddings. In addition to spectacular flora representing every continent, the Arboretum's resident peafowl treat guests to a colorful show when the peacocks attempt to impress passing hens. Avid gardeners will want to visit the nursery-like gift shop. Entry is free every third Tuesday, but note that there is no tram on these days.

301 N. Baldwin Ave. (Baldwin Ave. exit from I-210 follow the signs), Arcadia. www.arboretum.org. ✆ **626/821-3222.** Admission $9 adults, $6 students and seniors 62 and over, $4 children 5–12, free for kids 4 and under. Daily 9am–5pm (last admission 4:30pm). Closed Christmas. Free parking.

Norton Simon Museum of Art ★★★ ART MUSEUM   The serene garden setting is a perfect backdrop for one of the world's finest private collections of European, American, and Asian art. Neither as big nor as architecturally imposing as LACMA or the Getty (though Frank Gehry redesigned the interior in 2000), it's unmatched in masterpieces per square foot. You're treated to Rodin's "Burghers of Calais" upon arrival; other standouts include Diego Rivera's "The Flower Vendor/Girl with Lilies," Van Gogh's "Mulberry Tree," Rembrandt's "Portrait of a Boy," and Monet's "The Artist's Garden at Vétheuil." That's a short list from collections of important works by Degas, Picasso, Rembrandt, Degas, and many others. The "Blue Four" collection of European avant-garde artists Kandinsky, Jawlensky, Klee, and Feininger is splendid, and the museum is also strong in postwar and pop art. In short, every name you learned in your Art 101 class is represented here, and unless you've progressed beyond the basics, the audio tour is well worth the $3 fee.

411 W. Colorado Blvd. (corner of Orange Grove and Colorado Blvd. at the intersection of the Foothill [I-210] and Ventura [Calif. 134] freeways), Pasadena. www.nortonsimon.org. © **626/449-6840.** Admission $12 adults, $9 seniors 62 and up, free for students and children 17 and under; free for everyone 6–9pm 1st Fri of every month. Mon and Wed–Thurs noon–5pm; Fri–Sat 11am–8pm; Sun 11am–5pm; closed Tues. Free parking. Metro Gold Line to Memorial Park.

USC Pacific Asia Museum ★ ART MUSEUM/ARCHITECTURE   This small museum, which grew from one woman's curio shop, has been affiliated with the University of Southern California since November 2013. When her collection outgrew its shop in 1924, Grace Nicholson commissioned a new building strictly following China's Imperial Palace Courtyard style, with roof tiles, stone, marble carvings, bronze and copper imported from China and handmade by local craftsmen; its arched entrance is a replica of the Buddhist library in Beijing. Given to the city in 1943, it housed the institute that would become the Norton Simon Museum. The elaborate building and traditional courtyard garden are the museum's most notable features, but rotating exhibits of the 15,000-piece collection—ranging from 100 B.C. to the present, including one of the largest collections of Japanese folk art outside of Japan—will appeal to those interested in Asia and the Pacific Islands in general, and Buddhism and Hinduism in particular.

46 N. Los Robles Ave. (at E. Colorado), Pasadena. www.pacificasiamuseum.org. © **626/449-2742.** Admission $10 adults, $7 students and seniors, free for children 11 and under; free for everyone 4th Fri of every month. Wed–Mon 10am–6pm; closed Tues. Free parking. Metro Gold Line to Memorial Park.

L.A.'s Ethnic Neighborhoods

Los Angeles has the highest concentration of Mexicans outside Mexico, Koreans outside Korea, and even Samoans outside Samoa. Tiny Russian, Ethiopian, Armenian, and even British enclaves also coexist throughout L.A. But to call the city a "melting pot" wouldn't be quite accurate; to paraphrase Alex Haley, it's really more of a tossed salad, composed of distinct, albeit overlapping, cultures. The following neighborhoods are all in the Downtown area.

BOYLE HEIGHTS ★

East of Downtown; bounded by U.S. 101, I-10, Calif. 60, and Indiana St.

In the first decades of the 20th century, Boyle Heights was inhabited by Jewish immigrants. They later migrated west to the Fairfax district and beyond, leaving behind L.A.'s oldest orthodox synagogue and Brooklyn Avenue, now renamed Cesar E. Chavez Avenue. Boyle Heights is now the heart of the Latino barrio.

mission POSSIBLE

In the late 18th century, Franciscan friars established 21 missions along the California coast from San Diego to Sonoma in Northern California. Each stood a day's trek from the next on El Camino Real, "the Royal Road". (U.S. 101 roughly follows this path, remnants of which remain.) This was the beginning of European settlement in California and displacement of its native population. The two L.A.-area missions are named for the valleys where they were located: the San Gabriel Valley and the San Fernando Valley. A third, San Juan Capistrano, is in Orange County (p. 158).

Mission San Gabriel Arcangel ★

Founded in 1771, the fourth mission retains its original facade, notable for high oblong windows and large capped buttresses said to have been influenced by the cathedral in Cordova, Spain. The self-contained compound encompasses an aqueduct, a cemetery, a tannery, and a working winery. A copper font inside the church has the distinction of being the first one used to baptize a native Californian. The museum is most notable for Native American paintings of the Stations of the Cross, done on sailcloth in colors made from crushed desert flower petals.

428 S. Mission Dr., San Gabriel (6 mi. south of Pasadena). www.sangabrielmission.org. © **626/ 457-3035.** Admission $6 adults, $5 seniors 62 and over and students, $3 children 6–17, free for kids 5 and under. Daily 9am–4:30pm. Closed holidays.

Mission San Fernando Rey de España ★

Established in 1797, California's 17th mission once controlled more than 1½ million acres, employed 1,500 Native Americans, and more than 22,000 head of cattle. The fragile adobe complex was destroyed several times but always faithfully rebuilt. The aging church was replaced in the 1940s and again after an earthquake in the 1970s. The Convento, a 250-foot-long colonnaded structure dating from 1810, is the oldest remaining building. The old library, the private salon of the first bishop of California, and some other rooms have been restored to their late-18th-century appearance. A half-dozen padres and many hundreds of Shoshone Indians are buried in the adjacent cemetery.

15151 San Fernando Mission Blvd. (12 mi. north of Burbank on I-5), Mission Hills. www.missions california.com. © **626/457-3048.** Admission $6 adults, $5 seniors 62 and over; $3 children 6–17, free for ages 5 and under. Mon–Sat 9am–4:30pm, Sun 9am–4pm.

Westsiders come for cheap Mexican food, yet many miss the colorful **Mariachi Plaza,** near the corner of Boyle Avenue and First Street, where mariachi bands are prepared to entertain every afternoon and evening. Resplendent in matching ruffled shirts and bolero jackets with kaleidoscopic embroidery, they loiter under three-story murals of their forebears with guitars at the ready. More often than not, someone drives up in a minivan, offers a price, and carries off the whole ensemble to play for a private gathering. *Tip:* For an authentic meal in the neighborhood, try the Jalisco-style goat stew at **Birrieria de Don Boni,** 1845 E. 1st St. (www.birrieriadedonboni.com; © **323/ 262-4552**)—it's the only thing on the menu. (Known for decades as Birrieria Jalisco, the name changed in June 2014 when the original owner's daughter, who now runs the business, renamed it in her father's memory.)

CHINATOWN ★

Downtown; bounded by N. Broadway, N. Hill St., Bernard St., and Sunset Blvd.

Many Chinese settled in this once-rural area during the second half of the 19th century. Though the neighborhood hardly compares to the Chinese quarters of London, San

Francisco, or New York, Chinatown's bustling mom-and-pop shops and profusion of ethnic restaurants provide an interesting Downtown diversion.

Chinatown's center is the **Mandarin Plaza** mall, 970 N. Broadway, reconstructed in 1938 a few blocks from its original site just south of Dodger Stadium. Go for Sunday morning dim sum at **Empress Pavilion,** 988 N. Hill St. (www.empresspavilion. com; ✆ **213/617-9898**), then browse shops jammed with Chinese slippers, cheap jewelry, and china, which are interspersed with upscale stores specializing in inlaid furniture, Asian art, fine silks, and other imports.

During the monthlong **Chinese New Year** celebration, usually beginning in late January, Chinatown explodes into a colorful fantasy of sights and sounds: the Golden Dragon Parade, a beauty pageant, and a 5K/10K run. For more neighborhood information, visit www.chinatownla.com.

EL PUEBLO DE LOS ANGELES HISTORIC MONUMENT ★★

Enter El Pueblo Historic Monument via Alameda St. across from Union Station.

To avoid razing what had become an unsightly slum, this historic district was built in the 1930s on the site where the city was founded, and L.A. Latinos have since adopted it as a major cultural monument. Despite its nostalgic, somewhat Disney-fied version of the city's birth, El Pueblo has some claim to authenticity; some of L.A.'s oldest buildings are here, and the area exudes Old Mexico atmosphere.

A Mexican-style marketplace lines old, brick-paved **Olvera Street** (www.olvera-street.com), the primary pedestrian street. Weekends are a carnival of mariachis, piñatas, and folkloric performances from Aztec drumming to Ballet Folklorico. Olvera Street and adjacent Main Street are home to about two-dozen 19th-century buildings, most occupied by shops and restaurants. A recent addition is the **America Tropical Interpretive Center** (125 Paseo de La Plaza; www.americatropical.org; ✆ **213/485-6855**), a museum and viewing platform for David Alfaro Siqueiros and his mural on a neighboring building. The 1818 **Avila Adobe,** E-10 Olvera St. (www.calleolvera.com/history/adobe; ✆ **213/680-2525**), is the oldest building in the city. Free El Pueblo walking tours are offered Tuesday through Saturday; contact **El Pueblo Visitor Center** (622 N. Main St.; www.lasangelitas.org; ✆ **213/628-1274**).

KOREATOWN ★★

West of Downtown; bounded by Wilshire Ave., Crenshaw Blvd., Olympic Blvd., and Vermont Ave.

Roughly 100,000 Koreans live in Los Angeles, more than anywhere else in the world outside of Korea. They aren't all in Koreatown, of course, but a drive down Western Avenue between Olympic and Wilshire boulevards makes it easy to imagine you've wandered into the streets of Seoul. Signs in Korean script are bolted onto dozens of minimalls and office buildings within the vibrant commercial district. It's dense with edgy nightlife, but you can also while away hours in elixir shops, bargain stores, and authentic Korean barbecue joints. The museum within the **Korean Cultural Center,** 5505 Wilshire Blvd. (Mon–Fri 9am–5pm, Sat 10am–1pm; www.kccla.org; ✆ **323/936-7141**) houses historical photographs, Korean antiques, and rotating exhibits.

LEIMERT PARK VILLAGE ★

Southwest of Downtown; bounded by Crenshaw Blvd., Vernon Ave., Leimert Blvd., and 43rd Place.

The neighborhood around tiny Leimert Park, designed by the Olmsted Brothers in 1928 to be a model community, has become a center of African-American artistic life and culture. Its leafy, curving streets are lined with galleries, restaurants, and shops filled with local crafts and African imports. Folks flock here to jazz clubs that evoke

ESPECIALLY FOR kids

Much of larger-than-life L.A. is as appealing to kids as it is to adults. Many of the city's best attractions, like Venice Beach's **Ocean Front Walk** (p. 82), Hollywood's **Farmers Market** (p. 92), and Downtown's **Olvera Street** (p. 109) have a kid-friendly, carnival-like atmosphere. The novelty of sights such as the **Walk of Fame** (p. 89) and **Grauman's Chinese Theatre** (p. 87) appeals to kids as well. Older kids in particular love to go on **studio tours** (p. 111) and to **TV tapings** (p. 111).

Kid-centric museums are everywhere. Youngsters always dig the **La Brea Tar Pits** (p. 93) and the cool prehistoric creatures at the adjoining Page Museum. The **California Science Center** (p. 98) entertains, stimulates, and surreptitiously educates youngsters about science, technology, and their world. Its neighbor in Exposition Park, the **Natural History Museum** (p. 101), has giant dinosaur skeletons, an insect zoo, and a museum shop packed with irresistible model kits and toys. The **Petersen Automotive Museum** (p. 96) is packed with cool-looking cars and motorcycles, and its science-themed Discovery Center was designed just for kids.

The exemplary **Winnick Family Children's Zoo** (p. 95), within the Los Angeles Zoo, includes a top-notch petting zoo, exhibition animal-care center, Adventure Theater, and other kid-cool attractions. **Horseback riding** (p. 118) through the Hollywood hills might be just the thing for a little cowboy. And don't dismiss all art museums for family time; the **J. Paul Getty Museum** at the Getty Center (p. 83) cleverly disguises educational programs as games, and sets the entire family loose in a family room filled with picture books, games, storytellers, and workshops. Its audio guides include a special edition just for families.

Young tourists love the carousel and arcade at **Santa Monica Pier** (p. 82), and the miniature train ride at **Travel Town** in Griffith Park (p. 116). Then there are the big ones: **Universal Studios Hollywood** (p. 103), **Disneyland** (p. 142), **Knott's Berry Farm** (p. 150), and **Six Flags California** (p. 84) amusement parks.

Or you could do the simple thing and grab a bucket and shovel and head for the beach—pick a beach, any beach. Works every time.

---

the heyday of L.A.'s Central Avenue jazz scene, when greats like Ella Fitzgerald mesmerized audiences.

LITTLE TOKYO ★

Downtown, southeast of the Civic Center; bounded by 1st, 2nd, San Pedro, and Los Angeles sts.

Like nearby Chinatown, this redeveloped ethnic neighborhood isn't home to the majority of Angelenos of Japanese ancestry (suburban Gardena has that distinction), but Little Tokyo is the community's cultural center. Though the neighborhood is shabby compared with Japan's capital, its shops, restaurants, bakeries, bookshops, restaurants, boutiques, a few Buddhist temples, and the **Japanese American National Museum** (p. 99) are worth exploring. The **Japanese American Cultural and Community Center,** 244 S. San Pedro St. (www.jaccc.org; © 213/628-2725), regularly offers traditional Kabuki dramas and modern music concerts, and the **Cherry Blossom Festival** in spring and **Nisei Week** in late summer celebrate Japanese heritage with parades, traditional Ondo street dancing, a carnival, and an arts fair. Contact the **Little Tokyo Community Council** (www.littletokyola.org; © 213/293-5822) for more information.

Live-Audience TV Tapings

Being part of the audience for the taping of a television show lets you see how your favorite sitcom or talk show is made and glimpse your favorite TV personalities. Timing is important—most series go on hiatus between March and July. And tickets to the top shows are high in demand, so getting one takes advance planning—and possibly some waiting in line.

Request tickets as far in advance as possible. Several episodes may be shot on a single day, so you may be in the theater for up to 4 hours on top of the recommended 1-hour early check-in. You *might* luck into your top choice if you phone at the last moment, but you're more likely to get a list of shows that are currently filming, and you won't recognize many of the titles. Studios are always taping pilots that will never air, but you you never know who may be starring in them. Tickets are always free, are usually limited to two per person, and are distributed first-come, first-served. Many shows don't admit children under age 10; in some cases, minimum age is 18.

Tickets are sometimes given away outside popular tourist sites and at L.A.'s visitor centers. But if you want to see a particular show, contact the following suppliers:

Audiences Unlimited, Inc. (www.tvtickets.com), distributes tickets for about 30 major network shows filmed in L.A. It handles most of the top sitcoms, including "Big Bang Theory" "2 Broke Girls,"and "Two and a Half Men," as well as "Dr. Phil" and "Let's Make a Deal." The service is organized and informative (as is its website), and fully sanctioned by production companies and networks. **TVTix** (www.tvtix.com; ℃ 323/653-4105) also studio-authorized, distributes tickets for several game shows, reality shows and talk shows produced in the Los Angeles area.

CBS Television City, 7800 Beverly Blvd. at N. Fairfax, Los Angeles, distributes tickets for "The Price Is Right" and "Real Time with Bill Maher" through www. cbstelevisioncity.com/tickets. Tickets for many CBS sitcoms are also available from Audiences Unlimited (above).

Reerved tickets for TV shows produced at **Warner Bros. Studios,** 3400 Riverside Dr., Burbank, are distributed through the shows' individual websites. For the syndicated "Ellen DeGeneres Show" go to www.ellentv.com/tickets; for standby seats, call ℃ **818/954-5929** before noon the day of the show. Minimum age is 14. For "Conan," which airs on TBS, go to www.teamcoco.com/tickets; for standby, call ℃ **818/977-3056** between 10:30am and 2pm the day of the show. Minimum age is 16.

Paramount Studios also offers free tickets to its live audience shows. Call Guest Relations (℃ **323/956-1777**) between 9am and 5pm weekdays. **Universal Studios** (www.universalstudios.com; ℃ **800/864-8377**), now part of NBCUniversal, also offers free tickets for its live audience shows; if you're at the amusement park, obtain tickets for shows taping during your visit (subject to availability) at Universal Plaza.

Organized Tours
STUDIO TOURS
In addition to the studios listed below, the **Universal Studios Hollywood** amusement park (p. 103) includes daily tram tours of its studio lot in its admission price.

Body Double

For a cheap, easy way to get a great seat at a fancy Hollywood award ceremony, go to Seatfiller.com and sign up to be one of those people who makes sure all the front seats are occupied.

HOW TO BE A game show CONTESTANT

Thinking of taking a chance on fame and fortune while you're in Los Angeles? Make sure you have some flexibility in your schedule. Although most production companies give priority to out-of-town contestants, you might have to to return to L.A. one or more times for a final audition and/or taping. These tips might help you prepare:

The Bubblier, the Better: Be cheerful, and bright, good-natured when you lose or make mistakes, and above all, exuberant if you win the "big money."

Dress for Success: Contestant coordinators want players who won't alienate viewers, so dress conservatively. Avoid avoid wearing white, black, stripes, or metallics, which require lighting and camera adjustments.

The Cold, Hard Truth: Most talk show sets are kept very cool (hot lights raise the temperature on stage), so bring a sweater or jacket.

Money Matters: Should you be one of the lucky ones, keep in mind that all cash winnings, plus the retail value of all your prizes, will be reported to the IRS as earnings.

Some Game Shows Currently in Production:

o **Jeopardy!** www.sonypictures.com/tv/shows/jeopardy; ⓒ 310/244-5367

o **Wheel of Fortune** www.wheeloffortune.com; ⓒ 213/520-5555

o **The Price Is Right** www.cbs.com/daytime/price/tickets; ⓒ 310/244-5367

Paramount Pictures ★★★ Paramount is the only major studio still located in Hollywood, and the 2-hour "cart tour" around its Hollywood headquarters a journey into history (even the wrought-iron gates Gloria Swanson motored through in *Sunset Boulevard* are still there). The tour is both an ode to filmmaking and a behind-the-scenes look at movie and television facilities in production; no two tours are alike, and chances of spotting a celebrity are pretty good. Visits typically include a walk-through of the soundstages of TV shows or feature films, though you can't enter while shows are taping. Advance reservations are required, and children must be at least 10. Recording equipment is forbidden (still cameras are ok in certain areas). VIP tours (4½ hr., $178) are also available.

5555 Melrose Ave. (btw. N. Gower St. and Van Ness Ave.), Hollywood. www.paramountstudios.com. ⓒ **323/956-1777.** $53 per person by reservation only. Daily 9:30am–2pm. Follow signs to parking garages.

Sony Pictures Studio Tour ★ Although it doesn't have quite the historical cachet of Warner Bros. or Paramount, plenty of movie history was made at this Culver City lot. You could see the soundstage where Dorothy followed the Yellow Brick Road when this was MGM Studios, where Spider-Man battled bad guys, and the RV where meth was cooked in "Breaking Bad." You might visit the sets of "Jeopardy!" and "Wheel of Fortune" if they're not in use, visit the scoring stage where your favorite movie's music was recorded, or see a set for the next blockbuster under construction. And you could very well glimpse a movie star working on a nearby set. Reservations, though not required, are strongly recommended. Children must be 12 or older.

10000 W. Washington Blvd. (btw. Venice and Culver blvds.), Culver City. ⓒ **310/244-8687.** www.sonypicturesstudios.com. Reservations recommended; children under 12 not admitted. Tours $40 per person. Tours Mon–Fri at 9:30, 10:30am, 1:30, and 2:30pm, but are subject to change. Free parking.

Warner Bros. Studios ★★ The Warner Brothers' "VIP Tour" is a 2¼-hour jaunt around the world's busiest movie and TV studio. After a brief introductory film on WB history, groups of 12 pile into stretch golf carts for a view of the studio's back-lot streets, soundstages, sets, and craft shops. Nothing is staged, and there's no telling what or who you'll encounter. The tour includes a visit to the Warner Bros. Museum, displaying original costumes, props, sets, and scripts from classic films and television shows. Advance tickets are recommended and available online through the website, or by calling ℂ **818/972-8687;** otherwise, tickets are sold the day of the tour first-come, first-served. *Note:* Children 7 and under are not admitted, you must bring a valid photo ID, and you arrive about 30 minutes before the tour starts.

3400 Riverside Dr. (at Warner Blvd.), Burbank. ℂ **818/972-8687.** www.wbstudiotour.com. Tours $48 per person. Tours Mon–Fri every 20 min. 8:20am–4pm (extended hours during spring and summer). Parking $7 (follow signs to VIP tour parking).

BUS/VAN TOURS

L.A. Tours (www.latours.net; ℂ **323/460-6490**) operates regularly scheduled city tours in plush shuttle buses. They pick up from major hotels for tours taking in the Sunset Strip, the movie studios, Hollywood, homes of the stars, the Farmers Market, and other attractions. Various itineraries cover the Greater L.A. area and range from a half day, such as Beaches & Shopping ($55 adult, $45 child) to all day, such as the Los Angeles Grand Tour plus the Getty Museum ($99 adult, $89 child). Universal Studios, Disneyland and Six Flags Magic Mountain tours are also available.

The other major tour company in L.A. is **Starline Tours** (www.starlinetours.com; ℂ **800/959-3131** or 323/463-3333), which started the first-ever Movie Stars' Homes tour in 1935. Its popular Hop-On, Hop-Off narrated tour offers four routes ranging from Hollywood to Venice Beach and costing $39 to $69 ($22 to $42 children 3–11) when booked online. The 5½-hour Grand Tour of Los Angeles is the most popular, costing $55 ($42 children). Single-attraction tours, such as the Getty and Madame Tussaud's, are also available, as are many combination tours.

Esotouric (www.esotouric.com, ℂ **323/223-2767**), a small family operation, pokes into forgotten corners of the city and its lore. The founders' passion for their city's *noir*-ish past produces intensively researched tours such as Echo Park Book of the Dead, The Real Black Dahlia, and James M. Cain's Southern California Nightmare. These are as popular with locals as with tourists. A different tour is offered each Saturday at noon; the cost is $58 (discounted six-packs and 12-packs available).

WALKING TOURS

For the classic Hollywood walking tour, **Red Line Tours** (www.redlinetours.com; ℂ **323/402-1074**) offers daily sightseeing strolls to Hollywood's famous (and infamous) landmarks. Trips depart from the Egyptian Theatre (6708 Hollywood Blvd.) four times a day, seven days a week. Rates are $25 for adults, $18 for students and seniors, and $15 for children ages 9 to 15.

The **L.A. Conservancy** (www.laconservancy.org; ℂ **213/623-2489**) conducts informative and entertaining walking tours of Downtown L.A. The most popular is Broadway Historic Theatre & Commercial District, but other intriguing themes include Angelino Heights, Art Deco, Downtown's Modern Skyline, and Union Station. The fee is $10; some require advance reservations. Most start at 10am Saturdays.

Santa Monica Conservancy Walking Tours (www.smconservancy.org; ℂ **310/496-3146**) explore the distinct history, architecture, and culture of Santa Monica. Docent-guided tours take place at 10am Saturdays and cost $10 (cash, at beginning of

4

Los Angeles Attractions

tour); reservations recommended. Self-guided tour booklets are $3 (also available around town), and group tours can be arranged with two weeks' notice.

OTHER TOURS

BY BICYCLE   **Perry's Beach Cafe & Rentals** (www.perryscafe.com; © **310/939-0000**) in Santa Monica offers bike bicycle tours of Santa Monica's and Venice's beach communities, covering their history and landmark architecture. The $45 per person fee includes a tour guide and an additional 1½-hour bike rental with gear. *Note:* Tours given by reservation only October through May; minimum three people.

BY AIR   For a bird's-eye view of L.A., **Celebrity Helicopters** (www.celebheli.com; © **877/999-2099**) offers a variety of themed trips, from a 35-minute Celebrity Home Tour ($219) to a 25-minute fly-by of the the beach cities ($169) to a little bit of everything in L.A. ($199). Airplane tours are also available.

BY FOOT   **Off 'N Running Tours** (www.offnrunningtours.com; © **310/246-1418**) guides joggers on themed sightseeing runs through the region's most entertaining areas. The 4-mile "Running from the Paparazzi" tour zips through Los Angeles, Beverly Hills and Hollywood, including some (very) quick window shopping. "Pacific Pleasure" takes in Santa Monica, Venice and other beach cities. Tours cost $60 and include bottled water and a technical T-shirt; "Paraparazzi" participants also get a cupcake at the end.

BY TROLLEY   The city-run Beverly Hills Trolley Tours (www.beverlyhills.org; © **310/285-2442**) detail the city's art, architecture and history, divulging little-known facts and celebrity tidbits along the way. The 40-minute tour takes in Rodeo Drive and the Golden Triangle. Tours depart from the "Trolley Stop" at Rodeo Drive and Dayton Way and cost $5 for adults, $1 per child up to 12.

Beaches

Los Angeles County's 72-mile coastline sports more than 30 miles of beaches. County-run beaches usually charge for parking ($3–$12). Alcohol, bonfires, and pets are prohibited. For **surf conditions** (and coastal weather forecast), go to www.watchthewater. org. The following are the county's best beaches, listed from north to south.

EL PESCADOR, L.A. PIEDRA & EL MATADOR BEACHES ★   These rugged and isolated beaches, marked only by small highway signs, front a 2-mile stretch of the Pacific Coast Highway (Calif. 1, or PCH) between Broad Beach and Decker Canyon roads, 10 minutes from the Malibu Pier. Picturesque coves with unusual rock formations invite sunbathing and picnicking, but swimmers beware; there are no lifeguards. Parking atop the bluffs is limited. Stairs lead down cliffs to the beach.

ZUMA BEACH COUNTY PARK ★★   Jampacked on warm weekends, L.A. County's largest beach park is located off PCH, a mile past Kanan Dume Road. Zuma isn't the Southland's most scenic beach, but it has plenty of restrooms, lifeguards, playgrounds, volleyball courts, and snack bars. Westward Beach, the southern stretch toward Point Dume, is separated from the noisy highway by sandstone cliffs. A trail leads over the point's headlands to Pirate's Cove, once a popular nude beach.

MALIBU LAGOON STATE BEACH ★★★   Not just a pretty white-sand beach, but an estuary and wetlands area as well, Malibu Lagoon is the historic home of the Chumash Indians. The entrance is on PCH south of Cross Creek Road ($12 day use fee). Marine life and shorebirds teem where the creek empties into the sea, and the waves are always mild. The historic **Adamson House,** a showplace of Malibu tile, is operated as a museum.

SURFRIDER BEACH ★   L.A.'s best waves roll ashore here, making this one of L.A.'s most popular surfing spots. The beach is located between the Malibu Pier and the lagoon. Few "locals-only" wave wars break out here—surfing is not as territorial as it can be in other areas. Surfrider is surrounded by all of Malibu's hustle and bustle; don't come here for peace and quiet, as the surf is always crowded.

TOPANGA STATE BEACH ★   This short, narrow strip of sand, where Topanga Canyon Boulevard emerges from the mountains, gets significant highway noise, but that doesn't deter the surfers who wait in line to catch its excellent right point breaks. The beach has restrooms and lifeguard services, and across the street, the **Reel Inn,** 18661 Pacific Coast Hwy. (btw. Topanga Canyon Blvd. and Tuna Canyon Rd.), Malibu (✆ **310/456-8221**) is one of the best fresh fish restaurants around.

WILL ROGERS STATE BEACH ★   Three miles of sandy shoreline along PCH, between Sunset Boulevard and the Santa Monica city line, are named for the American humorist whose ranch-turned-state-historic-park (see "Parks," below) is hunkered above the palisades that provide the backdrop for this popular beach. A pay parking lot ($15) extends the length of the beach, whose facilities include restrooms, lifeguards, a snack hut (in season), volleyball courts, and a playground. It's not the best surfing beach, but the waves are friendly to swimmers and divers, and it's less crowded than Santa Monica next door.

SANTA MONICA STATE BEACH ★   The family-friendly beaches on either side of the Santa Monica Pier (p. 82) are popular for their white sands and accessibility. It offers big parking lots, cafes, and well-maintained restrooms. A paved path runs along the beach for walking, biking, or skating to Venice and points south. Colorado Boulevard leads to the pier; turn north on PCH below the coastline's bluffs, or south along Ocean Avenue—you can find parking in both directions.

VENICE BEACH ★★★   Moving south from Santa Monica, the paved pedestrian Promenade becomes Ocean Front Walk and gets progressively weirder until it reaches an apex at Washington Boulevard and the Venice fishing pier. Some people do just swim and sunbathe, but Venice Beach is defined by the sea of humanity on the Ocean Front Walk, plus the bevy of boardwalk vendors and old-fashioned pedestrian streets a block away. Park on the side streets or in the plentiful lots west of Pacific Avenue.

MANHATTAN STATE BEACH ★★   The Beach Boys once hung out at this wide, friendly beach. Ample parking on 36 blocks of side streets (btw. Rosecrans Ave. and the Hermosa Beach border) draws weekend crowds from the L.A. area. Manhattan has some of the best surfing around as well as restrooms, lifeguards, and volleyball courts. Manhattan Beach Boulevard leads west to the fishing pier with its adjacent seafood restaurants, aquarium, and perfect sunset vantage point.

HERMOSA CITY BEACH ★★★   This wide white-sand beach, extending to either side of the fishing pier, is one of the best in Southern California. The Strand, a wide, smooth pedestrian lane, runs the length of the beach. Main access is at the foot of Pier Avenue, which is lined with interesting shops and outdoor cafes. There's plenty of street parking, as well as restrooms, lifeguards, volleyball courts, playgrounds, and good surfing.

REDONDO STATE BEACH ★   Popular with surfers, bicyclists, and joggers, Redondo's white sand and ice-plant-carpeted dunes are just south of tiny King Harbor, along the Esplanade (S. Esplanade Dr.), offering a quiet respite. Get there via PCH or Torrance Boulevard. Facilities include restrooms, lifeguards, and volleyball courts.

Outdoor Activities

PARKS

Descanso Gardens ★ GARDEN   Los Angeles Daily News publisher, and amateur gardener E. Manchester Boddy, began planting evergreen camelia bushes from China and Japan here in 1941. Today his 150-acre Descanso Gardens contain more than than 600 camelia varieties, blooming under a canopy of California oaks. They share the limelight with a 5-acre International Rosarium. Descanso means "rest," and this is indeed a restful place, with paths and streams winding through a towering forest; it borders a lake, bird sanctuary, Japanese Garden & Tea House, and Boddy House museum. Each season features different plants: daffodils, azaleas, tulips, and lilacs in spring; chrysanthemums in fall; and so on. Art exhibits in the Sturt Haaga Gallery rotate every four months, and the Descanso Café offers light meals daily from 9am to 4:30pm. Daily guided walking tours cost $10 per person. Picnicking is allowed in specified areas. *Tip:* Kids (at least 30 inches tall) love the mini Enchanted Railroad, which travels around a section of the park near the promenade. Cost is $3.

1418 Descanso Dr., La Cañada Flintridge (near the intersection of the 2 and 210 freeways). www. descansogardens.org. (℗) **818/949-4200.** Admission $8 adults, $6 students and seniors 62 and over, $3 children 5–12, free for kids 4 and under. Daily 9am–5pm. Closed Christmas. Free parking.

Griffith Park ★★★ PARK   Donated to the city in 1896, this is one of America's largest urban parks. Even leaving aside its most famous attractions—the **Griffith Observatory** (p. 88), the **Autry National Center of the American West** (p. 91), the **Los Angeles Zoo** (p. 95), and the **Hollywood sign** (p. 90), there's a lot to do in these more than 4,200 acres at the edge of the Santa Monica Mountains. The prettiest of its 53 miles of hiking paths is the shady **Fern Dell trail** near the Western Avenue entrance, cooled by waterfalls and ferns. Other options include horseback riding, golfing, swimming, biking, and picnicking (see "Outdoor Activities" later in this chapter). For a general overview of the park, drive the mountainous loop road that winds from the top of Western Avenue, past Griffith Observatory, and down to Vermont Avenue. For a more extensive foray, turn north at the loop road's midsection, onto Mount Hollywood Drive. To reach the golf courses, Autry Center, and zoo, take Los Feliz Boulevard to Riverside Drive, which runs along the park's western edge.

Near the zoo, in a dusty corner of the park, the **Travel Town Transportation Museum,** 5200 Zoo Dr. (www.traveltown.org; (℗) **323/662-5874**) is a little-known outdoor museum with a small collection of vintage locomotives and old airplanes. Kids love the miniature train ride that circles the free museum, which is open Monday through Friday 10am to 4pm, and Saturday and Sunday 10am to 6pm.

4730 Crystal Springs Dr., (Los Feliz exit from I-5) Los Angeles. www.laparks.org. (℗) **323/913-4688.** Daily 6am–10pm.

Will Rogers State Historic Park ★★★ PARK/HISTORIC HOME   Wild West showman and humorist Will Rogers, who moved to Los Angeles in 1919 and became a movie actor and author of books detailing his down-home "cowboy philosophy," willed his ranch and grounds to the state in 1944. Charles and Anne Morrow Lindbergh hid out here in the 1930s in the aftermath of the kidnapping and murder of their son. The 168-acre estate overlooking the Pacific is now both a park and a historic site. Visitors may explore the grounds, the former stables, and the 31-room house filled with original furnishings, including a porch swing in the living room and many Native American rugs and baskets. Docent tours of the Ranch house are available, and self-guided tours can be downloaded from the website. Trail rides show off the estate as Rogers knew it—from the back of a horse.

1501 Will Rogers State Park Rd., Pacific Palisades, btw. Santa Monica and Malibu. *©* **310/454-8212.** From Santa Monica, take the Pacific Coast Hwy. (Calif. 1) north, turn right onto Sunset Blvd., and continue to the park entrance. $12 per vehicle. The park is open daily from 8am–sunset; the house, Thurs–Fri 11am–3pm, Sat–Sun 10am–4pm; and guided Ranch House tours are offered every hr., on the hour, up until 1 hr. before closing. Parking $12 ($11 seniors).

OTHER OUTDOOR ACTIVIES

BICYCLING   A flat, paved bicycle trail follows about 22 miles of state beaches, harbors, LAX, and laid-back beach towns such as Venice, Manhattan Beach, Hermosa Beach, and Redondo Beach. The first stretch starts at Will Rogers State Beach in Pacific Palisades and runs south through Santa Monica and Venice to Marina del Rey—about 8 miles. The second stretch—called the **South Bay Bike Trail**—starts at the south end of Marina del Rey and takes you to Torrance Beach. If you want to ride the entire path, you'll have to detour around Marina del Rey, which takes only about 15 minutes. The bike path attracts all levels of riders and gets pretty busy on weekends. There are plenty of fountains, snack stands, and public restrooms along the trail. For information on this and other city bike routes, go to www.labikepaths.com.

FISHING   No permit is required to cast from shore or drop a line from most public piers. The best saltwater fishing spot in L.A. is at the foot of Torrance Boulevard in Redondo Beach. **Del Rey Sport Fishing,** 13552 Fiji Way, Marina del Rey (www.marina delreysportfishing.com; *©* **800/822-3625** or 310/822-3635), runs half- and full-day deep-sea fishing trips every day, starting at $35 ($25 for kids under 12). Barracuda, halibut, and yellowtail are the most common catches. *Note:* Anyone 16 years and up needs a fishing license, available at most sporting goods stores.

GOLF   Most of L.A.'s public courses are administered by the Department of Recreation and Parks, whose online reservation system allows any player to book a tee time up to 8 days in advance, for a $5 fee (www.golf.lacity.org). You're also welcome to show up and get on the call sheet (much easier for nine-hole than 18-hole courses). Expect to wait for the most popular tee times.

Of the city's seven 18-hole and three 9-hole courses, you can't get more central than the **Rancho Park Golf Course ★★,** 10460 W. Pico Blvd. (www.rancho.lagolfclubs. com; *©* **310/838-7373**), in L.A.'s Westside. The par-71 course is an oasis contrasting with towering Century City buildings next door. It also has a 9-hole, par-3 course and a driving range that was renovated in 2014.

For a genuinely woodsy experience, try one of the three courses inside Griffith Park, northeast of Hollywood (see "Parks," earlier in this chapter). They are well maintained and challenging but not frustrating. The nine-hole **Roosevelt,** on Vermont Avenue across from the Greek Theatre, is especially bucolic, with deer, rabbits, raccoons, and skunks (fore!) often appearing early in the morning. **Wilson** and **Harding** are each 18 holes and start from the main clubhouse off Riverside Drive, the park's main entrance.

Greens fee for city courses range from $16 to $48 for non-residents, depending on day and size of course, and demand is high during peak times. Contact the Department of Recreation and Parks (www.laparks.org; *©* **213/625-1040**) for full details.

The public **Trump National Golf Club,** 1 Ocean Trails Drive, Rancho Palos Verdes (www.trumpnationallosangeles.com; *©* **310/265-5000**) occupies a blufff overlooking the Pacific and provides spectacular views from every hole. The course, 30 minutes south of Downtown, also offers a 45,000-square-foot clubhouse with locker rooms, a pro shop, three dining options, conference rooms, and a grand ballroom. Green fees are $275 peak, $215 midday, $160 afternoon, and $80 after 2:30pm. For more information on regional golf courses, see www.golfcalifornia.com.

HIKING　The **Santa Monica Mountains,** running only 50 miles from Griffith Park to Point Mugu (on the coast north of Malibu), offers great hiking. Peaking at 3,111 feet, they are part of the Santa Monica Mountains National Recreation Area, a conglomeration of 350 public parks and 65,000 acres. Hiking is best after spring rains, when the hills are green, flowers are in bloom, and the air is clear. Summers can be very hot; hikers should always carry fresh water and beware of poison oak.

Santa Ynez Canyon, in Pacific Palisades, is a long and relentless 3-mile climb that rewards hikers with fantastic ocean views. At the top is **Trippet Ranch,** a public facility providing water, restrooms, and picnic tables. From Santa Monica, take Pacific Coast Highway (Calif. 1) north; turn right onto Sunset Boulevard and then left onto Palisades Drive. Continue for 2½ miles, turn left onto Verenda de la Montura, and park near the trail head in the cul-de-sac at the end of the street.

Temescal Canyon, in Pacific Palisades, is one of the quickest routes into the wilderness. It's easier than the Santa Ynez trail and far more popular, especially among locals. Hikes here are anywhere from 1 to 5 miles. From Santa Monica, take PCH north; turn right onto Temescal Canyon Road and follow it to the end. Sign in with the gatekeeper, who can also answer any questions.

Will Rogers State Historic Park, in Pacific Palisades, is also terrific for hiking. An intermediate-level hike from the park entrance ends at Inspiration Point, a plateau that offers a view of much of L.A.'s Westside. (See "Parks," earlier in this secton.)

For more information on hiking in the L.A. region, go to www.latrails.com.

SAILING　Marina del Rey, the world's largest manmade marina, is the launch point for **Paradise Bound Yacht Charters** (www.aaparadiseboundyacht.com; ✆ **800/655-0850**). Book Captain Alex's 42-foot sailing vessel for a minimum of 2 hours for $340

A horse, **OF COURSE**

If there's anything more romantic than riding a horse through the Hollywood Hills at sunset, with a million lights twinking far below, I haven't found it. Just under the HOLLYWOOD sign at the edge of Griffith Park, with access to all its trails, the popular **Sunset Ranch** horse riding outfit, 3400 Beachwood Dr. off Franklin Ave. (www.sunsetranch hollywood.com; ✆ 323/469-5450) offers early-evening rides every day. Choose from a ride to the peak of Mount Hollywood; ($75 per person), a dinner ride that stops at a Mexican restaurant ($100 plus cost of meal), or a barbecue tour ($95) that rides to Griffith Park's highest peak and ends with a barbecue at the ranch.

Sunset Ranch also offers riding lessons and horse rentals by day. Another option for guided rides in Griffith Park is **Griffith Park Horse Rentals** in the Los Angeles Equestrian Center, 480 Riverside Dr., Burbank (www.griffithparkhorse rental.com; ✆ 818/840-8401), which has also added sunset dinner rides.

Closer to the ocean is **Los Angeles Horseback Riding,** 2623 Old Topanga Canyon Rd., Topanga (www.losangeles horsebackriding.com; ✆ 818/591-2032), at the top of a 1,800-foot ridge. Panoramic views of the ocean and San Fernando Valley are seen to best effect on their sunset or full-moon rides.

Also see **Will Rogers State Beach** (p. 115) for horseback rides.

---

an hour for up to six people, including the services of captain, crew, and a hostess (see website for special offers, packages, and coupons). Another option is **Marina Boat Rentals** (℃ 310/574-2822) in Marina del Rey, starting at $80 an hour for a six-person boat (no crew).

SEA KAYAKING   Sea kayaking is a simple and serene way to explore the southern coastline. **Southwind Kayak Center** (17855 Skypark Circle, Irvine; www.southwind kayaks.com; ℃ 800/768-8494 or 949/261-0200) rents a variety of kayaks for use in the bay or open ocean at its Newport Beach rental base. Rates start at $50 per day; kayaking classes and guided outings are also available.

SKATING   The 22-mile-long **South Beach Trail** that runs from Pacific Palisades to Torrance is one of the country's premier skating spots. In-line skating is especially popular, but conventional skates are common. Skating is allowed just about everywhere bicycling is (cyclists have right of way). Rent skates at **JS Rentals,** 1501 Ocean Front Walk, Venice (www.jaysrentalsvb.com; ℃ 310/392-7306), **Hermosa Cyclery,** 20 13th St., a block from The Strand in Hermosa Beach (www.hermosacyclery.com; ℃ 310/374-7816), or any of numerous outlets along the trail. Expect to pay $6 to $7 per hour or $20-$21 per day for most types of skates.

SURFING   George Freeth (1883–1918), who first surfed Redondo Beach in 1907, is widely credited with introducing the sport to California. It didn't catch on until the 1950s, but ever since the Beach Boys and other surf-music groups arrived on the scene, Southern California and surfing have been joined at the hip.

First-timers should contact the highly respected school **Learn to Surf L.A.** (www. learntosurfla.com; ℃ 310/663-2479) or **Malibu Longboards** (www.malibulongboards. com; ℃ 310/467-6898 or 818/990-7633) Private lessons run $99 to $120, group lessons around $75. Experienced surfers can rent boards for about $20 per day at shops near all top surfing beaches in the L.A. area. **Zuma Jay Surfboards** (22775 Pacific Coast Hwy., Malibu; www.zumajays.com; ℃ 310/456-8044), about a half-mile south of Malibu Pier, is Malibu's oldest surf shop. See www.surfline.com for more information about surfing in Southern California.

WINDSURFING   This challenging sport, also called sailboarding, was invented and patented in Torrance in 1968. **Long Beach Windsurf & Kayak Center,** 3850 E. Ocean Blvd., Long Beach (www.windsurfcenter.com; ℃ 562/433-1014), offers lessons and rentals in Alamitos Bay. A $199 learner's package includes instruction from 8am to noon and use of board and wet suit.

SHOPPING

Whether you're looking for trendsetting fashions or just some tourist schlock mementos, Los Angeles has your shopping needs covered like no other place in the world. This is the place that practically *invented* the shopping mall.

A note on shopping hours: Street shops are generally open Monday through Saturday from 10 or 11am to 5 or 6pm. Many are open Sunday, particularly those near the beaches, movie theaters, or clusters of other stores. Quite a few offer extended evening hours one night a week. Mall shops generally open from 10am to 8 or 9pm; shave an hour or from off each side on Sundays. Mall hours increase substantially during holiday periods.

Sales tax in Los Angeles is 9%; savvy out-of-state shoppers have larger items shipped directly home to save the tax.

Shopping By 'Hood

If addresses and phone numbers are not given here, refer to the store's expanded listing by category in "Shopping A to Z," later in this chapter.

L.A.'S WESTSIDE & BEVERLY HILLS

Beverly Boulevard ★   Beverly is L.A.'s premier boulevard for mid-20th-century furnishings. Expensive showrooms now line the street, but the shop that started it all is **Modernica,** 7366 Beverly Blvd. (www.modernica.net; © **323/933-0383**). British designer and rock royalty **Stella McCartney,** 8823 Beverly Blvd. (© **310/273-7051**), sells her entire fashion and acessories collecton from an ivy-covered 1920s cottage. From Robertson Blvd. to La Brea Ave.

La Brea Avenue ★   L.A.'s artiest shopping strip is anchored by the giant American Rag-Maison Midi-Alterna-complex and is also home to great urban antiques stores dealing in Art Deco, Arts and Crafts, 1950s modern, and the like. You'll also find vintage clothiers and furniture furniture galleries; custom, handcrafted furniture is available at **Mortise & Tenon,** 446 S. La Brea Ave. (© **323/937-7654;** www.mortise tenon.com). North of Wilshire Blvd.

Robertson Boulevard ★   The star-gazing is prodigious on this most popular of L.A.'s shopping streets. It's common to see the likes of Jessica Simpson and Lindsay Lohan picking out duds at trend-obsessed boutiques like **Kitson** and the splashy **Dolce & Gabbana** flagship at 147 N. Robertson Blvd. (www.dolcegabbana.com; © **310/247-1571**). Btw. Wilshire and Beverly blvds.

Rodeo Drive & Beverly Hills's Golden Triangle ★★   The 3 hallowed blocks of the city's most famous shopping street offer a mix of couture shops from high fashion's old guard, newer high-end labels, and two uniquely Beverly Hills-style minimals: the **Rodeo Collection,** 421 N. Rodeo Dr. (www.rodeocollection.net), a contemporary center with towering palms; and **2 Rodeo** (www.tworodeo.com), a cobblestoned Italianate piazza at Wilshire Boulevard. Here you'll find Prada, Chenel, Gucci, Hermès, Luis Vuitton, Polo/Ralph Lauren, Burburry, and one of the largest Tiffany & Co. stores in the world.

The 16-square-block area surrounding Rodeo Drive is known as the Golden Triangle. Shops off Rodeo are less name-conscious as those on the strip, and they're sometimes even affordable (but still plenty upscale). South Santa Monica Boulevard has a particularly colorful line of specialty stores, and Brighton Way is as young and hip as relatively staid Beverly Hills gets. Wilshire Boulevard is home to New York–style department stores in spectacular landmark buildings, such as Saks Fifth Avenue and Barneys New York. Btw. Santa Monica and Wilshire blvds., and Crescent Dr., Beverly Hills.

West 3rd Street ★   You can shop until you drop on this trendy strip, anchored on the east end by the **Farmers Market** (p. 92) and **The Grove** (see Shopping Malls, later in this chapter). Many of Melrose Avenue's shops have relocated here, along with terrific up-and-comers. Shops here, including the vintage-clothing stores, are a bit more refined than those on Melrose. Btw. Fairfax and Robertson blvds.

HOLLYWOOD & WEST HOLLYWOOD

Hollywood Boulevard ★   This is not one of Los Angeles's most famous streets for its shopping, but it's not all cheesy T-shirt shops and greasy pizzerias. Some excellent poster shops, souvenir stores, and Hollywood-memorabilia dealers are hiding out along the Walk of Fame—and of course, you can find devilish dainties at the legendary

Fredericks of Hollywood, 6751 Hollywood Blvd. (www.fredericks.com; © **323/957-5953**). Btw. Gower St. and La Brea Ave.

Larchmont Boulevard ★★ L.A.'s most pleasant shopping strip lies just east of busy Vine Avenue. Neighbors congregating on shady sidewalks lined by outdoor bistro tables lend charming, old fashioned air to Larchmont, which has grown more stylish as neighboring Hancock Park draws more artists and young industry types. Some chains have infiltrated the formerly mom-and-pop domain, but there's still plenty of unique shopping here. Case in point: 60-year-old **Chevalier's Books,** 126 N. Larchmont Blvd. (www.chevaliersbooks.com; © **323/465-1334**), one of L.A.'s landmark independent bookstores. Btw. Melrose Ave. and 3rd St.

Melrose Avenue ★★ It's showing some wear, but this is still one of the most exciting shopping streets in the country for cutting-edge fashions such as the leather, denim, and classic vintage at the L.A. branch of San Francisco's **Wasteland,** 7248 Melrose Ave. (www.wastelandclothing.com; © **323/653-3028**). Melrose is always an entertaining stroll, dotted with hip restaurants and funky shops selling the latest in clothes, gifts, jewelry, and accessories. Where else could you find green patent-leather cowboy boots, a 19th-century pocket watch, an inflatable girlfriend, and glow-in-the-dark condoms on the same block? Btw. Fairfax and La Brea aves.

Melrose Heights ★★ This posh section of Melrose, anchored by the venerable **Fred Segal,** houses designer boutiques such as **Diane Von Furstenberg,** 8407 Melrose Ave. and **Paul Smith** at 8221. L.A. jewelry designer **Suzanne Felsen,** 8332 Melrose Ave. (www.suzannefelsen.com; © **323/653-5400**), is a celebrity favorite, and **Marc Jacobs** has three stores at 8400, 8409, and 8410 Melrose Ave., featuring ready-to-wear, accessories, and menswear. Btw. La Cienega Blvd. and Fairfax Ave.

The Sunset Strip ★ Under monster-size billboards advertising the latest rock god, the Strip is lined with trendy restaurants, industry-oriented hotels, and dozens of shops offering outrageous fashions and stage accessories. **Sunset Plaza** is an anomaly—an upscale cluster of Georgian-style shops resembling Beverly Hills at its snootiest. Btw. La Cienega Blvd. and Doheny Dr., West Hollywood.

SANTA MONICA & THE BEACHES

Main Street ★ An excellent street for strolling, Main Street is bursts with mall standards mixed with upscale, left-of-center individual boutiques and casually hip cafes and restaurants. The primary strip connecting Santa Monica and Venice, Main Street has a relaxed, beachy vibe that sets it apart from similar strips. Stores here straddle the fashion fence between upscale trendy and beach-bum edgy. Btw. Pacific St. and Rose Ave., and Santa Monica and Venice blvds.

Montana Avenue This stretch of Montana has become an enclave of upscale stroller-pushing moms on the prowl for pricey designer fashions, country home decor, and gourmet takeout. It's still distinctive enough to warrant a special trip across town to shops such as minimalist **Savannah,** 706 Montana Ave. (savannahsantamonica. com; © **310/458-2095**); ultrahip **Jill Roberts,** 920 Montana Ave. (www.jillroberts.com; © **310/260-1966**); sleekly professional **Weathervane,** 1209 Montana Ave. (www. weathervaneforwomen.com; © **310/393-5344**), and the second-largest **Kiehl's** store outside of New York City, 1516 Montana Ave. (www.kiehls.com; © **310/255-0055**). Btw. 17th and 7th sts., Santa Monica; www.montanaave.com.

Santa Monica Place ★ This new outdoor mall straddles the Third Street Promenade and the Santa Monica Pier, offering high-end shopping 2 blocks from the beach.

THE ANTI-RODEO DRIVE: abbot kinney boulevard

If Rodeo Drive attitude and megamall conformity wear on you, flee to Venice and stroll the eclectic shops along **Abbot Kinney Boulevard.** This refreshingly anti-establishment stretch of street has the most diverse array of shops, galleries, and restaurants in Los Angeles, without the chain stores. You can easily spend the entire afternoon here poring over vintage clothing, antique furniture, vintage Vespas, local art, and amusing gifts. For a unique gift, try **Strange Invisible Perfumes,** 1138 Abbot Kinney Blvd. (www.siperfumes.com; ✆ **310/314-1505**), where they can custom-make a scent to match your musk. **Firefly,** 1409 Abbot Kinney Blvd. (www.shopfirefly.com; ✆ **310/450-6288**), a local favorite, sells everything from great baby gifts, stationery, and books to quirky handbags and cool clothing. **DNA Clothing Co.,** 411 Rose Ave. (www.dnaclothing.com; ✆ **310/399-0341**), specializes in the latest styles for men and women at great prices (it's a resource for many films and TV shows). When you need a breather, the boulevard is full of restaurants, including **Joe's** (the best California cuisine in L.A.; p. 58), You even get 2 hours of free street parking.

Anchored by **Bloomingdale's** and **Nordstrom,** and featuring the likes of **Hugo Boss, Burberry,** and **Kitson,** it's distinguished by a pretty view over Santa Monica Beach and fine rooftop dining and drinking. 300 block of Colorado Ave. www.santamonicaplace.com.

Third Street Promenade ★   Packed with corporate chain stores and restaurants, Santa Monica's enormously popular pedestrians-only shopping strip seethes all day and well into the evening with assorted street performers among the shoppers, bored teens, and home-challenged. However, a few gems are squeezed between Gap, Abercrombie & Fitch, and Old Navy, such as **Puzzle Zoo** and **Hennessey & Ingalls,** specializing in art and architecture books around the corner at 214 Wilshire Blvd. (www.hennesseyingalls.com; ✆ **310/458-9074**). 3rd St. btw. Wilshire Blvd. and Broadway Ave. www.downtownsm.com.

SILVER LAKE & LOS FELIZ

At the eastern end of Hollywood (and technically part of Los Angeles), these two communities have become increasingly hip. **Silver Lake,** named for the manmade reservoir at its center, is a bohemian enclave of artists and ethnic families that's popular for clubbing. To the northwest, the slightly tamer **Los Feliz** is filled with 1920s and '30s buildings. Together, they offer dozens of unique boutiques, music stores, and furniture dealers. Vintage clothing and home decor is an especially big draw, and Silver Lake, with many alternative bands in residence, has cutting-edge music stores around every corner. Silver Lake, bounded by Atwater Village and Elysian Valley to the northeast, Echo Park to the southeast, Westlake to the southwest, East Hollywood to the west, Los Feliz to the northwest. Los Feliz, bounded by Griffith Park to the north, Atwater Village to the northeast, Silver Lake to the southeast, East Hollywood to the south, Hollywood and Hollywood Hills to the northwest.

DOWNTOWN

Although many of Downtown's once-splendid streets are lined with cut-rate luggage and electronics stores, shopping here can be rewarding for the adventuresome, especially in the garment and fabric districts (see "Discount," later in this chapter). Florists and bargain hunters arrive before dawn at the vast **Los Angeles Flower District,** 766 Wall St. (btw. E. 8th and E. 7th sts.; www.laflowerdistrict.com; ✆ **213/622-1966**), for the city's best selection of fresh blooms; the **Southern California Flower Market,** 755 Wall St., between E. 7th and E. 8th streets (✆ **213/627-2482**), where flowers by the bundle go for amazingly low prices, is one of its primary draws. Families of all ethnicities stroll the bustling **Grand Central Market.**

Another favorite Downtown shopping zone is **Olvera Street** ★★★ (see p. 109), a lively brick pedestrian lane near Union Station where stalls have been selling Mexican wares since the 1930s. Everything sold south of the border is available here—custom leather accessories, huarache sandals, maracas, and of course, fresh churros. Weekends bring strolling musicians, mariachis, folk dancers, and Aztec performances.

For *the* best deals in handbags, luggage, shoes, costume jewelry, and trendy fashions, head for **Santee Alley,** between Santee Street and Maple Avenue. Often called the heart of the fashion district, it sells everything you've ever wanted at bargain prices. Go when the locals do, early on Saturday mornings.

PASADENA & ENVIRONS

Pretty, compact Pasadena is a breeze compared with L.A.'s megamalls. Stores generally open daily around 10am, and many stay open until 8 or 9pm to accommodate the dinner/movie crowd. Dating back to the 1880s, the 22-block-long **Old Pasadena district** (www.oldpasadena.com; centered on the intersection of Colorado Blvd. and Fair Oaks Ave.) historically has offered some of L.A.'s best shopping, though Banana Republic and Crate & Barrel, et al., are coming on strong. More upscale shopping has moved in; Tiffany & Co. has become more of an attraction than a store, and the hugely popular H&M fashion store is now a neighborhood anchor. Moving eastward, you'll find more eclectic shops and galleries commingling with pre-yuppie relics as the strip segues into the **Paseo Colorado** mall (below).

Several good hunting grounds surround Old Pasadena. Antiques hounds can find a rich concentration of collectibles at the **Green Street Antique Row,** 985–1005 E. Green St. (east of Lake Ave.), or the **Pasadena Antique Center,** on South Fair Oaks Boulevard (south of Del Mar Blvd.). And you never know what you might find at the **Rose Bowl Flea Market** (www.rgcshows.com; ✆ **323/560-7469**), California's largest monthly swap meet.

Shopping Malls
L.A.'S WESTSIDE & BEVERLY HILLS

The Beverly Center ★   Loved for its convenience and disdained for its penitentiary-style architecture (and the "no validations" parking fee), the eight-story Beverly Center contains about 160 standard mall shops, including the wildly popular **H&M,** and even a few boutiques that are open by advance reservation only (*so* L.A.). It's anchored on opposite sides by Macy's and Bloomingdale's department stores. You can see it from blocks away, looking like a gigantic climbing wall. 8500 Beverly Blvd. (at La Cienega Blvd.), Los Angeles. www.beverlycenter.com. ✆ **310/854-0070.**

The Grove ★   This massive, Vegas-style retail complex at the east end of the Farmers Market is one of L.A.'s most popular megamalls. Its eclectic architectural styles, ranging from Art Deco to Italian Renaissance, and miniature streets linked to the Market by a double-deck electric trolley are more than a little Disney-esque, but Angelenos love it—you can power-shop all morning, check your bags at a drop-off station, catch a movie at the 14-screen **Grove Theatre** (www.thegrovela.com ; ✆ **323/692-0829**), have a concierge secure you an early dinner reservation, and be home by 7pm. 189 The Grove Dr. (6333 W. 3rd St. at S. Fairfax Ave), Hollywood. www.thegrovela.com. ℂ **888/315-8883** or 323/900-8080. Parking in the Grove parking structure (enter on The Grove Drive or off Fairfax Ave.) or the Farmers Market parking lot.

Westside Pavilion ★   This shopping center has the only **Nordstrom** in the area and attracts a very style-conscious crowd with a taste for the finest in women's fashions, handbags, and shoes. Within easy access of the major arterials of I-405 and I-10, it houses more than 160 specialty shops, such as **BCBG, Aeropostale, Aldo, Banana Republic,** and **Nine West,** as well as the anchor restaurant **Westside Tavern,** a food court, and the two-story **Landmark Theatres.** This mall is big on community and kids' events. 10800 W. Pico Blvd. (btw. Westwood Blvd. and Overland Dr.), Los Angeles. www. westsidepavilion.com. ℂ **310/470-8752.**

HOLLYWOOD & WEST HOLLYWOO

Hollywood & Highland ★   This massive entertainment complex embodies this once-seedy area's rapid rehabilitation. Surrounded by souvenir shops and tattoo parlors, the gleaming 8¾-acre center has not only top-end stores such as Guess, Louis Vuitton, and bebe, but studio broadcast facilities and the gorgeous **Dolby Theatre** (p. 130). Its over-the-top, open-air Babylon Court, designed after the 1916 film "Intolerance," attempts to re-create a Golden Age movie set, complete with giant pillars topped with 13,500-pound elephants and a colossal arch framing the HOLLYWOOD sign in the distance. The six-level underground lot can pack in 3,000 cars. 6801 Hollywood Blvd. (at N. Highland), Hollywood. www.hollywoodandhighland.com. ℂ **323/817-0200.** Metro Red Line to Hollywood/Highland.

Pacific Design Center ★★   Something of an architectural and cultural landmark, this is the West Coast's largest facility for interior design goods and fine furnishings. It houses more than 200 showrooms filled with furniture, fabrics, flooring, wall coverings, kitchen and bath fixtures, lighting, art, and accessories. Technically, businesses here sell to the trade only, and their wholesale prices reflect that. *Tip:* For a fee, the center will provide a decorator-for-the-day to serve as official broker for your purchases. 8687 Melrose Ave. (btw. N San Vicente and Huntley), West Hollywood. www.pacific designcenter.com. ℂ **310/657-0800.**

PASADENA

Paseo Colorado ★   This monolithic open-air mall in the heart of Pasadena, anchored by Macy's, houses about 140 retailers and restaurants (but few men's fashions), a Gelson's market, a fitness center, a full-service day spa, and a 14-screen multiplex theater. It's unique for the dozens of offices, apartments, and studios on top, which allows residents easy access to all their daily necessities. 280 E. Colorado Blvd. (at Marengo Ave.), Pasadena. www.paseocoloradopasadena.com. ℂ **626/795-9100** or 626/795-8891. Metro Gold Line to Memorial Park.

Shopping A to Z
ANTIQUES & COLLECTIBLES

Modernica ★   Expensive home furnishing showrooms line Beverly Boulevard now, but this is the shop that started it all. You can still find vintage pieces, but Modernica is now best-known for the authentic—and more affordable—replicas it designs, such as Eames storage units and fiberglass chairs. 7366 Beverly Blvd. www.modernica.net. ℂ **323/933-0383.**

Obsolete ★★★   Anything but obsolete, this is one of the hippest antiques stores in the L.A. area or anywhere else. Inventory is always changing, but collectibles may range from antique carnival curios to 1920s Westinghouse pendant lamps to a19th-century anatomical chart from Belgium. 222 Main St. (near Rose Ave.) Venice. www.obsolete inc.com. ✆ **310/399-0024.**

Off the Wall ★★   There's nothing musty about this iconoclastic antique shop, which has helped create the interiors of the Hard Rock Cafe and Planet Hollywood. Its range encompasses the 20th century, but its strength is the Art Deco era, from curvy couches to neon bar signs, to Wurlitzers and pinball machines. Inventory is dominated by furnishings but includes folk art, clothing and jewelry. Most prices are well into four figures, but eagle-eyed shoppers will spot some small items for less than $100. 737 N. La Cienega Blvd. (at Sherwood), West Hollywood. www.offthewallantiques.com. ✆ **310/652-1185.**

ART

Bergamot Station ★★★   This lively arts complex, anchored by the **Santa Monica Museum of Art** (p. 82), housing more than 40 galleries (nearly double what it had in 2012), celebrated its 20th anniversary in 2014. The wide variety of styles and media include some mediocre and even dreadful art, but also some brilliant and innovative work. The **Rosamund Felsen Gallery** (rosamundfelsen.com; ✆ **310/828-8488**) is known for its shows of local contemporary artists, while the **Gallery of Functional Art** (www.galleryoffunctionalart.net; ✆ **310/829-6990**) displays one-of-a-kind and limited-edition furniture, lighting, and fixtures, as well as jewelry, ceramics, and other smaller items. Most galleries are closed Monday. 2525 Michigan Ave. (east of Cloverfield Blvd.), Santa Monica. www.bergamotstation.com. ✆ **310/453-7535.**

Soap Plant/Wacko/La Luz de Jesus Art Gallery ★★   This is so typical of Los Feliz: The wacky (just look at the name) and eclectic three-in-one business with candles, art books, Japanese robots, soap, and lava lamps for sale also includes owner Billy Shire's groundbreaking gallery, whose devotion to post-pop underground art earned him the moniker, "The Peggy Guggenheim of Lowbrow." Narrative paintings and unusual sculpture are the gallery's mainstay. 4633 Hollywood Blvd. (west of Hillhurst Ave.), Los Angeles. www.laluzdejesus.com. ✆ **323/666-7667.**

BOOKS

Barnes & Noble ★★★   A highlight of The Grove, this massive, three-story bookstore will carry every book you've ever wanted to read, and the books your aunt and daughter are pining after, too. Its size and long hours (9am–11pm daily) are its strengths, and if you need to take a break from browsing, there's a Starbucks onsite. 189 Grove Dr K30, Hollywood. www.barnesandnoble.com. ✆ **323/525-0270.** Parking in The Grove parking structure (enter on The Grove Drive or off Fairfax Ave.) or the Farmers Market parking lot.

Book Soup ★★★   This Sunset Strip landmark is L.A.'s best indie bookshop, with a thoughtfully curated selection of more than 60,000 mainstream and small-press titles on topics from show business to political screeds to high-minded literature. Staff picks are excellent, as are the book signings and readings. The shop also has an extensive old-fashioned newsstand. 8818 Sunset Blvd. (btw. Palm and Larabee), West Hollywood. www. booksoup.com. ✆ **310/659-3110.**

Distant Lands ★★   A combination travel accessory shop and bookstore, Distant Lands is a family-run institution with an expert staff who are always happy to tell you where to go. 20 S. Raymond Ave., Pasadena. www.distantlands.com. ✆ **646/449-3220.**

Traveler's Bookcase ★★★   Besides the vast selection of guidebooks, travel literature, international cookbooks and other destination-themed titles, you'll find globes, maps, antique travel posters and other accessories at this shop and reading room, which ranks among the best travel bookstores in the West. Prominent travel writers make regular appearances. 8375 W. 3rd St. (btw. S. Orlando and S. Kings), Los Angeles. www.travel books.com. ✆ **323/655-0575.**

Vroman's Bookstore ★★   A Pasadena institution since 1894, this is Southern California's oldest and largest independent bookstore, run by the great-grandson of its second owner. The cavernous, two-level space is clean, up to date, and well-organized; among the superstore authors who have appeared at its renowned author events are President Clinton, Irving Stone, Upton Sinclair, Ray Bradbury, Salman Rushdie, Joan Didion, and Anne Rice. The Pen and Stationery Department sells Montblanc and other fine pens, cards and stationery that scream "Gift!" 695 E. Colorado Blvd. (btw. Oak Knoll and El Molino aves.), Pasadena. www.vromansbookstore.com. ✆ **626/449-5320.** Metro Gold Line to Lake.

MUSIC

Amoeba Music ★★   This branch of the iconic Berkeley store is panacea to music junkies, in large part because of its knowledgeable staff. The huge assortment of music and movies goes well beyond the mainstream; it's unlikely you can think of any music (or movie) they don't have. Genres range from underground rock and electronica to jazz and classical. Amoeba also has the largest selection of vinyl on the planet—even 78s—and can sell you a turntable to play them on. It's also a trove of vintage and current concert and movie posters. 6400 Sunset Blvd. (at Ivar), Los Angeles. www.amoebamusic. com. ✆ **323/245-6400.** Metro Red Line to Hollywood/Vine.

Rockaway Records ★   It makes sense that Silver Lake, which many alternative bands call home, would have a trove of cutting-edge music stores. While this neighborhood mainstay is full of used CDs, collectible disks, vinyl, and new releases, they excel at weird and rare and priced to sell. 2395 Glendale Blvd. (south of Silver Lake Blvd.), Silver Lake. www.rockaway.com. ✆ **323/664-3232.**

CLOTHING & SHOES

Fred Segal ★★   Looking like cubes wearing an ivy buzz cut, this is not a store but a compound of breezy individual boutiques with their own specialties: Fred Segal Baggage; Fred Segal Feet; Apothia beauty products; Ron Herman (trendy sportswear); Ron Robinson (hard-to-find international and L.A. labels, and home and gift items); and the Fred Segal shop (men's organic cotton sportswear). Starting in 1960 as a small jeans shop, the brand has evolved into an L.A. powerhouse. It has appeared in movies and TV shows such as "Clueless," "Less Than Zero," and "The Closer," and its name has been dropped in many more. Celebrities stream through on a regular basis. Prices tend toward heights only a movie star could pay, but more affordable items are scattered throughout the shops. A second complex is located in Santa Monica. 8118 Melrose Ave. (at Crescent Heights), West Hollywood. www.fredsegal.com. ✆ **323/655-3734.** Also: 500 Broadway (at 5th St.), Santa Monica. ✆ **310/394-8509.**

Kitson's ★★   To my eye, Kitson's flagship store (it has branches all over L.A.), looks like an old, freshly repainted Thrifty drugstore, but make no mistake—this is a trend-obsessed boutique adored by young women all over the Southland. Its greatest asset is a staff that knows the merchandise and can visualize how it will look on you. Another virtue is a wide range of prices; no one need leave empty-handed. Women's fashion is the big ticket, but Kitson's also sells men's and children's wear, gifts, books and beauty products. 115 S. Robertson Blvd. www.shopkitson.com. ✆ **310/859-2652.**

HOME DESIGN & HOUSEWARES

Liz's Antique Hardware ★ Visitors in search of doorknobs or a drawer pulls for a home built in another era have high odds of success here. The place is stuffed to the rafters with knobs, latches, finials, and sconces from the past century—just about any home hardware you can think of, as long as you're willing to sift through bags and crates. Recent finds have included perfect sets of Bakelite drawer pulls and antique ceramic bathroom fixtures. 453 S. La Brea Ave. www.lahardware.com. ✆ **323/939-4403.**

Rachel Ashwell Shabby Chic Couture ★★ The formula of impeccably made custom slipcovered furniture and hand-picked vintage accessories has been widely imitated, but this original (since 1989) is still going strong. It also sells tableware, lighting, and fabric by the yeard, but what most customers love it for is their cloud-soft bedding. 1013 Montana Ave. (btw. 10th and 11th sts.), Santa Monica. www.shabbychic.com. ✆ **310/394-1975.**

JUST FOR KIDS

Oilily ★ This Dutch fashion house, which turned 50 in 2013, started as a reaction to children's clothing that was just a scaled-down versionof adult fashions. Its Crayola colors, playful florals and multicultural designs won over celebrity moms and dads such as John Travolta, Madonna, and Michael Jackson; now kids all over town sport the colorful duds. Once exclusively for kids, the store has added mom's fashions, cosmetics, and even bikes and strollers. 9520 Brighton Way (at Rodeo), Beverly Hills. www.oilily-world.com ✆ **310/859-9145.**

Puzzle Zoo ★★★ The original location of what is now a regional chain started out selling only puzzles, began adding toys (Mighty Morphin' Power Rangers were the first addition) and is now packed with puzzles, board games, toys, science kits, brain-teasers and coveted Marvel Comics action figures. Prices are higher than Walmart, but many these items just aren't available anywhere else. 1411 Third Street Promenade, Santa Monica. www.toyzoo.com. ✆ **310/393-9201.**

VINTAGE & CONSIGNMENT CLOTHING

Golyester ★★ Fashions and fabrics from the turn of the 20th century through the '80s are in mint condition here, and prices reflect that—this is not the place to grab a cheap used prom dress that will have wine stains by the end of the night. Vintage lingerie, embroidered sweaters, Joan Crawford-style suits, beaded 1920s drop-waist dresses, and an unusually robust selection of shoes are all well organized. You'll also find more men's clothes than at most vintage shops. 450 S. La Brea Ave. (at W. 6th), Los Angeles. www.golyester.com. ✆ **323/931-1339.**

Re-Mix They do make 'em like they used to here: This shop sells not only vintage (1920s–70s) shoes but new reproductions of popular styles (classic pinup-girl heels, Hollywood stilettos, spectator pumps, wedgies . . .). The smaller men's selection includes wingtips, penny loafers, white bucks, and blue suede shoes. They are very well made from soft, comfortable leather, and prices are surprisingly reasonable. 7607 Beverly Blvd. (east of Fairfax, btw. N. Stanley and N. Curson), Los Angeles. www.remixvintageshoes.com. ✆ **323/936-6210.**

SPECIALTY

Hustler Hollywood ★ Forget for a moment that the owner, Theresa Flynt, is the daughter of Hustler Magazine's Larry Flynt; her erotica store, the largest in the country, has not a whit of the raunchiness associated with dad's magazine. Adult toys and movies—along with clothing, jewelry, candles, and other home products—are artfully displayed in a tasteful boutique shop flooded with light from floor-to-ceiling windows. This shop has expanded to 13 shops nationwide since it opened here in 1998. 8920 Sunset Blvd. (at Hilldale), West Hollywood. www.hustlerhollywood.com. ℂ **310/860-9009.**

ENTERTAINMENT & NIGHTLIFE

It might not be the city that never sleeps, but as the center of the entertainment industry, Los Angeles boasts an ever-growing number of 24-hour and after-midnight eateries catering to night-crawlers who take advantage of the most plentiful live music, club, performing arts, and (of course) movie offerings this side of New York. Countless major events featuring national and international acts are on tap every day, but you do need to plan ahead and snag tickets well in advance.

Performing Arts

CLASSICAL MUSIC & OPERA

While best known for pop culture, L.A. also hosts top-flight orchestras and an opera company on the rise. The world-class **Los Angeles Philharmonic** (www.laphil.org; ℂ **323/850-2000**), got a huge boost with the opening of the **Walt Disney Concert Hall** (p. 101), which celebrated its 10th anniversary in Sept. 2013. Acclaimed conductor **Gustavo Dudamel** became the Philharmonic's music director in 2009. Tickets are scarce when celebrities like Itzhak Perlman, Emanuel Ax, and Yo-Yo Ma are in town. The Philharmonic plays a summer season at the **Hollywood Bowl** (see "Concerts Under the Stars," below).

A plan OF ATTACK

To find out what's going on during your stay, check **L.A. Weekly** (www.laweekly. com) or **TimeOut Los Angeles** (www. timeout.com/los-angeles). The nonprofit **LA Stage Alliance** (www.lastagealliance. com; ℂ **213/614-0556**) keeps an up-to-date list of stage productions. To find a specific performer, **Ticketmaster** (www. ticketmaster.com; ℂ **800/745-3000**) and concert trade publication **Pollstar** (www. pollstar.com) have tour itineraries. L.A.'s **tourism bureau** lists events at www. discoverlosangeles.com/what-to-do/ events, and **Los Angeles Magazine** (www. lamag.com/theguide/listings.aspx), runs selected listings for the current month.

To avoid surcharges, try to get tickets directly from the venue. Plan B: Try **Stub-Hub** (www.stubhub.com; ℂ **866/788-2482**) or **Prestige Tickets** (www. prestigetickets.com; ℂ **888/595-6260**). Both companies broker sales between buyers and sellers, usually at an average markup of 25% (spiking dramatically for big events). The difference is that Stub-Hub's quoted ticket prices include service charges, and it offers a guarantee to protect buyers against invalid tickets and other mishaps. Ticketmaster, a distant Plan C, buys blocks of tickets and then resells them; close to half the ticket price goes to service charges.

The **LA Stage Alliance** (above) offers half-price tickets to more than 100 venues online (www.lastagetix.com); the only catch is that you have to take whatever seats the theater assigns you.

Tip: As a last-ditch effort, go to the box office before show time to see if last-minute tickets have become available. If not, you can try "negotiating" with locals hawking tickets on the sidewalk, but be aware that not all those tickets are legitimate.

Slowly but surely, the **Los Angeles Opera** (www.laopera.org; ✆ **213/972-8001**), performing at the **Dorothy Chandler Pavilion,** is earning respect and popularity with inventive staging of classic and modern operas, visiting divas, and the contributions of high-profile general director **Plácido Domingo.**

The **UCLA Center for the Performing Arts** (www.uclalive.org; ✆ **310/825-2101**) presents top-quality music, dance, and theatrical performances at its **Royce Hall,** often compared to New York's Carnegie Hall, as well as several off-campus theaters.

CONCERTS UNDER THE STARS

Also see "The Live Music Scene," later in this chapter.

The Greek Theatre ★★   Ensconced among the trees in Griffith Park, this 5,800-seat venue in a natural amphitheater built in 1929 repeatedly captures trade publication Pollstar Magazine's award for North America's Best Small Outdoor Venue. The 2014 lineup included Ringo Star, Goo Goo Dolls, Tori Amos, and Sara Bareilles. The natural-gas Greek Shuttle ($7; advance reservation required) also was introduced in 2014, along with off-site parking on Crystal Springs Drive, north of Los Feliz Boulevard near the I-5 freeway. 2700 N. Vermont Ave. (at Commonwealth Canyon Dr.), Los Angeles. www.greektheatrela.com. ✆ **323/665-3125.**

Hollywood Bowl ★★★   The image of the multi-arched band shell, tucked into a natural amphitheater, is synonymous with warm nights and good music. Internationally known conductors and soloists appear for classical Tuesday and Thursday nights. The summer Wednesday jazz series included Herbie Hancock, the Count Basie Orchestra and Peter Frampton with Buddy Guy in 2014. Other events included the counterculture classic "Hair," Dave Stewart presiding over the 50th anniversary celebration of the Beatles' first show here, and an Elvis Costello concert with the Philharmonic playing backup. Lease events (not produced by the Bowl) have comprised the annual Mariachi Festival and rockers OneRepublic, Bruno Mars, Soundgarden, and Kings of Leon.

Indulging in a pre-concert picnic dinner and wine is a cherished local tradition; bring your own or order from the onsite caterers, **Patina** (www.patinagroup.com/bowl; ✆ **323/850-1885**) by 4pm the day before. 2301 N. Highland Ave. (at Pat Moore Way), Hollywood. www.hollywoodbowl.org. ✆ **323/850-2000.**

THEATER
Major Theaters & Companies

The all-purpose **Music Center of Los Angeles County** houses the city's top two playhouses: the **Ahmanson Theatre** and **Mark Taper Forum.** Both are at 601 W. Temple

4

EXPLORING LOS ANGELES

Entertainment & Nightlife

St., at N. Grand, Los Angeles (www.centertheatregroup.org; © 213/628-2772). They're home to the Center Theater Group, and also host traveling productions.

Every season, the Ahmanson hosts a handful of high-profile shows, such as the Queen extravaganza "We Will Rock You." The Mark Taper Forum is a more intimate theater that hosts contemporary works by international and local playwrights, such as Neil Simon's "The Dinner Party" and Tom Stoppard's prize-winning "Arcadia."

Tip: Try to nab one of the theaters' $25 "Hot Tix" at the box office or by phone beginning three weeks before the performance. These are less desirable seats, and exact locations are not disclosed, but it's a great way to attend the theater on a tight budget.

The recently restored 1926 landmark **Orpheum Theatre,** 842 S. Broadway, at 9th Street, Los Angeles (www.laorpheum.com; © 213/749-5171) hosts theatrical productions, concerts, film festivals, and TV and movie shoots—from Judy Garland's 1933 vaudeville performance to "American Idol." The 2,000-seat theater's Mighty Wurlitzer is one of three original theater organs remaining in Southern California.

Across town, the moderate-size **Geffen Playhouse,** 10886 Le Conte Ave., east of Westwood Blvd., Westwood (www.geffenplayhouse.com; © 310/208-5454), presents drama and comedy by prominent and emerging writers. Built in 1929 as a Masonic temple, the Geffen is now owned by UCLA and attracts many acclaimed off-Broadway shows and local TV and movie actors. Jennifer Garner, William Petersen, Annette Bening, Blythe Danner, and Mel Brooks appeared in 2014.

The former Kodak Theatre, home of the Academy Awards since 2002, became the **Dolby Theatre,** 6834 Hollywood Blvd., at N. Highland, Los Angeles (www.dolby theatre.com; © 323/308-6300), after Eastman Kodak filed for bankruptcy protection in 2012. The crown jewel of the Hollywood & Highland entertainment complex hosts international performances, from Melissa Etheridge to the Moscow Stanislavsky Ballet. Guided tours are offered daily, 10:30am to 4pm.

The restored **Pantages Theatre,** 6233 Hollywood Blvd., between Vine and Argyle, Los Angeles (www.pantages-theater.com; © 323/468-1770), built in 1930, was the country's first Art Deco movie palace and site of the Academy Awards from 1949 to 1959. Recent productions include "War Horse," "Jersey Boys," and "Kinky Boots."

At the foot of the Hollywood Hills, the 1,245-seat outdoor **John Anson Ford Amphitheatre,** 2580 Cahuenga Blvd. (across Hwy. 101 from the Hollywood Bowl) Hollywood (www.fordamphitheater.org; © 323/461-3673) has a backdrop of cypress trees and chaparral. No seat is farther than 96 feet from the stage. Music, dance, film, theater, and family programs run May through September. **Ford Theatres** (www. fordtheatres.org), a cozy 87-seat indoor theater, features live music and theater year-round. It went on hiatus for the 2014–15 winter season for renovation.

Smaller Playhouses & Companies

L.A. Theatre Works, 235 Charles E Young Dr., south of Sunset Boulevard (www.latw. org; © 310/827-0808), performs simultaneously for viewers and radio audiences. Shows are held at the Skirball Cultural Center (p. 87). Richard Dreyfuss, Julia Louis-Dreyfus, Jason Robards, Annette Bening, and John Lithgow are among hundreds of actors who have worked with the company.

In the same complex as Walt Disney Concert Hall, the state-of-the-art **REDCAT,** 631 W. 2nd St. at the southwest corner of the Walt Disney Concert Hall (www.redcat. org; © 213/237-2800) presents cutting-edge performance and media arts. (The name is an acronym for the Roy and Edna Disney/CalArts Theater.)

Other companies doing interesting work include the **Colony Studio Theatre,** 555 N. 3rd St. at E. Cypress, Burbank (www.colonytheatre.org; ℂ **818/558-7000**), performing at the 276-seat Burbank Center Stage; and **East West Players,** 120 N. Judge John Aiso St., north of E. 1st Street, Los Angeles (www.eastwestplayers.org; ℂ **213/625-7000**), performing in the David Henry Hwang Theater in Little Tokyo.

Comedy

In addition to the clubs below, check out the comedy and stand-up nights at **Largo at the Coronet** (see "Mostly Rock," p. 134).

The Comedy & Magic Club ★ Best known for Jay Leno's regular Sunday night gigs, this longtime Hermosa Beach favorite also sees the likes of Jerry Seinfeld, Kevin Nealon, Jon Lovitz, and Ray Romano. And yes, the schedule does include magic acts. Don't bother coming early for dinner—the food is average and the drinks are weak. 18 and up admitted. 1018 Hermosa Ave, Hermosa Beach (btw. 10th St. and 11th Court.). www. comedyandmagicclub.com. ℂ **310/372-1193.**

The Comedy Store ★★ Established comics polish their routines and new ones develop their material at this landmark owned by Pauly Shore's mom Mitzi. If there are a few clunkers, the nightly mix here means you'll still walk away laughing. The pros play in the 350-seat **Main Room** Friday and Saturday nights, while the 150-seat **Original Room** rotates as many as a dozen acts nightly. Developing comedians work the smaller **Belly Room.** Anyone—even you—can take the stage on Monday Potluck night. 8433 Sunset Blvd. (at N. Olive), West Hollywood. www.thecomedystore.com. ℂ **323/650-6268.**

Groundlings Theater ★★★ The training ground for the likes of Melissa McCarthy, Will Ferrell, Kristen Wiig, Phil Hartman, and Lisa Kudrow, this improvisation and sketch club remains one of the funniest around after 40 years. Skits rife with ferocious satire take new improvisational twists each night. 7307 Melrose Ave. (west of N. Poinsettia), Los Angeles. www.groundlings.com. ℂ **323/934-4747.**

The Hollywood Improv ★★ If you know only one comedy club by name, this is probably it. For a place where such legends as Jay Leno and Billy Crystal might pop up without warning, it has a loose, workshop-like atmosphere. It has showcased top comics since 1975, but with a different show every night, a lot of unknowns share the bill. 8162 Melrose Ave. (btw. N. Kilkea and N. La Jolla), West Hollywood. www.hollywood.improv. com. ℂ **323/651-2583.**

Laugh Factory ★ From Rodney Dangerfield to Dave Chappelle, most every comedian you've ever heard of has been a regular here. The big names who frequently sneak onstage to try out a new routine aren't posted on the schedule; your best bet will be one of the frequent All Star Comedy shows. But the comics you've never heard of will likely be every bit as funny. The laughs will make you forget the club's cramped seating, sometimes inept management and weak drinks. 8001 Sunset Blvd. (at N. Laurel Ave.), Hollywood. www.laughfactory.com. ℂ **323/656-1336.**

Movies: Play It Again, Sam

Chain megaplexes showing the latest big studio films—you know, just like those you have at home—are plentiful in L.A., and easy to find. We're here to point you toward indie gems and classics that reside outside of the mainstream. The L.A. Weekly (www. laweekly.com) can tell you what's playing when you're in town.

Cinema at the Cemetery

It's not nearly as macabre as it might sound: Every Saturday in the summer, the **Hollywood Forever Cemetery,** 6000 Santa Monica Blvd., between Gower Street and Van Ness Avenue (www.cine spia.org), hosts screenings of movie classics, which are projected against the cemetery's massive mausoleum wall.

Guests are encouraged to arrive early for a BYOB picnic on the lush lawn. Admission is $14 per person; parking is $15 per car within the cemetery, $8 in the lot around the corner at 801 N. Gower. Bring a sweater, a flashlight, and—if you're picnicking—a trash bag.

The **American Cinematheque** in Hollywood (www.americancinematheque.com; ℂ 323/466-3456) screens rarely-seen arts films and old classics. Since relocating to the historic and beautifully refurbished 1923 **Egyptian Theatre,** 6712 Hollywood Blvd., in Hollywood, it has hosted such themed events as alien and outer space films, and cinematic variations on Orwell's "1984." Tribute events usually include audience Q-and-A sessions with the honoree. *Note:* The company presents similar programming at the **Aero Theatre,** 1328 Montana Ave., Santa Monica (ℂ 310/260-1528).

The **Leo S. Bing Theater** at the L.A. County Museum of Art (p. 93) screens classics, new releases, documentaries and retrospectives, usually in conjunction with an exhibit. "Malcom X" and "It Happened One Night " were among 2014's titles.

Other theaters worth a look include **Laemmle's Sunset 5,** 8000 Sunset Blvd., West Hollywood (www.laemmle.com; ℂ 323/848-3500), showing independent art films; The **Nuart Theatre,** 11272 Santa Monica Blvd., Los Angeles (www.landmarktheatres.com; ℂ 310/473-8530), showing classics, foreign language films, and documentaries—plus the "The Rocky Horror Picture Show" every Saturday at midnight; and the historic **Silent Movie Theatre,** 611 N. Fairfax Ave., ½ block south of Melrose, Los Angeles (www.cinefamily.org; ℂ 323/655-2520 or 655-2510), showing rare pre-sound movies the first Saturday of each month and a wide variety of films the rest of the time.

The Live Music Scene
LARGE CONCERT VENUES

The pride of Downtown and home to the Lakers and Clippers pro basketball teams is the **Staples Center,** 1111 S. Figueroa St. (www.staplescenter.com; ℂ 213/742-7340). Along with the 7,200-seat **Nokia Theatre,** part of L.A. LIVE next door at 777 Chick Hearn Court (www.nokiatheatre.com; ℂ 213/763-6030), this combination sports/event stadium is the city's primary concert venue.

The 6,000-seat outdoor **Greek Theatre** in Griffith Park, 2700 N. Vermont Ave., Los Angeles (www.greektheatrela.com; ℂ 323/665-5857), is nearly as beautiful as the Hollywood Bowl. It books a full season of national acts such as Ringo Starr, the Goo Goo Dolls and Sara Bareilles. *Tip:* Getting out of the packed lots after a show can be a painfully slow process; consider taking the shuttle.

Orange County's **Verizon Wireless Amphitheatre** (formerly Irvine Meadows), 8800 Irvine Center Dr., Irvine (www.verizonwirelessamphitheatreirvine.com; ℂ 949/855-8095), holds 16,000, including a general-admission lawn *way* in the back. It has a steady lineup of touring rock and country acts, such as 2014 Fall Out Boy and Keith Urban. Allow plenty of time to get there from L.A.; Irvine sits at one of the most country's most heavily traveled freeway junctions.

Entertainment & Nightlife

EXPLORING LOS ANGELES

A most private **PUBLIC THEATER**

For those of us who have had enough of rowdy audiences and cramped seats, **ArcLight Cinemas**, 6360 W. Sunset Blvd., between Vine and Ivar streets (www.arclightcinemas.com; ✆ **323/464-4226**), eliminates rude patrons (remember ushers?), late arrivals (forbidden), searching for seats (reserved), uncomfortable chairs (think La-Z-Boy), and neck strain (the first row is 25 ft. from the screen). And it adds themed cocktails and appetizers in a groovy lounge.

Shows are a mix of indie and Hollywood, and ticket prices aren't much higher than average: $16 adults, $12 for children and $14 for seniors, with a $4 surcharge for 3D films. Four hours of parking is free. The sound and picture quality are impeccable, and filmmakers host Q-and-A sessions. **Note:** Additional locations in Sherman Oaks (✆ **818/501-7033**), Pasadena (✆ **626/568-9651**); and El Segundo/Beach Cities (✆ **310/607-9630**).

The **Honda Center,** 2695 E. Katella Ave. (1 mi. east of I-5), Anaheim (www.hondacenter.com; ✆ **714/940-2900**), a combination sports/event stadium, is becoming another primary concert venue. It's about an hour from Los Angeles via the always-crowded I-5 freeway, but it's convenient to Disneyland-goers.

MIDSIZE CONCERT VENUES

The Avalon Hollywood ★ This 1,100-seat landmark 1927 Art Deco theater and nightclub, thoroughly renovated in May 2014, has hosted shows ranging from Frank Sinatra to Snoop Dogg in its more than 60 years. These days it's primarily a dance club, drawing EDM aficionados with ground-breaking DJs like Wolfgang Gartner. 1735 N. Vine St., Hollywood (north of Hollywood Blvd.). www.avalonhollywood.com. ✆ **323/462-8900.** DASH Hollywood to Vine St./Hollywood Blvd.

Club Nokia ★ Bad views are scarce at the smaller of Nokia's two L.A. LIVE venues, which holds 2,300, but be aware that floor seats are fold-up chairs. Flamenco guitarist Benise, electronic rockers Lucent Dossier Experience, and Dutch symphonic rockers Within Temptation mixed it up recently. 800 W. Olympic Blvd. (west of S. Figueroa), Los Angeles. www.clubnokia.com. ✆ **213/765-7000.** Metro Red Line 802 to 7th St./Metro Center.

El Rey Theatre ★★ Upstairs or down, it's mostly standing room only at this restored Art Deco relic of Hollywood's golden days. Still, with a capacity of just 1,500, you get intimate shows by a steady stream of indie bands—the likes of Lauren Mvula, Radical Something, and Superchunk—in elegant surroundings. Bathroom lines can get frightfully long. 5515 Wilshire Blvd. (west of S. Dunsmuir). www.theelrey.com. ✆ **323/936-6400.**

Hollywood Palladium ★★★ This 1940 Streamline Moderne-style Art Deco venue, which holds 4,000 and boasts one of the region's largest dance floors, has hosted a range of musical acts from Tommy Dorsey with Frank Sinatra to the Grateful Dead to Megadeath. These days, it's mostly EDM and touring indie bands such as Atmosphere and Cosmic Gate. 6215 W. Sunset Blvd. (at N. El Centro), Hollywood. www.livenation.com. ✆ **323/962-7600.** Metro Red Line 802 to Hollywood/Vine.

The Wiltern ★★ A stunning Art Deco palace, this Koreatown club presents a wide range of national and international acts such as Emmylou Harris, Lebowski Fest, Imagine Dragons, and Switchfoot, with other types of entertainment filling out the schedule. Both assigned and general seating are available. 3790 Wilshire Blvd. (at Western), Los Angeles. www.livenation.com. ℭ **213/388-1400.** Metro Purple Line 805 to Wilshire/Western.

THE CLUB SCENE

Unless otherwise noted, listed clubs admit only patrons 21 and over and have a cover charge, which could range from $5 to $40, varying with the day of week, time of night and whims of the keeper of the door.

Mostly Rock

King King ★★ This exposed-brick renovated warehouse space offers a welcome reprieve from the Hollywood see-and-be-seen mentality. The red and black decor is as unpretentious as the eclectic, easygoing crowd—you're not likely to be turned away at the door for having the wrong "look." The varied program includes electronic music dance nights, cabaret, theater and live music. 6555 Hollywood Blvd. (btw. Hudson and Whitley), Hollywood. www.kingkinghollywood.com. ℭ **323/960-5765.** Metro Red Line 802 to Hollywood/Highland.

Largo at the Coronet ★★ Open to all ages, this club's 280-seat main stage is an intimate space to see some well-known performers—the Cowboy Junkies and Jackson Browne played here in 2014, and Sarah Silverman is a regular—within a lineup of rock, cabaret, theater, comedy, and spoken word. Check the website to catch resident musician, songwriter and producer Jon Brion's awe-inspiring monthly one-man show, which involves playing numerous instruments simultaneously and composing songs on the spot from titles tossed out by the audience. 366 N. La Cienega Blvd. (1 block north of Beverly Center), Los Angeles. www.largo-la.com. ℭ **310/855-0350.**

McCabe's Guitar Shop ★★ The back room of a nondescript music shop has drawn big names ever since the '60s. A short list of established artists who have been happy to play to just 150 people includes John Lee Hooker and T-Bone Burnett. No alcohol is served, and all ages are allowed. ***Fun fact:*** Owner Bob Riskin's mother was Fay Wray. 3101 Pico Blvd. (at 31st), Santa Monica. www.mccabes.com. ℭ **310/828-4497.**

The Troubadour ★★ Elton John (in his first U.S. show), Linda Ronstadt, Buffalo Springfield, Bonnie Raitt, Van Morrison . . . acts who owe their start to this intimate club read like a Who's Who of classic rock. Lenny Bruce was infamously arrested on obscenity charges after a 1961 show, and John Lennon and Harry Nilsson were booted for heckling the Smothers Brothers in '74. Established and emerging artists still treat audiences to memorable shows; all ages admitted. 9081 Santa Monica Blvd. (east of N. Doheny), West Hollywood. www.troubadour.com. ℭ **310/276-6168.**

Villains Tavern ★★ Steampunk meets Gothic at this club by the L.A. River, on the fringe of Downtown's Arts District. Though the name, sketchy surroundings, and decor are vaguely scary, it's friendlier than the average hipster bar. Bartenders give an expert spin to inventive cocktails, and talented bands play on the patios most nights. 1356 Palmetto St. (at S. Santa Fe), Los Angeles, www.villainstavern.com. ℭ **213/613-0766.**

Whisky A Go-Go ★ Los Angeles' rock scene was born with this legendary Sunset Strip club (you can blame it for the go-go dancing craze), which jump started countless careers: Jim Morrison, The Byrds, Van Morrison, Janis Joplin, Led Zeppelin . . . the list goes on. Lately, the club has emphasized local talent. All ages admitted. 8901 Sunset Blvd. (at N. Clark), West Hollywood. www.whiskyagogo.com. ℭ **310/652-4202.**

Blues & Jazz

The Baked Potato ★★ All ages are welcome at this restaurant/club a few blocks from Universal City. The restaurant offers more than 20 variations on the lowly (but enormous) potato to fuel you through jazz concerts by talented local and visiting performers. The friendly staff is a welcome departure from the typical L.A. club, and you never know when a well-known musician such as former Police guitarist Andy Summers will stop by to jam. 3787 Cahuenga Blvd. (east of Lankershim), Studio City. www.thebakedpotato.com. © 818/980-1615. Metro Red Line 802 to Universal/Studio City.

Cafe-Club Fais Do-Do ★ The faded opulence and declining Westside location are so very New Orleans, much like its name (Cajun dialect for "dance party"). The club offers a gumbo of Cajun, Zydeco, blues, jazz, soul, rock, salsa and comedy; the only rule is that it must be a good time. The former bank building creates a memorable atmosphere, and the kitchen turns out good Cajun and soul food. 5257 W. Adams Blvd. (at S. Cloverdale), Los Angeles. www.faisdodo.com. © 323/931-4636.

Harvelles Blues Club ★ The vibe is cool, dark and sexy, in a Jazz Age kind of way, at this stalwart, which opened in 1931 and claims to be L.A.'s oldest. This is an old-school club where the audience actually listens to the music; the crowd tends toward 30 and over. You'll find a good local band here any night of the week. 1432 4th St. (south of Santa Monica Blvd.), Santa Monica. www.harvelles.com. © 310/395-1676.

Bars, Cocktail Lounges & Dance Clubs
SANTA MONICA & THE BEACHES

Circle Bar ★★ This trendy Santa Monica hang is more casual than most dance clubs—just right for students, post-grads, locals and aspiring creative types to dance the night away and meet new people. It comes by its name honestly—all the action revolves around the large circular bar. It gets jam-packed on weekends; stick to weekdays to avoid waiting in line. 2926 Main St. (south of Kinney), Santa Monica. www.thecirclebar. com. © 310/450-0508.

Library Alehouse ★★★ When chef Tom Hugenberger took over this neighborhood spot, it was all about the stellar selection of international draft beers and about two dozen bottled brews. In 2013, he unveiled new salads, a killer burger, light fare, and entrees—nothing fancy, just hyper fresh, reasonably priced food that's now in the same league with the beer. The tranquil patio feels like anywhere but Los Angeles. 2911 Main St., Santa Monica. www.libraryalehouse.com. © 310/314-4855.

O'Brien's Pub ★★ With a great range of whiskeys, spirits, and tap beer, eight large screens dishing up a wide variety of sports, and a ready supply of good food, this local favorite is the quintessential Irish pub. It's bigger than it looks from out front; beyond the restaurant, there's a stage hosting live bands most nights and a relaxing patio. The crowd tends young, but the hospitality extends to everyone. 2941 Main St. (north of Pier Ave.), Santa Monica. www.obriensonmain.com. © 310/396-4725.

out & about: THE GAY & LESBIAN SCENE

Often referred to as Boys Town, **West Hollywood** (WeHo) is the best-known gay neighborhood in Los Angeles, but **Silver Lake** has a longstanding gay community that's worked hard to preserve the area's beautiful homes. The area's last women's bar, The Palms, closed in 2013 after nearly 50 years, leaving lesbians to look for women's nights or special events at the plenitude of gay bars.

The Abbey ★★★ Gay WeHo's social nexus is a large coffeehouse/restaurant with four full bars and an open-air design conducive to lingering from morning lattes to afternoon cocktails—high-octane, 10-ounce drinks. "Hen nights" and bachelorette parties were recently banned to restore the balance between regulars and tourists. 692 N. Robertson Blvd. (at Santa Monica), West Hollywood. www.abbeyfoodandbar.com. *C* **310/289-8410.**

Akbar See "Bars & Cocktail Lounges," below.

Micky's ★★ This cavernous West Hollywood stalwart bounced back from a 2007 fire with bigger dance floors (top 40 and pop on the first floor, hip-hop and rap on the second) and a new second-story VIP bar. Legions of scantily clad boys appeal more to a younger crowd. Open until 4am on Fridays and Saturdays. 8857 Santa Monica Blvd (btw. Larrabee and N. San Vicente), West Hollywood. www.mickys.com. *C* **310/657-1176.**

Mother Lode ★ One of WeHo's friendlier, lower-key spots, this is like a gay Cheers, with warm lighting and brass accents. Cute bartenders pour strong drinks, and the pop-rock soundtrack has coordinating video. The bar boycotted Stolichnaya in 2013 to protest Russia's treatment of gays, but basically it's a live-and-let-live kind of place. In 2014, it addressed customers' one consistent complaint: It now accepts credit cards. 8944 Santa Monica Blvd. (east of N. Robertson), West Hollywood. *C* **310/659-0700.**

Rage ★ After a 20-year reign over the WeHo circuit, this high-energy, high-attitude disco undertook a facelift and acquired a new owner in May 2014. The crowd has become more diverse, with gay men, a few lesbians, and young straights who just feel like dancing. It admits 18-year-olds on Fridays but won't serve them alcohol. 8911 Santa Monica Blvd. (at N. San Vicente), West Hollywood. www.theragenightclub.com. *C* **310/652-7055.**

L.A.'S WESTSIDE & BEVERLY HILLS

Nic's Beverly Hills ★★ Whatever your preconceptions about Beverly Hills, this attitude-free place embraces the stereotype then turns it on its head. Laid-back locals partake of fancy cuisine while jazz bands, big-band trios or eclectic DJ mixes play. Vodka is the star here, and you'll find the world's best in the Vodbox, a walk-in freezer where you're swaddled in faux fur coats for flights and bottle tastings (reserve in advance). The kitchen is known for luscious, vodka-infused small plates and appetizers, though dinner is just average. Happy hour lasts all day on Mondays. 453 N. Canon Dr. (at N. Santa Monica), Beverly Hills. www.nicsbeverlyhills.com. *C* **310/550-5707.**

HOLLYWOOD

Brickyard Pub ★★★ With more than 150 varieties of bottled beer (no draft), Brickyard typically hosts young professionals playing pool (8 tables available), shuffleboard (2), darts (4), or beer pong (3). Food trucks are often out front, and the Brickyard's happy hour (7–9pm) runs later than most. 11130 Magnolia Blvd. (east of Lankershim),

North Hollywood. www.brickyardnoho.com. ℭ **818/505-0460.** Metro Red Line to North Hollywood Station.

DBA ★★   This "concept nightclub" is equal parts dance club, art gallery, and performance space intended to be reinvented every few months. Summer of 2014 brought jazz from actor Jeff Goldblum; a rock musical based on Quentin Tarantino's movies; a discussion with screenwriters adapting "Fifty Shades of Grey;" and a dance party with deep discounts for guests wearing cat faces. 7969 Santa Monica Blvd. (btw. N. Laurel and N. Hayworth), West Hollywood. www.dbahollywood.com. ℭ **855/367-7969.**

Hemingway's ★★   "Papa" would fit right in among walls piled high with books, notebooks, and typewriters, and he'd surely approve of cocktails dubbed "The Old Man and the Sea," "Death in the Afternoon"…well, you get it. This place draws quite a diverse crowd. Get here before 9pm to snag a booth or sofa when local bands take the stage (DJs are on duty other nights), and you'll find most bartenders happy to concoct a drink to suit your taste. 6356 Hollywood Blvd. (east of Cahuenga), Hollywood. www.hemingwayslounge.com. ℭ **323/469-0040.** Metro Red Line 802 to Hollywood/Vine station.

La Descarga ★★★   Dress shirts are required for men and cocktail dresses and heels are encouraged for women (though dressy blouses with dark pants are accepted) at this little slice of Old Havana. It's a rare place in L.A. that offers a cigar lounge and fully stocked rum bar, let alone burlesque-style salsa acts. Just be sure to lock down a reservation—this place gets packed, especially on the weekend. 1159 N. Western Ave. (north of Santa Monica Blvd.), Hollywood. www.ladescargala.com. ℭ **323/466-1324.**

Next Door Lounge ★★   With its secret password and doorman in top hat and spats, this well-known Hollywood lounge transports you to the shady glamour of the speakeasy age. Classic 1920s drinks and modern cocktails of mescal, absinthe, and agave nectar prevail in the energetic, brick-lined den, where jazz plays while silent black-and-white films play on a wall. Catch a burlesque show or, on Wednesdays, try whiskey flights paired with flatbread pizza. Reservations are recommended, but walk-in singles can usually find space at the bar. Dress code applies. 1154 N. Highland Ave. (north of Santa Monica), Hollywood. www.nextdoorhollywood.com. ℭ **323/465-5505.**

Original Barney's Beanery ★   Once a proud component of Route 66, this place oozes rock and roll history: a placard on frequent patron Jim Morrison's favorite barstool, the table where Janis Joplin had her last drinks (nailed to the ceiling). The reasonably priced pub grub is serviceable—Barney's is known for its chili—making this a good cheap night out. Newer Santa Monica, Westwood, and other L.A. locations are more stylish but also more ordinary. 8447 Santa Monica Blvd. (at Holloway Ave.), West Hollywood. www.barneysbeanery.com. ℭ **323/654-2287.**

Three Clubs ★★   This down-to-earth lounge, aka "Three of Clubs," is Hollywood's original martini lounge, grown into a multifaceted entertainment venue and dance club. Eschewing a flashy sign, it keeps a low profile. The dark, two-room interior offers plenty of cushy seating and two long bars. It's usually packed with young characters of all kinds, dancing, mingling and taking in live music, burlesque, karaoke, or comedy in the back room ($5 cover). A food truck is usually stationed next door. 1123 N. Vine St. (north of Santa Monica), Hollywood. www.threeclubs.com. ℭ **323/462-6441.**

DOWNTOWN

Lock & Key ★★   Only the big neon keyhole sign offers a clue to what you're in for at this small mixology bar in up-and-coming Koreatown. The fun starts in the small, dark entry with walls covered by vintage doorknobs that cleverly conceal the one that opens the door. Once you're in, there's no more messing around. Fine wines and craft beers are available, but the specialty is cocktails, such as the Razzle Dazzle (rye gin, elderflower liqueur and cucumber juice) and the popular Strawberry Mule. Try the ramen burger (you can thank me later). 239 S. Vermont Ave. (north of W. 3rd St.; entrance next to Stall 239 food window), Los Angeles. lockandkey.la. ✆ 213/389-5625.

Perch ★★★   Like the better-known Standard, Perch is a rooftop bar, but in a classier atmosphere. The French-inspired rooftop bistro overlooks Pershing Square, with panoramic views of the Downtown skyline that are worth enduring the frequent lines and pricey dining and cocktails (beer is affordable, though). Outdoor fire pits and a choice of indoor or outdoor seating create a comfortable, upscale atmosphere for friends or couples. 448 S. Hill St. (south of Lexington), Los Angeles. www.perchla.com. ✆ 213/802-1770. Metro Purple Line or Red Line to Pershing Square.

LOS FELIZ/SILVER LAKE

Akbar ★   "It's a trap!". . . No, this is not a Star Wars-themed lounge, but a congenial bar that's primarily gay while welcoming straights as well. Within a plain exterior that borders on dingy, the bartenders concocting strong cocktails behind the mirrored bar are friendly, and the dance floor in back has plenty of room. 4356 W. Sunset Blvd. (at Fountain Ave.), Silver Lake. www.akbarsilverlake.com. ✆ 323/665-6810. Metro Red Line to Vermont/Sunset Station.

Red Lion Tavern ★   This large German beer hall and restaurant, a Silver Lake fixture, may be kitschy with its dirndl-clad waitresses, but it's good fun, especially during German sporting events—it was the place to be when Germany took the 2014 World Cup. Hearty half-liters, or 1.5-liter boots, of popular German beers pair with exemplary schnitzel, bratwurst, and potato pancakes. For a change of pace, delve into the vast world of German schnapps. 2366 Glendale Blvd. (btw. Deane and Brier), Silver Lake. www.redliontavern.net. ✆ 323/662-5337.

Thirsty Crow ★   This tiny, antique-filled Silver Lake bar is named for Aesop's fable about a resourceful bird. It's dimly lit and favors dark spirits, aiming squarely at whiskey aficionados, with more than 100 to choose from. Recommended for first-timers: the signature Thirsty Crow cocktail, a blend of Old Overholt rye whiskey, maraschino, lemon, and ginger beer. 2939 W. Sunset Blvd. (north of Silver Lake), Los Angeles. www.thirstycrowbar.com. ✆ 323/661-6007.

Spectator Sports

BASEBALL   The National League **Los Angeles Dodgers** (www.dodgers.com; ✆ 866/DODGERS [363-4377]) play at the old-school Dodger Stadium, 1000 Elysian Park, near Sunset Boulevard. The **Los Angeles Angels of Anaheim** (www.laangels.com; ✆ 888/796-HALO [796-4256]) play American League ball at Anaheim Stadium, 2000 Gene Autry Way, east of S. State College Boulevard. It's about 30 minutes from Downtown L.A.; the Metrolink train makes special Angels Express runs from L.A.'s Union Station. Regular baseball season is April to October. Call or visit the team websites for ticket pricing and availability.

BASKETBALL   Los Angeles has two NBA franchises: the **L.A. Lakers** (www.lakers.com) and the **L.A. Clippers** (www.clippers.com). Both teams play in the **Staples Center** in Downtown L.A., 1111 S. Figueroa St. between W. 12th and W. 11th streets (www.staplescenter.com; ✆ 213/742-7340), October to April, followed by 2 months of playoffs. Metro Silver Line to Flower/Pico.

FOOTBALL   Lacking a major-league team, L.A. focuses its football hopes and dreams on two dominant college teams, the **UCLA Bruins** (www.uclabruins.com; ☏ **310/825-2101**) and **USC Trojans** (www.usctrojans.com; ☏ **213/740-2311**). The season runs September through November.

HORSE RACING   Set against the San Gabriel Mountains, **Santa Anita Racetrack,** 285 W. Huntington Dr., Arcadia (www.santaanita.com; ☏ **626/574-7223**), is one of the most beautiful tracks in the country. Racing runs late December through mid-April.

ICE HOCKEY   The **L.A. Kings** (www.lakings.com; ☏ **888/546-4752**) hold court at their Staples Center home (see above); in Orange County, the **Anaheim Ducks** (www.anaheimducks.com; ☏ **714/704-2400**) play at the Honda Center (p. 133). Hockey season is typically October through mid-April, followed by playoffs.

SOCCER   **Los Angeles Galaxy** (www.lagalaxy.com; ☏ **877/3-GALAXY** [877/342-5299]), best known for superstar David Beckham, plays March through November at the StubHub Center, 18400 Avalon Blvd. at E. 184th St. Carson.

SIDE TRIPS FROM LOS ANGELES

by Christine Delsol

Los Angeles may be one of the world's most stimulating cities, but don't let it monopolize you to the point of ignoring its diverse, scenic side trips—from sun-filled South Coast beach towns to the island oasis of Catalina. And, of course, Disneyland.

THE DISNEYLAND RESORT

The Disneyland Resort is the undisputed front-runner in family-friendly vacation destinations in Southern California. Often-overlooked Knott's Berry Farm (see box), a short drive away, actually hosts a better selection of high-speed roller coasters, making it hugely popular with thrill-seeking teens.

5

The Disneyland Resort

33 miles S of Los Angeles

There are newer and larger Disney parks in Florida, Tokyo, France and Hong Kong, but none has the personal stamp of Walt Disney found in the original. (Walt and Lillian even lived in an apartment above the Main Street Fire Station while the park was being built.) In 2001, Disney unveiled a sister theme park, Disney California Adventure, along with the shopping/dining/entertainment district called Downtown Disney.

ESSENTIALS

GETTING THERE   To reach Disneyland by car from LAX, take I-105 east to I-605 south, then California. 91 east to I-5 south. From Downtown Los Angeles, take I-5 south until you see signs for Disneyland. The drive from Downtown L.A. or LAX takes approximately 40 minutes in the best of all possible worlds, but double that to allow for traffic.

If Anaheim is your first—or only—destination and you want to avoid L.A., consider flying directly into **John Wayne Airport** in Santa Ana (p. 18), Orange County's largest airport. It's about 15 miles from Disneyland at the intersection of I-405 and California 55. Check to see if your hotel has a free shuttle, or call a shuttle service such as **Disneyland Resort Express** (www.coachamerica.com; ✆ **714/978-8855**); or **SuperShuttle** (www.supershuttle.com; ✆ **800/258-3826**). Major car-rental agencies operate out of John Wayne Airport; to reach Anaheim, take California 55 north to I-5 north, take the Harbor Boulevard exit and follow signs to THEME PARKS.

VISITOR INFORMATION   For show schedules, ride closures and information for the day of your visit, go to www.disneyland.com (it also has an interactive trip planner), call ✆ **714/781-4565** for automated information or ✆ **714/781-7290** to talk to a live human in Guest Relations (expect a long wait).

ADMISSION, HOURS & INFORMATION   As of press time, admission to *either* Disneyland or Disney California Adventure, including unlimited rides and all festivities and entertainment, is $96 for adults and children 10 and over, $90 for children 3 to 9, and free for children 2 and under. Parking is $17. A **1-Day Park Hopper ticket,** which allows you to go back and forth as much as you'd like, is an additional $39 per ticket. A **2-day Park Hopper ticket** is $217 for adults and children 10 and over, and $204 for children 3 to 9. Other multiday, multipark combination passes are available as well. In addition, many area accommodations offer lodging packages that include admission for one or more days. Check the Disney website, www.disneyland.com, for seasonal ticket specials.

If you're also planning to visit Universal Studios Hollywood, look into buying a **Southern California CityPass** (p. 94)—it can save you serious money. One more money-saving tip for those with friends or relatives in Southern California: Disney offers some generous discounts to local residents, especially in winter. Visit the park with someone who lives here, and you also get the discount.

To get a jump on the crowds at the ticket counters, buy tickets in advance at the Disneyland website, by calling the ticket mail-order line (✆ **714/781-4043**), at any nearby Disneyland Resort Good Neighbor Hotel (the Disney site has a list), or as part of a travel package.

Disneyland and Disney California Adventure are open every day of the year, but operating hours vary, so check **www.disneyland.com** or call ✆ **714/781-7290** before your visit. Generally speaking, the parks are open from 9 or 10am to 6 or 7pm on weekdays, fall to spring; and from 8 or 9am to midnight or 1am on weekends, holidays, and during winter, spring, or summer vacation periods. *Tip:* The parks' hours are

---

THE ART OF THE package DEAL

If you plan to spend two or more nights in Disney territory, investigate the bevy of packaged vacation options. Start by perusing the standard package offers from Disney hotel properties on www.disneyland.com. (Personalized travel planning services are also available by calling **Walt Disney Travel Co.** at ✆ **714/520-6425**). Get online price quotes for customized, date-specific packages that can include airline tickets. The packages are quite flexible, and you *do* want to customize them: On a typical featured package of four days and three nights with a four-day park ticket, you'd pay for one day (possibly two, depending on your travel plans) of park admission that you won't be able to use. After you choose your hotel, be sure to change the default ticket to the number of days you'll actually be able to use. Rates are competitive, when you factor in such perks as multiday and multipark tickets, admission an hour before the park's public opening, preferred seating at Disney shows, and discount cards. Many non-Disney hotels, even those in Los Angeles or San Diego, also offer inclusive vacation packages that include the Disney parks. Compare their deals with the Disney quotes before you decide.

a clue to what kinds of crowds Disney planners are expecting: The later they close, the more people will be there.

WHEN TO GO The Disneyland Resort is busiest in summer between Memorial Day and Labor Day, on holidays (Thanksgiving week, Christmas week, Presidents' Day weekend, and Easter week), and on weekends year-round. All other periods are considered off season. Peak hours are from noon to 5pm; visit the most popular rides (see below) before and after these hours, and you'll cut your waiting times substantially.

Another timesaving tip: Enter Disneyland from the turnstile at the Monorail Station in Downtown Disney. The line is usually shorter, and the Monorail will take you straight into Tomorrowland (but it doesn't stop in California Adventure). The Disney parks have so much to do that it's tempting to attack them systematically, starting at the entrance and working your way around the park. Here's a better idea: Arrive early and run, don't walk, to the most popular rides—the Indiana Jones Adventure, Star Tours, Big Thunder Mountain Railroad, Splash Mountain, the Haunted Mansion, and Pirates of the Caribbean, all in Disneyland; and Radiator Springs Reserve, Twilight Zone Tower of Terror, Soarin' Over California, California Screamin', Grizzly River Run, and It's Tough to Be a Bug in Disney California Adventure. Waits for these rides can last an hour or more in the middle of the day.

Disney's **FASTPASS** system can also help you minimize time waiting in line. If the ride you want has a long line, go to the automated FASTPASS ticket dispenser, pop in your park ticket and receive a free voucher with a computer-assigned boarding time later in the day. At your assigned time, enter through the FASTPASS gate and wait maybe 10 minutes. To find the ticket dispensers, check your official map/guide when you enter the park and look for the red FP symbols. *Note:* You can obtain a FASTPASS for only one attraction at a time. And you still need to arrive at the park early, because each attraction has a limited supply of FASTPASSes each day. If you arrive in the middle of the afternoon, all the FASTPASSes might be gone.

Disneyland ★★★

Disneyland is divided into eight "lands" arranged around a central hub, each of which has a number of rides and attractions that are, more or less, related to that land's theme. Pick up a free park map on the way in, or you'll probably get lost in short order.

MAIN STREET U.S.A. Main Street U.S.A., at the park's entrance, is an idealized version of a turn-of-the-20th-century small-town street inspired by Marceline, Mo., (Walt Disney's childhood home), built to ⅞ scale. The attention to detail is exquisite, from architecture to furnishings to fixtures. Basically a collection of shops and eating places, it has a city hall, a fire station, and an old-time silent cinema (forever playing "Steamboat Willie," Mickey Mouse's debut). A mixed-media attraction combines "The Walt Disney Story" with a patriotic remembrance of Abraham Lincoln. Horse-drawn trolleys, fire engines, and horseless carriages carry visitors along Main Street to the Central Plaza, the park's hub.

The main station of the **Disneyland Railroad** is here, embarking on an 18-mile tour of the park's perimeter with stops at New Orleans Square, Mickey's Toontown, and Tomorrowland. It's an easy and pleasant way to get around when your feet tire out, and there's an endlessly fascinating diorama of the Grand Canyon, prehistoric past and present, between the Tomorrowland and Main Street stations.

Because there are no major rides, it's best to tour Main Street in mid-afternoon, when lines for rides are longest, and in the evening, when the streets fill with visitors viewing Disneyland's parades and shows. Stop at the information booth to the left of the Main Entrance for a schedule of the day's events.

ADVENTURELAND ★★   This is home to one of the park's original (but updated with new technology) rides, the still-entertaining **Jungle Cruise ★,** where you board a weathered tramp steamer and "risk your life" on an amalgam of the Mekong, Congo, Nile and Amazon rivers, fending off cobras, crocodiles, hippos and headhunters as you go. Kids can also inspect **Tarzan's Treehouse,** and may enjoy the animated birds, flowers and "Tiki gods" in the tame **Enchanted Tiki Room.** But the star of Adventureland is **Indiana Jones Adventure ★★★**, based on the Steven Spielberg films. Visitors venture into the Temple of the Forbidden Eye in jouncy all-terrain vehicles, following Indy into a morass of bubbling lava pits, whizzing arrows, collapsing bridges, and the familiar rampaging boulder. It's full of surprisingly realistic thrills but not likely to be too scary for most kids.

NEW ORLEANS SQUARE   A large, grassy green dotted with gas lamps, New Orleans Square evokes the French Quarter's timeless charm, from antebellum mansions to sidewalk cafes and lakefront terraces. One of Disneyland's most popular rides, **Pirates of the Caribbean,** ★ has been updated with Captain Jack Sparrow and his cohorts, from hit the movies based on the ride, battling Davy Jones as visitors ride through mock underground caves. The venerable **Haunted Mansion** also looms over the square, and while the effects are dated, the masterful re-creation of a decaying antebellum mansion is still compelling. On a sweltering summer day, you can dine by the cool moonlight to the sound of crickets in the **Blue Bayou** restaurant (the "bayou" being the start of the Pirates of the Caribbean ride). It's the only Disney eatery that requires reservations, so stop by early in the day.

CRITTER COUNTRY   There's exactly one reason to visit this ode to the backwoods if you don't have kids: **Splash Mountain ★★**, one of the world's largest water flume rides, based very loosely on the Disney movie "Song of the South." The mountain's innards reverberate with "Zip-A-Dee-Doo-Dah," inexplicably belted out by characters no one has seen for 25 years, but the ride is exhilarating—and wet. If you do have kids, the spellbinding **Many Adventures of Winnie the Pooh** is a slow journey via "beehive" to Hundred Acre Wood, living through pitfalls and pratfalls with Pooh and the gang on a quest for "hunny." It's hugely popular and a good candidate for FASTPASS. The somewhat anachronistic **Davy Crockett's Explorer Canoes**—you row your own boat around Tom Sawyer Island—are more fun than you might think.

FRONTIERLAND   One of the few overhauls Disney undertook in 2014 was refurbishing the biggest attraction in this bucolic vision of 19th-century America: the runaway-train roller coaster **Big Thunder Mountain Railroad ★★**. Most of the work won't be visible to riders, save for a smoother, quieter ride through the bowels of a deserted gold mine. But the end sets off new sound, light, and fog effects that create a pretty convincing explosion. It's pretty mild as grown-up coasters go and could be a good transition from kiddie coasters for children who meet the 40-inch minimum. Young kids will enjoy the raft to the **Pirate's Lair at Tom Sawyer's Island,** a play area where they encounter live pirates and search for buried treasure, and the island's petting zoo and Abe Lincoln-style log cabin. Two beautifully crafted reproduction riverboats—the 19th century Mississippi paddlewheeler **Mark Twain** (being refurbished at press time) and the three-masted 18th century **Sailing Ship Columbia**—that circle Tom Sawyer's Island appeals to all ages, offering great views of Frontierland and New Orleans Square. Both suspend operations at dusk.

MICKEY'S TOONTOWN ★ The wacky world of the movie "Who Framed Roger Rabbit" inspired this trippy cartoon come to life—there's not a straight line or right angle in sight. Crawling with Disney characters at all times of day, it serves as an elaborate interactive playground where kids can run, climb, and let off steam. **Goofy's Playhouse** is whimsical and surreal, **Roger Rabbit's Car Toon Spin** manic and disjointed, and **Mickey's House & Minnie's House** make the characters more real than ever. Everything in Toontown brims such imagination that I am certain it was designed by a 5-year-old. *Tip:* Because of its popularity with families, Toontown is most crowded during the day but often deserted after dinnertime.

FANTASYLAND Storybook characters of all kinds have a home here. Of the "dark rides" that are geared toward the youngest children, the adult favorite is **Peter Pan's Flight,** with its giddy sensation of flying and visualization of London from high above. **Mr. Toad's Wild Ride** is a close second; both have been with the park since day one. You'll also find the **King Arthur Carousel, Mad Tea Party, Dumbo the Flying Elephant, Casey Jr. Circus Train, Alice in Wonderland, Snow White's Scary Adventures, Pinocchio's Daring Journey,** and more.

The best-known attraction is **It's A Small World,** a slow indoor river ride through a saccharine scenario of the world's children singing the song everybody loves to hate. It is, however, a quick way to cool off when you've had too much sun. The **Matterhorn Bobsleds,** a zippy roller coaster through the Abominable Snowman's icy mountain lair, was the park's first roller coaster and remains one of its most popular rides.

TOMORROWLAND ★ Conceived as an optimistic look at the future, Tomorrowland today has a retro-futuristic, steampunk look inspired by Jules Verne. The revamped **Space Mountain ★★**, a disorienting pitch-black indoor roller coaster. The latest evolution of **Star Tours,** ★ the original Disney-George Lucas joint venture, is a 3D version of misadventures in a Starspeeder as you and familiar Star Wars characters try to get to the Moon of Endor. The **Finding Nemo Submarine Voyage** is themed as an undersea research expedition that encounters Dory, Marlin and other characters from the movie along the way; the "subs" are just as claustrophobia-inducing as the original ride was, but it has better animation and young kids eat it up.

Other attractions include: **Buzz Lightyear Astro Blasters,** where guests pilot a Star Cruiser through a comical interactive space mission; **Captain EO,** the 17-minute interactive 3D film starring Michael Jackson in the music video to end all music videos; and **Innoventions,** a huge rotating building that recently added Captain America and a cadre of superheroes to the hands-on exhibits of technological wonders such as the futuristic, high-tech **Dream Home.** The venerable elevated **Disneyland Monorail** was a futuristic marvel when introduced in 1959; now it's basic transportation to Downtown Disney and back.

Disney California Adventure ★★

Disneyland's new sister park, unveiled in 2001 with three themed lands, completed its expansion to eight lands with the addition of Cars Land and Buena Vista Street in 2012. With the twin missions of bringing Disney and Pixar stories and characters to life and celebrating California's heritage and natural attributes, it seems less focused and harder to grasp than Disneyland. Even so, it has some terrific rides and attractions, designed with the same incomparable attention to detail that defines the original park. The entrance harks back to the old Pan Pacific Auditorium, a 1930s L.A. landmark.

A BUG'S LAND ★ This bug-themed land encompasses **It's Tough to Be a Bug ★★**, **Flik's Fun Fair,** and **Bountiful Valley Farm.** Inspired by the movie "A Bug's Life,"

It's Tough to Be a Bug uses 3D technology to lead the audience on an underground romp with bees, termites, grasshoppers, stink bugs, spiders, and a few surprises. (Little kids might find this scary.) The **Flik's Fun Fair** area features bug-themed rides and a water playground designed for little ones ages 4 to 7, but sized so their parents can ride along. **Bountiful Farm** pays tribute to California's agriculture.

BUENA VISTA STREET ★ Named after the street in Burbank where the Disney studios are located, this could have been called Art Deco street—the details are that gorgeous and true. Just as Disneyland's Main Street was modeled after Walt Disney's hometown, this is an equally idealized version of his adopted home, Los Angeles, in the 1920s and '30s. Also like Main Street, the focus is on shops and restaurants. With no rides, it won't thrill young children, but there are enough ice cream shops, popcorn wagons and a five-and-dime to stave off boredom. The Red Car Trolley (a nod to the Big Red Cars of the old Pacific Electric Railway), with singing newsboys hanging out the windows, keeps things lively.

CONDOR FLATS Condor Flats is a tribute to daring test pilots in the early days of aeronautics; inside a weathered corrugated hangar is **Soarin' Over California** ★★★, the simulated hang-glider ride that immediately rose to the top of everyone's FASTPASS list. It combines elevated seats with a spectacular IMAX-style surround-movie—riders "soar" over California's scenic lands, feeling the Malibu ocean breeze and smelling the Central Valley orange groves and Yosemite pines.

CARS LAND You need to be a fan of the "Cars" movies to truly appreciate this Route 66-themed land, with the exception of **Radiator Springs Racers,** a combination of a dark ride with an engaging story and a thrill ride acting out a perilous high-speed race through a finely detailed Sonoran desert setting (kids who meet the 40-inch height minimum will be fine). Definitely a FASTPASS ride—get them early. Beyond that, you have **Luigi's Flying Tires,** where you climb aboard a giant tire and literally float on air around a garden and tire storage yard—kind of fun, but mostly for kids—and **Mater's Junkyard Jamboree,** which has you riding in dancing tractor trailers.

GRIZZLY PEAK An instant icon, Grizzly Peak towers over the **Grizzly River Run** ★, a splashy gold-country ride through caverns, mine shafts, and water slides; it culminates with a wet plunge into a spouting geyser. Children must be 42 inches tall, and riders of any age should be prepared for a lot of spinning. Kids of all sizes can cavort nearby on the **Redwood Creek Challenge Trail,** a forest playground with smoke-jumper cable slides, net climbing, and swaying bridges.

HOLLYWOOD LAND ★★ The big attraction here is the truly scary **Twilight Zone Tower of Terror** ★★★, based on the story that an entire wing and an elevator full of people vanished from the Hollywood Tower Hotel during a violent storm on Halloween night 1939, and you're about to retrace their steps as you star in a special Disney episode of . . . "The Twilight Zone." In the eerily vacant hotel, you tour the lobby, library, and boiler room, ultimately boarding the elevator to plunge 13 stories to the fifth dimension and beyond. The sudden free-fall will be too much for most young children; I wouldn't recommend it for those under 10.

Popular shows include **Monsters, Inc. Mike & Sully to the Rescue!,** where guests ride taxis through Monstropolis on a mission to safely return "Boo" to her bedroom; and **Jim Henson's MuppetVision 3D** ★, an on-screen comedy romp featuring Kermit, Miss Piggy, and friends. At the end of the street, the replica movie palace **Hyperion Theater** presents Broadway-caliber live-action shows of classic Disney films, most recently Aladdin. All aimed squarely at young kids, of course, but the **Disney**

Animation building, a series of interactive galleries where visitors see how stories become animated features, is fun for adults as well.

PACIFIC WHARF   This food-focused land was inspired by Monterey's Cannery Row and features tours of the bread factory at **Boudin Bakery,** and wine pairings on the terrace of the **Golden Vine Winery,** and sundaes, cones and shakes made with premium chocolate at the **Ghirardelli Soda Fountain.** If you're still hungry, a phalanx of restaurants draws on California's culinary heritage.

PARADISE PIER ★★   This fantasy boardwalk recalls the glory days of the beachfront amusement parks that once lined California's coast. The highlight is **California Screamin' ★★**, a roller coaster replicating the wooden white-knucklers of the past, but on smooth state-of-the-art steel rails that catapult you from zero to 55 mph in less than 5 seconds and into a loop-de-loop over the boardwalk. Height minimum is 48 inches, and it may be too intense even for some bigger kids. **Mickey's Fun Wheel** adds unique zigzagging cars to the familiar Ferris wheel; there's no height limit, but if your little ones (or you) have sensitive stomachs, opt for the stationary cars—the barf bags aren't there for nothing. There's also **Silly Symphony Swings,** a musical wave swing ride; **Toy Story Mania,** which "shrinks" you to the size of a toy and tests your skill in 3D carnival games; and **Ariel's Undersea Adventure,** which loads you into a giant clam shell and sends you into the deep to cavort with "The Little Mermaid" cast. You'll also find all the familiar boardwalk games, corn dogs and other guilty-pleasure food, and a full-service ocean-themed restaurant.

Downtown Disney District ★

This colorful (and very sanitized) "street scene" is filled with restaurants, shops, live music venues, and entertainment for all ages. You can window-shop with kids in tow, dine at a rainforest temple, watch the big game from inside an ESPN studio, or party into the night. The promenade begins at the park gates and stretches toward the Disneyland Hotel.

Highlights include **House of Blues,** the restaurant/club that features Delta-inspired cuisine, big-name musicians, and the hand-clapping Sunday Gospel Brunch; **Ralph Brennan's Jazz Kitchen,** a spicy mix of New Orleans traditional foods and live jazz; **ESPN Zone,** the ultimate sports, dining, and entertainment experience; and **World of Disney**'s enormous range of toys, souvenirs, and collectibles. There is also an AMC Theatres 12-screen multiplex and the LEGO Imagination Center.

Where to Stay

Whether to choose a Disney hotel or nearby off-site lodging—dozens of hotels and motels line Harbor Boulevard as you approach the park entrance—is largely a matter of checks and balances. Disney hotels are expensive, but perks such as early park admission, no-hassle park entry, top-quality diversions for kids, and a discount card may be worth it. Most offsite lodging is considerably less costly, and sometimes downright cheap, and many offer free park shuttles. Some are even closer to the front entrance than Disney's hotels. When my daughter was little, we always stayed at the Disneyland Hotel so that if she had a meltdown, we could zip back to the hotel on the Monorail for a rest, and return when we were ready. Now, we stay off-site and just spend all day at the park.

EXPENSIVE

Disney's Grand Californian Hotel & Spa ★★   Grand it is, from its design to its size to its price. Authentic Arts and Crafts details, from the unique tiles to the furnishings to the period-specific artwork, are all the more impressive for being applied on such a scale. The vast lobby was inspired by national park lodges of a more gracious era, yet the hotel's bones and its service are state of the art. While not as opulent as the public areas, guest rooms are spacious and display handsome Arts and Crafts accents such as simple lines, heavy wooden headboards with tree silhouette cut-outs, and mission-style light fixtures. The varied configurations include several that are ideal for families. The best rooms overlook the park, but at a steep premium. The Grand Californian comes with a long list of amenities, but what guests will care most about is its private entrance to Disney California Adventure Park and Downtown Disney. The two main restaurants are the upscale **Napa Rose** and the **Storytellers Cafe,** a "character dining" restaurant that's always buzzing with excited kids (be sure to make a reservation). Its **Mandara Spa** offers a full array of spa services for men and women.

1600 S. Disneyland Dr., Anaheim. www.disneyland.com. ℂ **714/956-MICKEY** (956-6425) or 635-2300. 948 units. $379–$733 double; from $920 suite. Valet parking $25; self-parking $17. **Amenities:** 3 restaurants; 2 lounges; children's center; concierge; concierge-level rooms; Jacuzzi; 2 outdoor pools; room service; spa; business center; free Wi-Fi.

Disney's Paradise Pier Hotel ★   In a way, the Paradise Pier Hotel is an extension of the Paradise Pier land of the California Adventure park across the street, with its whimsical beach boardwalk theme and a water slide modeled after a classic wooden roller coaster. The ungainly building is the legacy of an older hotel that was on the property when Disney bought it for expansion. The theme is toned down in guest rooms, limited to the airy blue and green decor, a "beachball" bed pillow, a sunburst-shaped mirror, and nostalgic California artwork. It doesn't hold a candle to the Grand Californian, but may be a better choice if you're traveling with children. Family suites are comfortable for six or more people, and breakfast at the hotel's **PCH Grill** is guaranteed to be attended by Mickey Mouse and other popular Disney characters.

1717 S. Disneyland Dr., Anaheim. www.disneyland.com. ℂ **714/956-MICKEY** (956-6425) or 999-0990. 489 units. $271–$452 double; from $627 suite. Valet parking $25; Self-parking $17. **Amenities:** 2 restaurants (1 seasonal); lounge; use of Grand Californian private entrance to park; children's programs; fitness center; Jacuzzi; outdoor pool; room service; business center; free Wi-Fi.

MODERATE

The Anabella Hotel ★   Three former motels were merged and renovated to create this leafy, low-rise Spanish mission-style hotel across from Disney California Adventure Park. The resulting guest rooms vary greatly in size and layout, but they all feature contemporary decor, pillow-top mattresses, work desks, and a choice of carpeted or hardwood floors. Most bathrooms are roomy and have a combination tub and shower, and granite counters. "Kids' suites" have a queen bed, a day bed, and a bunk bed in a separate bedroom with Disney decor. It's worth spending time on a phone call to be sure you get the features you want. Parking takes up most of the grounds, but the main swimming pool and whirlpool are surrounded by a pleasant garden. A smaller pool for adults only lies next to the street-side fitness room. *Tip:* It's a 10- to 15-minute walk to the park entrance at the Grand Californian hotel. The city's ART (Anaheim Resort Transit) bus ($2; www.rideart.org) stops about every 20 minutes for the 18-minute ride to the park's main gate, if you want to save your feet.

1030 W. Katella Ave. (at S. West St.), Anaheim. www.anabellahotel.com. ℂ **800/863-4888** or 714/905-1050. 360 units. $99–$215 double. Parking $15. **Amenities:** Restaurant; lounge; concierge; exercise room; Jacuzzi; 2 outdoor heated pools (1 adults-only); room service; free Wi-Fi.

Portofino Inn & Suites ★★   Directly across from California Adventure's back side, this butter-yellow, all-suite hotel is designed for business travelers headed to the nearby convention center as well as vacationing families. You can either walk or take the ART bus to Disney's front gate. The recently updated guest rooms are sleek and stylish; standard ("deluxe") rooms have balconies or patios, and king suites have microwaves, refrigerators and coffeemakers. Kids' Suites have bunk beds, a sleeper sofa, and TV in a separate room, plus a fridge and microwave. Parking and Internet access are included in the $10 daily resort fee.

1831 S. Harbor Blvd. (at Katella), Anaheim. www.portofinoinnanaheim.com. © **800/398-3963** or 714/782-7600. 190 units. $117–$200 double; from $135 suite. Disneyland shuttle ($5 adults, $ children). **Amenities:** Exercise room; Jacuzzi; outdoor heated pool; arcade; free Wi-Fi.

INEXPENSIVE

Candy Cane Inn ★★   The secret's out about this longtime bargain-hunters go-to place, and rates have crept up to the point where it just barely qualifies as inexpensive, but it's still the best of the bunch. Flowering vines, cobblestone drives and walkways, and old-fashioned street lamps turned a former run-of-the-mill motel into a cheery, attractive inn near Disneyland's main gate. Rooms have comfortable, tasteful furniture with tropical floral-print spreads, plantation-style wood shutters, and separate dressing/vanity areas. Breakfast is served in the courtyard, which also has a heated pool, whirlpool, and kids' wading pool.

1747 S. Harbor Blvd. (at Katella), Anaheim. www.candycaneinn.net. © **800/345-7057** or 714/774-5284. 171 units. $109–$189 double. Rates include expanded continental breakfast. Free parking and Disneyland shuttle. **Amenities:** Exercise room; Jacuzzi; outdoor heated pool and wading pool; free Wi-Fi.

Where to Dine

For dining reservations at any place throughout the Disneyland Resort, go to www.disneyland.com or call © **714/781-DINE** (781-3463).

EXPENSIVE

Napa Rose ★★★ CALIFORNIAN   In Disney's Grand Californian Hotel, the first Disney restaurant that foodies could take seriously shares the warm lighting, stained glass and mission-style furnishings of the hotel's Arts-and-Crafts style. Executive Chef Andrew Sutton (formerly with Napa's Auberge du Soleil) injects a wine-country sensibility and passion for fresh ingredients that change with the seasons, such as Sierra trout, Humboldt artisan cheese, and Sonoma rabbit. Even the kids' menu is refined, while still covering the basics. A record-breaking 40-plus sommeliers tend to the impressive and balanced wine list. Outdoor seating around a rustic fire pit faces California Adventure's Grizzly Peak. *Tip:* For a more casual experience, dine in the restaurant's lounge, which offers full menu service.

> ## Healthy Snack Options
>
> Both the Disneyland and California Adventure parks offer rustic wooden **fruit stands** teeming with a variety of seasonal fresh fruit and juices that sell for a fraction of the price you'd pay for a hot dog, fries, and a Coke. Ask a Disney "Cast Member" (any employee) for the location of the nearest stand.

1600 S. Disneyland Dr. (in Disney's Grand Californian Hotel). © **714/300-7170.** www.disneyland.com. Reservations strongly recommended. Main courses $30–$45. V. Daily 5:30–10pm (last seating 9:15pm).

MODERATE

Catal Restaurant/Uva Bar & Cafe ★★ MEDITERRANEAN/TAPAS   Joachim Splichal of L.A.'s acclaimed Patina (p. 71) is behind this Spanish-inspired restaurant/ tapas bar-cafe combo in the middle of Downtown Disney. Catal, the second-floor fine-dining option, has a rustic feel but a sophisticated menu borrowing flavors from the Mediterranean and the Middle East. Seasonal dishes may include Catalan seafood stew or braised lamb shoulder with spicy red lentil curry. Uva (Spanish for "grape") Bar & Cafe, originally a simple tapas bar, expanded in 2012, adding even more Barcelona-style sidewalk tables and yellow umbrellas, breakfasts, entrees, and the "cafe" in its name. The new "street" fries with Chorizo Bilbao, melted cheese, green onions and pickled garlic are a runaway favorite, along with lamb burgers with feta cheese and piquillo peppers. ***Note:*** For a more kid-friendly Italian meal, try another Patina Group restaurant, **Naples Ristorante e Pizzeria,** at 1550 Downtown Disney Dr. (**714/ 776-6200**).

1580 Disneyland Dr. (Downtown Disney). www.patinagroup.com. ℭ **714/774-4442.** Reservations recommended Sun–Thurs, not accepted Fri–Sat for Catal; not accepted for Uva Bar. Main courses $23–$41; tapas $13–$22. Daily 8am–3pm and 5–10pm. (Catal); 8am–11pm (Uva Bar).

Ralph Brennan's Jazz Kitchen ★★ CAJUN/CREOLE   The New Orleans food dynasty responsible for the Big Easy's Commander's Palace commissioned New Orleans artists to create handcrafted furnishings for this multifaceted two-story replica of traditional French Quarter architecture, embellished with wrought-iron grillwork, cascading ferns, and stone fountains. The quick-bite Jazz Kitchen turns out classics like gumbo ya ya red beans and rice with ham and sausage, and the all-important beignet. It shares the ground floor with Flambeaux's, a casual New Orleans-style jazz club with a bead-encrusted grand piano. The elegant traditional dining rooms upstairs include an outdoor Jazz Balcony where you can dine overlooking the Downtown Disney action. Entrees range from Southern fried chicken to the unique Paneed Chicken & Grits, a Parmesan-herb crusted chicken breast with andouille sausage grits and crawfish sauce.

For Sports Lovers

Sports fans may prefer Downtown Disney's **ESPN Zone,** 1545 Disneyland Dr. (www. espnzone.com; ℭ **714/300-3776**), with more than 175 TVs showing just about every current U.S. sporting event with your American grill food and pub fare.

1590 S. Disneyland Dr. (Downtown Disney). www.rbjazzkitchen.com. ℭ **714/776-5200.** Reservations strongly recommended. Main courses $24–$35; Express items $7–$10. Mon–Thurs 11am–10pm; Fri–Sat 11am–11pm; Sun brunch 10am–10pm. Jazz Kitchen Express 8am–10pm.

INEXPENSIVE

Tortilla Jo's MEXICAN   Even if it's the 100-plus types of tequila that reel you in to this festive indoor/outdoor restaurant, you'll appreciate the variety of fresh, authentic Mexican food that appeals to both kids (mini quesadillas, tostado bowls) and adults (all the usual suspects, plus the signature Jo's Carnitas, made from citrus-braised pork, and less often seen gorditas and huaraches). The guacamole is prepared fresh at your table any way you like it, and the fresh tortillas are made by hand.

1510 Disneyland Dr. (Downtown Disney). www.patinagroup.com. ℭ **714/535-5000.** Main courses $13–$24. Sun–Thurs 11am–9pm; Fri–Sat 11am–10pm.

5

SIDE TRIPS FROM LOS ANGELES

Disneyland

knott's berry farm, FOR THE THRILL

Destined to forever be Disneyland's unappreciated stepsister, Knott's actually outdoes the Magic Kingdom in one important (and profitable) area: It attracts droves of young Southern Californians with a much wider array of scream-inducing thrill rides.

The park's roots are in land the Walter Knott family began farming in 1920. Mrs. Knott began selling pies, preserves, and home-cooked meals during the Depression, and lines became so long that Walter created an Old West ghost Town as a diversion for waiting customers. It is widely recognized as America's first theme park.

Today's Knott's Berry Farm offers no less than 165 shows, attractions and intense, state-of-the-art thrill rides but retains much of its original Old West flavor. Snoopy, Charlie Brown and friends are the park's official costumed characters. Knott's is divided into five themed areas, each featuring at least one of the roller coasters that set the park apart from Disneyland.

Old West Ghost Town The park's original attraction is a collection of authentic 19th-century buildings relocated from deserted Old West towns. The **GhostRider ★★★** is the park's single biggest attraction, one of the longest and tallest wooden coasters in the world speeding through a replica mine. **Bigfoot**

Rapids ★★ is styled as a whitewater river raging through a turn-of-the-20th-century wilderness park (you *will* get wet).The tamer **Calico Railroad ★** steam train was thoroughly refurbished in mid-2014 with new state-of-the-art animatronic characters and embellished scenery.

The Boardwalk This section is an ode to beach culture, with colorful architecture and lots of palm trees. The big gun here is the super-scary **Xcelerator ★★★**. It resembles a 1950s roller coaster, but its high-tech inner workings launch you to 83mph in just over 2 seconds, whips you straight up 20 stories and almost straight down again. The **Boomerang ★** is a corkscrew scream machine with three head-over-heels loops in less than a minute—forward first, then backward.

Camp Snoopy Six acres just for kids re-create a rustic Sierra wilderness camp that hosts Snoopy and his cohorts. It acquired six new scenes and more than a dozen Peanuts characters in summer 2014. On **Charlie Brown's Kite Flyer ★** (replacing Snoopy Bounce), you ride on the "kite" itself, soaring above winding paths and burbling streams. Several of the more than a dozen rides are designed for small children; the new **Linus Launcher ★** (replacing Charlie

LONG BEACH & THE QUEEN MARY ★

21 miles S of Downtown Los Angeles

Long Beach, California's fifth-largest city, is best known as the home of the former cruise liner Queen Mary. But while you're in the vicinity, take a detour to **Naples Island,** which calls Venice, Italy to mind.

Essentials

GETTING THERE See chapter 9 for airport and airline information. Driving from Los Angeles, take I-5 or I-405 to I-710 south, which leads to downtown Long Beach

Brown's Speedway) flings riders on a wild ride as they grip their flying blankets.

OTHER ATTRACTIONS **Fiesta Village** is a kind of south-of-the-border arcade, with markets, carnival rides (including the mild but entertaining **Jaguar! ★★** and stomach-churning **La Revolución**), a century-old merry-go-round and high-tech electronic versions of old-time carnival games. **Indian Trails** is a cultural area featuring native dance and music by costumed American and Aztec performers.

8039 Beach Blvd. (btw. La Palma and Crescent aves.), Buena Park. www.knotts.com. ✆ **714/220-5200.** The park is about 10 minutes north of Disneyland; exit south onto Beach Boulevard from I-5 or California 91. Admission (purchased online) $65 adults ($39 3-day advance), $35 ages 3–11 and 62 and older, free for children 2 and under. Parking $15. Tickets are also available at many Southern California hotels, often at a discount. Also check the website for discounts. Daily 10am–6 or 7pm, until 10 or 11pm Saturdays. Hours vary from week to week and often change with seasonal promotions, so call ahead.

Knott's Soak City Water Park
This 13-acre water park, next door to Knott's Berry Farm, takes its theme from the surf woodies and longboards of 1950s Southern California. The fun includes the **Pacific Spin,** a raft that drops riders 75 feet into a six-story funnel tube, as well as body slides, speed slides, an artificial wave lagoon, and an area for youngsters with their own pool and beach-shack fun house. Admission is $32 for ages 12 and up, $22 for ages 3–11, and free for children 2 and under; parking is $12. After 3pm, tickets for all ages are $20. Special promotions and discount coupons are often available. The park is open mid-May through early September, opening at 10am and closes between 5 and 7pm, based on the season.

WHERE TO STAY & EAT Within an easy walk of the park, **Knott's Berry Farm Resort Hotel,** 7675 Crescent Ave., at Grand Avenue (www.knottshotel.com; ✆ **866/752-2444** or 714/995-1111) offers the only lodging close to the park. Despite the name, it looks very much like a business hotel, despite its water play structure, arcade, and Peanuts-themed rooms with bedtime stories piped into the phone.

Mrs. Knott's Chicken Dinner Restaurant, 8039 Beach Blvd., near La Palma (✆ **714/220-5080**), recalls the park's origins as a roadside diner. It features Cordelia Knott's original fried-chicken dinner and her famous pie (the boysenberry is fantastic), as well as chicken pot pie, country-fried steak, pot roast, roast turkey, and pork ribs.

and the Queen Mary Seaport. Downtown Long Beach is at the eastern end of the vast Port of Los Angeles. Pine Avenue, the central restaurant and shopping street, extends south to Shoreline Park and the Aquarium. The Queen Mary is docked just across the waterway, gazing south toward tiny Long Beach marina and Naples Island.

VISITOR INFORMATION Contact the **Long Beach Area Convention & Visitors Bureau,** 301 E. Ocean Blvd, Suite 1900 (www.visitlongbeach.com; ✆ **800/452-7829** or 562/436-3645).

The Major Attractions

Aquarium of the Pacific ★ One of the country's largest aquariums, this is the cornerstone of Long Beach's ever-changing waterfront. Just across the harbor from the "Queen Mary," more than 11,000 ocean creatures, from sharks (some you can touch) to penguins to delicate sea horses and moon jellies—plus gaggles of tropical birds in Lorikeet Forest—occupy enough exhibit space to fill three football fields. The aquarium re-creates three areas of the Pacific: the warm Baja and Southern California regions, the Bering Sea and chilly northern Pacific, and faraway tropical climes, including impressive re-creations of a lagoon and barrier reef. Educational multimedia displays and hands-on activities pop up everywhere, reeling in kids and adults alike.

100 Aquarium Way (off Shoreline Dr.), Long Beach. www.aquariumofpacific.org. ✆ **562/590-3100.** Admission $29 adults, $26 seniors 62 and over, $15 children 3–11, free for kids 2 and under. Daily 9am–6pm except Christmas and Toyota Grand Prix weekend (mid-Apr). Parking $8.

Naples Island ★★ This former duck-hunting club, created from swampland in the early 1900s, is now home to some of Long Beach's priciest real estate. Walking or biking along waterways lined with Mediterranean, Craftsman and '60s-style beach homes (each with its own boat dock) is a delight, especially on evenings between Christmas and New Year's, when homeowners go all out with lights. But the best views are from the water. Numerous outlets rent kayaks and pedal boats, but for the full effect, take a gondola tour. **Gondola Getaway** (www.gondolagetawayinc.com; ✆ **562/ 433-9595**) has a fleet of custom-made boats based on authentic Venetian gondolas with adaptations for Naples Island. (Some gondoliers sing; others play taped music.) Basic hourlong tours cost $85 for two and $20 for each additional passenger up to six. I recommend embarking about an hour before sunset; the sight of the sinking sun staining the water orange as you head back to shore is a perfect way to end a day.

E. 2nd St. crosses Naples Island btw. Bay Shore Ave. and E. Marina Dr. From the Queen Mary, take Queens Hwy. toward downtown and continue as it become Queens Way, turn right on Ocean Blvd. and drive east to E. Livingston Dr., then turn right onto E. 2nd St.

The Queen Mary ★★ This Art Deco luxury liner, with staterooms paneled in now-extinct tropical hardwoods, perfectly preserved crew quarters, and miles of handrails made of once-pedestrian Bakelite, is the only survivor from an era of elegant travel. Strolling the teakwood decks or catching live jazz in the Streamline Moderne observation lounge takes you back to the ship's 1936 maiden voyage from Southampton, England. Photos and memorabilia show up everywhere, while the Glory Days Historical Tour takes you behind the scenes, dishing up anecdotes from the Queen Mary's eventful past. Rotating exhibitions, such as those on Princess Diana and Bob Hope, are available as part of certain combination tickets. The Cold War–era Soviet submarine "Scorpion" is moored alongside the ship and requires separate admission ($14 adult, $12 child), but is also included in some combination tickets. Aquarium/ Queen Mary combo tickets are also available.

1126 Queen's Hwy. (end of I-710), Long Beach. www.queenmary.com. ✆ **877/342-0738.** Basic admission $25 adults, $14 children 4–11, free for kids 3 and under; First Class Historic Passport $31 adults, $20 children, free for kids 3 and under. Themed packages, some including admission to special exhibits, are available. Daily 10am–6pm. Parking $15.

Where to Stay

Hotel Queen Mary ★★ The Queen Mary is a hotel as well as a slice of history, and it's fascinating to discover that the accommodations and amenities on the most luxurious vessel ever to sail the Atlantic are only average by today's standards. The charm is in the details, such as original bathtub faucets with "cold salt," "cold fresh," "hot salt," and "hot fresh" options, and dressers whose top drawers actually are desktops. The beautifully carved interior is a feast for the eye, and weekday rates are hard to beat. Onboard restaurants are good but overpriced, though the expansive Sunday champagne brunch served in the Grand Salon, complete with ice sculpture and harpist, provides enough atmosphere justify its price. Don't miss having a cocktail in the Art Deco Observation Bar. The shopping arcade, fittingly, has a British feel.

1126 Queen's Hwy. (end of I-710), Long Beach. www.queenmary.com. © **877/342-0742.** 365 units. $99–$189 double; from $360 suite. Many packages available. Resort fee $15 per room. Valet parking $20; self-parking $17. **Amenities:** 4 restaurants; bar; spa; Wi-Fi (included in resort fee).

Where to Dine
EXPENSIVE

The Sky Room ★★ CALIFORNIAN/FRENCH   This restored 1926 Art Deco restaurant's brilliant white interior, with its massive pillars, curvaceous ramps, glimmering brass, elevated maple-and-ebony dance floor, and classic jazz band create a sense of luxury liner, admittedly enhanced by a view of the "Queen Mary." The opulence extends to Frette linens, custom black-rimmed china, and a *"Wine Spectator"* award-winning wine list. The Californian/French menu offers a pleasing presentation of the classics—king salmon, game hen, duck breast—with bison short rib added for good measure.

40 S. Locust Ave. (at Ocean Blvd.), Long Beach. www.theskyroom.com. © **562/983-2703.** Reservations recommended. Main courses $27–$47. Mon 5:30–9pm; Tue–Thurs 5:30–9pm; Fri–Sat 5:30–10pm; Sun 4:30–9pm. Valet parking $7.

MODERATE

Yard House ★ AMERICAN ECLECTIC   In addition to being one of Long Beach's best outdoor dining venues, the Yard House features one of the world's largest selections of draft beers; all 1,000 gallons are visible through a glass door as they make their way through nylon tubes to dozens of taps at the oval bar. The name comes from the early colonial tradition of serving beer in 36-inch-tall glasses, or yards, to weary stagecoach drivers. Customers can order yards, half-yards or traditional pint glasses. in addition to a wide range of sandwiches, burgers, pizza, chicken, steaks and seafood. The many appetizers—fried calamari, jerk wings, blue crab cakes, sushi rolls, lettuce wraps and sliders—cry out to be matched up for a tapas-style meal. Try to get a table on the deck overlooking the harbor on a sunny day.

401 Shoreline Village Dr., Long Beach. www.yardhouse.com. © **562/628-0455.** Main courses $12–$34. Sun–Thurs 11am–midnight; Fri–Sat 11am–2am.

THE SOUTH COAST ★★★

Huntington Beach, 36 miles S of Los Angeles; Newport Beach, 44 miles; Dana Point, 59 miles

In stark contrast with Orange County's inland industrial parks and cookie-cutter housing tracts, this 42-mile coast is a dazzling stretch of beguiling seaside towns, pristine beaches, ecological preserves, secluded coves, picturesque harbors, and legendary surf breaks. You could cruise this coast, which inspires comparisons to the French Riviera or Costa del Sol, on a day trip from L.A. But who wants to end a pleasant day at the beach snarled in traffic on the way back? My advice is to take a day or two to relax and enjoy the area.

Essentials

GETTING THERE   You'll most likely be exploring the coast by car, so I've organized beach communities in order from north to south, featuring my favorites for their character and natural beauty. From Los Angeles, take I-5 or I-405 south. The

South Coast

Balboa Pavilion **8**	International Surfing Museum **4**
Bolsa Chica Ecological Reserve **3**	Knott's Berry Farm **1**
Dana Point **9**	Mission San Juan Capistrano **6**
Disneyland Resort **2**	South Coast Plaza **5**
Fashion Island Newport Beach **7**	

shore-hugging Pacific Coast Highway (Hwy. 1, or PCH) links many Orange Coast communities and is a gorgeous, if somewhat time-consuming drive. To reach the beaches directly, take the following freeway exits: **Huntington Beach,** Beach Boulevard/Hwy. 39 from I-405 or I-5; **Newport Beach,** Hwy. 55 from I-405 or I-5; **Laguna Beach,** Hwy. 133 from I-5; **San Juan Capistrano,** Ortega Highway/Hwy. 74 from I-5; **Dana Point,** Hwy. 1 from I-5.; and **San Clemente** from I-5. You can also reach San Juan Capistrano and San Clemente by train on the Amtrak (www.amtrak.com; © **800/ 872-7245**) route running between L.A. and San Diego.

VISITOR INFORMATION   For information on all the coastal areas check the **Orange County Visitor Center**'s website at www.visittheoc.com. **Huntington Beach** has a visitor info kiosk at the base of the Huntington Pier at 325 Pacific Coast Highway (surfcityusa.com). **Newport Beach** has tourism information at www.visitnewport beach.com. The Visitor Center for **Laguna Beach** is located at 381 Forest Ave. (www. visitlagunabeach.com). For **San Juan Capistrano** check www.sanjuancapistrano.org, and for **Dana Point** www.danapointbeach.com.

Huntington Beach ★★

Huntington Beach claims the moniker Surf City; Hawaiian-born George Freeth is credited with bringing the sport here in 1907, and some say the breaks around the pier and Bolsa Chica are the best in California. The world's top wave riders flock to Huntington every August for the rowdy but professional **U.S. Open of Surfing.** Nostalgic Gidgets and Moondoggies shouldn't miss the **International Surfing Museum,** 411 Olive Ave. (www.surfingmuseum.org; © **714/960-3483**), with gargantuan longboards from the early days, memorabilia of surfing greats represented on the Walk of Fame near Huntington Pier, and a gift shop where a copy of the "Surfin'ary" can help you bone up on surfer slang.

Huntington City Beach, adjacent to Huntington Pier, is a haven for volleyball players and surfers; dense crowds abound, but so do amenities such as outdoor showers, beach rentals, and restrooms. Just south of the city beach is 3-mile-long **Huntington State Beach.** Both have lifeguards and concession stands seasonally; the state beach also has restrooms and showers. The main entrance is on Beach Boulevard, with access points all along Pacific Coast Highway (Hwy 1). The **Bolsa Chica Ecological Reserve** (www.bolsachica.org; © **714/846-1114**) is a 900-acre restored urban salt marsh that harbors more than 200 bird species and a wide variety of protected plants and animals. An easy 1.5-mile loop trail begins from a parking lot on Pacific Coast Highway a mile south of Warner Boulevard; docents lead a narrated walk the first Saturday of every month.

Newport Beach ★★

Orange County's classy, wealthy side is juxtaposed with a laid-back SoCal beach attitude in Newport Beach. The main beach area runs along the **Balboa Peninsula** about 5 miles along the narrow, often clogged Newport Beach Boulevard, which becomes West Balboa Boulevard. Several beach areas have facilities. The peninsula's **Balboa Pavilion & Fun Zone,** 400 Main St. (www.balboapavilion.com; © **800/830-7744**), includes a vintage boardwalk and historic cupola-topped structure built in 1906 as a bathhouse for swimmers in ankle-length bathing costumes. Now it's the terminal for Catalina Island passenger service, harbor and whale-watching cruises, and fishing charters. The **Balboa Fun Zone** boardwalk (www.thebalboafunzone.com; © **949/673-0408**) is a collection of carnival rides, games, and food stands.

Man-made **Balboa Island** (www.balboaisland.com), one of Newport Beach's main attractions, is reached by ferry from Balboa Peninsula (www.balboaislandferry.com) and by car on Jamboree Road. Million-dollar clapboard cottages in the island's center, and modern houses with two-story windows and private docks along the perimeter, make a colorful, romantic sight. Shops and cafes lining **Marine Avenue,** the main commercial street, evoke a New England fishing village. Elegant inland shopping malls such as **Fashion Island** and **South Coast Plaza** draw fashionable socialites, celebrities, and dedicated shoppers. The area is filled with gourmet and theme restaurants, and take out fast food joints; moderate and expensive hotels line Hwy. 1.

WHERE TO STAY
Expensive
Pelican Hill Resort ★★   The truly wealthy retreat to this resort's bungalows and villas tricked out with luxe furnishings, marble bathrooms, private patios, and all the comforts that come with the price tag. The two championship golf courses were designed by the celebrated Tom Fazio, the 23,000-square-foot spa provides a blissful escape, and the Coliseum pool with more than a million hand-laid glass tiles is dazzling. The Northern Italian Andrea restaurant is one of the best on the South Coast.

22701 Pelican Hill Rd. www.pelicanhill.com. ℭ **800/315-8214** or 949/467-6800. 204 bungalows, 128 villas. $395–$495 double bungalow; from $845 suite; from $525 villa. Complimentary valet parking. **Amenities:** 5 restaurants; children's programs; concierge; fitness facilities and spa; 2 championship golf courses; 3 pools; free Wi-Fi.

Inexpensive
Newport Channel Inn ★★   For the price, this small motel, a block from the beach, hits all the right marks, and more. Clean, comfy rooms are carpeted to reduce noise and a dining-size table with chairs, microwave, small fridge, coffeemaker, and powerful showers. The beds are cozy, the pillows a step above the norm, and the staff accommodating and friendly. Go for a second story room to avoid parking and street noise. Though it's on the highway, you just have to cross the street and walk a short path to beach. Reserve well in advance during holidays and summer. *Tip:* **Cappy's Cafe,** one of Newport's best breakfast places, is next door at 5930 West Coast Hwy. (www.cappyscafe.com; ℭ **949/646-0202**).

6030 W. Coast Hwy. www.newportchannelinn.com. ℭ **800/255-8614** or 949/642-3030. 30 units. $80–$139. Free Parking. **Amenities:** Free Wi-Fi.

WHERE TO DINE
Moderate
Crab Cooker SEAFOOD **★★**   Folks in search of fresh, well-prepared seafood have headed to this bright-red former bank building since 1951. As you enter, check out the catch of the day at the fish market by the front door. As befits a beach landmark, the vibe is super casual, with humble wooden tables, uncomplicated smoked and grilled preparations, and meticulously selected fresh fare. Lobster and crab dishes are pricey, but other generous choices, including side dishes, are reasonably priced.

2200 Newport Blvd., Newport Beach. www.crabcooker.com. ℭ **949/673-0100.** Main courses $12–$20. Sun–Thurs 10am–9pm; Fri–Sat 11am–10pm.

Laguna Beach ★★★
Breathtakingly beautiful elevated headlands, coastal bluffs, pocket coves, and a very inviting beach make **Laguna Beach** a haven for artists and other creative types. Artists in the original colony created plein-air Impressionist paintings in early 1900s, and art

remains one of the Laguna's main attractions. The annual **Festival of Arts & Pageant of the Masters** (see box) draws thousands annually. The **Laguna Art Museum,** 307 Cliff Dr. (www.lagunaartmuseum.org; ℂ **949/494-8971**) is the community's artistic cornerstone. In addition to a small but intriguing permanent collection, the museum's special exhibitions of works by regional artists are definitely worth a detour. Past examples include a display of surf photography from the coast's 1930s and '40s golden era, and dozens of plein-air paintings. In addition to its abundant natural beauty, much of the town's appeal lies in the proliferation of art galleries mingling with high-priced boutiques. In warm weather, Laguna Beach's Mediterranean island ambience can make you forget which continent you're on.

Life Imitates Art

A tradition for more than seven decades in arts-friendly Laguna, the **Festival of Arts & Pageant of the Masters** is held every summer throughout July and August. The oddly fascinating pageant consists of costumed people posing to exactly re-create famous paintings. Order tickets well in advance at www. foapom.com.

Crystal Cove State Park (www.crystalcovestatepark.com; ℂ **949/494-3539**), which stretches 3 coastal miles between Corona del Mar and Laguna Beach to the south, beckons seekers of solitude. The winding, sandy strip of beach is backed with grassy terraces, and the entire area offshore is an underwater nature preserve. An enclave of vintage, rustic beach cottages from the 1930's and '40s are clustered in the **Crystal Cove Historic District,** (www.crystalcovebeachcottages.org) which preserves a coastal lifestyle lost to modern development. Some cottages are available for nightly rental, while others are being refurbished. Contact Reserve America (www.reserve america.com; ℂ **800/444-7275**).

WHERE TO STAY
Expensive

Montage Resort & Spa ★★★   This 30-acre Arts and Crafts beauty is all about style. The neo-Craftsman-style guest rooms are spacious, immaculate, and tastefully decorated with museum-quality plein-air artwork, huge marble bathrooms with over-size tubs, feather-top beds with goose-down pillows, and balconies. Distractions include swimming pools, tide pools at the beach, manicured park areas, an oceanfront spa, and the signature restaurant, **Studio.**

30801 S. Coast Hwy (btw. Shreve and Wesley drives). www.montagelagunabeach.com. ℂ **866/271-6953** or 949/715-6000. 248 units. $895–$1,100 double; from $2,190 suite. Valet parking $36. **Amenities:** 3 restaurants; spa; pool and kiddie pool; Wi-Fi ($16 per day).

Surf and Sand Resort ★★   The nine-story Surf and Sand Resort has come a long way since it started in 1948 as a beachside motel. Still occupying the same fantastic location smack on the sand, it now features 167 guest rooms that, despite their simplicity and standard size, feel enormously decadent. They're all very bright and beachy; each has a private balcony with a dreamy ocean view, a marble bathroom accented handsomely with granite, and earplugs for anyone disturbed by the surf's. There's a spa and restaurant, and the hotel is within easy walking distance of Laguna's commercial core. *Tip:* Try getting one of the deluxe corner rooms, with an expanded 90-degree view of the California coastline.

1555 S. Coast Hwy. (btw. Calliope St. and Bluebird Canyon Dr.). www.surfandsandresort.com. ℂ **877/741-5908** or 949/497-4477. 167 units. $460–$560 double; from $645 suite. **Amenities:** Restaurant; bar; pool; spa; free Wi-Fi.

The Ramos House Café

If you're anywhere near San Juan Capistrano early in the day, have a bite at the **Ramos House Cafe** (www.ramoshouse. com; ℰ **949/443-1342**), in a little old house on California's oldest residential street, in the historic Los Rios district. The Southern-influenced menu changes daily, and everything is made from scratch (even the ice cream is turned by hand). Its bloody marys are legendary. The cafe, near the train depot at 31752 Los Rios St., is open for breakfast and lunch Tuesday through Sunday from 8:30am to 3pm; $40 brunch only Saturday and Sunday.

San Juan Capistrano & Dana Point ★★

San Juan Capistrano is defined by its Spanish mission and loyal swallows. The **Mission San Juan Capistrano,** 26801 Ortega Hwy./Hwy. 74 (www.missionsjc.com; ℰ **949/234-1300**), dominates the town center with its adobe walls enclosing an Old World courtyard with gardens and fountains and a mix of old ruins, working buildings, and an intimate mission chapel still used for religious services. The mission doubles as a community center, hosting concerts and cultural events year-round. Beyond town, it's known primarily for the **swallows** said to return to nest every March. In reality, you'll probably see the well-fed birds here all the time, with fewer and fewer leaving and returning in the spring.

Dana Point is a picturesque boating community with a yacht-filled harbor and million-dollar homes hidden on bluffs. Bordering the harbor is **Doheny State Beach,** with a seaside park where tree-shaded lawns give way to the mile-long beach. With some tent sites a few steps from the sand, stellar surf breaks, and tide pools, it offers some of the best beach camping to be found in California. For info and camping availability, call ℰ **949/496-6172.**

San Clemente ★★

Conveniently located right off I-5 at the south end of the Orange Coast and near the north end of San Diego County, San Clemente is often overshadowed by its more glamorous neighbors. But its coastline is lovely, with 20 acres of beach, a long fishing pier jutting over the ocean with a sweet little park above, and classic SoCal coastal Spanish-style architecture, with red tile roofs above simple white buildings. The surf scene is legendary—even the pros are willing to hike a mile-long trail to reach the famed surf break called **Trestles.**

WHERE TO STAY

Inexpensive

Beachcomber Inn ★ It's hard to find a room by the beach at this price, especially one with a full, albeit small, kitchen and pretty cottage decor. Rooms, which were starting to look a bit shabby, got a complete makeover in 2014. They lack air-conditioning, but ceiling fans stir the ocean breezes. The Spanish Revival building, sitting on a bluff above the beach just south of the pier, feels like a private estate with barbecue grills, a firepit, and Adirondack chairs overlooking the sea. The neighborhood has plenty of dining options. There's one drawback—Amtrak trains run right below the bluff. Bring earplugs and think of the train whistle as part of the town's charm.

533 Avenida Victoria. www.thebeachcomberinn.com. ℰ **949/492-5457.** 12 rooms. $135–$160 double. **Amenities:** Free Wi-Fi.

SANTA CATALINA ISLAND ★★

A dose of Santa Catalina Island's clean air, crystal-clear water, and blissful absence of cars can fool you into thinking that you're a continent away from city hustle and bustle, even though you're only 22 miles off the Southern California coast and *still* in L.A. County. There's plenty of room to fish, swim, sail, scuba, and snorkel, plus miles of hiking and biking trails.

Chewing-gum magnate William Wrigley, Jr. bought the remote, unspoiled island in 1919, planning to develop a fashionable pleasure resort. To promote the new vacation-land, Wrigley brought big-name bands to the Avalon Ballroom and moved his Chicago Cubs to the island for spring training. Soon Catalina was a world-renowned playground, luring such celebrities as Laurel and Hardy, Cecil B. DeMille, John Wayne, and even Winston Churchill.

In 1975 the Santa Catalina Island Conservancy—a nonprofit organized to preserve and protect the island's natural habitat—acquired about 88% of Catalina Island, protecting virtually all of the hilly acreage and rugged coastline that make up what is known as the interior; some of the most spec-tacular areas can be reached only by organized tour (see "Exploring the Island," p. 161).

Cart Culture

When you arrive in Avalon, the island's only city, you'll immediately notice the abundance of golf carts in a comical array of styles and colors. Avalon is the only California city with state authoriza-tion to regulate the number of vehicles allowed on city streets. It has no rental cars and only a handful of private vehi-cles; most residents use golf carts, and many homes' driveways are only big enough for the carts. To rent a golf cart, see "Getting Around," below.

Essentials

GETTING THERE   The most common way to reach the island is on the **Catalina Express** ferry (www.catalinaexpress.com; ✆ **800/481-3470**), with roughly 30 daily departures year-round from Long Beach, San Pedro, and Dana Point. High-speed cata-marans make the trip in about an hour. Captain's and Commodore Lounge upgrades are available. Round-trip fares are $74.50 for adults, $68 for seniors 55 and over, $59 for children ages 2 to 11, and $5 for infants. Fares for Dana Point are $2 higher, except for infants. Check-in at the ticket window begins 1 hour prior to each departure at the following terminals:

- **San Pedro:** The **Sea and Air Terminal,** Berth 95; take the Harbor Freeway (I-110) south to Harbor Boulevard exit and follow the signs. Parking first hour is free, $1 per hour thereafter up to $12 maximum.
- **Long Beach:** The **Catalina Landing,** 320 Golden Shore. Take I-710 south into Long Beach. Stay left, follow signs to downtown, and exit at Golden Shore. Turn right at the stop sign and continue around to the terminal on the right; parking ($15) is in the structure on the left.
- **Dana Point: Dana Wharf Sportfishing,** 34675 Golden Lantern St. Parking is $12 per day.

The **Catalina Flyer,** 400 Main St., Newport Beach (www.catalinainfo.com; ✆ **800/830-7744**), the West Coast's largest passenger catamaran, departs once a day from Newport Beach's Balboa Pavilion, leaving at 9am and returning at 4:30pm.

Santa Catalina

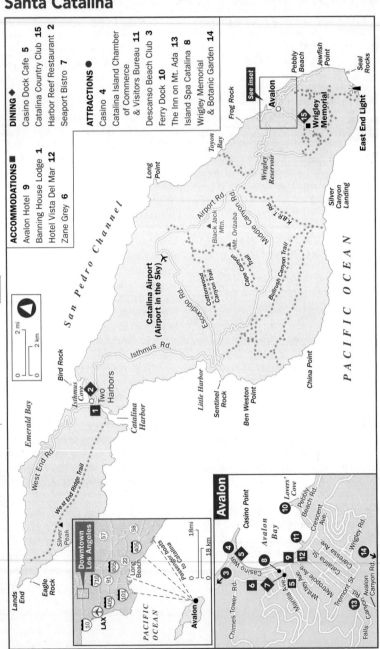

ACCOMMODATIONS ■

Avalon Hotel **9**
Banning House Lodge **1**
Hotel Vista Del Mar **12**
Zane Grey **6**

DINING ◆

Casino Dock Cafe **5**
Catalina Country Club **15**
Harbor Reef Restaurant **2**
Seaport Bistro **7**

ATTRACTIONS ●

Casino **4**
Catalina Island Chamber
of Commerce
& Visitors Bureau **11**
Descanso Beach Club **3**
Ferry Dock **10**
The Inn on Mt. Ada **13**
Island Spa Catalina **8**
Wrigley Memorial
& Botanic Garden **14**

Travel time is about 75 minutes each way. Round trips are $70 for adults, $65 for seniors, $53 for children 3 to 12, and $6 for infants. Pets are not allowed.

Island Express Helicopter Service, 1175 Queens Way Dr., Long Beach (www.islandexpress.com; $\mathcal{C}$ **800/228-2566** or 310/510-2525), flies from Long Beach (regularly) or San Pedro (seasonally) to Avalon in 15 minutes. The expense may be worth the thrill and convenience, particularly if you're prone to seasickness. It flies on demand between 8am and sunset year-round for $125 plus tax each way, or $250 round-trip. The heliport is a few hundred yards southwest of the Queen Mary.

VISITOR INFORMATION The **Catalina Island Chamber of Commerce and Visitors Bureau** is on the Green Pleasure Pier (www.catalinachamber.com; $\mathcal{C}$ **310/510-1520**) at the foot of Catalina Avenue.

GETTING AROUND When you land, take a **Catalina Transportation Service** (www.catalinatransportationservices.com; $\mathcal{C}$ **310/510-0025** for dispatch or 310/510-0342 for information) taxi or shuttle to your hotel. Most visitors get everywhere they want to go by foot; if you get worn down, hop on the red **Avalon Trolley,** which will run you around town for $2 each way or $7 for an all-day pass.

To explore beyond where your feet can comfortably carry you, you can rent a bike from **Brown's Bikes,** 107 Pebbly Beach Rd. (www.catalinabiking.com; $\mathcal{C}$ **310/510-0986**), between the ferry dock and town. Golf carts are available from **Catalina Island Golf Carts,** 635 Crescent Ave. at Pebbly Beach Road (www.catalinaislandgolfcart.com; $\mathcal{C}$ **310/510-1600**), or **Island Rentals,** between the ferry dock and Crescent Avenue at 125 Pebbly Beach Rd. (www.catalinagolfcartrentals.com; $\mathcal{C}$ **310/510-1456**). Both offer a town map for a self-guided tour. Rates are about $40 per hour plus a deposit; drivers must be 25 or older and have auto insurance.

Exploring the Island

Picturesque **Avalon,** whose permanent population is less than 4,000, is both the island's port of entry and its only city. You can walk along Crescent Avenue, the main beachfront road, and easily explore the side streets. Northwest of Avalon, the village of **Two Harbors** is accessible by boat or shuttle bus. Its twin bays are favored by pleasure crafts from L.A., so there's a lot of camaraderie and a less touristy ambience.

ORGANIZED TOURS **Santa Catalina Island Company** tours (www.visitcatalinaisland.com; $\mathcal{C}$ **877/778-8322**) offer the greatest variety of excursions in Avalon and around the island. The most comprehensive is the **Cape Canyon,** which takes you into the heart of Catalina's "outback" in an all-terrain, biofuel-powered Hummer. The

CATALINA'S GRAND casino

The **Casino Building,** Avalon's world-famous Art Deco landmark, is not a gambling palace; "casino" is an Italian word for a place of entertainment or gathering. The ornate structure, with exquisite the craftsmanship inside and out, houses the island's only movie theater and the world's largest circular ballroom (diameter 158 feet). Nearly every big band of the 1930s and '40s played here after it opened May 1929. Today, the ballroom is a coveted venue for weddings, dances and special events such as the three-week **JazzTrax Festival** (www.jazztrax.com; $\mathcal{C}$ **866/872-9849**) every October (book tickets and accommodations as far in advance as possible).

rugged route includes American bald eagle and Catalina Island fox habitats at scenic Middle Ranch and Airport-in-the-Sky for lunch and a visit to the nature center. It costs $125 for adults, $112 for seniors and children in summer ($115 and $103 fall winter and spring).

Many tours last 2 hours or less and don't monopolize your whole day. For example, the 1-hour **Behind the Scenes Casino Tour** includes the "green rooms" used by Errol Flynn, Cary Grant, and all the big bands, and the projection room with the original 1929 equipment on display. The shorter **Casino Tour** focuses on the the Casino's magnificent ballroom (see "Catalina's Grand Casino," below). Other shorter tours include the **Zip Line Eco Tour** through Descanso Canyon and down to the beach, and my favorite, the **Skyline Drive,** which takes you high and deep into the island's protected wilderness for stupendous views, possible buffalo sightings, and a light lunch at the nature center at the Airport-in-the-Sky. These trips cost from $10 to $78, except for the zip line, which is $120 for adults, $109 seniors and children.

Most boating excursions are an hour or less, such as the **Undersea Tour,** a leisurely cruise of Lover's Cove Marine Preserve in a semi-submersible to view view kelp forests and sea life from 5 feet below the surface; the nighttime **Flying Fish Boat Trips** (seasonal) in searchlight-equipped open boats; and of course, the classic **Glass-Bottom Boat** tour. These are $16 to $45.

WHAT TO SEE & DO IN AVALON Walk along horseshoe-shaped Crescent Avenue, past private yachting and fishing clubs, toward the landmark Casino building. You can see the Art Deco theater for the price of a movie ticket any night, and the recently renovated **Catalina Island Museum** (www.catalinamuseum.org; ✆ 310/510-2414), on the ground floor explores 7,000 years of island history, from archaeology to big bands, as well as special exhibits such as "Chaplin and Goddard: A Secret Love Affair," from 2014. Admission is $5 for adults, $4 for seniors, and free for kids 15 and under. The museum is open daily from 10am to 5pm.

The **Descanso Beach Club** (www.visitcatalinaisland.com; ✆ 310/510-7410), a mini-Club Med in a private cove just past the Casino, unveiled an extensive renovation in fall 2014, including a new kitchen and a clubhouse with a ballroom. It's much nicer beach than the public town beaches, but service easily gets bogged down. Though you can play on the beach year-round, club facilities—a pricey open-air restaurant, bars, live music, volleyball lawns, dance area, fire rings on the beach, cabana and lounge rentals—are available only from spring to October. The club also rents kayaks and other watersports gear and books massages, golf tee times and tours. Admission is $2.

About 1½ miles from downtown Avalon is **Wrigley Memorial and Botanic Garden** (www.catalinaconservancy.org; ✆ 310/510-2897). Ada Wrigley's specialized gardens showcase plants endemic to California's coastal islands. It's open daily from 8am to 5pm; admission is $7 for adults, $5 seniors and veterans with ID, $3 free for children 5 to 12, free for children under 5 and active military.

The Catalina Island Co. opened the island's first resort spa, the 15,000-square-foot. **Island Spa Catalina** (www.visitcatalinaisland.com; ✆ 877/778-8322) in fall 2014. Occupying the historic oceanview El Encanto Building on Crescent Avenue at Marilla (a block north of Hotel Metropole), it includes a spa shop, cafe and salon. Treatments incorporate indigenous elements such as yarrow sea salt.

VISITING TWO HARBORS For a better look at the rugged natural beauty of Catalina, head to Two Harbors, the quarter-mile "neck" at the island's northwest end. The name comes from the harbors on either side, known as the Isthmus and Catalina

Harbor. It's an excellent starting point for campers and hikers but also offers just enough civilization for less intrepid travelers.

The **Banning House Lodge** (www.visitcatalinaisland.com; ✆ **877/778-8322**) is a 12-room B&B on the Isthmus. The 1910 Craftsman-style house served as on-location lodging for movie stars like Errol Flynn and Dorothy Lamour. Peaceful and isolated, the simply furnished but comfortable inn has spectacular views of both harbors. Peak season rates start at $134 (2-night minimum on weekends, 3 on holidays) and $108 off-peak. Continental breakfast and transportation from the pier are included.

Everyone here eats at the **Harbor Reef Restaurant** (www.visitcatalinaisland.com; ✆ **310/510-4215**) on the beach. The tropical-themed saloon/restaurant serves breakfast, lunch, and dinner, specializing in hearty steaks, ribs, swordfish, and buffalo burgers. The house drink is "buffalo milk," a potent concoction of vodka, crème de cacao, banana liqueur, milk, whipped cream, and nutmeg.

Diving, Snorkeling & Kayaking

Catalina's clean water and giant kelp forests teeming with marine life have made it a renowned snorkeling and diving destination for experts and beginners alike, while kayaking takes you to otherwise inaccessible coastline along magnificent cliffs. The state-protected underwater **Casino Point Marine Park,** a divers' favorite, is conveniently located behind the Casino and can get outrageously crowded in summer. It's also one of the best snorkeling spots, along with **Descanso Beach Club** (p. 162) and **Lover's Cove Marine Reserve,** another state underwater park off Pebbly Beach Road southeast of the ferry dock.

For tours, gear rentals and instruction, contact **Catalina Divers Supply** (www.catalinadiverssupply.com; ✆ **800/353-0330**) or **Joe's Rent-a-Boat** (www.joesrentaboat.com; ✆ **310/510-0455**) on the Green Pier; or **Catalina Snorkeling Adventures** at Lover's Cove (www.snorkelingcatalina.com; ✆ **877/766-7535**). At Two Harbors, contact **Two Harbors Dive & Recreation Center** (www.visitcatalinaisland.com; ✆ **310/510-4272**).

Hiking

Hikers head for the island's interior to find secluded coves, rolling hills, and sheer peace. Look for giant buffalo roaming the hills, scions of 14 movie extras that were left behind in the 1920s. The granddaddy of the more than 200 miles of trails is the Trans-Catalina Trail, a 37.2-mile trek along the island's spine. Obtain a free **hiking permit** online or from the friendly Conservancy Office, 125 Clarissa Ave., Avalon (www.catalinaconservancy.org; ✆ **310/510-2595**). Guided walks to the most popular trails are available as iPhone or Droid apps.

Beaches

Unfortunately, Avalon's beaches leave much to be desired. The town's central beach, off Crescent Avenue, is small and completely congested in peak season; claim your spot early in the morning before it fills up. **Descanso Beach Club** (p. 162) offers the best beach in town but also gets crowded very quickly, and services are expensive. Best bet: Rent a kayak and find a secluded cove that you'll have virtually to yourself.

Where to Stay

Only a handful of hotels can justify the island's high rates. Reserve well in advance, because most places fill up quickly in summer and holiday seasons. The best time is in September or October when the water is warm, crowds have subsided, and lodging is easier to find. If can't find a vacancy, check with the Catalina Chamber of Commerce (see "Visitor Information," p. 161), for last-minute cancellations. *Note:* At press time, the **Inn on Mt. Ada,** long recognized as one of California's finest hotels, was scheduled to close. Catalina Island Conservancy and USC, which oversee the historic property, were seeking new operators. If and when it reopens, add it to your list.

EXPENSIVE

The Avalon Hotel ★★　Originally a gentleman's club developed at the turn of the 20th century, this property is a luxurious Craftsman-style hotel replete with rich, hand-carved mahogany and imported slate etched with the island's silhouette, accented with handmade tile, local artwork, and island memorabilia. Large, modern but homey guest rooms come in a variety of sizes and feature garden or ocean views (some with balconies) and supremely comfortable queen- or king-size memory foam beds. The rooftop lounge is a fantastic place to sip wine and watch the action at the harbor.

124 Whittley Ave., Avalon. www.theavalonhotel.com. ℂ **310/510-7070.** 15 units. Mid-Nov to mid-June $195–$495 double; mid-June to mid-Sept $349–$649 double. Rates include continental breakfast. **Amenities:** Free harbor/heliport transfer; GPS units; free laptops and high-speed Internet connection.

MODERATE

Hotel Vista Del Mar ★★　A favorite with families and couples alike, this Mediterranean-style hotel is smack-dab in the middle of town. A lush garden atrium courtyard, a large public balcony with arches framing views of the harbor, and a friendly, efficient staff raise it above the norm. Large, modern guest rooms have ocean or courtyard views. The oceanview suites with double Jacuzzi tubs are fantastic but hard to get, as the only two are booked by regulars most of the time.

417 Crescent Ave. (btw. Catalina and Sumner aves.), Avalon. www.hotel-vistadelmar.com. ℂ **800/601-6836** or 310/510-1452. 15 units. Apr–Nov $250–$295 double, from $425 suite; Dec–Mar $175–$200 double, from $325 suite. Rates include continental breakfast and evening refreshments. **Amenities:** Free Wi-Fi.

> ### For Travelers With Wheelchairs
>
> Visitors who use wheelchairs should look into **Hotel Metropole** (www.hotel-metropole.com; ℂ **800/300-8528** or 310/510-1884). One of the Avalon's most modern properties, it has an elevator, a large sun deck overlooking Avalon Bay, a shopping complex, and a convenient location in the heart of Avalon.

INEXPENSIVE

Good choices for affordable lodgings are **Zane Grey** (www.zanegreypueblohotel.com; ℂ **310/510-0966**), a hilltop 1926 Hopi-style abode and former home of Western author Zane Grey, with its cozy living room with fireplace and piano, free shuttle service, and a pool; and **Hermit Gulch Campground** (www.visitcatalinaisland.com; ℂ **310/510-8368**), the best of Avalon's three campgrounds (though also subject to crowding and noise in peak season). Reserve in advance. The red Avalon Trolley (p. 161) can run you back and forth to town.

Where to Dine

Besides the choices below, Avalon options include the waterfront **Avalon Grille,** with patio seating and a full bar in the center of town, across from the Green Pleasure Pier (ℂ **310/510-7494**). The **Harbor Reef Restaurant** (p. 163) is the place to eat on the Two Harbors side of the island.

EXPENSIVE

Catalina Country Club ★★ CALIFORNIAN   Some of Avalon's most elegant meals are served at the landmark, Spanish-Mediterranean clubhouse built by Wrigley in 1920s. The menu is peppered with historical photos and vintage celebrity anecdotes. The cuisine, emphasizing seafood, is infused with influences from around the world and prepared with sustainable seafood, free-range, organic meats, and fresh produce. Choose a seat outdoors in the Catalina tile-Fountain Terrace courtyard or inside the chic, intimate dining room. *Note to walkers:* The club is only a few minutes from the waterfront but uphill.

1 Country Club Dr. (above Sumner Ave.). ℰ **310/510-7404.** Reservations recommended. Main courses $19–$35 dinner. Daily 11am–10pm.

MODERATE

Seaport Bistro ★ INTERNATIONAL   Tucked away in a quiet residential neighborhood, just far enough from Avalon's bustle to be romantic, this restaurant is new by Catalina standards (open since summer 2013). Its theme is food from seaports around the world, including California's shores. That broad canvas allows for a varied menu that may include eggplant parmesan, turkey meatloaf, tagine, paella, and dessert fondue. There's no ambience to speak of unless you count a partial view of the harbor, but if you can't find something you like here, you just aren't trying.

119 Maiden Lane (1 block west of Crescent, btw. Marilla Ave. and Upper Olive St.). www.seaportbistro. com. ℰ **310/510-3663.** Reservations recommended. Main courses $16–$25. Thurs–Tues 5–9pm.

INEXPENSIVE

You can get a good low-bucks meal at the **Casino Dock Cafe** (ℰ **310/510-2755**), with live summertime entertainment, marina views from the sunny deck, breakfast burritos loaded with homemade salsa, and kicking bloody marys.

SANTA BARBARA ★★★

92 miles NW of Los Angeles; 45 miles S of Solvang; 105 miles S of San Luis Obispo

Between palm-lined Pacific beaches and the foothills of the Santa Ynez Mountains, this prosperous small city presents a mosaic of whitewashed stucco and red-tile roofs, and a gracious, relaxed attitude that has earned it the sobriquet American Riviera. It's ideal for kicking back on gold-sand beaches, prowling the shops and galleries that line its historic streets, and relaxing over a meal in one of many top-notch restaurants.

Downtown Santa Barbara is distinctive for its Spanish-Mediterranean architecture, legacy of a devastating 1925 earthquake that forced the city to rebuilt its entire business district. Out of the rubble rose a stylish planned community that enforced strict building codes to this day.

Essentials

GETTING THERE   By car, U.S. 101, running straight through Santa Barbara, is the qickest route from north or south (1½ hr. from Los Angeles, 6 hr. from San Francisco). **Amtrak** (p. 270) offers daily rail service to Santa Barbara out of the **Santa Barbara Train Station,** 209 State St. (ℰ **805/963-1015**). Fares can be as low as $31 (round-trip) from Los Angeles's Union Station.

GETTING AROUND   State Street, the primary commercial thoroughfare, ends at Stearns Wharf and Cabrillo Boulevard; the latter runs along the ocean. **MTD** (www. sbmtd.gov) runs frequent electric shuttles (50¢; 25¢ for ages 60 and over and people with disabilities; free for children less than 45 in. tall) in the downtown and waterfront areas, if you'd rather leave the car behind.

VISITOR INFORMATION The **Santa Barbara Visitors Center,** 1 Garden Street at Cabrillo Boulevard (www.santabarbaraca.com; © **805/965-3021** or 805/568-1811), is open Monday through Saturday from 9am to 5pm and Sunday from 10am to 5pm; it closes at 4pm November through January.

Pick up the free weekly Independent for events listings, and "Explore Santa Barbara," the visitor's guide published by the Santa Barbara News-Press, at shops and sidewalk racks around town.

Seeing the Sights
HISTORIC DOWNTOWN
Red Tile Walking Tour ★★★ The Mediterranean-style red tile roofs decreed by city planners after the 1925 earthquake provided the name for this self-guided survey of landmark buildings built with adobe-textured walls, rounded archways, tile work and terra-cotta rooftops that now symbolize the city's Mediterranean atmosphere. The visitor center (above) has a map/guide of the tour, which covers about 12 blocks and takes 1 to 3 hours, depending on how often you stop.

Btw. State and Santa Barbara sts. and Ortega and Anapamu sts. www.santabarbaracarfree.org (select "Car Free Maps"). © **(805) 696-1100.**

Santa Barbara County Courthouse ★★ Built in 1929, this grand "palace" is the local benchmark for Spanish colonial revival architecture, with its formidable facades, beamed ceilings, striking murals, an 85-foot-high observation clock tower, and formal sunken gardens. Free guided tours are offered on Monday, Tuesday, Wednesday, and Friday at 2pm.

1100 Anacapa St. (btw. E. Figueroa and E. Anapamu). www.santabarbaracourthouse.org. © **805/962-6464.** Free admission (donations appreciated). Mon–Fri 8am–5pm; Sat–Sun and holidays 10am–4:30pm.

Santa Barbara Museum of Art ★★ This jewel of a museum feels like the private gallery of a wealthy collector. It leans toward early 20th-century Western American paintings and 19th- and 20th-century Asian art, but the best displays might be the antiquities and Chinese ceramics. Visiting exhibits often feature small but excellent collections such as the Armand Hammer Foundation's French Impressionist and Post-Impressionist paintings and the Glasgow Museums' Botticellis and other Italian masterpieces. Check the website for free and half-price days.

1130 State St. (at E. Anapamu). www.sbmuseart.org. © **805/963-4364.** Admission $10 adults; $6 seniors 65 and over, students, and children 6–17; free for children 5 and under. Tues–Sun 11am–5pm, Thurs 11am–8pm.

ELSEWHERE IN THE CITY
Ganna Walska Lotusland ★ This secluded, lavishly landscaped 37-acre estate is renowned for exotic plants, mysterious garden paths, and lotus-filled ponds. The estate's eccentric European-born mistress was fond of succulents and cactuses, interspersing them artistically among native plants. Assembled mostly in the 1940s, the garden's priceless rare specimens include prehistoric plants now extinct in the wild. Montecito is a 5-minute freeway drive south of Santa Barbara. *Note:* Admission is by tour only; reservations are required and available up to six months in advance.

Santa Barbara

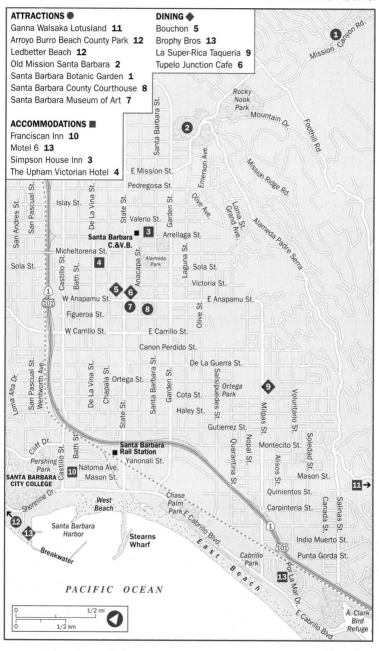

ATTRACTIONS ●
Ganna Walsaka Lotusland **11**
Arroyo Burro Beach County Park **12**
Ledbetter Beach **12**
Old Mission Santa Barbara **2**
Santa Barbara Botanic Garden **1**
Santa Barbara County Courthouse **8**
Santa Barbara Museum of Art **7**

ACCOMMODATIONS ■
Franciscan Inn **10**
Motel 6 **13**
Simpson House Inn **3**
The Upham Victorian Hotel **4**

DINING ◆
Bouchon **5**
Brophy Bros **13**
La Super-Rica Taqueria **9**
Tupelo Junction Cafe **6**

695 Ashley Rd. (At Sycamore Canyon Rd.), Montecito. www.lotusland.org. ✆ **805/969-9990.** Admission $45 adults, $20 children 3–18, free for ages 2 and under. 2-hr. guided tours mid-Feb to mid-Nov, Wed–Sat 10am and 1:30pm.

Old Mission Santa Barbara ★ Established in 1786 by Father Junípero Serra and built by the Chumash Indians, this is a stunning example in physical form of the blending of Indian and Hispanic spirituality.This hilltop structure, overlooking the town and the Channel Islands beyond, is called the Queen of the Missions in recognition of its twin bell towers and beauty. Self-guided tour booklets are available.

2201 Laguna St. (at Los Olivos St.). www.santabarbaramission.org. ✆ **805/682-4713,** ext. 166. Admission $7 adults, $5 seniors, $2 children 5–15, free for 4 and under. Mon–Fri 9am–4:30pm; closes 4:14pm fall and winter. Guided tours $2 in addition to admission. Thurs–Fri 11am, Sat 10:30am.

Santa Barbara Botanic Garden ★ The Botanic Garden is devoted to indigenous California plants. More than 5½ miles of meandering trails on 65 acres offer glimpses of cactuses, redwoods, wildflowers, and much more, many arranged in representational habitats or landscapes. The gardens were established in 1926. You'll catch the very best color and aroma just after spring showers.

1212 Mission Canyon Rd. (.8 mi. N. of Foothill Rd., 5 min. drive from the mission). www.sbbg.org. ✆ **805/682-4726.** Admission $108 adults, $8 seniors 60 and over and children 13–17, $6 children 2–12, free for children 1 and under. Daily 9am–5pm (until 6pm Mar–Oct).

Stearns Wharf ★★ California's oldest working wharf attracts visitors for strolling, shopping, dining, and exploring its exhibits, which include a Sea Center with aquariums and an outdoor touch-tank. Although it no longer serves passenger and freight ships as it did when built in 1872, local fishing boats still unload their daily catch here. *Note:* Grassy **Chase Palm Park,** a half-mile east on Cabrillo Boulevard, hosts the Arts and Crafts Show every Sunday, a cherished city tradition since 1965.

End of State St., west of W. Cabrillo Blvd. Parking free with validation. www.stearnswharf.org.

Beaches

East Beach is Santa Barbara's favorite, stretching from the Santa Barbara Zoological Gardens to Chase Palm Park and the wharf. Nearer the pier you'll find manicured lawns, tall palms, and abundant facilities; to the east are many volleyball courts, plus the Cabrillo Pavilion, a recreational center, bathhouse, and architectural landmark dating from 1925. Picnic areas with barbecue grills, showers, and clean, well-patrolled sands make this beach a good choice for everyone.

On the other side of Santa Barbara Harbor, the less sheltered **Leadbetter Beach** off Shoreline Drive is popular with surfers and a great place to watch pleasure boats going in and out of the harbor. Basic facilities include restrooms and picnic areas.

Two miles west of Leadbetter is secluded but popular **Arroyo Burro Beach County Park,** also called Hendry's Beach. It has a grassy park beneath the cliffs and a white crescent beach with waves ideal for surfing and bodysurfing.There are volleyball nets, picnic areas, and restrooms.

Outdoor Activities

BIKING & SKATING A relatively flat, palm-lined 2-mile coastal pathway, perfect for biking and in-line skating, runs along the beach. (Adventurous cyclists can also pedal through town, where painted bike lanes line many major routes.) These routes and many others are outlined in the free Santa Barbara County Bike Map, available from the visitor center or **Traffic Solutions** (www.trafficsolutions.info; ✆ **805/963-7283**). For bike or skate rentals, contact **Wheel Fun Rentals,** 23 E. Cabrillo St. (www.wheelfunrentals.com; ✆ **805/966-2282**).

BOATING The **Santa Barbara Sailing Center,** 133 Harbor Way at the Santa Barbara Harbor (www.sbsail.com; ✆ **805/962-2826**), rents sailboats (lessons available), kayaks, pedal boats, and motorboats. Skippered and bareboat charters, as well as a variety of sightseeing cruises, are also available.

GOLF The 18-hole, par 70 **Santa Barbara Golf Club,** 3500 McCaw Ave. at Las Positas Road (www.sbgolf.com; ✆ **805/687-7087**), is one of the best-maintained and more challenging municipal courses you'll find. There's a great 6,009-yard, 18-hole course and a driving range. Greens fees range from $35 to $60. The scenic 18-hole, par 70 **Sandpiper,** 7925 Hollister Ave. (www.sandpipergolf.com; ✆ **805/968-1541**), is rated as one of the top U.S. public courses. Rates range from $140 to $180.

HIKING The moderately strenuous foothill trails in the Santa Ynez Mountains above Santa Barbara are perfect for day hikes. One of the most popular hikes is the **Seven Falls/Inspiration Point Trail,** an easy trek that begins on Tunnel Road, passes the mission, and skirts the edge of Santa Barbara's Botanic Garden (with its own pleasant hikes). Though they are not the easiest sites to navigate, **Santa Barbara Hikes** (www.santabarbarahikes.com) and **Santa Barbara Trail Guide** (www.santabarbara trailguide.com) have comprehensive details on hiking the area.

Shopping

State Street from the beach to Victoria Street is the city's main thoroughfare and has the largest concentration of shops, with a number of boutiques among the T-shirts and postcards. (If your feet wear out, hop on one of the electric shuttle buses.) **Brinkerhoff Avenue** (off Cota St., btw. Chapala and De La Vina sts.) is Santa Barbara's antiques row; most shops are open Tuesday through Sunday from 11am to 5pm. **El Paseo** (814 State St.) is a picturesque shopping arcade built around an 1827 adobe home and is reminiscent of an old Spanish street. **Paseo Nuevo,** on the other side of State Street, is a modern outdoor mall anchored by a Nordstrom department store.

Where to Stay

Santa Barbara's accommodations are expensive, especially in summer. Decide first whether you'd like to stay beachside (even more expensive) or downtown; you won't be able to happily stroll between the two areas.

The free reservations service **Santa Barbara Hot Spots** (www.hotspotsusa.com; ✆ **800/793-7666** or 805/564-1637) keeps an updated availability list for about 90% of the area's lodgings. Call Monday through Thursday from 9am to 7pm, Friday and Saturday 9am to 8pm; winter hours are Monday through Friday 9am to 5pm and Saturday 9am to 4pm. It's closed Sundays and holidays.

EXPENSIVE

Simpson House Inn ★★★ Set in an acre of English gardens, the Simpson House is the epitome of Victorian luxury. Rooms within the landmark 1874 house enjoy such extras as claw-foot tubs and antique brass showers; each is different and may have a private balcony, or a wood-burning fireplace. While the lavish decor takes its cues from the architecture, the amenities are pure 21st century. Book one of the romantic cottages, tucked into niches within the gardens, for a heightened feeling of country elegance and exclusivity.

121 E. Arrellaga St. (btw. Santa Barbara and Anacapa sts.), Santa Barbara. www.simpsonhouseinn. com. ✆ **800/676-1280** or 805/963-7067. 15 units. $275–$550 double; $395–$550 cottage. 2-night weekend minimum. Rates include full breakfast, afternoon refreshments, evening hors d'oeuvres, and wine. **Amenities:** Concierge; complimentary bikes and beach equipment; video library; free Wi-Fi.

MODERATE

The Upham Victorian Hotel and Garden Cottages ★★
Whether you're here for business or a romatic getaway, this conveniently located inn has you covered. With its warm lobby, sweeping redwood verandas and Victorian cupola, it has the intimate atmosphere of a B&B while also offering the business and conference facilities of a full-service hotel. Built in 1871, the Upham is Southern California's oldest continuously operating hostelry, yet accommodations are sleekly decorated and offer all the modern comforts. There's also a cozy bistro on site.

1404 De La Vina St. (at Sola St.), Santa Barbara. www.uphamhotel.com. ✆ **800/727-0876** or 805/962-0058. 50 units. $206–$315 double; from $255 suite and cottage. Rates include continental breakfast and afternoon wine and cheese. **Amenities:** Restaurant.; business center; free Wi-Fi.

INEXPENSIVE

The **Motel 6** near East Beach, at 443 Corona del Mar Dr. (www.motel6.com; ✆ **800/466-8356** or 805/564-1392), is famous for being the chain's first property. The renovated rooms look nice, but like its bretheren it still lacks such basics as Kleenex and shampoo. While winter rates are reasonable, it's unconscionably overpriced the rest of the year.

Franciscan Inn ★
One block from the beach, in a quiet residential neighborhood near Stearns Wharf, this meticulously maintained Spanish-style hotel is an affordable retreat with some frills, such as free local calls and a book and video library. Comfortable rooms are a bit old-fashioned with their country-tinged decor, while bathrooms feature fresh tile. Most second-floor rooms have unobstructed mountain views, and some suites have fully equipped kitchenettes. A great choice for families, the Franciscan will also suit a romantic couple on a budget.

109 Bath St. (at Mason St.), Santa Barbara. www.franciscaninn.com. ✆ **800/663-5288** or 805/963-8845. 53 units. $145–$235 double, from $200 suite. Extra person $10. Rates include continental breakfast and afternoon refreshments. Free parking. **Amenities:** Heated outdoor pool; whirlpool; free Wi-Fi.

Where to Dine

EXPENSIVE

Bouchon ★★ CALIFORNIAN   This warm, inviting restaurant is passionate about Santa Barbara County wines (*bouchon* is French for "wine cork"), and knowledgeable servers will help you match vintages to menu options. The local, seasonal menu changes frequently but has recently included smoked Santa Barbara albacore "carpaccio" with vinaigrette and shaved imported Parmesan; sliced local venison on cumin spaetzle; and herbed monkfish saddle with a creamy Gruyère gratin. Request a table on the heated front patio, and do try the signature chocolate "molten lava" cake.

9 W. Victoria St. (off State St.). www.bouchonsantabarbara.com. ✆ **805/730-1160.** Reservations recommended. Main courses $25–$48. Daily 5–10pm.

MODERATE

Brophy Bros. Clam Bar & Restaurant ★★ SEAFOOD   Best-known for its unbeatable view of the marina, Bophy Bros. earns repeat visits with huge portions of fresh seafood. Favorites include New England clam chowder, cioppino, and any one of the seafood salads. The scampi and garlic-baked clams are consistently good, as is all the fresh fish. The crab cakes with roasted red pepper aioli is a standout. Ask for a table on the narrow deck overlooking the harbor. *Note:* This place is small, and the wait can be up to 2 hours on a weekend night.

119 Harbor Way (off Cabrillo Blvd. in the Waterfront Center). www.brophybros.com. (C) **805/966-4418.** Reservations not accepted. Main courses $10–$25. Daily 11am–10pm.

Tupelo Junction Café ★★★ SOUTHERN   This friendly restaurant, standing modestly among State Street's European labels and designer boutiques, produces Southern cuisine with a healthy California touch, such as wild salmon with andouille sausage and their signature fried chicken salad. Tempting small plates include cheddar hush puppies with pepper jam and dungeness crab cakes with smoked chili remoulade. Sinful beignets with crème anglaise show up at breakfast and for dessert with lunch and dinner. Eat here early in your vacation, because you'll surely want to come back.

1218 State St. www.tupelojunction.com. (C) **805/899-3100.** Small plates $8–$15, main courses $14–$22. Tues–Sun 8am–2pm and 5–9pm; closed Monday.

INEXPENSIVE

La Super-Rica Taqueria ★★ MEXICAN   This unassuming street-corner shack hasn't let its famous endorsement by the late Julia Child go to its head. The no-nonsense tacos are fat with *adobado* (marinated pork), *bistec* (grilled flank steak), and other fillings heaped on fresh, grainy corn tortillas. Stray from the tacos and you'll also find wonderful *quesadilla con chorizo* (grilled Spanish sausage and melted cheese between two tortillas). Check the daily specials for such treats as *pozole,* a stew of pork and hominy in red-chile sauce, and Dover sole tamales—and ask for extra tortillas.

622 N. Milpas St. (btw. Cota and Ortega sts.). (C) **805/963-4940.** Most items $3–$10. No credit cards. Daily 11am–9pm.

SAN DIEGO ESSENTIALS

by Maribeth Mellin

Creativity blossoms in San Diego's gentle climate. No wonder Dr. Seuss and Dr. Salk both chose to live here. Director Cameron Crowe attended high school (and graduated at 15) in San Diego, chemist and Nobel Prize laureate Kary Mullis conjured theories while surfing in La Jolla, and singer Jason Mraz lives on an avocado ranch in North San Diego County. Must be something in the weather, or water, or easy lifestyle. When the overall mood is mellow, the style casual, and the attitude decidedly laid back, the mind is free to wander.

Visitors needn't worry about packing dressy clothes or fancy cosmetics. Sure, some bankers, lawyers, and the like wear suits and even stockings (horrors!) at work. But you can bet their wardrobes contain plenty of shorts, T-shirts, bathing suits, sandals, and well-worn flip-flops. San Diego's average temperature is 70.5°F (21.4 Celsius) and the thermometer rarely dips below 60° along the coast. The sun shines in clear skies more than 250 days of the year and even when it's cloudy or foggy, a few rays usually peak out by noon. Visitors typically begin shedding extraneous clothing and worries within 24 hours of their arrivals, settling into the San Diego vibe quickly. Fun is the focus, whether you're waiting in line to see young pandas roll about at the zoo, studying a Matisse at Balboa Park, or listening to the symphony or B.B. King under the stars.

Most of central and coastal San Diego is carefully landscaped and manicured, but lawns quickly give way to rocky hills, forested mountains, and moonscape desert east of the city. You can drive for less than 2 hours to hike along pine-scented trails at Mount Palomar, 6,000 feet above sea level, or wander amid towering desert cactus and boulders to an oasis in the Anza Borrego desert, and be back downtown for dinner. To experience San Diego's heart and soul, however, you must head to the beach. The Pacific Ocean splashes and slithers over 70 miles of coast lined with funky and ritzy beach towns; sample as many as possible. Head to La Jolla if you're looking for high style, or the Mission Beach boardwalk for the classic funky SoCal scene, or Coronado for absolute breathtaking natural beauty. Admiring the sunset is practically mandatory—just turn west to catch the show.

GETTING THERE

Arriving

BY PLANE   San Diegans have a love-hate relationship with **San Diego International Airport** (SAN; www.san.org; ✆ **619/400-2404**). The location— just 3 miles northwest of downtown—is convenient, but has drawbacks.

Planes fly directly over several neighborhoods, including Point Loma, Ocean Beach, and Uptown, and pilots thread a passage between high-rise buildings and Balboa Park on descent, giving passengers a somewhat scary birds-eye view of San Diego. The airport has two main terminals and a Commuter Terminal a half-mile from the main airport for short flights from Los Angeles. The Airport Loop shuttle provides free, 24-hour service from the main airport to the Commuter Terminal.

International carriers serving San Diego include Air Canada, Volaris, Japan Airlines, and British Airways. Domestically, the city is served by most national and regional airlines; none use it as a hub. In North County, the **McClellan-Palomar Airport** (www.sdcounty.ca.gov; ✆ **877/848-7766** or 760/431-4646) in Carlsbad (CLD), 42 miles north of downtown San Diego, is served by **United Express** from Los Angeles.

> ### Need a Lift?
>
> Some hotels often offer free **airport shuttles**; request a pickup by using the hotel phones in baggage claim. **SuperShuttle** (www.supershuttle.com; ✆ **800-258-3826**) offers shared vans to most county areas; advance reservations required to the airport, not from the airport. **Uber** (www.uber.com/cities/san-diego) is available for trips and from the airport and around town.

The **Metropolitan Transit System** (MTS; www.sdmts.com; ✆ **619/233-3004**) operates the San Diego Transit Flyer—bus route no. 992—between the airport and downtown San Diego. The one-way fare is $2.25, and exact change is required. The ride takes about 15 minutes, and buses come at 15-minute intervals. **Taxis** line up outside terminals 1 and 2. The 10-minute trip to downtown is about $15; budget $25-$30 for Coronado or Mission Beach, and $35 or more for La Jolla.

By Bus

Greyhound buses serve San Diego from downtown Los Angeles and other Southwestern cities, arriving at the downtown terminal, at 120 W. Broadway (www.greyhound.com; ✆ **800/231-2222** or 619/515-1100). Buses from Los Angeles are as frequent as every hour, and the ride takes about 2 to 3 hours. One-way fare is $24 and round-trips are $38.

By Car

Three main interstates lead into San Diego. **I-5** runs south from Los Angeles to the Tijuana border crossing. **I-8** cuts across California from points east such as Phoenix, **I-15** runs through inland San Diego; **Highway 163** branches off 15 south to central parts of the city. San Diego is 130 miles (2–3 hr.) south of **Los Angeles.**

By Train

Amtrak (www.amtrak.com; ✆ **800/872-7245**) trains run between downtown Los Angeles and San Diego 12 times daily, making stops in Orange County and North San Diego County before arriving at downtown's **Santa Fe Station** at 1050 Kettner Boulevard (✆ **619/239-9021.** The travel time from Los Angeles is about 2 hours and 45 minutes and a one-way ticket to San Diego is $37, or $51 for a reserved seat in business class.

Visitor Information

The San Diego Tourism Authority's **International Visitor Information Center,** 1140 N. Harbor Dr., along the downtown Embarcadero (www.sandiego.org; ✆ **619/236-1212**), disseminates information on attractions, hotels, and other interests and can provide maps. Daily summer hours are from 9am to 5pm; from October through May 9am to 4pm There's also abundant info on their website. You can also find staffed information booths at the airport, train station, and cruise terminal.

In La Jolla, the center is at 1162 Prospect St. (© **858/454-1718;** open daily 11am–4pm in winter from 10am to 6pm in summer. The **Coronado Visitor Center,** 1100 Orange Ave. (www.coronadovisitorcenter.com; © **866/599-7242** or 619/437-8788), dispenses maps, newsletters, and brochures. It's open Monday through Friday from 9am to 5pm, Saturday and Sunday from 10am to 5pm.

GETTING AROUND
On Foot

Walking within neighborhoods is advised, since parking is typically in short supply. But distances between main destinations are significant; you'll have to get around by car or public transport.

By Bus

Though it's improving, public transportation by bus in San Diego tends to be inefficient and time consuming. The **MTS Transit Store,** 102 Broadway at First Avenue (www.sdmts.com; © **619/234-1060**), dispenses passes, timetables, and maps, and issues ID cards for seniors 60 and older, as well as for travelers with disabilities—all of whom pay $1.10 per ride. Most bus **fares** are $2.25. For connections with another bus or trolley, purchase a $5 day pass giving you unlimited use of most bus and trolley routes for the day. The office is open Monday through Friday from 9am to 5pm. For assistance with route information from a living, breathing entity, call MTS at © **619/233-3004.** View timetables, maps, and fares online at www.transit.511sd.com and www.sdmts.com

By Trolley

Getting around on the bright red San Diego Trolley is easy and practical if you're staying downtown or, to a lesser degree, in Mission Valley. The **Blue Line** is handiest for most visitors and travels through downtown and runs south to San Ysidro at the Mexico border. The **Green Line** runs from downtown to Old Town, Mission Valley, and farther east to Santee. The trolley doesn't serve any beach communities or Balboa Park. Buy your ticket at machines in stations; it's a flat fare of $2.50. A $5 day pass is also available. Fare inspectors board trains at random to check tickets. For recorded information, call © **619/685-4900.** To speak with a customer service representative,

---

Curb Appeal: Check Your Colors

Street-parking rules are color-coded. A **red curb** means no stopping at any time. **Blue curbs** are for people with disabilities placards. A **white curb** signifies a passenger-loading zone; the time limit is 3 minutes, or 10 minutes in front of a hotel. A **yellow curb** is a commercial loading zone. A **green curb** designates short-term parking only—usually 15 or 30 minutes (as posted). Unpainted curbs are subject to parking rules on signs or meters.

If you plan on taking three or more trips in one day, buying a pass will be less expensive than anteing up regular fares. **Day Passes** allow unlimited rides on most MTS (bus) and trolley routes. Passes are good for 1, 2, 3, and 4 consecutive days, and cost $5, $9, $12, and $15, respectively. They can be bought at the Transit Store and all transit station automated ticket vending machines and must be loaded on a Compass Card,

available online, by phone, or in person at the Transit Store (bus drivers sell 1-day passes only). The regular trolley fare is $2.50 one-way for most routes; rural routes cost $5 to $10 each way. The one-way bus fare is $2.25 for urban routes and $2.50 for express routes. Exact fare is required on buses; drivers do not make change. See www.transit. 511sd.com or for more information.

call ✆ **619/233-3004** daily from 5:30am to 8:30pm; check the website at www.sdmts. com/trolley/trolley.asp for details.

By Car

Traffic congestion gets worse each year, but San Diego is still easy to navigate by car. Car rental companies have desks at the airport and offices around town. For up-to-the-minute traffic info, dial ✆ **511.** Metered parking spaces and pay lots are found in downtown, Hillcrest, and the beach communities. Many areas restrict street parking to 1 or 2 hours. Check out **Breezenet.com,** which can land you car-rental discounts with some of the most competitive rates around from Mom & Pop agencies. Also worth visiting are **Orbitz.com, Hotwire.com, Travelocity.com,** or **Priceline.com,** all of which offer competitive online car-rental rates (especially if you "bid blind" on Priceline or Hotwire).

By Train

Amtrak (www.amtrak.com; ✆ **800/872-7245**) stops in Solana beach and Oceanside en route to Orange County (with a Disneyland stop at Anaheim) and L.A. A one-way ticket from San Diego to Solana Beach is $12; to Oceanside, $18; and to Anaheim, $28.

San Diego's express rail commuter service, the **Coaster,** travels between the Santa Fe Depot station and the Oceanside Transit Center, with stops at Old Town, Sorrento Valley, Solana Beach, Encinitas, and Carlsbad. Fares range from $4 to $5.50 each way, with discounts for seniors and children. Check www.transit.511sd.com, or call ✆ **800/262-7837** for the schedule. The **Sprinter** rail service runs west to east alongside Highway 78, from Oceanside to Escondido, but doesn't access any major tourist attractions.

By Taxi

Half a dozen taxi companies serve the area. Rates are based on mileage and can add up quickly in sprawling San Diego—a trip from downtown to La Jolla will cost about $35 to $50. Other than in the Gaslamp Quarter after dark, taxis don't cruise the streets. Cabs do gather at major attractions but you have to call ahead for pickup elsewhere. Among the local companies are **Orange Cab** (✆ **619/291-3333**), **San Diego Cab** (✆ **619/226-8294**), and **Yellow Cab** (✆ **619/444-4444**). The **Coronado Cab Company** (✆ **619/435-6211**) serves Coronado. You can also dial ✆ **511** and say "taxi" to be connected to a dispatcher. **Uber** is available in San Diego www.uber.com/cities/san-diego.

By Water

BY FERRY   Ferries run between downtown San Diego and Coronado (www.flagshipsd.com; ℂ **800/442-7847** or 619/234-4111) departing from Broadway Pier (990 N. Harbor Dr.) hourly from 9am to 9pm and the Fifth Avenue Landing (600 Convention Way, located behind the Convention Center) about every 2 hours from 9:25am to 8:25pm. Times are extended an hour on Friday and Saturday nights. The Broadway Pier ferry departs Coronado's Ferry Landing hourly from 9:30am to 9:30pm. The Fifth Avenue ferry return trips every tow hours from 9:17am. The fare is $4.25 each way (free for children under 4); buy tickets at kiosks at departure points. The ferries do not accommodate cars; bikes are allowed.

[FastFACTS] SAN DIEGO

ATMs/Banks   You can usually find a bank—or at least an ATM—wherever crowds gather, especially at major attractions and shopping districts. Most permit cash withdrawals, and many are linked to international networks. Very few banks exchange foreign cash. There is an exchange place at Horton Plaza.

Business Hours   Banks are open weekdays from 9am to 4pm or later, and sometimes Saturday morning. Stores in shopping malls tend to operate from 10 or 11am until about 9pm weekdays and until 6pm weekends, and are open on secondary holidays.

Consulates   Mexico has the only consulate in San Diego, it's at 1549 India St. ℂ **619/231-8414.**

Disabled Travelers
San Diego's major attractions are wheelchair friendly, and manual wheelchairs with balloon tires are available free of charge at the main lifeguard stations in Ocean Beach, Mission

Beach, Pacific Beach, La Jolla, and Del Mar, among others. Beach conditions permitting, the Mission Beach, Coronado, and Oceanside lifeguard stations have electric wheelchairs available. Obtain more specific information from **Accessible San Diego** (www.asd.travel; ℂ **619/325-7550.**

Doctors & Dentists
For a doctor referral, contact the **San Diego County Medical Society** (www.sdcms.org; ℂ **858/565-8888**). Convenient hospitals **UCSD Medical Center–Hillcrest,** 200 W. Arbor Dr. (health.ucsd.edu; ℂ **619/543-6222**), in the center city; **UCSD Thornton Hospital,** 9300 Campus Point Dr. (health.ucsd.edu; ℂ **858/657-7000**), in La Jolla, and find another in Coronado, at **Sharp Coronado Hospital,** 250 Prospect Pl. (www.sharp.com; ℂ **619/522-3600**). For dental referrals, contact the **San Diego County Dental Society** at ℂ **800/201-0244** or 619/275-0244 (www.sdcds.

org), or call ℂ **800/DENTIST** (336-8478 or 855/294-9614; www.1800dentist.com).

Drinking Laws   The legal age for purchase and consumption of alcoholic beverages in California is 21. Alcohol is forbidden at all city beaches, boardwalks, and coastal parks.

Emergencies   Call ℂ **911** for fire, police, and ambulance. The TTY/TDD emergency number is ℂ **619/233-3323.** The main police station is at 1401 Broadway, at 14th Street (ℂ **858/484-3154.** If you encounter serious problems, contact the San Diego chapter of **Traveler's Aid International** (www.travelersaid.org), which has locations at the airport (ℂ **619/295-1277**).

Internet & Wi-Fi
Downtown's Gaslamp Quarter offers 2 hours of free Wi-Fi from any public space (go to www.freewifisandiego.com for information), and there's also free Wi-Fi at the airport. To find other public Wi-Fi hotspots,

check www.jiwire.com; its Hotspot Finder holds the world's largest directory of public wireless hotspots. Try www.cybercaptive.com or www.cybercafe.

LGBT Travelers Despite its reputation for conservative local politics, San Diego is one of America's gay-friendliest destinations, with several openly gay politicians and public officials. Hillcrest, near Balboa Park, is the city's most prominent "out" community. The free San Diego Gay and Lesbian Times (www.gaylesbiantimes.com), published every Thursday, is packed with info. For matters of health and wellness contact the San Diego LGBT Community Center,

3909 Centre St. (www.the centersd.org; ☏ **619/692-2077**); it's open Monday through Friday 9am to 10pm, Saturday 9am to 7pm.

Mail At press time, domestic postage rates were 32¢ for a postcard and 45¢ for a letter. For international mail, a first-class letter of up to 1 ounce costs $1.05 (85¢ to Canada); a first-class postcard costs the same as a letter. For more information, go to www.usps.com and click on "Calculate Postage." Convenient post offices include 815 E St. (Mon–Fri 9am–5pm) in downtown, an office in the Mission Valley Shopping Center, next to Macy's

(Mon–Fri 9:30am–6pm, Sat 9:30am–4pm). Most small communities also have offices.

Pharmacies Pharmaceuticals and nonprescription products are readily available at **Walgreens** (www.walgreens.com), **Rite-Aid** (www.riteaid.com), and **CVS** (www.cvs.com), all with several locations, including some open 24 hours.

Safety San Diego is an extremely safe destination, by big-city standards. Follow the common precautions: leave valuables at home; lock your doors; stash belongings out of sight in car trunks; and stay away from illegal drugs.

Neighborhoods in Brief

Coronado Locals refer to Coronado as an island, but it's actually on a peninsula connected to the mainland by a long, sandy isthmus known as the **Silver Strand.** It's a wealthy, self-contained community inhabited by lots of retired Navy brass. The northern portion is home to **U.S. Naval Air Station, North Island**), in use since World War I. Shops line Orange Avenue, and you'll find several resorts, including the landmark **Hotel del Coronado,** referred to locally as "the Del." Coronado has a lovely dune beach, plenty of restaurants, and a downtown reminiscent of a small New England town.

Downtown After decades of intense development and restoration, downtown San Diego has emerged as a vibrant community with several attractions including the Gaslamp Quarter, the **Embarcadero** (waterfront), the Convention Center, and Little Italy, all sprawling over eight individual "neighborhoods." The **Gaslamp Quarter** features renovated historic buildings housing top restaurants and clubs. The trendy **East Village** is home **PETCO Park** and the stunning **Central Library,** opened in 2014. **Little Italy** at the

northern edge of downtown is a great place to find a variety of restaurants (especially Italian) and boutiques.

Hillcrest & Uptown As the city's original self-contained suburb, Hillcrest was first developed in 1907 along with Banker's Hill as a desirable address for bigwigs to erect their mansions. Now it's the heart of San Diego's LGBT community, as well as an inclusive neighborhood, with an eclectic blend of popular shops and cafes. It's the closest neighborhood to **Balboa Park** (home of the **San Diego Zoo** and numerous **museums**). Other old Uptown neighborhoods of interest are **Mission Hills** to the west of Hillcrest, and **University Heights, Normal Heights, North Park, South Park, Golden Hill,** and **Kensington** to the east. These areas lack major hotels.

Mission Bay & the Beaches Come here when you want to wiggle your toes in the sand and play in bay and ocean waters. Mission Bay is a watery playground perfect for waterskiing, sailing, kayaking, and windsurfing, and is home to **SeaWorld.** The adjacent communities of **Ocean Beach, Mission Beach,** and **Pacific Beach** are known for their wide stretches of sand, active nightlife, and informal dining. The boardwalk running from South Mission Beach to Pacific Beach, is a popular place for in-line skating, bike riding, people-watching, and sunsets. Partying is a way of life here.

La Jolla Mediterranean in design and ambience, La Jolla pronounced La-*hoy*-ya) is home to an inordinate number of wealthy folks who choose La Jolla for its gorgeous coastline, outstanding restaurants, upscale shops, galleries, and some of the world's best medical and research facilities, as well as the **University of California, San Diego (UCSD).** The heart of La Jolla is referred to

as the **Village,** a picturesque neighborhood perfect for simply strolling about. Although nightlife is lacking, there's so much to do and see here, you may not even notice.

Old Town & Mission Valley These two busy areas northeast of downtown offer easy access to freeways and public transportation to downtown. Old Town State Historic Park (where California "began") contains several museums that document the city's beginnings. Just east is the vast suburban sprawl of Mission Valley, a tribute to the automobile and consumerism with car dealerships and shopping malls. Its main street, aptly named Hotel Circle, is lined with moderately priced hotels.

San Diego Calendar of Events

JANUARY

San Diego Restaurant Week: For 2 weeks in mid-January, with a second week in mid-September. www.sandiegorestaurantweek.com.

Farmers Insurance Open, Torrey Pines Golf Course: La Jolla. www.farmersinsurance open.com.

FEBRUARY

Mardi Gras in the Gaslamp Quarter: www.gaslamp.org.

St. Patrick's Day Parade: Hillcrest. www.stpatsparade.org.

APRIL

ArtWalk: Little Italy. www.missionfederalartwalk.org.

MAY

Fiesta Cinco de Mayo: Old Town. May 5. www.oldtownsandiego.org.

JUNE

The Rock 'n' Roll Marathon and Half Marathon: www.san-diego.competitor.com.

San Diego County Fair: Del Mar. www.sdfair.com.

Summer Organ Festival: Balboa Park. www.balboapark.org.

San Diego Symphony Summer Pops: Downtown. www.sandiegosymphony.org.

JULY

World Championship Over-the-Line Tournament: Mission Bay. www.ombac.org.

Thoroughbred Racing Season: Del Mar Racetrack. www.dmtc.com.

San Diego LGBT Pride Parade: Rally, and Festival: Hillcrest. www.sdpride.org.

Comic-Con International: Downtown. www.comic-con.org.

the sunshine **TAX**

San Diegans make wallet-busting concessions for the privilege of living amid so much natural beauty in the country's best climate. The median home costs nearly $500,000 and the cost of living is more than 30% higher than the national average. Every day necessities are costly.

For example, the price of gas is 5% higher than the national average. Yet more than three million people live in San Diego County, and the city of San Diego, with 1.3 million residents, is the nation's seventh largest.

AUGUST
La Jolla SummerFest: La Jolla. www.ljms.org.

SEPTEMBER
Fleet Week: Downtown and Coronado. www.fleetweeksandiego.org.

OCTOBER
Little Italy Festa: www.littleitalysd.com.

NOVEMBER
San Diego Beer Week: www.sdbw.org.

San Diego Bay Wine & Food Festival: www.worldofwineevents.com.

DECEMBER
Balboa Park December Nights: First Friday and Saturday in December. www.balboapark.org.

College bowl games: Holiday Bowl (www.holidaybowl.com) and the Poinsettia Bowl (www.poinsettiabowl.com).

WHERE TO STAY

San Diego accommodations are as varied as the county's diverse topography. From beaches, to mountains, to desert, you'll find hip high-rises, spa- and golf-blessed resorts, and properties rife with history, as well as backpacker hostels and out-of-the-ordinary B&Bs.

Downtown and the beaches have the largest variety; Mission Valley is filled with chains; and La Jolla and Coronado have some of the finest luxury resorts. Certain details are standard—most places charge for an extra person in the room but allow children under a certain age to stay for free. All are non-smoking and some small places don't allow smoking anywhere on property. Ask about any loyalty programs wherever you go; join and you could get an upgrade, free nights or extras like free W-Fi and hotel credits.

Vacation rental homes, condos, beach cottages, and apartments abound. **VRBO** (www.vrbo.com) lists more than 4,000 units available for rent by owner. **Mission Sands** (www.missionsands.com) manages some luxury as well as moderately priced rentals. If you're looking for multiple bedrooms and kitchens, **Resortime** (resortime.com) arranges rentals in timeshare units. In addition to rooms in private homes, **AirBnB** (www.airbnb.com) lists some fabulous seaside studios.

Note: This chapter explores all the options within the city proper. Lodging for Del Mar, Encinitas, and Carlsbad (all beautifully situated along the coast and within 40 min. of the city) are found in chapter 8.

Price Categories

Room rates vary greatly, especially given the many websites with special deals. We've listed the lowest possible rate for a double room in high and low season, which means the rooms with the least amenities, views, and space. In many places there isn't much difference, since San Diego is a year-round destination. Both summer and winter are considered high season at most hotels; shoulder season in fall and spring usually have the best rates. Do surf the Internet as prices can shift significantly by seller.

Inexpensive: $150 and under
Moderate: $175 to $300
Expensive: $300 and up

Downtown, Gaslamp Quarter & Little Italy
EXPENSIVE

Hard Rock Hotel San Diego ★★ This party playground draws fun-loving, sometimes rowdy guests—stay away if you're looking for a peaceful retreat. The room decor sets the mood; even the smallest studios have sexy, backlit wood-framed beds at center stage facing wide screen TVs plus elaborate sound systems with an endless selection of movies, music channels, and custom playlists. Suites are kitted out with low leather couches, bar stools at a wet bar, and a second TV in the living area. The bathroom separates the two other rooms—an awkward arrangement if you prefer privacy while primping. Some Rock Star suites feature wraparound terraces with fire pits. There's always a party at Float, the large rooftop pool lounge with private cabanas and furnished seating areas by the bar. Weekend afternoon pool parties are hugely popular—ask for a room away from the pool unless you want to be in the middle of the fun. A branch of Nobu, Nobuyuki Matsuhisa, and Robert De Niro's chi chi, pricey Japanese restaurant, adds class to the ground floor. Maryjane's 24-hour diner fuels revelers with hearty burgers and steak and eggs served 24/7. With its prime placement as the anchor for the Gaslamp Quarter, near the convention center and PETCO Park, the Hard Rock attracts a lot of tourists checking out the guitars, costumes and other rock memorabilia in the lobby. Ask if there are any special events planned during your stay—be prepared for wedding, convention, and Spring Break parties.

207 Fifth Ave. www.hardrockhotelsd.com. ✆ **866/751-7625** or 619/702-3000. 420 units. From $249–$269 double; from $289 suite. $19 resort fee. Valet parking $40. **Amenities:** 2 restaurants, 2 bars; music venue; concierge; exercise room; outdoor pool; room service; spa; free Wi-Fi.

Omni San Diego Hotel ★★★ The attractive yet sensible design of this 32-story hotel's rooms make it my favorite near the convention center. Sleek wood headboards replace tacky hotel art, the simple desk and night tables are uncluttered, and floor-to-ceiling windows, many with bay views, actually open a tad. Best of all, a corner set of glass shelves in the bathroom provides ample, uncluttered space for necessities. Others say the highlight is the hotel's fourth-floor sky bridge to PETCO Park and suites overlooking the ball field, certainly a plus when the Padres are in town. Baseball memorabilia lines hallways by the bridge, and packages with tickets are popular (plus, you needn't worry about parking close to the ballpark).

675 L St. www.omnihotels.com. ✆ **888/444-6664** or 619/231-6664. 511 units. $219 double; from $329 suite. Valet parking $38. **Amenities:** Restaurant; 2 bars; concierge; exercise room; Jacuzzi; outdoor pool; room service. Wi-Fi $10/day or complimentary with free loyalty program sign-up.

The US Grant ★★★ Downtown San Diego's grand dame, built in 1910 by the son of Ulysses S. Grant, has been rescued from near dilapidation many times over. The most recent fix came in 2006, when the Sycuan Band of the Kumeyaay Nation, a thriving local community, purchased the property and invested $56 million in renovations. The Grant is now as glorious as ever, with its grand sweeping lobby, glistening glass chandeliers, filigreed iron railings, and velvet couches. Though the rooms have lovely historic accents, including 9-foot ceilings and all sorts of curlicue moldings and accents, many are cramped and have tiny bathrooms. But the larger suites, featuring elegant salons and large bathrooms, are lovely and spacious enough to serve as dressing rooms for the bridal parties celebrating in the many ballrooms. The hotel's historic Grant Grill has long been one of downtown's most elegant dining spaces—so old school that women weren't allowed to dine there until a gutsy group of businesswomen

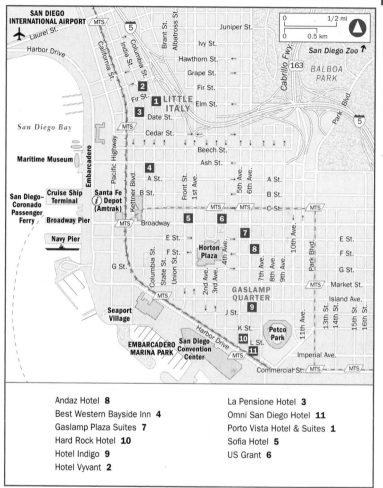

Andaz Hotel **8**	La Pensione Hotel **3**
Best Western Bayside Inn **4**	Omni San Diego Hotel **11**
Gaslamp Plaza Suites **7**	Porto Vista Hotel & Suites **1**
Hard Rock Hotel **10**	Sofia Hotel **5**
Hotel Indigo **9**	US Grant **6**
Hotel Vyvant **2**	

refused to leave in 1969. A redesign updated the grill's dark leather and wood men's club feel with high-backed chairs covered in light beige upholstery replacing most booths and window shutters adding light—but the rooms still glows with the light from crystal chandeliers at night. The old-fashioned mock turtle soup is still on the menu, but curried coconut broth, fennel, violet mustard, and other gourmet touches appeal to more adventuresome palates. The Art Deco cocktail lounge's mixologist takes signature cocktails to delicious, seasonal levels—try the Smashing Pumpkin in autumn.

326 Broadway. www.usgrant.net. ℂ **866/837-4270** or 619/232-3121. 270 units. $249–$278 double, suites from $324. Valet parking $39. Dogs less than 40 lb. accepted with no fee. **Amenities:** Restaurant; bar; babysitting; 24-hr. concierge; exercise room; room service; Wi-Fi $12/day.

TRAVELING WITH pets

Many of us wouldn't dream of going on vacation without our pets. We've pointed out which hotels accept them. As for activities, many San Diegans congregate with their canine friends at **Dog Beach,** at the north end of Ocean Beach, where dogs can swim, play, and socialize. After your pooch is thoroughly coated in seawater and sand, take him to the do-it-yourself **Dog Beach Dog Wash,** 2 blocks away at 4933 Voltaire St. (www.dogwash.com; ℂ **619/523-1700**). Nate's Point in Balboa Park is another favored place to let your pooch run loose. It's at the west end of the park, on the south side of Cabrillo Bridge.

MODERATE

Andaz Hotel ★★   When the sexy, beyond hip Ivy Hotel moved under the Hyatt hotel's umbrella in 2010, regulars feared their hangout would become uptight and staid. Their worries proved unfounded. Yes, gone are the long lines of scantily dressed young revelers seeking entrance to the underground club (now closed). Instead, a more casual crowd gathers at RoofTop600, a glam lounge with private cabanas, bottle service, and fire pits (open Thurs–Sat nights). And some rooms still have the glass-enclosed bedside bathtubs and showers that were the talk of the town when Ivy opened in 2007. The sleek rooms with polished wood walls and ceilings framing low king-sized beds combine sensuality and sophistication (some overlook downtown, but most face other buildings). Luxury hits the mini-bars, too, which are stocked with full-sized bottles of Grey Goose and Jack Daniels, along with free soft drinks and snacks. When not cast in London lounge mode, RoofTop600 serves brunch, lunch, and sandwiches, salads and pizzas. The downstairs restaurant is closed but the wine bar serves appetizers along with a whopping 88 wines by the glass. Business travelers and couples enjoy the youthful, fun vibe but it's not a good choice for families or sensible, practical types.

600 F St. www.andaz.com. ℂ **800/492-8804** or 619/849-1234. 159 units. $229-323 double; suite from $379. Valet parking $40. Pets less than 50 lb. accepted for $100 for stay up to 6 nights. **Amenities:** Restaurant; 2 bars; nightclub; 24-hr. concierge; fitness center; outdoor pool; room service; spa services; free Wi-Fi.

Hotel Indigo ★★   You needn't hock your jewels for a room close to the convention center and ball park. Just look toward the East Village, downtown's fastest-growing neighborhood. Ahead of the times in location and style, the Indigo is just a few blocks from most of downtown's main draws—but a few streets east of most hotels. It's surrounded by modern condo towers housing young professionals, meaning the neighborhood's loaded with trendy coffee houses, restaurants, and lounges. Thoughtful touches in the rooms include bedside area rugs on the hardwood floors, comfy reading chairs with tableside reading lamps, ample outlets at the desk, and a wet bar with coffee and tea maker. Pets are welcome without a deposit and are allowed to roam around specific areas by the rooftop garden. And on the subject of the roof: the Level 9 rooftop lounge shuns hip pretension, offering a fab spot for sunset cocktails.

509 Ninth Ave. www.hotelindigo.com/sandiego. ℂ **877/834-3613** or 619/727-4000. 215 units $188–$250. Valet parking $41. **Amenities:** Restaurant; 2 bars; concierge; exercise room; room service; free Wi-Fi.

The Sofia Hotel ★   This remake of one of San Diego's oldest, and one-time seediest, hotels takes full advantage of the building's 1920s Gothic brick architecture.

Carpeting, intricate molding, cushy club chaises and heavy drapes give a sense of stately, old-fashioned city dwellings. Travelers accustomed to bright, airy, modernistic rooms might feel penned in here (many of the rooms are quite small); those who appreciate coziness and reasonable rates will do just fine. The location is ideal for busy travelers, with the Santa Fe Depot, trolley station, and waterfront practically next door. It's a 5 to 10 minute walk to the Gaslamp's hot spots, with no notable restaurants or bars nearby. The in-house Currant American Brasserie is a pleasant find, however.

150 W. Broadway. www.thesofiahotel.com. *©* **800/826-0009** or 619/234-9200. 211 units. $112–$149 double; from $229 suite. Valet parking $34. Small pets accepted with $25 per night. **Amenities:** Restaurant; bar; 24-hr. concierge; exercise room; spa services, free Wi-Fi.

INEXPENSIVE

Best Western Bayside Inn ★   Given the reasonable room rates, this standard chain hotel deserves consideration. It's within a 5 to 10 minute walk of the Embarcadero, Little Italy, the train station, and Gaslamp Quarter, and the hotel's location on a side street lessens street noise. Rooms are standard, clean, and functional, with one or two beds and small desks, cabinets with mini-fridge and microwave, mirrored sliding doors on the foyer closet, and a tub-shower combo in the bathroom. Carpeting, linens, and drapes are all fresh and clean and even the smallest rooms have enough space for a couple of suitcases. Some larger rooms have balconies and seating areas. Naturally, views are best from the highest of the 14 stories; ask ahead for a bay view (the Bayside name is misleading). The courtesy shuttle to the airport, train station, and cruise ship pier is a big plus, and though the outdoor pool is small, it's a pleasant place to cool off after sightseeing.

555 W. Ash St. www.baysideinn.com. *©* **800/341-1818** or 619/233-7500. 122 units. $150–$190 double. Rates include continental breakfast. Parking $14. **Amenities:** Restaurant (breakfast daily, dinner Mon–Fri 5–9pm, no lunch); bar; pool and hot tub; room service; free Wi-Fi.

Gaslamp Plaza Suites ★★   San Diego's first skyscraper, 11 stories tall, rises above Fifth Avenue in historic marble sturdiness. It's no gleaming steel and glass tower, but fits in with the Gaslamp Quater's blend of period architecture. Built in 1913 to house one of San Diego's first banks, it's now a 60-suite hotel on one of downtown's busiest avenues. The lobby has retained its elegance, with Australian gumwood carpentry, marble walls, mirrored ceilings above crystal chandeliers, and etched glass windows. Similar touches add a bit of glamour to the suites, all with kitchenettes including microwave, fridge, dishes, and utensils. Floral swag drapes, Art Deco patterned rugs, and marble bathrooms reflect the historic ambience, without being fussy. Rooms on the top floors have spectacular views of downtown's skyline; those on lower floors in the back overlook parking lots and drab buildings. A modest continental breakfast is served in the breakfast room, and the rooftop terrace is a good spot for relaxing and hooking into someone else's free Wi-Fi (hint, hint). The Melting Pot restaurant and Vin de Syrah wine bar on the hotel's ground floor are dependable dining choices, but there are so many options nearby that you'll want to explore. Despite heavy windows, noise can be a problem, especially on weekend nights when the surrounding clubs and restaurants are in full swing. Beware of major holidays, as well—the Gaslamp's Mardi Gras celebration is one of the country's largest and the neighborhood is party central for any occasion.

520 E St. www.gaslampplaza.com. *©* **800/874-8770** or 619/232-9500. 64 units. $111–$149 double; from $149 suite. Rates include continental breakfast. Valet parking $30. **Amenities:** 2 restaurants, concierge; Wi-Fi $12/day, $30/week.

Hotel Vyvant ★   If you want to feel like a local, choose this restored 1910 home (formerly called the Little Italy Inn). With 23 rooms, it's not quite a B&B, though the staff and other guests make it feel that way, especially during the sociable breakfasts and weekend cocktail hours in the living room. A few inexpensive, tastefully decorated rooms have shared bathroom. Larger en-suite rooms have an Old World ambiance, with glowing table lamps, polished antique furnishings, and heavy drapes. Most rooms lack fridges; if you're staying a while go for a room or suite with kitchenette. Complimentary breakfast includes breads, granola, and coffee from local artisan businesses. The location is ideal, steps from Little Italy's restaurants and shops. Highway access is a breeze, since I-5 runs close by. Despite the proximity to roads, the airport and train stops, the rooms are peaceful. Parking is tough, though.

505 W. Grape St. www.hotelvyvant.com. ℅ **800/518-9930** or 619/230-1600. 23 units. $89–$109. Rates include continental breakfast. Pets allowed for $50 fee. Limited street parking. **Amenities:** Free Wi-Fi.

La Pensione Hotel ★★   Guests get maximum style for moderate prices at this European-inspired boutique hotel. Developers were just beginning to cast eager eyes on Little Italy back in 1991, when San Diego star architect Rob Quigley remodeled a historic India Street fixture into the downtown area's coolest inn. A 2011 makeover refreshed the property, and today glam touches incudes silver foil wall coverings, Italian glass pendant lamps, polished nickel furnishings, and rainshowers. The downside to staying here? Most rooms are tiny and late-night noise can mandate earplugs—try for an upper-floor bay. Surrounded by Little Italy's abundant restaurants and bars (and with a restaurant and café on site), near a trolley station, and close to the airport, La Pensione fits the bill for travelers seeking moderate rates, access to public transportation and a decent hip quotient.

606 W. Date St. www.lapensionehotel.com. ℅ **800/232-4683** or 619/236-8000. 68 units. $100 double. Limited free underground parking. **Amenities:** 2 restaurants; exercise room; free Wi-Fi.

Porto Vista Hotel & Suites ★★   Proving you needn't have wads of cash to be stylish, the owners of this Little Italy inn managed to dress up an old motel with enough extras to make it a fun place to do more than simply sleep. Granted, the least-expensive rooms are small and simple, but the ice-blue tufted headboard mounted over the bed, and black-and-white glamour photos on the walls, add a touch of class. As the price climbs added amenities include include bathtubs, balconies with bay views, and expanded wet bars with microwave and fridge. Happy hour at the fourth-floor Glass Door restaurant and lounge attracts neighbors from nearby condos; grab an outdoor table for views of the harbor. The food gets mixed reviews, so order sparingly. Packages including free Wi-Fi and full breakfast are worth a few extra bucks.

1835 Columbia St. www.portovistasd.com. ℅ **800/537-9902** or 619/544-0164. 189 units. $111–$139 double; suite from $150. Valet parking $22. Dogs up to 40 lb. accepted with $75 fee. **Amenities:** Restaurant; bar; free airport shuttle; Wi-Fi $20 (or free with packages).

Hillcrest & Uptown
INEXPENSIVE

Balboa Park Inn ★   An elephant's trunk drapes over the headboard above a jaguar in the "Zoo Room's" wall-length mural. Stenciled fish and framed egret paintings dot the sea blue walls in "The Aruba." Standard rooms are non-existent at this quirky B&B, just steps from the San Diego Zoo, and a few blocks from Hillcrest's abundant clubs and restaurants. The owners took a small neighborhood apartment complex and created 26 wacky suites with private bathrooms and kitchenettes. Your choices are limited only by your imagination. Wanted to pretend you're in Paris in the '30s, or on the Orient Express? No problem. Various rooms have faux fireplaces, whirlpools, or garden views. The decor helps mask the lack of space in the smallest units. The court-yard and rooftop terrace add room for resting and ruminating.

3402 Park Blvd. www.balboaparkinn.com. ℂ **619/298-0823.** 26 units. $99 double; from $149 suites. Street parking. Rates include continental breakfast. **Amenities:** Free Wi-Fi.

Inn at the Park ★ Hillcrest and the entire uptown area are sorely lacking accom-modations, unfortunately, as there are a number of great restaurants and bars in these neighborhoods. This sturdy brick hostelry, however, has been housing guests since 1926, and it's still your best Uptown option, just a block from Balboa Park. The over-sized rooms (ranging from 524–1,100 sq. ft.) are now part of the Shell Hospitality timeshare group (but still available by the night) and are outfitted for guests staying multiple days or weeks. All have full kitchens with electric stovetops, fridges, and tableware along with separate dining areas, plus Sealy Posturpedic beds. The rooms also feature electronic blackout shades, and updated entertainment systems. Larger units have separate bedrooms and walk-in closets. Painted moldings, floral stencils, long couches with glass coffee tables, and wall-hung Formica dining tables make the units feel like urbane city apartments rather than simple hotel rooms. (That's with the exception of a few that are oddly glammed with gilded bedframes set against purple walls; ask to move if you draw one of those). The restaurant is closed, but breakfast is served (for a fee) in the rooftop dining room and there are plenty of dining options all around.

525 Spruce St. www.shellhospitality.com. ℂ **800/874-2649** or 619/291-0999. 82 units. $110–$134. Rates include continental breakfast. Valet $15; free street parking. **Amenities:** Kitchens; free Wi-Fi.

Keating House ★★ The epitome of 1880s elegance and style, this faithfully restored Queen Anne Victorian mansion is the star of this Banker's Hill neighborhood dotted with similar historic homes. Flowering jasmine and roses, wild bursts of scarlet bougainvillea, and tall cacti fill the grounds both street side and in the back courtyard, providing bucolic shade for the wicker chairs scattered around porches in the main house and the remodeled carriage house. Each of the 9 units has its merits, from the French doors opening to the garden in the aptly named Garden Suite to gas fireplaces, towel warmers, soaking tubs, and porches in other suites. All have high ceilings, are tastefully decorated with antiques including iron beds, and are painted various deep colors. Breakfast is served in a formal dining room and guests gather to share tips in the parlor. Balboa Park is just 3 blocks away, and it's a downhill walk to downtown and the Gaslamp (with plenty of taxis around for the return trip). Be aware that planes do fly overhead on approaching the airport, but the noise is usually insignificant.

2331 Second Ave. www.keatinghouse.com. ℂ **619/239-8585.** 9 units. $119–$169 double. Free street parking. Rates include full breakfast. **Amenities:** Free Wi-Fi.

Lafayette Hotel, Swim Club & Bungalows ★★ Spirited, fun-loving guests adore this redesigned 1946 hotel. In its early years, it was a 25-acre resort with mul-tiple restaurants, clubs, and shops, and attracted a Hollywood set. It fell into disrepair over subsequent decades and became a favorite of ladies of the night and their com-panions. After a $6 million remodel of the historic building, the Lafayette is once again, we're happy to say, a place for the chic set to hang their hats. Poolside suites are bright white and airy, with wood rocking chairs by the beds and striped awnings over terraces. A more formal mood prevails in the manor rooms and suites, some with art deco wallpaper, others in classy cream and burgundy. Whimsical two-story bungalows with multiple bedrooms are perfect for girl and/or guy getaways, encouraging a fun time with their retro meets edgy design. As for the public areas: Johnny Weissmuller (the original Tarzan and gold medal winner) designed the nearly Olympic sized swimming pool; today Sunday Rockabilly Pool Parties draw crowds of locals, some dressed in 50s style to bop along with pop songs. The **Red Fox Steakhouse and Piano Bar** is as fabulous, with a devoted crowd belting out jazz standards and showtunes come nightfall; while **Hope 46** (named for Bob Hope) is more modern and serves classic American cuisine. There's always live music somewhere, from Rolling Stones cover bands in the lounge to jazz groups by the pool. Don't be intimidated by the vibe: oldsters with hip attitudes are welcome. Check the app **Hotel Tonight** for lower rates.

2223 El Cajon Blvd. www.lafayettehotelsd.com. ✆ **619/296-2102.** 131 units. $82–$139 double; from $149 suites. Self-parking on-site $8. **Amenities:** 2 restaurants; 2 bars; live music; room service; pool; free Wi-Fi.

Old Town & Mission Valley
MODERATE
Cosmopolitan Hotel and Restaurant ★ History buffs and romantics enjoy this perfectly situated Old Town B&B. Peruvian Juan Bandini commissioned the Spanish hacienda-style home in 1829. Despite many reincarnations, its original architecture remains much the same. For many years it housed the colorful Mexican restaurant Casa de Bandini; when that closed, the building was transformed into a charming inn with a courtyard restaurant. As befits the house, rooms have floral wallpaper and antique furnishings, and some have claw-foot tubs. All open to the wraparound, second-story verandah overlooking the courtyard restaurant or the streets of Old Town. Rooms lack phones and TV, but there is complimentary Wi-Fi. Touring Old Town is a breeze from here, and you're lucky to be able to escape to your cool room when the streets get crowded. Jam, sweet breads, and coffee are served at tables outside each room in the morning. Parking is abundant at lots around Old Town.

2660 Calhoun St. www.oldtowncosmopolitan.com. ✆ **619/297-1874.** 10 units. $149–$295 double. Rates include continental breakfast. Free parking. **Amenities:** Restaurant; 2 bars; room service; free Wi-Fi.

Crowne Plaza San Diego ★ The tropical setting beside a golf course makes the Crowne Plaza stand out amid the area's dozens of chain hotels, as most are surrounded by asphalt parking lots. It's perfect for families who want reasonably priced accommodations without feeling like they could be staying anywhere from Amarillo to Chicago. At a minimum 322 square feet, the standard rooms are large enough for two plus luggage and accumulated stuff. Suites are double in size, and executive club level rooms include free continental breakfast in a private lounge. Striped wallpaper, floral prints in gilded frames, and double sinks in the bathrooms add a few stylish touches, and all rooms have balconies or terraces. The pool area, surrounded by palms and flowering bushes, is a pleasant oasis after busy days. Befitting its luau theme, the Islands restaurants serves pupus and sushi in the evening along with three standard meals. Join the free loyalty program when you check in for free Wi-Fi and other perks.

2270 Hotel Circle N. www.cp-sandiego.com. ✆ **800/227-6963** or 619/297-1101. 417 units. $121–$179. Pets accepted with $75 fee. Parking $12. **Amenities:** 2 restaurants; bar; exercise room; pool; whirlpool; room service; spa; complimentary shuttle; comp Wi-Fi for free loyalty club members or $10/day.

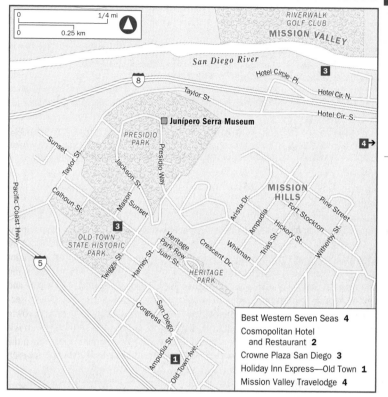

Best Western Seven Seas **4**
Cosmopolitan Hotel
 and Restaurant **2**
Crowne Plaza San Diego **3**
Holiday Inn Express—Old Town **1**
Mission Valley Travelodge **4**

INEXPENSIVE

Holiday Inn Express–Old Town ★   The I-5 interstate runs close to this efficient, yet pleasant hotel, giving guests easy access to the airport, beaches, and popular
attractions. Fortunately, most rooms face a courtyard and traffic noise is surprisingly
subdued. The facade is mock Spanish colonial, but rooms look like most standard business quarters. Accouterments include a small desk with proper outlets, plus microwaves, coffeemakers, small fridges, decent mattresses, and clean, well-maintained
bathrooms. Those who pay a bit more get a balcony and/or whirlpool tub. There's a
small pool and free shuttle to the airport and other locations. The free hot breakfast is
a boon and Old Town's eateries are scattered around nearby streets.

3900 Old Town Ave. www.hioldtownhotel.com. (*C*) **855/212-0196** or 619/543-1130. 123 units. From
$114–$120; double; from $166 suite. Rates include breakfast. Complimentary underground park-
ing. **Amenities:** Outdoor pool and whirlpool; deli/market; shuttle; free Wi-Fi.

Mission Valley Resort ★   Impressions are mixed when it comes to this 20-acre
Mission Valley property surrounded by nondescript motels. Some units are plagued
with worn furnishings or noisy air conditioning. Others, however, are in fine condition.
There seems to be little rhyme or reason regarding room remodels; ask to look at a few

before settling in. The 202 rooms are spread on hillsides, beside the two pools, and near the parking lots, which gives guests a lot of room to roam. I prefer the quieter hillside units with nearby parking. The on-site coffee shop, lounge, and convenience market come in handy. In short: it's not fancy, but you can't beat the price, which includes free parking.

875 Hotel Circle South. www.missionvalleyresort.com. (📞) **800/362-7871** or 619/543-1130. 202 units. $71–$139 double. Complimentary parking. **Amenities:** Restaurant; bar; 2 pools; fitness center; convenience/liquor store; guest laundry; free Wi-Fi.

Mission Bay & the Beaches
EXPENSIVE

Paradise Point Resort & Spa ★★★   You'd be hard put to find a better water-side resort for families . . . and romantics. The 44-acre tropical retreat covers a man-made island constructed when the Army Corps of Engineers dredged a channel deep enough for boats to enter Mission Bay. Hollywood producer Jack Skirball visited the island in 1962 and transformed it into his version of paradise. His concept has endured through several changes in management, and families who arrived shortly after the original resort opened gather here annually for multi-generational vacations. Many of the staff have remained for decades and greet returnees like old friends.

Much of the success of Paradise Point is due to its low-key ambience and abundant room to roam. Low-rise buildings with adjacent parking spaces are spread about the large property amid lawns, flower gardens, streams, pools, and the beach. Each structure contains only a few rooms; several stand alone. Many of the units with fridges and microwaves can be expanded by booking adjoining rooms and are well suited for large families and group getaways. If you can splurge, go for waterfront cottage with a view of the bay from the bed, plus a fireplace, separate living area, and terrace by the sand and fire rings.

The formal restaurant was redesigned with a more casual style in 2014 and renamed Tidal. The outdoor deck fills with families (kids have their own menu) before sunset; couples tend to wander in a bit later, dine on the terrace, and linger over cocktails in couches beside fire pits.

There are plenty of distractions, including a full-service marina with all kinds of watercraft and an 18-hole putting course. Bikes and surreys are available for rent beside the large sundries and souvenir shop. Naturally, a serene spa adds the pampering element.

1404 Vacation Rd. www.paradisepoint.com. (📞) **800/344-2626** or 858/274-4630. 462 units. $167–$301 double; from $295 suite. Valet $20 or self-parking $34. Pets less than 15 lb. accepted with $100 fee. **Amenities:** 2 restaurants; 2 bars; bikes; concierge; exercise room; 18-hole golf putting course; 5 outdoor pools; limited room service; full-service spa; tennis/basketball courts; marina w/ watersports equipment/rentals; laundry facilities; resort fee $24/day includes Wi-Fi.

Tower 23 ★★★   Though it opened back in 2005, this sleek glass-wrapped cube on the Pacific Beach boardwalk is still the hippest hotel at the beach. It's got all the right elements for an awesome getaway: A top-notch restaurant and bar filled with sunlight in the day and bands of purple, pink and blue lights at night; a Sunset Patio on the boardwalk; roof-top deck with teak lounges and cocktail service—you get the picture. The six types of cutely named rooms (sanctuary suite, surf pad) have the same basic design with balconies or terraces (no ocean views for least expensive), glass-enclosed rainshowers, Tempur-Pedic mattresses wrapped with puffy white duvets, minimalist furnishings, and a sea and sky blue and tan palette. At the top of the line, the Sweet Suite's perks include two ocean-view balconies and a chromotherapy whirlpool tub. Despite the stylish surroundings, the casual, beach-friendly vibe makes it a decent choice for families with older children who'll enjoy the youthful energy.

723 Felspar St. www.t23hotel.com. © **866/869-3723** or 858/273-8440. 44 units. $229–$389 double; from $419 suite. Valet parking $20. Pets less than 25 lb. accepted with $150 fee. **Amenities:** Restaurant; bar; room service; spa services; free Wi-Fi.

MODERATE

Catamaran Resort Hotel ★★ With Mission Bay at one end and Pacific Beach on the other, this venerable 1950s resort attracts families, couples, small meeting groups, and locals on hometown getaways. All find just what they need, including kitchenettes in some rooms, easy access to Pacific Beach's vibrant (read: wild) nightlife, bountiful activities, and a full-service spa. A fun Polynesian theme prevails throughout the resort, with koi ponds, waterfalls, squawking macaws, nightly torch lightings, lei-making classes, weekly luaus, and Hawaiian music in Moray's Lounge (complete with huge live eel). During the summer, guests have complimentary access to theme bay cruises on the hotel's Bahia Belle sternwheeler—families go for the early evening ride, while grownups wait for the 10pm cocktail cruise. Ground floor bay front rooms and suites beside the sand complete the island escape fantasy, but garden view rooms give a sense of tranquility. The casual furnishings and tan carpeting are the same wherever you land, whether in the 13-story tower or two-story buildings, all with balcony or terrace. The smallest rooms have coffeepot and small fridge, larger studios and suites have full kitchens. The Atoll restaurant serves all meals, including a popular Sunday brunch. Breaking ranks with most hotels these days, the Catamaran has no resort fee and Wi-Fi is free. Hooray!

3999 Mission Blvd. www.catamaranresort.com. © **800/422-8386** or 858/488-1081. 311 units. $149–$189 double, from $339 suite. Valet parking $23; self-parking $18. **Amenities:** Restaurant; 2 bars; children's programs; concierge; exercise room; hot tub; outdoor pool; room service; spa; sports equipment/rentals; free Wi-Fi.

Crystal Pier Hotel ★★★ Do your fantasies include falling asleeping to the ocean's rhythmic music? Wish you could float on the waves night and day? It's easy to make such dreams come true at this outstanding beach escape. Family-owned and faithfully tended, the complex includes cottages straight out of New England, lining a wooden pier jutting into the ocean. Wooden shutters and geraniums blooming in window boxes by front doors hint at pleasures inside, including beds covered with quilts, kitchens with full-sized refrigerators and, best of all, a deck with an umbrella-shaded table and chairs, plus lounge chairs, perched above the waves. A large percentage of guests return annually to the same cottage, parking their cars outside the front door, hanging their beach towels off the deck railings, and refusing to leave until the vacation account has run dry. Three suites on the boardwalk are similarly laid out, sans parking and overwater deck; one is a simple room without kitchen. The demand is so high it's best to reserve your cottage four to six months ahead for winter and 11 months for summer. That said, you can luck out and book a cottage at the last minute—it's always worth checking. Minimum stays required.

4500 Ocean Blvd. www.crystalpier.com. © **800/748-5894** or 858/483-6983. 29 units. $175–$525. **Amenities:** Beach equipment rental; free Wi-Fi.

Elsbree House ★ This five-room ocean-green house is as close as you can get to renting a vacation home by the beach without having to stay a week or more. Each room has a private entrance and private bathroom with tub and shower, and two can be connected to create a larger space, with two queen and two twin beds. An English country theme prevails inside the white picket fence, with geraniums and daisies blooming in pots beneath shade trees and beds dressed in floral linens and lace. It's not too fussy, though children under 12 aren't admitted and this certainly isn't the place for a rowdy celebration. An expanded continental breakfast (cereals, yogurt, hard-boiled eggs, muffins, fruit) is served in the antique-filled dining room each morning. There's also a three-bedroom condo with room for six available by the week. It's a 2-block walk to funky OB's busy Newport Avenue with all sorts of restaurants, bars and shops. *Warning:* OB is in the airport's flight path and plane noise, especially in early morning, is significant. But residents happy to be living by the beach manage to tune it out. Parking is tight, but there's a pay lot 1 block away.

5054 Narragansett Ave. www.bbinnob.com. ℭ **619/226-4133.** 6 units. $149–$199 double; condo $1,199–$2,700 per week. Rates include continental breakfast (except condo). No children under 12 allowed. **Amenities:** Free Wi-Fi.

Pacific Terrace Hotel ★   Since it's at the north end of Pacific beach, this hotel is quieter than most in the area. Wood shutters and wall art featuring palms and flowers give the rooms a serene, tropical feel. Separate vanity sinks outside the bathrooms are a nice touch, as are the Tommy Bahama toiletries and unlimited use of beach towels, umbrellas and toys. Several rooms have kitchenettes and dining areas. You can swim in the ocean right in front of the hotel, walk north and watch surfers tackle the waves at Tourmaline Beach, or simply lounge at the pool terrace beside the boardwalk. The mandatory resort fee ($24) includes 2-hour bike rental, free Wi-Fi, and a coupon book good for discounts at nearby hotels and shops. There's no restaurant, but a breakfast buffet (not complimentary) is served each morning, and a few nearby restaurants let you charge your meals to your room.

610 Diamond St. www.pacificterrace.com. ℭ **800/344-3370** or 858/581-3500. 73 units. From $188–$296 double; from $320 suite. Parking $22. **Amenities:** Concierge; exercise room; hot tub; pool; room service; spa services; resort fee $24 includes free Wi-Fi.

INEXPENSIVE

The Dana on Mission Bay ★★★   Among my favorite go-to lodgings for penny-pinching family and friends, this Mission Bay old-timer covers all the bases. The Sixties-era original buildings still hold small, modest, motel-like rooms where sandy kids can't destroy the dark carpeting and bedspreads. Many are located around the pool areas and gardens. All units have mini-fridge, microwave, and coffeemaker. The 74 rooms and 12 suites added during a 2004 remodel are located in two three-story buildings at the bay's edge. They're larger and brighter, with private terraces or balconies. The marina's boat slips, paddleboards, wave runners and other toys are a big draw, as are rental bikes for touring Mission Bay's endless bike paths and shuttles to local attractions including SeaWorld right across the water from the 10-acre resort. A resort fee covers the shuttle, Wi-Fi, a coupon book and other goodies.

1710 W. Mission Bay Dr. www.thedana.com. ℭ **800/455-3339** or 619/222-6440. 271 units. $99–$229 double; from $199 suites. Parking $20. Small dogs allowed for a $100 fee good for 6 days. **Amenities:** 2 restaurants; bar; bike rentals; concierge; fitness center; 2 hot tubs; 2 outdoor heated pools; room service; spa services; marina w/watersports equipment/rentals; guest laundry facilities; free Wi-Fi.

The Pearl Hotel ★   A risky gamble has paid off for the imaginative owners who took a 1959 motel and transformed it into a midcentury modern marvel on a busy Point

Loma street. "Rad" describes the transformation from drab and dreary to stylish and fun—only a few places can get away with mirrors over the beds and live fish floating in glass bowls. Making the most of limited motel-room space, the designers mounted the small desks and nightstands on the walls, added a divider separating the open closet from the low platform beds, and brightened the bathrooms with shiny tile and glass. Some rooms have balconies or patios (room 9 with its sitting area and larger balcony overlooking the pool is in high demand). In the evening, guests gather around the saltwater pool where films are shown on a large projection screen during "Dive In Theater" nights. Or they head to the on-property Eat at the Pearl restaurant; popular with locals, it serves a to-die-for burger with smoked Gouda, and large pork, chicken, and steak entrees. Point Loma's sportfishing pier, Shelter Island, and a few great restaurants are nearby, but there's no beach or other attractions. Here, staying and playing at The Pearl is the main event. *Tip:* Rooms by Rosecrans Street will get some noise but those in the back lack views.

1410 Rosecrans St. www.thepearlsd.com. © **877/732-7573** or 619/226-6100. 23 units. $99–$149 double. "Play & Stay" rate $79 after midnight (must be booked on-site, subject to availability). Parking $10, $5 for hybrids. **Amenities:** Restaurant; bar; bike rentals; outdoor saltwater pool; spa services; free Wi-Fi.

La Jolla

EXPENSIVE

The Bed & Breakfast Inn at La Jolla ★★   Guests tend to return to this gracious home frequently, enjoying the quiet historic neighborhood and the B&B's serene gardens. Architect Irving Gill designed the cubist building in 1913, and many of his loveliest buildings, with signature archways, built-in nooks and shelves, and simple, unadorned walls, are clustered nearby. All 15 rooms have small private bathrooms; some are bright and cheery with floral wallpaper, and lots of pillows and ruffles; others are more modern and minimalist with soft beige walls. All include a pleasingly eclectic combo of antique and modern furnishings. A few rooms have partial sea views, or clay foot tubs, or decorative fireplaces. Soft towels, crisp linens, fresh flowers, and fragrant toiletries add pampering touches. Days begin with a candlelit three-course breakfast and end with cheese and wine at sunset; beverages and snack are set out during the day. Birds and butterflies flit about the flower-filled gardens and terraces.

7753 Draper Ave. www.sandiegolajollabnb.com. © **888/988-8481** or 858/456-2066. 15 units. $210–$289 double Children under 12 not allowed. Rates include full breakfast. Limited free parking for small cars. One dog less than 35 lb. accepted with $200 deposit and $50 nightly fee, and can only stay in one particular suite. Reservations must be arranged in advance on the phone. **Amenities:** Beach chairs/umbrellas; CD players; free Wi-Fi is not dependable.

The Grande Colonial ★★★   Though first-time visitors in La Jolla gravitate toward the more famous La Valencia, second-timers pick this thoughtfully restored 1913 inn in a relatively quiet section of La Jolla's main street. Each room is different. In some rooms golden-hued carpeting and bedcovers set against aquamarine walls reflect the sunlit scenery; others set a handsome tone with an ochre, gold, and brown palette. All rooms are outfitted with goose down comforters and pillows and soft robes. Several have ocean views, but ask for one away from the condo tower blocking much of the scenery. Our favorites are the gracious suites with window seats that overlook the Scripps Park's palms and the sea. Relax in the brick courtyard and small pool tucked in a courtyard, and sip cocktails in the antique-filled lobby before dining at the hotel's superb **Nine-Ten** restaurant (p. 209), one of San Diego's finest. For stays of one week or more, the Grande Colonial's intimate **Little Hotel by the Sea** and **Garden Terrace** offer apartment-like suites with living rooms, kitchens, and a separate entrance.

910 Prospect St. www.thegrandecolonial.com. (Ⓒ) **888/828-5498** or 858/454-2181. 93 units. $219–$229 double; from $259 suite. Valet parking $25. **Amenities:** Restaurant; bar; concierge; outdoor pool; room service; free Wi-Fi.

La Jolla Beach and Tennis Club ★ Both a private club and a public resort with rooms available by the night, this 22-acre oceanfront property is among the most desirable destinations around if you want to dig your toes in the sand and wear your swimsuit all day long. Rooms set right along the beach are downright basic . . . but the sea views above La Jolla Shores are irresistible. Among the many types of units available are small studios (some with beds facing sea views), and multi-bedroom suites with kitchens. The least-expensive rooms face gardens and parking lots, but guests still have easy access to the beach and can hear waves crashing at night. Members of this exclusive club book the best rooms far in advance in summer; some families vacation with friends in the same adjacent rooms annually. It's possible to get an ocean front room in summer, but stay away from major holidays like July fourth.

Staff members are genial and helpful, setting up barbecues and picnic tables for family dinners (extra fee), setting up lounge chairs and striped umbrellas on the beach, and booking sunset dinner reservations at the famed Marine Room, a few steps down the beach. Tennis is hugely important here, and professional players partake in competitions on 12 championship hard courses. The long pool beside the courts is geared more toward exercise than lounging, especially in the early morning when members stop by to swim laps each morning.

The **La Jolla Shores Hotel** (www.ljshoreshotel.com) next door is run by the same management. It's not directly on the beach and is constructed in a hacienda style with many rooms facing a central courtyard. Rooms have newer furnishings than at the club, but the hotel feels more like a standard property rather than the sand in your toes, summer vacation home style of the club. The properties do not share facilities.

2000 Spindrift Dr. www.ljbtc.com. (Ⓒ) **888/828-0948** or 858/454-7126. 98 units. $231–$517 double; from $419 suite. 3-night minimum in summer. **Amenities:** 2 restaurants; seasonal beach snack bar; babysitting; children's programs; exercise room; 9-hole pitch-and-putt golf course; heated outdoor pool; room service; 12 lighted tennis courts; spa services; watersports equipment/rentals; free Wi-Fi.

La Valencia Hotel ★★★ The grande dame of La Jolla's village, "La V" was designed by architect William Templeton Johnson, in 1926 and has retained its rose-hued splendor through various renovations, including a major redo in 2013-2014. The building's Mediterranean style, tiled wall, and fountains, and other historic touches remain intact. But the dark wood and leather venerable Whaling Bar, gathering point for neighborhood bigwigs over decades, has been transformed into the bright, almost stark, Cafe La Rue with long orange banquettes beneath paintings of Parisian street scenes and a contemporary bistro menu. Rooms have been updated as well while keeping a grand Mediterranean style. The rooms vary greatly in size, view, and comfort and though the oldest section has a certain charm, newer areas are more comfortable. At the top of the options are the beach-cottage sized villas with spa tubs, fireplaces, and personalized butler service. George Clooney or Clark Gable would look right at home lounging beside the palm-shaded pool, and you expect to see ladies in broad-brimmed sunhats and floral dresses sipping tea in La Sala Lounge. It's a classic, and definitely worth a visit even if you're not staying here.

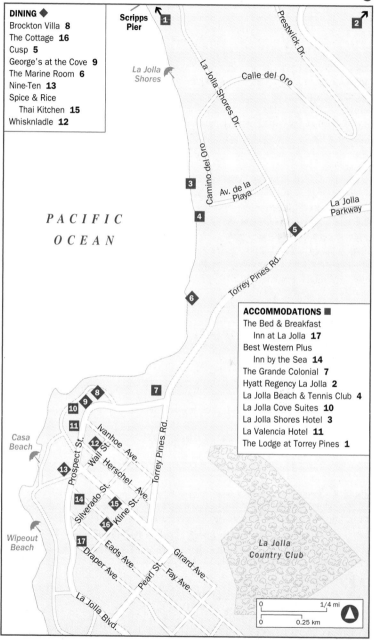

DINING ◆
Brockton Villa **8**
The Cottage **16**
Cusp **5**
George's at the Cove **9**
The Marine Room **6**
Nine-Ten **13**
Spice & Rice
   Thai Kitchen **15**
Whisknladle **12**

Scripps
Pier

La Jolla
Shores

Prestwick Dr.

La Jolla Shores Dr.

Calle del Oro

Camino del Oro

Av. de la
Playa

La Jolla
Parkway

PACIFIC
OCEAN

Torrey Pines Rd.

ACCOMMODATIONS ■
The Bed & Breakfast
   Inn at La Jolla **17**
Best Western Plus
   Inn by the Sea **14**
The Grande Colonial **7**
Hyatt Regency La Jolla **2**
La Jolla Beach & Tennis Club **4**
La Jolla Cove Suites **10**
La Jolla Shores Hotel **3**
La Valencia Hotel **11**
The Lodge at Torrey Pines **1**

Casa
Beach

Ivanhoe Ave.

Prospect St.

Wall St.

Herschel Ave.

Torrey Pines Rd.

Silverado St.

Kline St.

Wipeout
Beach

Eads Ave.

Draper Ave.

Girard Ave.

Pearl St.

Fay Ave.

La Jolla
Country Club

La Jolla Blvd.

0   1/4 mi
0   0.25 km

1132 Prospect St. www.lavalencia.com. ℂ **800/451-0772** or 858/454-0771. 112 units. $365–$385 double; from $595 suites and villas. Valet parking $30. Pets less than 75 lb. accepted with $30 nightly fee. **Amenities:** 3 restaurants; 2 bars; babysitting; concierge; exercise room; hot tub; outdoor pool; room service; sauna; spa services; free Wi-Fi.

The Lodge at Torrey Pines ★★★

A tribute to California Craftsman architecture and interior design, this handsome lodge on a cliff above the sea beside Torrey Pines State Reserve wows the eye with dozens of gorgeous details. Wood shingles and sandstone set the tone in the facade, with doors opening to a handsome atrium lobby that looks like it belongs in Yosemite. Sunlight glows on high-beamed ceilings and hardwood floors, and Stickley rocking chairs are clustered around a blazing fireplace. Similar furnishings, Tiffany-style lamps, and marble and stone bathrooms continue the Craftsman theme in rooms spread about the property in several buildings. Naturally, those on the highest floors have stunning views of the sea and sky, plus extras including large balconies and fireplaces. Duffers go for those facing the famed Torrey Pines Golf Course, home to many a championship tournament. Even the garden view rooms are lovely, especially those buried in pines and native grasses. There's little reason to leave the property, given the exceptional dining at the signature A.R. Valentien restaurant, the serene pool, and the luxurious spa. Take a hike along the hilltop to fully appreciate the reserve's wild beauty.

11480 N. Torrey Pines Rd. www.lodgetorreypines.com. ℂ **800/656-0087** or 858/453-4420. 169 units. $323 double; from $659 suite. No resort fee. Valet parking $30; self-parking $25. **Amenities:** 2 restaurants; bar; concierge; exercise room; preferential tee times at the golf course; hot tub; outdoor pool; room service; spa; free Wi-Fi.

MODERATE

Hyatt Regency La Jolla ★

Designed by architect Michael Graves, this 16-story tower, topped with a crescent-shaped roof, was a startling sight when it appeared beside I-5 in 1989. These days, a full-scale community with a sea of townhouses and condos, plus several shopping areas, surrounds the hotel. The area is a sensible base as it gives easy access to the interstate, UCSD, several world-class scientific institutes, and all of La Jolla's attractions. With 417 guestrooms, the Hyatt is a magnet for meeting groups, academic gatherings, and business travelers, but it works for vacationers as well. All you need is a room on one of the higher floors with stunning views of sky and sea. A renovation in 2014 added a coastal flair to the guestrooms, with walls and textiles in soft blues and greys and modernistic furnishings. All the benefits of a luxury chain hotel are at hand, including a club floor with complimentary beverages and food in a private lounge; a long outdoor pool with plenty of lounge chairs, cabanas, fire pits and other comforts; access to one of La Jolla's most prestigious health clubs; and proximity to some of the area's best restaurants in the Aventine complex, also designed by Graves.

377 La Jolla Village Dr. www.lajollahyatt.com. ℂ **888-591-1234** or 858/552-1234. 417 units. $161–$179 double. Regency Club rooms start at $216. Valet parking $25, self-parking $20. **Amenities:** Restaurant; bar; pool; hot tub; spa; gym; spa; Wi-Fi for a fee.

INEXPENSIVE

Best Western Plus Inn by the Sea ★

Upgrade to an ocean view on the fifth floor for the best experience at this standard motel in the heart of the village. It's not fancy or stylish, but offers excellent room rates within walking distance of the coastline and La Jolla's great restaurants and shops. Rooms are several steps above a basic motel style, but this isn't a swanky resort. Still, the decor is pleasant enough, with bright blue carpeting, decent mattresses with lightweight beige bedspreads, small tables and dressers, coffeemakers, and shower/tub combos with vanity sink outside the bathroom. They all also have balconies, a nice touch. Breakfast including cereals, scrambled eggs, and muffins is served each morning, and refrigerators are available on request. Business travelers take note: the Wi-Fi is not always dependable. Ask which rooms have the best reception. If you're on a strict budget and are more interested in exploring than hanging out at a resort, this place is perfect.

7830 Fay Ave. www.lajollainnbythesea.com. ✆ **800/526-4545** or 858/459-4461. 129 units. $129–$149 double. Rates include continental breakfast. Parking $12. **Amenities:** Pool; guest laundry; free Wi-Fi.

La Jolla Cove Suites ★★ Blessed are the prescient souls who purchased coastal La Jolla land in decades past. Take Max Heimburge, a shoe store magnate who constructed the La Jolla Cove Hotel directly across from what's arguably the most scenic beach in San Diego in the 1950s. A granddaughter now operates the hotel, and was struggling to keep it afloat when Anthony Melchiori of the TV show Hotel Impossible stepped in to help. He found the condition of the rooms and infrastructure appalling, of course, but whipped everybody into shape, oversaw a quick fix for the most obvious problems, and—in a move that cheered potential guests—suggested a lower room rate. His intervention worked, occupancy is up, and the entire operation has been spiffed up.

So what has changed? Balconies along the ocean-facing facade (95% of the units face the sea) have new furniture and fresh paint job. Inside, there's an enough space to feel you've rented a seaside apartment, with big living areas, small kitchen, bedrooms and bathroom. Soft aqua walls and furnishings with clean, simple lines modernize the units. The best rooms (where my husband and I spent the night after our La Jolla Cove wedding) are in cottages on a hill behind the hotel, though the climb up steep steps is a drawback. Rooms without a view are a bargain, given the neighborhood.

Guests tend to mingle on the terrace behind the building with a saltwater pool, hot tub, and three propane barbeque grills. The rooftop terrace, where continental breakfast is served, would be a great place to hang out were it not often booked for weddings. On-site parking is a huge plus, as street spots are nearly impossible to find. La Jolla village's shopping and dining district is a block uphill.

1155 Coast Blvd., La Jolla. www.lajollacove.com. ✆ **888/525-6552** or 858/459-2621. 113 units. $121–$139 double; from $175 suite. Rates include continental breakfast. Parking $20. **Amenities:** BBQ grills; access to nearby health club; hot tub; heated outdoor pool; free Wi-Fi.

Coronado
EXPENSIVE
Hotel del Coronado ★★★
A landmark for all of San Diego, the "Hotel Del" rose above the beach in all its glory in 1888. Now a National Historic Landmark, the Pacific Coast's oldest resort hotel reflects a grandeur only starry-eyed visionaries could imagine. Designed to attract tourists—and potential Coronado residents—from all over the country, the hotel was constructed from hundreds of thousands of feet of redwood, oak, and other woods shipped in to build the largest all-wood structure in the country. The result is a Queen Ann style castle bedecked with red-shingled turrets, towering cupolas, frothy gingerbread trim, circular ballrooms, and pristine white balconies facing Glorietta Bay on one side and the open sea on the other. Rooms in the original Victorian building are in high demand despite their quirks, be they tiny bathrooms or

ocean views so partial they requiring balancing on the furniture to see water. All retain a casual elegance, with sand-colored walls, wood-shutters on the windows, and French doors. Claim an ocean-view suite and you'll feel like royalty, especially while sitting on your balcony drinking Champagne while hordes of tourists checking out the grounds snap your photo. You need a guest key to access the grand pool or book one of the cabanas or lounges for two at the swanky Del Beach area. Guests seeking privacy opt for the plain seven-floor tower beside the main building, with its adults-only pool and quiet beach. Those with considerable spending power opt for the exclusive Beach Village's cottages and condos outfitted like private homes. Finding your way around the grounds can be confusing for the directionally challenged. Take time to check out the herb and rose gardens, relax on a bench beside the walkway edging the sand (a popular local jogging and biking path), and stop to admire the weddings that take place almost daily on emerald lawns and the sand. Maze-like underground tunnels in the Victorian building contain shops and historic photo galleries (look for shots of Jack Lemmon and Marilyn Monroe filming "Some Like it Hot" on the Del's beach). Sunday brunch in the opulent Crown Room never disappoints, even with its $80 tab, and sunsets are perfect viewed from the outdoor patio at ENO Pizzeria and Wine Bar.

1500 Orange Ave. www.hoteldel.com. © **800/468-3533** or 619/435-6611 757 rooms. $329–$739 double; from $599 suite; Beach Village from $900. Minimum stay requirements apply most weekends. $25 resort fee. Valet parking $47; self-parking $37. Pets less than 40 lb. welcome for a $125 fee. **Amenities:** 5 restaurants; 4 bars; airport transfers; babysitting; bike rentals; children's programs; concierge; health club; 2 hot tubs; 2 outdoor pools; room service; full-service spa; free Wi-Fi.

MODERATE

El Cordova Hotel ★★   Pretty Spanish touches like red-tiled roofs, archways, courtyards, and tiled stairways plus friendly service and proximity to Coronado's attractions, are just some reasons to stay at this 1930s hotel. It's undergone major renovations over the years but maintains its Old World style with Mexican tiles in the bathrooms and kitchenettes, wrought iron framed mirrors and lamps, and paintings of Spanish street scenes. There's nothing posh or pretentious, but it's a comfy spot with several shops and restaurants within the building complex including **Miguel's Cocina,** a popular Mexican restaurant.

1351 Orange Ave. www.elcordovahotel.com. © **800/229-2032** or 619/435-4131. 40 units. $105–$125 double, suite from $195. Street parking. **Amenities:** Restaurant; BBQ grill; bike rentals; hot tub; outdoor pool; watersports equipment/rentals; free Wi-Fi.

Glorietta Bay Inn ★★   This gracious historic mansion attracts romantics, while the hotel's adjacent motel-style buildings are perfect for families, travelers on a budget, and those staying a long while. The 11 rooms in the main building are outfitted much like a B&B with antiques, heavy drapes with fringed swags, and floral spreads and pillows. Some, including the water-view Penthouse Suite, have a more modern, airy style. Many of the rooms in the other buildings have balcony views of Glorietta Bay, though the least-expensive "snug" rooms face parking lots. All have mini fridges and microwaves; the accommodations are several steps above motel-style. Continental breakfast and afternoon refreshments are served in the mansion's living room.

1630 Glorietta Blvd. www.gloriettabayinn.com. © **800/283-9383** or 619/435-3101. 100 units. $149–$159 double; from $279 suite; mansion from $295. Rates include continental breakfast and afternoon refreshment. Self-parking $10. **Amenities:** Babysitting; concierge; access to nearby health club; hot tub; outdoor pool; spa services; free Wi-Fi.

WHERE TO DINE

Farm-to-table, locavore cuisine isn't just a concept here—it's the norm. Chefs rely on produce from small organic gardens for their seasonal menus. In fact, visiting chefs from around the country stop to admire the baby veggies at **Chino Farms** (6123 Calzado Del Bosque, Rancho Santa Fe; ℂ 858/756-3184), among the best produce farms in the country. Chefs rely on the sea's bounty as well, along with the ever-expanding creations from artisanal cheese, bread, and chocolate producers. Japanese, Indian, Thai, and French restaurants are opening in neighborhoods all over the county, providing access to ethnic cuisines that were hard to find until recently. Mexican food is omnipresent but, alas, rarely excellent.

Because San Diego is spread so far about, it's tough dining outside the neighborhood around your hotel. Public transportation is inconvenient, to say the least. Though there is minimal bus service to most neighborhoods, the last bus typically runs its full route around 10pm. Even locals rely on taxis for special nights out, willing to pay a bit more to avoid concerns over parking (often scarce) and imbibing and driving. *Note:* Some of the finest restaurants are located in North County. See chapter 7.

Downtown, Gaslamp Quarter & Little Italy
EXPENSIVE

Cowboy Star ★★ AMERICAN/STEAKHOUSE Should you feel like wrangling a steer or elk, this aptly named fancy saloon and butcher shop will fit the hefty bill. The dining room follows a gunslinger motif with its cow skulls, photos of John Wayne and Lee Marvin, and cowboy movie posters. But there's nothing cutesy about the food prepared by Victor Jimenez, who's overseen some of San Diego's finest restaurants. It's hard to be abstemious when faced with lamb sweetbreads, steak tartare, Muscovy duck breast and an 18-ounce rib chop—bring friends and count on leftovers. All meats come from family owned ranches and are free of antibiotics and growth hormones; in-house butchers hand-cut the steaks. Non-carnivores get palate pleasers like savory mushroom corn cake and wild sea bream confit. You can cut the bill by half or more by ordering steak and frites, roasted bone marrow or other delights from the bar menu.

650 10th Ave., East Village. www.thecowboystar.com. ℂ **619/450-5880.** Reservations recommended. Main courses $28–$52. Lunch Tues–Fri 11:30am–2:30pm; dinner Mon–Thurs 5–10pm, Fri–Sat 5–10:30pm, Sun 5–9pm.

Searsucker ★★ AMERICAN A stint on *Top Chef* put Brian Malarkey in the local star chef set, and he's expanded his dynasty widely, starting with one of the Gaslamp's hippest eateries. Menus change frequently, but you'll usually find the popular duck fat fries and egg and bacon pork belly. Ordering small plates is the best way to go here; though entrees are usually imaginative and tasty, you get a far better sampling of the chef's talents with appetizers. Malarkey has opened several other restaurants in San Diego with mixed results; the original is still the best. *Tip:* Tables on the sidewalk are best for conversation (the restaurant can get cacophonous) and people watching.

611 Fifth Ave., Gaslamp Quarter. www.searsucker.com. ℂ **619/233-7327.** Dinner reservations recommended. Entrees $24–$35. Mon–Fri 11:30am–2pm; Sun–Thurs 5:30–10pm; Fri–Sat 5:30–11pm; brunch Sat–Sun 10am–2pm.

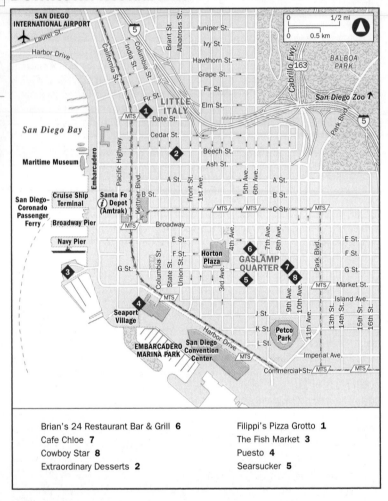

Brian's 24 Restaurant Bar & Grill **6**
Cafe Chloe **7**
Cowboy Star **8**
Extraordinary Desserts **2**

Filippi's Pizza Grotto **1**
The Fish Market **3**
Puesto **4**
Searsucker **5**

MODERATE

Brian's 24 Restaurant Bar & Grill ★ AMERICAN   With something for everyone on the menu and 24/7 schedule, Brian's is the go-to choice . . . when you can't decide where to go. All day and night breakfast service is a big plus in my book; there are times when a bacon and egg protein rush is just what my body craves. Hungry fans rave about the chicken and waffles, meatloaf and peanut butter topped burger and, when late-night cravings hit, the fries topped with carne asada. The décor is as eclectic as the menu, with antique touches like a gorgeous polished wood bar and chandeliers in a rather dark, cramped room.

828 Sixth Ave., Gaslamp Quarter. www.brians24.com. (℃ **619/702-8410.** Main courses $11–$17. Daily 24 hr.

Cafe Chloe ★★ FRENCH   Good luck grabbing a sidewalk table for a weekday or weekend brunch at this sweet East Village café; there's nothing else like it downtown. The daytime menu offers both breakfast and lunch choices, with standards like *croque madame* and steak *frites*. The bistro salad with poached egg is a personal favorite, as is the wild mushroom and truffle oil crepe. Dinner entrees include tender lamb chops with eggplant and the flavorful blend of mussels sautéed with chorizo. Café tables for two or four face large windows looking out to the sidewalk; tables in the back room by the kitchen are less pleasant. Service can be slow and food quality erratic, but the setting with its brick walls and cozy nooks is perfect for a foaming latte and croissant.

721 Ninth Ave., East Village. www.cafechloe.com. ℂ **619/232-3242.** Main courses $19–$28. Mon–Thurs 7:30am–10pm; Fri 7:30am–10:30pm; Sat 8:30am–10:30pm; Sun 8:30am–9:30pm.

The Fish Market/Top of the Market ★★ SEAFOOD/SUSHI   With its views of San Diego Bay and array of fresh seafood, it's no wonder this local Embarcadero tradition is frequently packed. Irresistible choices at the downstairs Fish Market include crispy salt and pepper calamari rings, a killer shrimp po'boy, panko crusted scallops or simple grilled local sea bass or, for the purists, at least a half-dozen oyster varieties. A festive mood prevails in the block-long dining room; getting a table beside the windows overlooking the bay is worth the wait. **Top of the Market** is far more subdued and classy, with white linen tablecloths, sparkly crystal and candles, and the seafood preparations are exceptional. Your decision's easy if the Chesapeake soft shell crabs are on the menu, and the chilled seafood platter is a must-do starter (unless lobster bisque better suits your tastes). Fresh fish is flown in daily, and choices could include Dover sole from Holland or Fijian yellowfin tuna. The few from the second story dining room is stunning, especially at sunset. There's another Fish Market in Del Mar at 640 Via de la Valle (ℂ **858/755-2277**).

750 N. Harbor Dr., Embarcadero. www.thefishmarket.com. ℂ **619/232-3474.** Fish Market Main courses $15–$40. Top of the Market main courses $24–$48. Daily 11am–9:30pm (Fri–Sat until 10pm).

INEXPENSIVE

Extraordinary Desserts ★★★ LIGHT FARE   Many San Diegans would be utterly bereft if Karen Krasne grew tired of creating intensely fresh, perfect cakes, pastries and pies. Her original shop in Mission Hills is still strictly a dessert stop, but the larger Little Italy location has a light food menu, along with sparkling and dessert wines and craft beers to help curb appetites before patrons dive into the sweets. Six choices of grilled cheese sandwiches include a fontina with grilled poblano chilies, though it gets mighty competition from the smoked salmon Panini. There are plenty of salads and small plates, too, but leave room: Devonshire berry tart or slice of salted caramel pecan cake—that's why you're here! Dare you to leave without a box of pastries or jar of Krasne's Maui mango chutney. The original location in Hillcrest, 2929 Fifth Ave. (ℂ **619/294-2132**), is more cozy but serves only desserts and does not have alcohol.

1430 Union St. (at Ash St.), Little Italy. www.extraordinarydesserts.com. ℂ **619/294-7001.** Desserts $2–$9, salads and sandwiches $8–$18. Mon–Thurs 8:30am–11pm; Fri 8:30am–midnight; Sat 10am–midnight; Sun 10am–11pm. Bus: 30.

Filippi's Pizza Grotto ★ ITALIAN   Sure, there are trendier and more refined restaurants in the new Little Italy, but nobody does Old World Italian like this venerable pizzeria behind a 1950s Italian market. Aromas of garlic, oil, salami and cheese spark appetites as diners walk through the cramped market to reach tables covered with red-checked cloths in the dark, crowded but convivial dining room. Meatballs the size of oranges top thick tomato sauce on spaghetti and the eggplant parmagiana is so delightfully dense I dare you to finish a serving. But it's the pizzas with their crisp browned crust, ample ingredients (anchovies, anyone?) and generous melted cheese that keep fans coming back to eat in or take out. The original of a dozen branches throughout the county, this Filippi's has some free parking. Other locations include one in Pacific Beach at 962 Garnet Ave.

1747 India St. Little Italy. www.realcheesepizza.com. © 619/232-5094. Main courses $6–13. Sun–Mon 11am–10pm; Tues–Thurs 11am–10:30pm; Fri–Sat 11am–11:30pm.

Puesto ★★ MEXICAN   L.A. design meets TJ street food in this slick hot spot. And how can you not have fun sipping the perfect margarita, nibbling chips with chunky guacamole, and gabbing with friend on a bright orange couch on a balmy afternoon? Puesto's glass door open to two levels, plus an umbrella shaded patio, all packed most days and nights with happy eaters. The food sets this place apart from other trendy spots—here, authentic regional Mexican street tacos take top billing and each one is a culinary work of art. Go for the $11 three-taco mix, choosing a chicken verde with jalapeño and caramelized onion, Baja fish with tempura crisp cod and the rajas veg (sautéed chilies, corn, and mushrooms with cheese). Or go wild and add a taco filled with lobster chunks or filet mignon for a few dollars more. Heartier entrees with black beans and Jasmine rice include a *cochinita pibil* worthy of its yucatecan roots. Beers on tap include six Mexican favorites, with nary a watery Corona in sight.

789 W. Harbor Dr., Embarcadero. www.eatpuesto.com. © 233-8880. Main courses $11–$19. Daily 11am–10pm.

Hillcrest & Uptown
EXPENSIVE

Bertrand at Mister A's ★★★ AMERICAN/MEDITERRANEAN   Few places hit as high marks for romance, elegance, cuisine and service as Mister A's, a San Diego landmark since 1965. The high-rise view alone earns raves, with its sweeping panorama of downtown's skyline and San Diego Bay. The cuisine is equally stellar, covering Mediterranean standards from escargots and pan sautéed duck breast to paella with aplomb. Servers glide about as if on stage in the simple room with its floor to ceiling windows, linen-draped tables and modern art. The bar/patio menu offers high-end comfort food (Kobe beef baby burgers, ahi sliders, and creamy chicken liver pate) and the imaginative Sunday brunch offerings include an insanely delish pork belly eggs benedict. Bertrand at Mister A's has an equally impressive sister restaurant in the North County neighborhood of Rancho Santa Fe, romantic **Mille Fleurs,** 6009 Paseo Delicias (© 858/756-3085; www.millefleurs.com).

2550 Fifth Ave. Hillcrest. www.bertrandatmisteras.com. © 619/239-1377. Reservations recommended. Main courses $27–$46. Lunch Mon–Fri 11:30am–2:15pm; dinner Mon–Thurs 5:30–9:30pm, Fri–Sun 5–9:30pm; brunch Sun 10am–2pm.

MODERATE

Bankers Hill Bar + Restaurant ★★ AMERICAN   Chef Carl Schroeder and restaurateur Teryle Garve, masterminds behind the Del Mar's outstanding **Market Restaurant + Bar** (p. 260), have a second winner in this airy, open, inviting bistro, with prices that encourage frequent visits and a constantly changing menu based on locally sourced ingredients. The BBQ pork tacos are too popular to delete from the

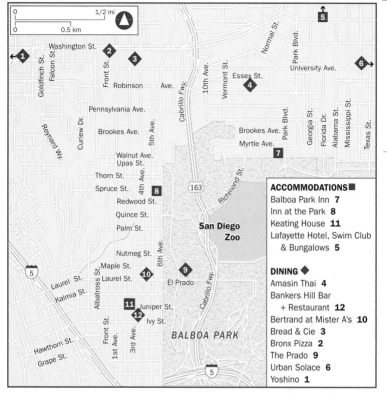

ACCOMMODATIONS ■
Balboa Park Inn **7**
Inn at the Park **8**
Keating House **11**
Lafayette Hotel, Swim Club
& Bungalows **5**

DINING ◆
Amasin Thai **4**
Bankers Hill Bar
+ Restaurant **12**
Bertrand at Mister A's **10**
Bread & Cie **3**
Bronx Pizza **2**
The Prado **9**
Urban Solace **6**
Yoshino **1**

menu, as is the beefy BH burger; other choices vary so often regulars never get bored; try the chili shrimp jambalaya if offered. Cleverly named craft cocktails (The Stalker, Sherry Cobbler, Talent Scout) also change with the seasons, and there's a good wine and beer selection. A happy hour menu appears in early evening and a late night menu after 9:30pm, though you can't be sure what time the place will close, since the owners rely on the crowd to tell them when to turn out the lights.

2202 Fourth Ave., Bankers Hill. www.bankershillsd.com. © **619/231-0222.** Reservations recommended. Main courses $14–$23. Nightly 5pm–closed (around 11).

The Prado ★★ ECLECTIC   The Cohn family, operators of more than a dozen San Diego restaurants of all types and cuisines, have worked wonders with one of Balboa Park's loveliest historic buildings. Their Prado takes full advantage of the building's attributes, with umbrella-shaded tables set beside tiled fountains on the outdoor terrace surrounded by trees and flowers, and linen-draped tables and leather booths filling the interior's dining rooms beneath filigreed chandeliers. A lunch of steak tacos or Portobello salad is a lovely break from museum hopping. The Prado is popular for dinner before attending plays at the Old Globe, but make reservations, or you may be turned away. The rosemary roasted Jidori chicken and olive oil poached salmon draw rave reviews. For a lighter pre-theater dinner try a Champagne cocktail and salmon and crème fraiche flatbread in the lounge beneath the hand painted wooden ceiling or discuss the play's highlights over coffee and cream cheese flan after the curtain falls.

1549 El Prado, Balboa Park. www.cohnrestaurants.com/theprado. ☏ **619/557-9441.** Main courses $24–$36. Lunch Mon–Fri 11:30am–3pm, Sat–Sun 11am–3pm; dinner Tues–Sun 5–10 pm.

Urban Solace ★★ AMERICAN   This 2008 pioneer in North Park's restaurant scene has stayed packed and popular as newcomers have opened and closed, thanks in a large art to chef Matt Gordon's devotion to artfully prepared, hearty New American fare made with natural, organic, carefully sourced ingredients. His dishes are like comfort food reborn—meatloaf with ground lamb, pork and figs; whiskey glazed chicken with biscuits; hangar steak with blue cheese potato puffs. Don't miss the warm cheese biscuits with orange honey butter and Les's'more with hazelnut ganache and malted milk marshmallow. Be prepared to stand in line for breakfast, especially during the Sunday bluegrass brunch. Décor takes second fiddle to the food, with tables packed close together alongside a long bar. Most wines and beers come from the West Coast and cocktails rely on clever use of spices and fruits.

3823 30th St., North Park. www.urbansolace.net. ☏ **619/295-6464.** Main courses $12–$27 dinner. Reservations available for lunch and brunch, not for breakfast or brunch. Mon–Thurs 11:30am–10pm; Fri 11:30am–11pm; Sat 10:30am–11pm; Sun 10am–2:30pm and 5–9pm.

INEXPENSIVE

Amarin Thai ★★ THAI   Wallet watchers fear not. Despite the wall-long wine cabinet, golden Buddha, and framed gilt panels you can dine regally here on a pauper's budget. Suree, the restaurant's much-loved chef, is a master at preparing yummy, rich, thick curry, noodles, and soup with plenty of flavor for less than $10; her Tom Yum soup in a steaming hot pot is a popular bargain. Once her imagination takes hold, though, Suree really shines. Her Mambo Mambo chicken with mango and red curry and sizzling Thai steak with dark plum sauce are amazing. The extensive wine list includes French, Italian, Australian and Chilean imports.

3843 Richmond St., Hillcrest. www.amarinsandiego.com. ☏ **619/296-6056.** Main courses $9–$19. Mon–Tues 11am–3pm, 5–10pm; Wed–Thurs 11am–3pm, 5pm–2am; Fri 11am–3pm, 5pm–3am; Sat noon–3am; Sun noon–2am.

Bread & Cie ★★ LIGHT FARE/MEDITERRANEAN   Owner and former film-maker Charles Kaufman was ahead of the artisan food wave when he opened this bread bakery in 1994. Using European techniques and high-quality ingredients made the breads stand out from anything around at the time; today, the company's products are sold in dozens of restaurants and shops. The original shop has become a small café serving quiche, paninis, and homemade granola and breakfast and sandwiches like roasted eggplant and feta on black olive bread or curried chicken salad on fig and anise bread. Croissants, muffins, and killer cookies are available to accompany an espresso or prosecco. Order at the counter, then find a seat in the small rooms facing the ovens.

350 University Ave., Hillcrest. www.breadandcie.com. ☏ **619/683-9322.** Reservations not accepted. Sandwiches and light meals $4–$11. Mon–Fri 7am–7pm; Sat 7am–6pm; Sun 8am–6pm.

Bronx Pizza ★ ITALIAN   Pizza lovers face ever-increasing options in San Diego, especially for fancy pies with an emphasis on artisan ingredients. But for the back-to-the-basics, good ol' fashioned, fuggedaboutit, fold-a-slice-and-stuff-your-face action, locals line up at Bronx Pizza. This cash-only, counter-service joint, a Hillcrest main-stay, is built for quick slices, with a takeout window and simple dining areas featuring red vinyl booths and Big Apple décor—subway murals, Yankees logos, and photos of Babe Ruth, boxers, and Rudy Guiliani. The menu is limited, as is the cashier's patience if you're looking for something they don't carry—distractions such as "creative" toppings, salads, pastas, or wings. Bronx Pizza specializes in simple, thin-crust, 18-inch pies; cheese and pepperoni are staples, but the white pie with spinach has its devotees. It's on a busy Hillcrest street, parking is tough, and there could be a long line for a table. Call in a take out order if you're in a hurry, have a friend rush in, then take your pie to the beach.

111 Washington St., Hillcrest. www.bronxpizza.com. ✆ **619/291-3341.** Pies $14–$20, $3 by the slice ($2 for cheese). Cash only. Sun–Thurs 11am–10pm; Fri–Sat 11am–11pm.

Saffron Noodles and Saté ★★ THAI   Su-Mei Yu opened her tiny Saffron Thai Grilled Chicken takeout in 1985 and quickly earned kudos for creating healthy, easy meals. She then opened Saffron Noodles and Saté next door in 2002, providing a place to sit and eat her expanded menu, including two-dozen varieties of soups and noodles. Both spots serve her signature saffron-marinated chicken, which comes by the piece or combo with jasmine rice, salad, and your choice of sauces (go for the peanut). The noodle restaurant has a long room with tables and chairs and offers two-dozen varieties of soups and noodles. There are five versions of Tom Yum soup and Monday's special is the Brain Booster stir-fry packed with veggies and tofu. Curries appear on each day's special menu, along with some sort of super-food salad, soup, or entrée. Yu has authored two Thai cookbooks and has become a passionate supporter of healthy eating to achieve harmony and health. She also hosts Savor San Diego, a weekly public TV show featuring local food producers and farms.

3731-B India St., Mission Hills. www.saffronsandiego.com ✆ **619/574-0177.** Main courses $6–$10. Mon–Sat 10:30am–9pm; Sun 11am–8pm.

Yoshino ★★ JAPANESE   This modest, family-run Japanese restaurant has been serving a small menu of favorites for decades, long before Japanese cuisine became standard fare. Early on, choices were limited to crunchy sesame chicken, veggie tempura, teriyaki, udon, and other basics, plus the largest, most reasonably priced plate of impeccably fresh tuna sashimi possible. They added a sushi bar a few years back and expanded the menu, but regulars (including lots of attorneys, doctors, and laborers) still go for the cooked specials with miso soup, simple lettuce salad, bean sprouts and rice. Slick Formica tables are set slightly askew (watch your teacups slide), and some booths are separated by screens, but I like the tables by the kitchen where I can watch waitresses in kimonos bowing constantly as they deliver meals. The restaurant sits in a reasonably-sized parking lot with absolutely no visual attributes, but the chorus of "thank you very much" from every worker in the place will leave you smiling.

1790 Washington St., Mission Hills. www.facebook.com/pages/Yoshino-Japanese-Restaurant/ 117438968274997. ✆ **619/295-2232.** Main courses $11–$30. Lunch Tues–Fri 11:30am–2:30pm; dinner Tues–Thurs and Sun 5–9pm, Fri–Sat 5–10pm; closed Mon.

Old Town & Mission Valley
EXPENSIVE

El Agave Tequileria ★★ MEXICAN   First-timers are typically surprised at the menu prices (high) at this hidden gem above a liquor store on the outskirts of Old Town. But this is gourmet cuisine and well worth the price. At El Agave, Mexican meatballs, called albondigas, are made with lobster, chicken is served in a rose-colored

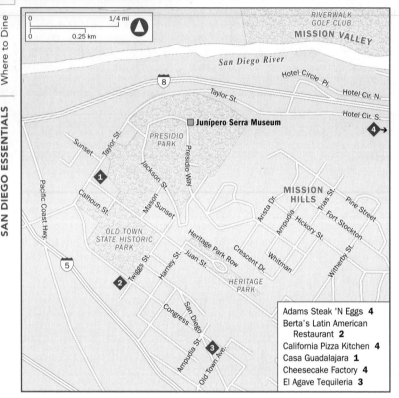

RIVERWALK
GOLF CLUB
MISSION VALLEY

San Diego River

Hotel Circle Pl.
Hotel Cir. N.
Taylor St.
Hotel Cir. S.

Junípero Serra Museum

PRESIDIO
PARK

Sunset
Taylor St.
Jackson St.
Presidio Way

MISSION
HILLS

Pacific Coast Hwy.
Calhoun St.
Mason Sunset

Arista Dr.
Ampudia
Hickory St.
Trias St.
Fort Stockton
Pine Street
Witherby St.

OLD TOWN
STATE HISTORIC
PARK

Heritage Park Row
Crescent Dr.
Whitman

Twiggs St.
Harney St.
Juan St.

HERITAGE
PARK

Congress
San Diego
Ampudia St.
Old Town Ave.

Adams Steak 'N Eggs **4**
Berta's Latin American
Restaurant **2**
California Pizza Kitchen **4**
Casa Guadalajara **1**
Cheesecake Factory **4**
El Agave Tequileria **3**

mole that's lighter and more palate-friendly than stronger traditional moles. Or create a wide-ranging meals just from appetizers like taquitos de cochinita, made with Yucatan-style pork; tiny tamales stuffed with shrimp and tlacoyos with cuitlacoche, a savory mushroom-like fungus grown on corn. As befits its name, El Agave stocks 2,000 different tequilas displayed in ceiling racks and glass-fronted cabinets. Though patio seating is pleasant enough, I prefer the upholstered banquettes in the handsome dining room with its polished wood floors, brick walls and subdued golden lighting.

2304 San Diego Ave., Old Town. www.elagave.com. © **619/220-0692.** Reservations recommended. Main courses $22–$75. Daily 11am–10pm.

MODERATE

Berta's Latin American Restaurant ★ LATIN AMERICAN   A few blocks from Old Town's Mexican restaurants (think: food tamed for timid palates), chefs at this little cottage remain faithful to their South American recipes and spices, though the staff will suggest milder dishes if asked. Nearly every Central and South American country is represented on the menu, making choices difficult for anyone who's traveled the region. The papas choriadas, a Peruvian potato salad, brings back memories of the Andes, while the Brazilian Vatapa is filled with the tropical flavors of coconut and ginger. Spain gets a nod with paella and tortilla español, but I prefer going for impossible-to-find-anywhere-else dishes such as Venezuelan arepas, the perfect vegetarian option with masa patties filled with cheese served with black beans and salad. The dining room is reminiscent of Latin America as well, with its simple high-backed wooden dining chairs, woven tablecloths, ruffled curtains, and paintings of famed landmarks. The menu's the same for lunch (smaller portions) and dinner.

3928 Twiggs St., Old Town. www.bertasinoldtown.com. © **619/295-2343.** Main courses $14–$20 dinner. Tues–Sun 11am–10pm (lunch menu until 3pm).

Casa Guadalajara ★ MEXICAN   First, be forewarned. This cavernous, Mexican fiesta-themed, multi-room restaurant is not your best choice for romance or conversation. But it is *the* place to go if you want to hear excellent mariachis amid a whirlwind of *papeles picado* (hanging paper cutouts), sombreros, piñatas and waitresses in ruffled, embroidered dresses. Bountiful servings of decent Mexican standards come on painted pottery plates, the most popular margaritas are birdbath sized (you can go smaller) and large tables of happy diners celebrating birthdays and such are common. All that said, the menu has some excellent dishes, including the carnitas (marinated pork), cochinita pibil (pork Yucatan-style) and shrimp with a spicy chipotle salsa. It's a great choice for kids and upbeat celebrations.

4105 Taylor St. (at Juan St.), Old Town. www.casaguadalajara.com. © **619/295-5111.** Reservations recommended. Main courses $10–$19. Mon–Thurs 11am–10pm; Fri–Sat 11am–11pm; Sun 8am–10pm.

Inexpensive

Adams Steak 'N Eggs ★★ AMERICAN   Choose a filet or carne asada, add eggs, potatoes, toast or tortillas and a spicy Bloody Mary and you've got a great start on the weekend. This Mission Valley standard serves the best breakfast in a valley packed with chain hotels, and you can easily spot the families headed to SeaWorld among the diehard regulars greeting staff like old friends. Along with hefty omelets, Adams serves fluffy corn fritters with honey butter (a personal favorite) and a cinnamon roll big enough to feed a table of four. There's little room between the wooden tables and chairs lined up in the long room; the umbrella-shaded patio tables are more inviting.

1201 Hotel Circle South, Mission Valley. © **619/291-1103.** adamssteakneggs.com. Main courses $8–$13. Mon–Fri 6:30–1:30am; Sat–Sun 7am–1pm.

farmer's MARKETS

Neighborhood farmer's markets around the county display the region's outstanding produce, including local avocados, strawberries, oranges, asparagus, and baby lettuces along with gorgeous gladiolas, calla lilies, and ranunculus. The selection changes with the season, and the quality is always impeccable. In addition, vendors supply some of the best street food around, from French crepes to South American pupusas and East African sambusas. Nearly every neighborhood has a weekly market. The **Little Italy Mercato** (www.littleitalymercato) on Saturday mornings is one of the largest, with a wide array of edibles. You get a real neighborhood feel at the Wednesday evening **Ocean Beach** market (www.oceanbeachsandiego.com) and **Hillcrest's** Sunday extravaganza (hillcrest farmersmarket.com). For a full list check with the San Diego Farm Bureau (www.sdfarmbureau.org).

Mission Bay & the Beaches
EXPENSIVE

Sushi Ota ★★★ SUSHI   Locals and savvy visitors rave about this simple sushi spot located in an ugly strip mall. The interior's simple black and white setting is equally unimpressive. But chef-owner Yukito Ota isn't concerned with appearances. His whole focus is on the most masterful, precisely prepared sushi and sashimi imaginable. Out-of-town Japanese businessmen stop by for their sushi fixes and at times it's nigh on impossible to snag a seat at the sushi bar at lunch. The menu includes teriyaki, tempura and a few other standards, but only a fool would ignore the day's special sashimi with up to seven fish varieties. If you're splurging, let the chef prepare whatever he feels is best, but be prepared to spend well over $100 for two.

4529 Mission Bay Dr., Pacific Beach. www.sushiota.com. (⌀ **858/270-5670.** Reservations strongly recommended. Main courses $17–$60. Mon 5:30–10:30pm; Tues–Fri 11:30am–2pm and 5:30–10:30pm; Sat–Sun 5–10:30pm.

Tidal ★★ MEDITERRANEAN/CALIFORNIAN   Located in what was originally a 1960s home, now part of the Paradise Point Resort, this bright, airy dining room incorporates a bar, lounge area with tangerine-colored couches, a patio with fire pits, and communal tables as well as plenty of private tables. A 2014 remodel makes the formerly formal Baleen restaurant casual enough for children with a kids' menu (this is a family resort) but the main menu is decidedly adult. Chef Amy DiBiase has loyal fans who've followed her to various restaurants and are happy to try her imaginative take on coastal cuisine. Her smoked salmon belly with horseradish cream is a winner, and her ricotta gnudi (like a cheese gnocchi) with roasted eggplant and braised lamb is a foodie favorite. The kid's menu includes simple spaghetti and organic chicken, plus a child's version of the outstanding cheese plate.

1404 Vacation Rd. (Paradise Point Resort), Mission Bay. www.paradisepoint.com. (⌀ **858/490-6363.** Reservations recommended. Main courses $21–$40. Daily 5–10pm; Sat–Sun brunch 10am–3pm.

MODERATE

The 3rd Corner ★★★ FRENCH   Chefs just off duty and serious oenophiles tend to linger at OB's classy wine bar until the wee hours, nibbling on fine cheeses and sipping one of 1,000 available wines stacked in cases and shelves around dining rooms. Early in the evening, friends settle in the lounge's leather couches for happy hour wines and munchies—the house salad, a true bargain, is one of the best I've ever tasted, as is the wild mushroom soup. More serious diners study their menus at tables and booths in two small dining rooms and a patio, trying to decide which tasty entrée sounds best. The baked Humboldt fog cheese with toasted brioche is my favorite appetizer; for mains I'm partial to the perfectly seasoned shrimp arrabiatta and the tender New York steak with salad and fries. I'm less impressed with the lunch salads and sandwiches—fortunately many of dinner's best apps and entrees are on the lunch menu. Choose a bottle from the stacks to accompany your meal for a mere $5 corkage fee. Parking is limited to a small lot and neighborhood streets, but there are large lots at Robb Field across the street. There's also an outpost in Encinitas at the Lumberyard shopping center, 897 S. Coast Hwy. (⌀ **760/942-2104**).

2265 Bacon St., Ocean Beach. www.the3rdcorner.com. (⌀ **619/223-2700.** Main courses $6–$21. Tues–Fri 11:30am–1am; Sat 10am–1am; Sun 10am–11pm (brunch until 3pm).

INEXPENSIVE

The Mission ★ BREAKFAST/LIGHT FARE   Fans wait in line outside this Mission Valley Hangout for heart healthy fare combining Asian, Latin, and American ingredients and techniques. There's soy chorizo, gluten-free blueberry cornmeal pancakes, egg whites, and braised tofu and generous bowls of fruit and granola for health-conscious types, and roast beef hash and eggs for hungry carnivores. Lunch offerings include green chili tamales with black beans and a filling Indo Chine Happiness Bowl with ginger sesame chicken, beef, or shrimp atop brown rice and veggies. Bring something to keep you occupied during the 30-minute or longer wait.

Other locations: 2801 University Ave., in North Park (𝒞 **619/220-8992**), and 1250 J St., Downtown (𝒞 **619/232-7662**); both have similar menus and hours.

3795 Mission Blvd., Mission Beach. www.themissionsd.com. 𝒞 **858/488-9060.** All items $7–$11. Daily 7am–3pm.

Point Loma Seafoods ★★★ SEAFOOD   Arrive before 11am or after 2pm to beat the lunch crowds at this landmark seafood market and restaurant at Point Loma's sport fishing docks. Fans lean over the glassed-in fish displays willy-nilly (no lines here) and shout out their orders to efficient white-aproned clerks, step back until their numbers are called, grab their tray and search for a table outside, inside or on the 2nd story terrace. I crave the crab sandwich with hunks of meat on thick sourdough, but sometimes order the Caesar salad with seared ahi or sashimi and sushi when in diet mode. Friends usually go for the lightly fried shrimp, cod or squid. After decades in the same small shop, the owners expanded the place to include the second story, which did noting to diminish the crowds.

2805 Emerson St., Point Loma. www.pointlomaseafoods.com. 𝒞 **619/223-1109.** Main courses $10–$15. Mon–Thurs 9am–7:30pm; Fri–Sat 9am–8pm; Sun 10am–8pm.

Rubio's ★★ MEXICAN/TACOS   Ralph Rubio opened his first taco stand in 1983, serving the fish tacos he'd come to love while surfing in Baja. The recipe is simple: take a soft corn tortilla, add a piece of beer-batter fried fresh fish (Alaskan Pollock in this case), and top with chopped cabbage, salsa, and a white sauce. Rubio's tacos were an instant hit, and there now are 190 Rubio's in four states. The quality remains the same, though the menu has expanded to include grilled fish tacos, seafood burritos, salads, and beef and chicken options. You could order one or two tacos alone, but might as well go all the way and get a plate with two tacos, beans, rice, and chips, and add other flavors from the red and green options at the salsa bar. Rubio's first stand near Mission Bay is small and parking is limited, but it's still a favorite with old-timers.

4504 East Mission Bay Dr., Pacific Beach. www.rubios.com. 𝒞 **858/272-2801.** Main courses $3–$8 Mon–Sat 10am–10pm; Sun 10: 30am–9pm.

Tender Greens ★★ NEW AMERICAN   Healthy and delicious food served with a smile might as well be the motto of this small farm-to-table chain with three San Diego restaurants. Diners order at a counter where most ingredients for salads, sandwiches, and "Big Plates" are displayed and workers briskly assemble each meal. Choose your ingredients from a long list, including herb-brushed albacore, marinated steak, grilled veggies, various breads and sides. Or go for a grilled Thai octopus or other large salad, or a simple bowl of Roma Tomato soup—and be prepared to face a tempting array of cookies and other desserts by the cash register. At the hugely popular Point Loma branch, seating is in a large, bright dining area with simple blonde wood tables and a few plants; sadly, it's deafeningly noisy when busy. Head for the outdoor patio to avoid the cacophony. Other locations: 110 W. Broadway, Downtown (© 619/795-2353), and UTC, 4545 La Jolla Village Dr., La Jolla (© 858/455-9395). There's also a small outlet, called Garden, at the San Diego International Airport Commuter Terminal.

Liberty Station, 2400 Historic Decatur Rd., Point Loma. www.tendergreens.com. © **619/226-6254.** Main courses $6–$12. Daily 11am–9pm.

Wonderland ★★★ ECLECTIC   Sun-loving diners claim stools at wall-length, open second story windows for a straight-on view of OB's surf and sand while those seeking conversation and shade settle in a tables and booths spread about the two large dining room at this creative take on the classic beach shack. A rotation of 30 local craft beers are served on tap at the center bar, and the wide-ranging menu covers everything from yummy ahi poke with macadamia nuts to chili verde, green coconut curry and tempura veggies. Burgers with fries and mac 'n cheese satisfy traditionalists, and hot beer cheese with salty pretzel balls help balance the brews. A doorway leads to an equally cavernous pub that's packed for televised sporting events. The reggae's always loud, but the food, drink, and views are worth the auditory assault.

5083 Santa Monica Ave., Ocean Beach. wonderlandob.com. © **619/255-3358.** Main courses $9–$18. Mon–Tues 11am–midnight; Wed–Thurs 11am–1am; Fri 11am–2am; Sat 9am–2am; Sun 9am–midnight.

La Jolla

EXPENSIVE

George's at the Cove ★★★ CALIFORNIAN   La Jolla is San Diego's fine dining epicenter, with George's smack in the bulls-eye. Three dining options cover all except the most stringent budgets, with **George's California Modern** topping the charts. Here, Chef Trey Foshee demonstrates his award-winning cuisine relying on the absolute finest local ingredients to enhance halibut, lamb, beef, veggies or whatever catches his imagination, all served with panache to ocean-view tables and more private high-backed royal purple booths in the no-jackets-required, chic dining room. Don't let the rooftop **Ocean Terrace**'s mind-blowing views of La Jolla Cove distract you from Foshee's superb bistro fare, also served in the indoor/outdoor **George's Bar.**

1250 Prospect St., La Jolla. www.georgesatthecove.com. © **858/454-4244.** Reservations strongly recommended. California Modern main courses $31–$50. Mon–Thurs 5:30–10pm; Fri–Sat 5–11pm; Sun 5–10pm. Ocean Terrace/George's Bar main courses $16–$26 dinner. Daily 11am–9pm (until 10:30pm on Fri–Sat). Valet parking.

The Marine Room ★★★ FRENCH/ECLECTIC   Combine a celebrated chef with a venerable seaside dining room, add impeccable service and an unfussy, elegant setting and you'll come close to imagining this quintessential ultimate dining experience. The restaurant's been drawing crowds since 1941, thanks to its location at the tide line in La Jolla Shores and the fierce waves that sometimes crash right against well-fortified windows. Executive Chef Bernard Guillas has become a San Diego culinary superstar since he took over the restaurant in 1994. His imaginative menus rely on local produce, the chef's Brittany heritage, and his worldwide travels. Never timid with ingredients, he'll put Gouda and cherries with beef carpaccio; quinoa and absinthe infusion with halibut; and hazelnut in lobster bisque. Reserve a window table during sunset for ultimate romance. Low on cash? Sample the scene and cuisine at the lounge while nibbling on braised pork cheeks or shrimp and Andouille lollipops.

2000 Spindrift Dr., La Jolla. www.marineroom.com. © **866/644-2351.** Reservations recommended, especially weekends. Main courses $26–$43. Sun–Thurs 5:30–9:30pm; Fri–Sat 5:30–10pm. Valet parking.

Nine-Ten ★★★ CALIFORNIAN   Chef Jason Knibb isn't one to rest on his many laurels as his "Mercy of the Chef" prixe-fix dinners confirm. Though not overly complex, his innovative farm-to-table creations hit all the right notes. His signature Jamaican Jerk Pork Belly, a tasty homage to his Montego Bay roots, is always on the menu. Everything else is determined by the ingredients fresh that day. I can vouch for the Hamachi sashimi with shitake mushrooms and whatever preparation he lands on for the beef short ribs. Unless you're a picky eater, go for the prix fixe menus with matching wines for the best take on Knibb's style. Save room for pastry chef Rachel King's varying flavors for panna cotta, mousse, or seasonal sorbets. The casual, sophisticated setting, in the aptly named **Grande Colonial Hotel** (p. 191), encourages lingering whether in the high-ceilinged, mahogany-accented dining room or the outdoor patio. Breakfast and lunch are available as well.

910 Prospect St., La Jolla. www.nine-ten.com. © **858/964-5400.** Reservations recommended. Main courses $20–$40. Sun 7:30am–9:30pm; Mon 6:30am–9:30pm; Tues–Sat 6:30am–10pm. Valet parking.

MODERATE

Brockton Villa ★ BREAKFAST/CALIFORNIAN   The closest restaurant to gorgeous La Jolla Cove is housed in one of the few historic beach bungalows still standing across from the sea, handsomely renovated a century after it was first built in 1894. The best views are from the front porch tables, but the rooms indoor are charming thanks to white wooden walls, shadow boxes with sea glass and shells and a fireplace covered with hand-painted plates. The puffy Coast Toast is by far the most popular breakfast item (ingredients include whipping cream and OJ), though someone at your table should order the artichoke and asparagus omelet with truffle goat cheese. Lunch segues into sandwiches and salads, starring the lamb wrap with feta and tapenade, while dinner brings out the heavy hitters like ginger-chili glazed salmon and macadamia crusted scallops. *Note:* Steep stairs from the street limit wheelchair access.

1235 Coast Blvd. (across from La Jolla Cove), La Jolla. www.brocktonvilla.com. © **858/454-7393.** Reservations recommended. Main courses $16–$25. Daily 8am–9pm.

Cusp ★★ AMERICAN   It's taken La Jolla a long time to get a truly stylish, hip nightspot; most places that try don't last long. But this trendy restaurant/lounge on the 11th floor of the Hotel La Jolla, overlooking La Jolla Shores, has created a lasting buzz. It helps that the older hotel underwent a complete makeover when Kimpton hotels took charge, turning the nondescript 70s style building into a super-chic haunt for trendy travelers from L.A. and beyond. As befits the scene, there are lots of shared plates including crab stuffed squash blossoms and a tapa-inspired flatbread with garlic roasted shrimp and, chorizo and manchego cheese. Several tables are set with all chairs facing the sea view. There's always something extra happening, including occasional Jazz Supper Club nights, lobster and crab specials, sunset menus, wine nights and more.

7955 La Jolla Shores Dr., La Jolla. www.cusprestaurant.com. © **858/551-3620.** Main courses $16–$30. Mon–Fri 7–10:30am, 5–10pm (open until 11pm on Fri); Sat–Sun 8am–2pm, 5–11pm (10pm on Sun).

Whisknladle ★★ CALIFORNIAN/FRENCH   Chef Ryan Johnston is a bit obsessive in his approach to gourmet foodie comfort food. His kitchen team cures sausages, pickles vegetables, churns ice cream, makes cheeses, bakes breads, butchers pigs and generally cooks as though as though cans and boxes were never invented. The results keep fans packing the roofed patio to share those artisanal cheeses and meats on the ultimate charcuterie board or hoard their charred bone marrow. A happy hour starting at 3pm bridges the gap between lunch and dinner, whetting appetites with tapas and acclaimed craft cocktails. The Whisknladle folks are also behind **Prepkitchen** ★★, 7556 Fay Ave. (© **858/875-7737;** www.prepkitchen.com), a great little spot where you can pick up soups, salads, and sandwiches to go; there are also Prepkitchens in Del Mar, 1201 Camino del Mar (© **858/792-7737**), and Little Italy, 1660 India St. (© **619/ 398-8383**).

1044 Wall St. (at Herschel), La Jolla. www.whisknladle.com. © **858/551-7575.** Reservations recommended. Main courses $18–$35. Mon–Thurs 11am–9pm; Fri 11:30am–10pm; Sat 10am–10pm; Sun 10am–9pm (brunch until 3pm). Validated parking available.

INEXPENSIVE

The Cottage ★ BREAKFAST/LIGHT FARE   Cobalt blue tile frames the open kitchen and a white picket-like fence edges the brick patio, highlighting this La Jolla bungalow's innate charms. The umbrella and tree-shaded patio is the perfect place for lingering and floor-to-ceiling windows let in plenty of sunlight inside for breakfast-lovers reading the paper over their blueberry pancakes, crab cake benedicts or roasted veggie omelets. Mimosas and Bloody Marys are popular on weekends, while most customers stick with foamy cappuccinos and lattes on workdays. Breakfast is served until 3pm; lunch items like crab fettuccini, stuffed avocado salad and grilled chicken sandwich with feta appear at 11:30am. Dinner is served in summer only.

7702 Fay Ave. (at Kline St.), La Jolla. www.cottagelajolla.com. © **858/454-8409.** Main courses $10–$20, dinner $13–$22. Daily 7:30am–3pm; dinner (May–Sept only).

Spice & Rice Thai Kitchen ★ THAI   Escape the crowds on La Jolla's busy shopping street and duck into the serene sidewalk patio with dozens of orchids in tiny bamboo baskets on the walls. The fragrance of lemongrass and curry tantalizes taste-buds with a sense of what's to come—excellently prepared standards including a slightly tangy lime-dressed grilled beef salad and perfect pad Thai. Several sautéed veggie dishes and curries start at a sensible $12, with add-ons including beef, chicken, tofu and shrimp upping the bill a dollar or two. Signature fried rice paper "gold bags" filled with finely chopped meats and veggies set the stage for delicious dinners of panang curry duck and spicy seafood with chili-garlic paste.

7734 Girard Ave., La Jolla. www.spiceandricethaikitchen.com. © **858/456-0466.** Main courses $12–$18. Mon–Fri 11am–3pm and 5–10pm (until 11pm on Fri); Sat 11:30am–3:30pm and 5–11pm; closed Sun.

Coronado

EXPENSIVE

1500 Ocean ★★ CALIFORNIAN   Executive Chef John Shelton relies on his California roots in creating his menu for the Hotel Del Coronado's special occasion restaurant. Duck, beef, pork and chicken are prepared with flair, but Shelton's passion for the sea comes through and Shelton's talents with seafood shine in his poached

Coronado Hotels & Restaurants 6

ACCOMMODATIONS ■
El Cordova Hotel **5**
Glorietta Bay Inn **7**
Hotel del Coronado **8**

DINING ◆
1500 Ocean **6**
The Brigantine **3**
Chez Loma **4**
Clayton's Coffee Shop **2**
Tartine **1**

prawns with chimichurri, seared diver scallops with English pea risotto, and fragrant black mussels. Most seafood comes from along the Pacific Coast from Alaska to the tip of Baja, and impeccable freshness is one key to each meal's quality. Though the dining room is stylish and sleek, the ambience is classy casual, with diners dressed SoCal style in shirtsleeves and sundresses (waiters do don ties). Ocean-view sunset dinners are best from the terrace, though the view's also great from tables by the large windows indoors. Shelton also oversees the Del's lavish Sunday brunch in the historic wood paneled Crown Room and the more casual Sheerwater restaurant.

1500 Orange Ave., Coronado. www.hoteldel.com. ✆ **619/522-8490.** Reservations recommended. Main courses $31–$48. Tues–Sun 5:30–9:30pm; closed Sun btw. Labor Day and Memorial Day.

Chez Loma ★ FRENCH A flashback to Coronado's genteel, high-society days, this small gem in a Victorian cottage exudes romance and intimacy. The glassed-in patio is particularly lovely with its reflected candlelight; inside tables are spread far enough for conversation. Each dish is perfectly prepared and presented. The scent of lavender and honey on the rack of lamb woos the taste buds, as does the vanilla infusion in the scallops. Chef Alejandro Martinez sticks with his tried and true recipes for the most part, and fans are happy knowing their favorite country pate and duck with

211

port cherry sauce are always available. The duck shows up in tacos on the brunch menu, which meanders from Mexican chilaquiles to mussels a la mariniere.

1132 Loma (off Orange Ave.), Coronado. www.chezloma.com. ℭ **619/435-0661.** Reservations recommended. Main courses $23–$33. Sun–Wed 5–8:30pm; Thurs–Sat 5–9pm; brunch Fri–Sun 9:30am–2pm.

Moderate

The Brigantine ★ AMERICAN/SEAFOOD   Islanders have relied on the Brig for dependable meals in a comfy setting among friends since 1973. Redesigns have added a horseshoe-shaped bar and banquet room but left the wood-paneled, nautical dining room much the same. The menu's reliable as well, with long-time favorites like the massive Brig burger, flambéed scallops and shrimp and crab Louie in big demand. There's nothing especially creative or nouveau about the cooking; it's more like going to a good friend's house for Sunday dinner. There are several other Brig locations, including Point Loma (the original), 2725 Shelter Island Dr. (ℭ **619/224-2871**), and Del Mar, 3263 Camino del Mar (ℭ **858/481-1166**).

1333 Orange Ave., Coronado. www.brigantine.com. ℭ **619/435-4166.** Main courses $15–$32. Mon–Sat 11am–2pm; dinner Mon–Thurs 5–9pm, Fri–Sat 5–9:30pm, Sun 4:30–10pm.

Clayton's Coffee Shop ★ AMERICAN/BREAKFAST   Jukeboxes, red vinyl booths and chrome stools at the counter are sure-fire signs this classic coffee shop has been serving up eggs, bacon and hashbrowns for many a decade. The food's about as basic as it gets—burgers, dogs, club sandwich at lunch and meatloaf or chicken fried steak at dinner. But it's usually well prepared, though not completely dependable. Still, if you slip a quarter in the jukebox you get two whole songs and can feel like you've flashbacked to the Fifties. There's also a takeout window around the corner for the regular menu's items.

979 Orange Ave., Coronado. ℭ **619/435-5425.** Main courses $7–$11. Mon–Sat 6am–9pm; Sun 6am–8pm.

Tartine ★★ CONTINENTAL/CAFE   There's something yummy on the menu day and night at this cheery café, from quiche or homemade granola at breakfast to the nicoise sandwich on a warm baguette at lunch to the sublime fisherman's stew at dinner. Though dinner specials are pricey, you can get a wonderfully healthy (or indulgent) meal here at very reasonable prices. Soups, pate and cheeses are available all day and evening, and you can stop by anytime for a lemon tart or slice of coconut cream cake with an espresso or Prosecco.

1106 First St., Coronado. tartinecoronado.com ℭ **619/435-4323.** Main courses $7–$25. Daily 6am–9pm.

EXPLORING SAN DIEGO

by Maribeth Mellin

S an Diego has the best climate and easiest lifestyle in the country—perhaps even in the world. Sound like an idle boast? Consider this—the temperature averages 70°F year round and humidity is usually nonexistent. We San Diegans freak out if the thermometer slides below 60 and crank up the heat. It's said that negative ions, which improve mood, sleep, and general health, are in abundance due to our proximity to the ocean. Sound like New Age malarkey? Who cares? We're happy to chill, hang loose, and shine on any worries.

That doesn't mean we're mindless fools. San Diego has produced more than a dozen Nobel laureates and a similar number of Broadway bound plays. Chefs love playing with our natural bounty, musicians happily perform beneath the stars, and architects let their imaginations run free. Diversity shapes our cultural scene—with 30% of the population Latino or Hispanic and 10% Asian, ethnic fairs and feasts occur at least once each month.

Let's not forget playtime. Beyond the 70 miles of beach, San Diego has three world-class animal parks, the largest urban cultural park in the U.S., and enough sporting possibilities to expand any Sunday warrior's skills. Beyond all that, relaxation is unavoidable. Tense muscles melt in the sun, worries drift away in warm air, and flagging spirits give way to smiles. Though you don't need to race around to enjoy San Diego, but you will want to sample our many pleasures.

SAN DIEGO ATTRACTIONS

San Diego's crown jewel is Balboa Park, a 1,174-acre playground and the nation's largest urban cultural park. It's also the country's second-oldest city park (after New York's Central Park), established in 1868 in the heart of the city, bordered by downtown to the southwest and fringed by the early communities of Hillcrest and Golden Hill to the north and east. Originally called City Park, the name was eventually changed to commemorate the Spanish explorer Balboa. Tree plantings started in the late 19th century, while the initial buildings were created to host the 1915–16 Panama-California Exposition; another expo in 1935–36 brought additional developments.

The park's most distinctive features are its mature landscaping, the architectural beauty of the Spanish Colonial Revival–style buildings lining El Prado (the park's east-west pedestrian thoroughfare), and the engaging and diverse museums contained within it. You'll also find more than a dozen gardens, 65 miles of hiking trails, an ornate pavilion with one of the

BALBOA PARK: full exposure

San Diego's city fathers demonstrated incredible ambition and prescience when planning the two Panama-California Expositions. The first, designed to celebrate the opening of the Panama Canal and bring national attention to the burgeoning city, established San Diego's architectural and cultural landscape; the Cabrillo Bridge and blue and white tile dome atop the California Building have become San Diego landmarks. Several of the fair's Spanish-style buildings house today's museums, where items gathered in 1915 are still on display. The 1935–36 California Exposition was a more prurient affair, with 76 little people living in a Midget Village, scantily clad burlesque dancer Sally Rand waving fans in front of her private parts, and actors presenting 40-minute versions of Shakespeare's greatest hits.

You'll learn about this history and more on **guided tours of the park.** They cater to a wide variety of interests, from historical to horticultural (most tours start from the **visitor center,** www.balboapark.org; (**C** **619/239-0512**). There are free rotating tours on Saturdays at 10am that highlight either the palm trees and vegetation or park

history. Park rangers lead free 1-hour tours focusing on the park's history, architecture, and botanical resources every Tuesday and Sunday at 11am. Rangers also conduct trail walks on the second Wednesday of the month. The **Committee of 100** (www.c100.org; (**C** **619/795-9362**), an organization dedicated to preserving the park's Spanish Colonial architecture, offers a free exploration of the historic structures on the first Wednesday of the month at 9:30am. A 90-minute self-guided audio tour with adult and children's' versions is also available at the visitor center costing $5 for adults; $4 for seniors, students, and military; and $3 for children 3 to 11.

Guides from the **San Diego History Center** add historical anecdotes and trivia to their 1-hour walking tour of El Prado every Thursday at 11am and 1pm; tickets are $10 and reservations advised (www.sandiegohistory.org/calendar; (**C** **619/232-6203**). The 90-minute **Old Globe Theatre Tour** visits the three performance venues and backstage areas on most Saturdays and Sundays at 10:30am; the tour costs $5 for adults and $3 for seniors and students (www.theoldglobe.org; (**C** **619/231-1941**).

world's largest outdoor organs, an IMAX domed theater, the acclaimed **Old Globe** (p. 252), and the **San Diego Zoo** (p. 221).

The park is divided into three distinct sections, separated by Hwy. 163 and Florida Canyon. The narrow western wing of the park consists of largely grassy open areas that parallel Sixth Avenue—it's a good place for picnics and dog-walking; the only museum in this section is the **Marston House** (p. 217). The eastern section is devoid of cultural attractions, but has the **Balboa Park Municipal Golf Course** (p. 244) and other ports venues including a velodrome. The central portion of the park, between Hwy. 163 and Florida Drive, contains the zoo and all of the museums.

If you really want to visit the zoo and a few of the park's museums, don't try to tackle it all in the same day. Allow at least 3 hours to tour the zoo; the amount of time you spend in the 15 major museums will vary depending on your personal interests. Check out the **walking tour** that takes in most of the park's highlights (p. 237). There are informal restaurants serving sandwiches and snacks throughout the park—for breakfast, **Tobey's 19th Hole** at the municipal golf course is a find (p. 244); try lunch at the Japanese Friendship Garden's **Tea Pavilion** (p. 217) or in the **San Diego**

Balboa Park

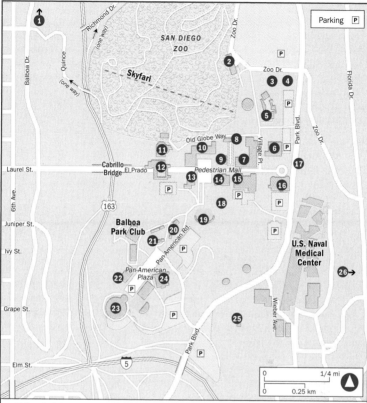

7

EXPLORING SAN DIEGO | San Diego Attractions

Balboa Park Miniature Railroad **3**
Balboa Park Municipal Golf Course **26**
Botanical Building and Lily Pond **8**
Carousel **4**
Casa de Balboa **15**
  Museum of Photographic Arts
  San Diego History Center
  San Diego Model Railroad Museum
Casa del Prado **7**
House of Charm **13**
  Mingei International Museum
  SDAI Museum of the Living Artist
House of Hospitality **14**
  Balboa Park Visitors Center
  Prado Restaurant
House of Pacific Relations
  International Cottages **21**
Japanese Friendship Garden **18**

Marston House **1**
Old Globe Theatre **11**
Reuben H. Fleet Science Center **16**
Rose and Desert Gardens **17**
San Diego Air & Space Museum **23**
San Diego Automotive Museum **22**
San Diego Hall of Champions
  Sports Museum **24**
San Diego Museum of Art **10**
San Diego Museum of Man **12**
San Diego Natural History Museum **6**
San Diego Zoo entrance **2**
Spanish Village Art Center **5**
Spreckels Organ Pavilion **19**
Timken Museum of Art **9**
United Nations Building **20**
Veterans Museum & Memorial Center **25**

If you plan to visit more than three of the park's museums in one day, buy the **One-Day Explorer** pass allowing admission for up to five museums in one day. It's $43 for adults and $25 for children 3 to 12. With some popular museums charging $15 and more for adult admission and $8 and more for children, it's a great deal. The **Multi-Day Explorer** allows entrance to 17 museums and is valid for 1 week. It's $53 for adults, $29 for children 3 to 12. The **Multi-Day Explorer with One Day Zoo Admission** adds a single-day ticket to the zoo (including the guided bus tour and Skyfari aerial tram) for $89 adults (normally $46 for the zoo alone), $52 children ($36 for zoo alone). The passes can be purchased at any participating attraction (but not the zoo), at the visitor center, or online at www.balboa park.org. The website also lists valuable coupons with discounted museum entry fees and restaurant deals. *Tip:* If you happen to visit in October, admission is free for children ages 3 to 11 at 17 museums and the zoo for the entire month. *Note:* Passes may not cover admission to special exhibitions.

Museum of Art's sculpture garden (p. 220). The **Prado Restaurant** is also a San Diego favorite for lunch or dinner.

There are two primary **road entrances** into the heart of the park. The most distinctive is from Sixth Avenue and Laurel Street: Laurel turns into El Prado as it traverses the beautiful **Cabrillo Bridge** ★ across Highway 163. You can also enter via Presidents Way from Park Boulevard. Major **parking areas** are at Inspiration Point just east of Park Boulevard at Presidents Way; in front of the zoo; and along Presidents Way between the Aerospace Museum and the Organ Pavilion. Other lots, though more centrally located, are small and in high demand, especially on weekends.

Free **tram** transportation within the park runs daily from 8:30am to 6pm, with extended hours in summer months. The red trolley trams originate at the Inspiration Point parking lot to circuit the park, arriving every 8 to 10 minutes and stopping at designated pickup areas. It's a sensible way to get around the park, as it's a long walk from one cluster of museums to another. Stop by the **Balboa Park Visitors Center,** in the House of Hospitality (www.balboapark.org; © **619/239-0512**), to learn about walking and museum **tours,** or to pick up a brochure about the **gardens** of the park; the visitor center is open daily, 9:30am to 4:30pm. To prepare for your visit, download a tram route map and a park map from the excellent website. *Note:* Some museums are closed on Mondays.

Botanical Building and Lily Pond ★★ PARK/GARDEN   Sunlight filters through tree ferns and moss creeps over fountains and waterfalls in this enchanting garden, the perfect place to escape the sun and please the senses. It's one of Balboa Park's most popular photo ops (hint, hint), with a 250-foot long redwood latticework, domed structure set behind a long lily pond. You're immediately surrounded by soothing scents as you step into the cool, shady building, first constructed for the 1915–16 Panama-California Exposition; visitors tend to speak in whispers while wandering along pathways beside some 2,100 exotic orchids, bromeliads, tropical ferns, flowering bushes, and fragrant herbs, all labeled for identification. Pastel pink and blue water lilies float in the 257-foot long lily pond fronting the Botanical Building. *Tip:* Bring snacks and take a picnic break on the broad lawns beside the pond.

El Prado. www.balboapark.org. © **619/235-1100.** Free admission. Fri–Wed 10am–4pm; closed Thurs and major holidays.

House of Pacific Relations International Cottages ★ CULTURAL INSTI-TUTION   This cluster of 17 charming one- and two-room cottages disseminates information about the culture, traditions, and history of more than 30 countries. Open houses are scheduled every Sunday from noon to 4pm, when hosts in native costume answer questions about their countries. Each group takes a turn presenting a lawn program with ethnic food, music, and dance on Sundays, from 2 to 3pm, March through October. The adjacent **United Nations Building** (www.unasd.org; © **619/233-5044**) houses an international gift shop.

Adjacent to Pan American Plaza. www.sdhpr.org. © **619/234-0739.** Free admission (donations welcome). Sun noon–4pm, gift shop open daily 10am–4:30 pm.

Japanese Friendship Garden ★ PARK/GARDEN   Streams splash over moss-covered rocks in this beautifully serene *San-Kei-En,* or "three-scene garden" beside a Japanese teahouse. The original tea garden, constructed for the 1915 Exposition, was destroyed in 1954, but devotees gradually acquired 12 acres, two of which have been developed so far. (Still to come are herb and tea gardens, a cherry tree grove, a lily pond, and an amphitheater.) From the main gate, a crooked path (to confound evil spirits, who move only in a straight line) threads its way to the information center in a traditional Japanese-style house. Here you can view the most ancient kind of garden, the *sekitei,* made only of sand and stone (a self-guided tour is available). Visitors are asked to respect the garden's purpose as a place of contemplation and to refrain from yelling, smoking, and otherwise disturbing the serenity. Noodles, salads, rice bowls, and sandwiches are on offer at the **Tea Pavilion** restaurant, which also offers an impressive array of fine teas. It gets crowded here at times, destroying the peaceful ambience. Try visiting late in the day.

2125 Park Blvd., adjacent to the Organ Pavilion. www.niwa.org. © **619/232-2721.** Admission $6 adults; $5 seniors, students, and military; free for children 6 and under. Daily 10am–3:30pm (garden closes at 4:30pm).

Marston House Museum & Gardens ★ HISTORIC HOME   Noted San Diego architects Irving Gill and William Hebbard designed this Craftsman house in 1905 for George Marston, a local businessman and philanthropist. The architecture shows the Asian influence of the Arts and Crafts movement as well as elements of Frank Lloyd Wright's Prairie School; the home is furnished with Roycroft, Stickley, and Limbert pieces, and a lovely collection of art pottery. The home and gardens, listed on the National Register of Historic Places, are complemented by a gift shop in the carriage house. Tours take 45 minutes and depart every half-hour.

3525 Seventh Ave. (northwest corner of Balboa Park at Balboa Dr. and Upas St.). www.soho sandiego.org. © **619/297-9327.** $10 adults, $7 seniors, $4 children 6–12, free for children 5 and under. Fri–Mon 10am–4pm.

Mingei International Museum ★★★ MUSEUM   This unique museum show-cases folk art and handmade functional objects from cultures around the globe. Why the odd name? Japanese writer Sets Yang coined the word Mingei (pronounced "*min-gay*") in the 1920s to describe an appreciation for folk crafts. The concept caught on with collectors and curators around the world, but San Diego has one of few museums solely devoted to the Mingei movement. That's thanks to San Diego State University professor and ceramics artist Martha Longenecker who opened the museum in a shop-ping center in 1978 with an enchanting collection of handcrafted carousel animals. She quickly gained an impassioned following, as well as generous benefactors, and gar-nered this prime locale in Balboa Park in 1996. Today, the Mingei has six galleries, an education center, an impressive art reference library, and some 26,000 objects of folk art, craft, and design from 141 countries. French artist Niki de Saint Phalle's fanciful sculptures beside the museum hint at the whimsical, amusing, and thought-provoking surprises inside. There are usually several exhibits on display simultaneously, covering such diverse topics as Mexican Día de los Muertos altars; hand-embroidered costumes from Romania; African American quilts; surfboard and surf gear design; and hats and headdresses from around the world. The gift shop is filled with tempting jewelry, textiles, pottery, and books. *Tip:* Complimentary docent-led tours are offered at 2pm in the museum's lobby, Tuesday through Sunday.

1439 El Prado. www.mingei.org. © **619/239-0003.** Admission $8 adults; $5 seniors, children 6–17, students, and military with ID; free for children 5 and under. Tues–Sun 10am–5pm.

Museum of Photographic Arts ★★ MUSEUM   At MOPA, one of the country's largest photography museums, you'll be exposed to the works of the planet's transformative shutterbugs, men and women who have changed the way we see the world. On exhibit is usually a small slice of the collection—it holds more than 7,000 images from 800 photographers; there are usually at least two exhibits running simultaneously. Photojournalism exhibits have included Margaret Bourke-White's 1950s *Life* magazine portraits of segregation in America and Los Angeles Times photographer Don Barletti's 2002 Pulitzer Prize winning series on undocumented immigrants undertaking the treacherous train journey from Central America to the U.S. Other exhibits have covered cutting-edge digital and photo montage works along with one-man shows from celebrities, including Jessica Lange and Graham Nash. Video installations are projected on the gallery's ceiling, and film festivals are held in the 226-seat theater. Photographers will surely want to spend time here, but casual shooters should check out the exhibits' descriptions before plunking down admission fees.

1649 El Prado. www.mopa.org. © **619/238-7559.** Admission $8 adults, $7 seniors and retired military (and their dependents), $6 students, free for active-duty military (and their dependents) and children 12 and under with adult. Tues–Sun 10am–5pm.

Reuben H. Fleet Science Center ★ MUSEUM   If you're traveling with future Einsteins (or just young science geeks), plan on spending an hour immersed in gadgets and gizmos at this often-cacophonous, but still educational, playground. Though not as impressive as L.A.'s California Science Center and similar museums, the Fleet does a decent job of exposing kids to various scientific principles—and gives them a break from more staid museums. Within the Science Center, toddlers under 5 years old get their own playground with chutes and ramps for directing balls, and a fire truck with pedals, steering wheels, and buttons setting off the truck's sirens. Older kids race between 12 hands-on exhibits, peering through microscopes at human tissue samples, standing inside a giant kaleidoscope, and building six-foot-high spiral towers with wooden planks. Should boredom set in at the mere mention of science, skip the exhibits and head straight for the IMAX Dome Theater. Tickets include both the theater and center. *Tip:* Keep an eye out for school groups before buying your ticket; you may want to save your visit for later in the day.

1875 El Prado. www.rhfleet.org. © **619/238-1233.** Admission plus an IMAX film $18 adults; $16 seniors; $15 children 3–12. Daily 10am–6pm.

San Diego Air & Space Museum ★★ MUSEUM   San Diego is considered the birthplace of naval aviation, so it's only fitting that the city is blessed with one of the largest and most comprehensive aviation museums in the country. The 1935-built venue, with its sleek, cylindrical design, is stuffed to the rafters with over 60 aircraft that illustrate the history of flight. On display are a mock-up of Da Vinci's ornithopter, full-scale models of a 1901 Wright glider and Charles Lindbergh's Spirit of St. Louis, plus authentic WWI- and WWII-era fighter planes. The jet and spacecraft collection is topped by the actual command module from the Apollo 9 mission. Now over 50 years old, the museum offers a few high-tech features; several realistic flight simulators put visitors in the hot seat, and a 4D theater (3D visuals plus seats that move with the action) screens adrenalin-pumping movies. Little ones love the Kid's Aviation Action Hangar, which offers little pedal planes to drive around and child-size flight simulators. Diehards may want to visit the museum's Gillespie Field Annex (*©* **619/258-1221**; Mon–Thurs 8am–3pm), which houses more planes, including many which are being restored.

2001 Pan American Plaza. www.sandiegoairandspace.org. *©* **619/234-8291.** Admission $18 adults; $15 seniors, retired military, and students with ID; $9 children 3–11; free for active military with ID and children 2 and under. Daily 10am–5pm.

San Diego Automotive Museum ★ MUSEUM

You have to love cars to enjoy this one-room museum devoted to classic, antique, and celebrity vehicles. The DMC Delorian, and a motorcycle exhibit centering on Steve McQueen's racing career, are the biggest draws. There a Cadillacs, low-riders, Fiats, and Ferraris and a kid's area with a scavenger hunt game. Outdoor shows or car rallies are held on many weekends. There's no set calendar—devotees should call ahead.

2080 Pan American Plaza. www.sdautomuseum.org. *©* **619/231-2886.** Admission $9 adults, $6 seniors and active military, $5 students, $4 children 6–15, free for children 5 and under. Daily 10am–5pm (last admission 4:30pm).

San Diego Hall of Champions Sports Museum ★ MUSEUM

Sports of all sorts are hugely popular in San Diego, and many a champ has been born and/or played here. Among the most famous are long-distance swimmer Florence Chadwick, who conquered the English Channel twice in the 1950s; four-time America's Cup winner (from 1974–88) Dennis Conner; and skateboarder Tony Hawk, who went pro in 1982 at the age of 14 and was the National Skateboard Association world champion for 12 consecutive years. Tony Gwynn, a beloved local hero who played for the San Diego Padres for 20 years, is honored with a special memorabilia collection, and 140 athletes are celebrated with plaques in the Breitbard Hall of Fame. But it's hard to sense the excitement and adulation these athletes garnered unless you're a die-hard sports fan with a fondness for photos, uniforms, and sports gear. If you decide to skip the exhibits, do check out the building's facade, designed by Richard Requa in 1934 to resemble the Mayan Palace of the Governor at Uxmal, Yucatán.

2131 Pan American Plaza. www.sdhoc.com. *©* **619/234-2544.** Admission $8 adults; $6 seniors 65 and older, students, and military; $4 children 7–17; free for children 6 and under. Daily 10am–4:30pm.

San Diego History Center ★ MUSEUM

While you're wandering through Balboa Park, spend a few minutes checking out the information and memorabilia collected by the San Diego Historical Society. Changing exhibits have focused on such varied themes as the local craft brew culture, the tuna fishing industry, and local artists, including Donal Hord and Belle Baranceanu. The gift shop has all sorts of themed wares, plus books and an excellent selection of historic photos.

1649 El Prado. www.sandiegohistory.org. *©* **619/232-6203.** Admission $8 adults; $6 seniors and students; $4 students, seniors, and retired military with ID and dependents; $3 children 6–17; free for children 5 and under and active-duty military. Mon–Sun 10am–5pm.

San Diego Model Railroad Museum ★ MUSEUM   Children and model train enthusiasts of all ages (and you know who you are) should chug on over to the largest indoor railroad museum on the continent, a Balboa Park tradition dating back to 1935. Passionate members of the several local model railroad clubs gather here for meetings and just plain fun; there's usually someone around to explain the layouts and point out the significance of various train cars. Club members operate a toy Lionel train layout, allowing kids to push a few buttons.

1649 El Prado. www.sdmrm.org. ✆ **619/696-0199.** Admission $9 adults; $7 seniors; $4 students; $5 military; $2 children 6–15 with adult admission; free for children 5 and under. Tues–Fri 11am–4pm; Sat–Sun 11am–5pm.

The San Diego Museum of Art ★★ ART MUSEUM   San Diego's oldest and largest fine art museum merits a thoughtful meander. Perhaps best known for its impressive array of Spanish art (notably El Greco's poignant, intense *The Penitent St. Peter*) the museum abounds in lesser-known works by diverse stars, including *Bouquet*, a vase of garden flowers by Matisse, *Haystacks at Chailly* (an early Monet landscape), and Diego Rivera's unusual portrait, *Hands of Dr. Moore,* reminiscent of Frida Kahlo's work with its depiction of the doctor's hands trimming the tree of life rooted in blood. The 12,000-piece permanent collection covers the ages, from an Egyptian statue of Ramesses II from the 13th century BC to Frank Stella's large (108 inches square) 1970 *Flin Flon VIII,* which tricks the eye kaleidoscopically with colored-filled geometric shapes. Recently renovated first-floor galleries feature a large Asian collection of paintings, ceramics, and metalwork. The courtyard Sculpture Garden's peaceful lawn serves as a gallery for several pieces including Henry Moore's smooth, undulating, bronze *Reclining Figure: Arch Leg* and Louise Nevelson's massive steel *Night Presence II,* a study in architecture forms that withstand the elements with a rusty patina. It's one of the few Balboa Park museums that have remained in residence since the building opened in 1926, with a gap during Word War II when the galleries were uses as military hospital wards. *Tip:* If you're worried about touring with bored children, ask for the Search & Find activity sheets.

1450 El Prado. www.sdmart.org. ✆ **619/232-7931.** Admission $12 adults, $9 seniors and military, $8 full-time students, $5 children 7–17, free for children 6 and under; family 4-pack (2 adults, 2 youths) $28. Admission to traveling exhibits varies. Mon–Tues, Thurs–Sat 10am–5pm; Sun noon–5pm; closed Wed.

San Diego Museum of Man ★★ MUSEUM   Housed in the ornate, California Building topped with a tiled dome and 200-foot-high bell tower, this small anthropology museum first opened for San Diego's 1915–16 Panama-California Exposition. The Smithsonian Institution helped fund the expeditions needed to collect 5,000 specimens of ethnological importance from around the world for the exhibit; many of those items remain in the museum's core collection of some 100,000 items. If you have a strong interest in archeology, anthropology, and modern foreign cultures you'll be happy roaming about for an hour or more. Casts of Guatemalan Maya stelae (pillars covered with symbols) have stood beneath the entry's Rotunda Gallery's blue dome since 1915 at the entrance to the *Maya: Heart of Sky, Heart of Earth.* In the interest of full disclosure, I've been fascinated by the Maya for decades, have explored most major archeological sites, and am always happy to visit this museum if only to wander amid the displays of pottery, ceramics, and textiles set against reproductions of murals depicting Maya cities and symbols painted in 1915.

Amateur Egyptologists (and a few sentimental experts) are drawn to the Mummies and Ancient Egypt galleries containing jewelry, ceramics, and tomb figurines from

Amara, where Queen Nefertiti reigned and young King Tut spent his childhood, plus a rare child's coffin, several mummies, and shrunken heads. The adjacent *Adventure Kids in Egypt* room gives children hands-on exposure to archeology through games and costumes. *Footsteps through Time* fills five galleries with exhibits covering 65 million years of primate and human evolution—creationists beware! More than 100 touchable replicas, plus dioramas, a hands-on Dig Site teaching archeological techniques, videos, and well-written descriptions hold most visitors' interest. Another gallery explores San Diego's native cultures. Special exhibits have included the hugely popular and gruesome *Instruments of Torture* collection and items from the museum's vaults, including Southwestern rugs and pottery, Samurai armor, and Latin American folk art.

1350 El Prado. www.museumofman.org. (*C*) **619/239-2001.** Admission $13 adults; $10 seniors and active-duty military, $8 students, $6 children 3–12; free for children 2 and under. Daily 10am–5pm.

San Diego Natural History ★★ MUSEUM   This esteemed institution, established in 1874, examines and preserves the history of the flora, fauna, and geology of Southern California and Baja, boasting a collection of over 7.3 million specimens. Younger folks and science buffs are drawn in by the life-sized T-Rex skeleton reproduction in the four-story atrium and other giant curiosities including a leering Megaladon (mega-toothed) shark suspended above the interior courtyard. Kids are typically happiest amid the Fossil Mysteries gallery's giant models, including ones of a mammoth and a mastodon (precursors of today's elephants) and the sharp-beaked pteranodon, one of the world's largest flying reptiles, dangling overhead. Hands-on opportunities abound, from manipulating the jaws and teeth of predators and prey to crouching in an Ice Age lion's cave.

Odd as it sounds, the Skulls gallery is worth a look, if only to compare the sizes of 200 skulls, ranging from a tiny snake to a rhino and giraffe. Several bilingual displays include information about the shared geology and natural history in Baja and San Diego. Temporary exhibits, on such topics as the Titanic, the Dead Sea Scrolls, and King Tut have been blockbusters (and carry an extra admission fee). In an attempt to modernize its image, the museum is now called theNAT on some brochures.

1788 El Prado. www.sdnhm.org. (*C*) **619/232-3821.** Admission $17 adults; $15 seniors; $12 students, children age 13–17, and active-duty military; $11 children 3–12; free for children 2 and under. Daily 10am–5pm.

San Diego Zoo ★★★ ZOO   Few visitors can resist this renowned zoo, committed to saving animal species and sharing expertise in animal care conservation. Beyond its lofty goals, the 100-acre property is just plain fun and a wonderful place to pass several hours. Visit in early morning or late afternoon for the best animal action and viewing access and you just might catch the zoo's famed giant pandas munching on bamboo or engage in staring contests with lowland gorillas. The zoo's first animals were left behind after the 1915–16 Expo, and rescued by surgeon Dr. Harry Wegeforth, who famously said "Wouldn't it be wonderful to have a zoo in San Diego? I think I'll build one." In 1921, the zoo was given land on the north side of Balboa Park and several buildings were constructed in the 1930s through the Works Projects Administration. Today, nearly 4,000 animals representing 660 species reside in state-of-the-art enclosures mimicking their natural habitats. The zoo is also a recognized botanical garden with more than 70,000 plants clustered in gardens—Fern Canyon and Orchid Basin are especially gorgeous.

Photo-op animal encounters begin at the entrance, where dozens of rosy pink flamingos pose beside a pond as if awaiting the next camera click. Lines nearby for the

35-minute, narrated **Guided Bus Tour** covering about 70% of the facility; start your visit here to plan your route along meandering trails to the animal ecosystems, as the exhibits are called. Among the most popular wildlife sightings are the Tasmanian Devils, kookaburras, and kangaroos in the **Australian Outback,** and the endangered species such as the mandrill monkey, clouded leopard, and pygmy hippopotamus in the zoo's most elaborate habitat, the **Lost Forest.** The icy **Polar Bear Plunge** is a perennial favorite, as is the 7½-acre **Elephant Odyssey.** Look through nursery windows for newborn animals in the **Children's Zoo** where kids can enter a petting paddock with sheep and goats. And of course, there's the overwhelmingly popular **Panda Trek** exhibit, where screens showing videos of the pandas keep those waiting in long lines from growing impatient.

Wandering about the zoo can be exhausting, as trails tend to wind down—and back up—steep canyons. An **Express Bus** allows you to get on and off at one of five different stops. Use the free **Skyfari** aerial tram to soar from the entry area to the **Northern Frontier** (polar bears, arctic foxes). In addition to several fast-food options and snack carts, **Albert's** restaurant is a beautiful oasis at the lip of a canyon and a lovely place to take a break.

Other zoo experiences include a "4D" movie ($6), sleepovers (from $139 per person ages 4 and up), and **Backstage Passes** ($105 plus admission), a 1½-hour, behind-the-scenes tour (ages 5 and up); call ✆ **619/718-3000** for more information.

2920 Zoo Dr., Balboa Park. www.sandiegozoo.org. ✆ **619/234-3153** (recorded info) or 619/231-1515. Admission $46 adults, $36 children 3–11, free for children 2 and under and active-duty military; discounted 2-day passes can be used for both the Zoo and Zoo Safari Park; children 11 and under are free in Oct. Mid-January to Mid-March and November to mid-December daily 9am–5pm (grounds close at 4pm); Mid-January to late March, Late April to late June, and early September to early November daily 9am–6pm; late March to late April 9am–7pm; late June to early September 9am–9pm; mid-December to mid-January 9am–8pm.

Now *That's* a Deal!

If you plan to visit both the zoo and the Zoo Safari Park, a 2-Visit Pass makes sense. It's $76 for adults, $56 for children ages 3 to 11. Regular admission is $46 adult and $36 child for the Safari Park and $46 adult, $36 child for the Zoo—so with the pass that's a savings of $16 each adult and child; passes are valid for 1 year (and can be used twice at the same attraction, if you choose). A 3-for-1 pass gives you 1-day passes to the zoo and Zoo Safari Park, and unlimited entry to SeaWorld for 7 days from first use. The cost is $149 adults, $119 children ages 3 to 9, a saving of $46 adult and $31 child. The regular single-day admission to SeaWorld is $84 adult, $78 child.

Other value options include the **Southern California CityPass**

(www.citypass.com; ✆ **888/330-5008**), which covers SeaWorld, Disneyland Resorts, and Universal Studios in Los Angeles; passes are $331 for adults, or $289 for kids age 3 to 9 (a savings of about 25%), and are valid for 14 days. The San Diego Zoo and Safari Park will be added to the pass in 2015. The **Go San Diego Card** (www.gosandiegocard. com; ✆ **866/628-9032**) offers general admission to more than 50 attractions, including the zoo and LEGOLAND, as well as deals on tours, shopping, and dining. One-day packages start at $80 for adults and $75 for children (ages 3–12). Regular single day admission to the Zoo and LEGOLAND is $132 adult, $122 child.

Spreckels Pavilion ★★ PERFORMING ARTS VENUE   Hearing haunting music in the air? Head for the ornate, curved pavilion just south of the Plaza de Panama, grab a seat, and soak in the sounds of civic organist Carol Williams playing the magnificent 1914 pipe organ. Presented to the citizens of San Diego in 1914 by brothers John D. and Adolph Spreckels (developers of Coronado) the organ is one of the world's largest. It's usually protected behind a 12-ton metal curtain, which opens for concerts on Sundays at 2pm, and Mondays at 7:30 and 9:30 pm during the summer. There's seating for 2,500 but little shade; bring sunscreen and a hat.

South of El Prado. spreckelsorgan.org. ℭ **619/702-8138.** Free admission.

Timken Museum of Art ★ ART MUSEUM   The Timken Museum is a good place to experience fine art without becoming overwhelmed; it's possible to roam the galleries in less than an hour, and admission is free. And the collection of 60 pieces, (including Russian icons and European and American paintings) includes such important works as San Diego's only Rembrandt, a brooding *St. Bartholomew,* painted in 1657; American Thomas Birch's large, dramatic *An American Ship in Distress,* from 1841; and Albert Bierstadt's 1864 painting *Cho-looke, the Yosemite Fall,* with its depiction of this pristine natural wonder sans modern-day crowds. Seventeenth century Parisian tapestries woven with gold threads hang in the museum's entryway, with small galleries devoted to art from various countries (Italy and Russia, notably) branching to each side. The museum's architecture is outstanding as well, with its modernist "see-through" glass and grillwork design allowing views of Balboa Park from within.

1500 El Prado. www.timkenmuseum.org. ℭ **619/239-5548.** Free admission. Tues–Sat 10am–4:30pm; Sun noon–4:30pm; closed Mon.

MORE ATTRACTIONS
Downtown & Beyond

Restaurant, clubs, and shops, many housed in historic buildings, line Fifth and Fourth avenues in the early 20th-century **Gaslamp Quarter ★★**. Visit in daylight to appreciate the historic aspects and stop at **Ghirardelli** (643 Fifth Ave.; ℭ **619/234-2449**) for hot fudge made with San Francisco's famous chocolate. Adjacent to the Gaslamp is burgeoning **East Village,** a hip, metrosexual neighborhood with **PETCO Park ★** (p. 257) and the nine-story innovative **Central Library ★★★** (9330 Park Blvd. www.sandiego.gov/public-library; ℭ **619/236-5800**). Designed by architect Rob Quigley, the library opened in 2013; it's topped with a steel mesh dome, altering downtown's skyline, which alternately pleases or dismays critical San Diegans.

Firehouse Museum ★ MUSEUM   If you happen to be roaming around downtown and Little Italy during the few hours this museum is open, stop by the see San Diego's first fire engine—a horse-drawn steamer—and other antique firefighting equipment. The museum features hydrants, helmets, axes, uniforms, and a 9/11 memorial inside a former working fire station. As in working firehouses, everything is polished to perfection, and volunteer firefighters are usually around to answer questions. Kids can climb aboard one of the trucks.

1572 Columbia St. (at Cedar St.). www.sandiegofirehousemuseum.com. ℭ **619/232-3473.** Admission $3 adults; $2 seniors, military in uniform, and ages 13–17; free for children 12 and under. Thurs–Fri 10am–2pm; Sat–Sun 10am–4pm.

Maritime Museum San Diego ★★ MUSEUM   Sail through nautical history with a tour of the classic vessels on display at the family friendly Maritime Museum on the bay. The 1863 *Star of India,* the world's oldest iron merchant ship still afloat, is the most popular attraction in the collection. In its day it managed 21 circumnavigations of the globe and survived a cyclone. The museum's model ships and nautical memorabilia are housed in another National Historic Landmark, the bright white 1898 propeller-driven *Berkeley* steamboat (it's moored beside the 1904 steam yacht *Medea).* Visitors can also tour a Soviet attack submarine, a pilot boat, and the HMS *Surprise,* a precise replica of an 18th-century British warship; it played a starring role in the Russell Crowe flick *Master and Commander.* The museum's ardent members are now building the *San Salvador,* an exact replica of the first recorded European ship, commanded by Juan Rodriguez Cabrillo, to arrive in San Diego. Construction is taking place at Spanish Landing Park, 3900 N. Harbor Dr., and is open daily 11am–4pm.

1492 N. Harbor Dr. www.sdmaritime.org. (C) **619/234-9153.** Admission $16 adults; $13 seniors 62 and over; students 13–17; and active military with ID; $8 children 3–12; free for children 2 and under. Daily 9am–8pm.

Museum of Contemporary Art San Diego Downtown ★★ ART MUSEUM Occupying the former baggage building of the 1915-built Santa Fe train station, the downtown outpost of the Museum of Contemporary Art presents works from 1950 and beyond, including installations by Richard Serra and others that were commissioned specifically for this majestic, cavernous space. Richard Gluckman (whose credits include Pittsburgh's Warhol museum and the Museo Picasso in Málaga, Spain) transformed the two-building complex in 2007. It's hard to miss the entrance, where artist Jenny Holzer's "truisms," or series of words, run down the building's facade in 61 feet of LED lights. On the building's backside, Richard Serra placed six 25-ton solid steel blocks beneath outdoor arcade arches facing the station's tracks in a work called, aptly enough, "Santa Fe Depot." A rotating series of installations in the three-story gallery features cutting-edge artists including James Drake, who covered the walls with 1,242 drawings. Exhibits complementing the installations are displayed at the museum's other downtown gallery, designed by Helmut Jahn in 1993 across the street from the depot at 1001 Kettner Blvd. The museums hosts lectures and special events frequently. Free tours are given every Saturday at 2pm, and admission is valid for seven days at the downtown and La Jolla locations.

1100 and 1001 Kettner Blvd. www.mcasd.org. (C) **858/454-3541.** Admission $10 adults; $5 seniors, students age 26 and over, and military; free for anyone 25 and under; free admission every 3rd Thurs 5–7pm; paid ticket valid for 7 days at all MCASD locations. Thurs–Tues 11am–5pm; closed Wed.

The New Children's Museum ★★ MUSEUM   Kids under 10 delight in the bounce house, and outdoor bubble fountain (bring an extra set of dry clothes), at this clever, arts–based museum. Local architect Rob Wellington Quigley, who also designed downtown's new public library, dreamt up the angular, glass fronted, three-level building, which opened in 2008. Vast airy spaces give kids room to race around interactive art exhibits including a recording studio with instruments made from kitchen utensils, and a pretend bakery where kids make treats out of clay. A large park across the street from the museum gives kids for running, playing, and family picnics.

200 W. Island Ave. www.thinkplaycreate.org. (C) **619/233-8792.** Admission $10 adults, $5 seniors and military; $5 children; free for children 11 months and under; free admission the 2nd Sun of the month. Mon–Sat 10am–4pm. Parking $10.

San Diego Chinese Historical Museum ★ MUSEUM   This small museum in the 1927 Chinese Mission is the heart of downtown's small Asian Pacific Historic District. With photos and text, the museum explains the history of a Chinatown that thrived in mid to late 1900s in the Stingaree red light district. The museum also serves as a cultural center, presenting concerts, lectures, neighborhood tours and celebrations for Chinese New Year and other holidays (check the website). There's a small garden with a statue of Confucius and a gift shop; allow a half-hour to tour.

404 Third Ave. www.sdchm.org. (℘ **619/338-9888.** Admission $2 adults; free for children under 12. Tues–Sat 10:30am–4pm; Sun noon–4pm.

USS *Midway* Museum ★★ HISTORIC SITE   After serving 47 proud years in the United States Navy, including stints in the Vietnam War and Operation Desert Storm, the aircraft carrier "USS *Midway*" is now a floating naval-aviation museum on the Embarcadero and a not-to-be-missed San Diego landmark. The massive flight deck—1,001-feet long and covering a whopping four acres—displays around 30 vintage restored aircraft, including an SBD Dive Bomber from WWII, a Vietnam-era Huey gunship helicopter and an F-14 Tomcat fighter; the newest addition is a rare F4F Wildcat which was restored over several years by dedicated museum volunteers. There are also two flight simulators, approximately 60 interactive exhibits, and several cockpits that kids love to explore.

In the fall of 2014 the museum debuts a new theater with a multi-media show on the battle of Midway. The free self-guided audio tour narrated by former sailors does an excellent job of detailing daily life aboard the warship; the tour covers a lot of ground, both historically and physically—make sure you're okay with lots of stairs, ladders, and tight spaces. The docents, many of whom are veterans, couldn't be more helpful and engaging.

910 Harbor Dr. www.midway.org. (℘ **619/544-9600.** Admission $20 adults, $17 seniors, $15 students, $10 retired military and children 6–12, free for children 6 and under and active-duty military. Daily 10am–5pm.

William Davis House ★ HISTORIC HOME   The oldest structure in the Gaslamp Quarter, this prefabricated "saltbox" house was shipped by boat in 1850 from Portland, Maine. A museum on the first and second floors documents life in early San Diego and profiles some of the city's first movers and shakers; you can tour the house in 30 minutes. The Gaslamp Quarter Historical Foundation sponsors several types of tours here, including a guided house tour every Tuesday at 1pm ($10 adults, $8 seniors, students), and walking tours of the neighborhood for $15, $12 for seniors, students, and military every Thursday and Saturday at 11am.

410 Island Ave. (at Fourth Ave.). www.gaslampquarter.org. (℘ **619/233-4692.** Admission $5 adults and children; $4 seniors, military, and students. Tues–Sat 10am–5pm; Sun 9am–4pm.

Old Town & Mission Valley

If you visited San Diego before 2005, you'll remember Old Town as the home to Bazaar del Mundo, a wildly colorful, vibrant place with artsy shops surrounding a courtyard where macaws squawked, folkloric dancers twirled their skirts, and mariachis strolled through restaurants. All that changed when, after more than three decades, businesswoman Diane Powers lost her hold on the park's concessions to a national operator. The complex is now more sedate and focused on the historical aspects of San Diego and the Mexican California of the mid-1800s. *Tip:* Bazaar del Mundo's shops still exist in a much smaller version at 4133 Taylor St.

Old Town Attractions

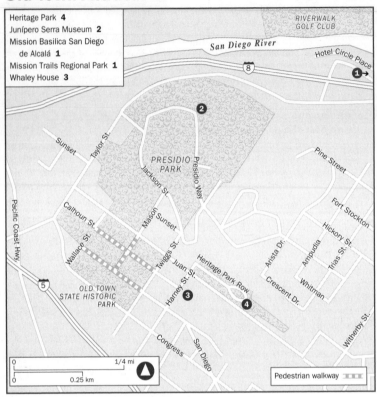

Heritage Park **4**
Junípero Serra Museum **2**
Mission Basilica San Diego
 de Alcalá **1**
Mission Trails Regional Park **1**
Whaley House **3**

RIVERWALK
GOLF CLUB

San Diego River

Hotel Circle Place

Sunset

Taylor St.

PRESIDIO
PARK

Presidio Way

Jackson St.

Pine Street

Fort Stockton

Pacific Coast Hwy

Calhoun St.

Mason

Sunset

Hickory St.

Wallace St.

Twiggs St.

Juan St.

Heritage Park Row

Arista Dr.

Ampudia

Trias St.

OLD TOWN
STATE HISTORIC
PARK

Harney St.

Crescent Dr.

Whitman

Witherby St.

Congress

San Diego

0   1/4 mi
0   0.25 km

Pedestrian walkway

Mission Valley, which starts just north of Presidio Park and heads straight east, is decidedly more modern; until I-8 was built in the 1950s, it was little more than cow pastures with a couple of dirt roads. Shopping malls, motels, a golf course, condos, car dealerships, and a massive sports stadium fill the expanse today. Farther upstream along the San Diego River is the **Mission Basilica San Diego,** and just a few miles beyond lies an outstanding park with walking trails. Few visitors make it this far, but **Mission Trails Regional Park** reveals what San Diego looked like before the Spanish (and the car dealers) arrived.

Heritage Park ★ ARCHITECTURE   Downtown's 19th century historic structures were threatened with demolition during San Diego's post World War II boom, but were rescued when public and private funds were raised to purchase several significant buildings and move them to this 7.8-acre park. A few, including San Diego's first synagogue, Temple Beth Israel, and a modest cottage lacking electricity, water, and other conveniences, are open to the public daily 9am to 5pm. A couple of ornate Victorian homes have been lovingly restored into real beauts. A 15-minute stroll through the park provides a pleasant respite from Old Town's busy shopping district.

2454 Heritage Park Row. www.co.san-diego.ca.us/parks/heritage.html. Free admission. Daily sunrise to sunset.

Junípero Serra Museum ★ MUSEUM   William Templeton Johnson (the architect for many of Balboa Park's buildings) designed this Spanish Revival mission, with its white arches and red-tiled roof, in 1929, commemorating San Diego's first mission. Displays cover San Diego's early days, including the native peoples, Spanish explorers, and Mexican residents who were here when Southern California was part of Mexico (many of the artifacts were uncovered during archeological digs). The 70-foot tower is sometimes open and visitors are allowed to climb to the top for spectacular views, though the 360-degree panorama from the front of the museum is outstanding on its own. Note: The place is staffed by volunteers and can occasionally be closed when it should be open, so call ahead before visiting.

2727 Presidio Dr., Presidio Park. www.sandiegohistory.org/serra_museum.html. ✆ **619/232-6203.** Admission $6 adults; $4 seniors, students, and retired military; $3 children 6–17; free for children 5 and under. Sat–Sun 10am–5pm (Sept–June), Fri–Sun 10am–5pm (June–Sept).

Mission Basilica San Diego de Alcalá ★ CHURCH   Inconveniently located on the east end of Mission Valley, this historic treasure is worth the trek if you're interested in the early California missions. Established in 1769, the mission was the first link of 21 California missions founded by Spanish missionary Junípero Serra. In 1774, the church was moved from Old Town to its present site for agricultural reasons. Archeological explorations have uncovered artifacts and bits of information about the church, community, and farming practices. Few of the original bits remain, but there is a bell dating to 1802 and century-old olive and citrus trees amid gardens. The church is an active Catholic parish. *Hint:* Take the trolley and walk about 5 minutes from stop. Other missions in San Diego County include **Mission San Luis Rey de Francia** in Oceanside, **Mission San Antonio de Pala** near Mount Palomar, and **Mission Santa Ysabel** near Julian.

10818 San Diego Mission Rd., Mission Valley. www.missionsandiego.com. ✆ **619/281-8449.** Admission $5 adults, $2 seniors and students, $1 children 11 and under. Free Sun for daily Masses. Museum and gift shop daily 9am–4:30pm; Mass daily 7am and 5:30pm, with additional Sun Mass hourly from 7am–noon and 5:30pm.

Mission Trails Regional Park ★ PARK/GARDEN   Well off the beaten track, but only 8 miles from downtown San Diego, this is one of the nation's largest urban parks. Encompassing some 5,800 acres, it includes abundant bird life, two lakes, a picturesque stretch of the San Diego River, and 1,592-foot Cowles Mountain. The park has hiking and mountain bike trails and a 46-space campground (activenet.active.com/sdparkandrec; ✆ **619/668-2748**) available for overnight camping on Friday and Saturday nights. Call ahead to make sure it's open. Go early for good bird-watching and comfortable hiking—the midday sun can be brutal.

1 Father Junípero Serra Trail, Mission Gorge. www.mtrp.org. ✆ **619/668-3281.** Free admission. Daily sunrise–sundown (visitor center 9am–5pm). Take I-8 to Mission Gorge Rd.; follow for 4 mi. to entrance.

Old Town State Historic Park ★ HISTORIC SITE   Devoted to re-creating San Diego from 1821 to 1872, the park contains some original structures, including homes made of adobe; the rest are reconstructed. La Casa de Estudillo, depicts the life of a wealthy family in 1872 and Seeley Stable has two floors of wagons, stagecoaches, and other memorabilia. California's first public schoolhouse and San Diego's first newspaper office are also open for touring. On Wednesdays and Saturdays, from 10am to 4pm, costumed park volunteers reenact life in the 1800s with cooking and crafts demonstrations. Free 1-hour walking tours leave the headquarters (address below) daily at 11am and 2pm. Plan on 90 minutes here. Southeast of the park's main plaza streets are lined with more shops, galleries, and restaurants.

4002 Wallace St., Old Town. www.parks.ca.gov. ℭ **619/220-5422.** Free admission (donations welcome). Museums daily 10am–5pm (until 4pm Oct–Apr); most restaurants until 9pm.

Whaley House ★ HISTORIC HOME In 1856, this brick two-story house was built for Thomas Whaley and his family. It's an urban legend that this house has four resident ghosts, including by the spirit of Yankee Jim Robinson, who was hanged in 1852 where the house now stands. Frankly, what's most interesting about the home are the ghost tales, though exhibits do include a life mask of Abraham Lincoln, one of only six made, and the spinet piano used in the movie *Gone With the Wind.*

2476 San Diego Ave. www.whaleyhouse.org. ℭ **619/297-7511.** Admission before 5pm $6 adults, $5 seniors 65 and older, $4 children 3–12; admission after 5pm $10 adults, $5 children 3–12. Free for children 2 and under. June–Aug daily 10am–9:30pm; Sept–May Sun–Tues 10am–5pm, Thurs– Sat 10am–9:30pm; closed Wed.

Mission Bay & the Beaches

Belmont Park ★ AMUSEMENT PARK It's hard to tell what this 1925 amusement park will look like come 2015, but admission is free and it's always worth a walk-through while you're strolling along the Miss Bay boardwalk. The latest owners, who took over the beleaguered park in 2012, have plans for all sorts of improvements. The wooden **Giant Dipper roller coaster ★**, a registered National Historic Landmark, still rattles as riders squeal, and the tiled 1920 **Plunge** indoor swimming pool is undergoing renovations. There are a variety of carny-style rides, games, and food stands, along with the **Wave House ★** (www.wavehousesandiego.com; ℭ **858/228-9304**). This self-described "royal palace of youth culture" features **FlowBarrel ★**, a wave machine for stand-up rides on a 10-foot wave, and **FlowRider,** with a less gnarly wave-riding experience for novices. Other attractions include a mini-golf course, rock-climbing wall, and zip line.

3146 Mission Blvd., corner of W. Mission Bay Dr. www.belmontpark.com. ℭ **858/488-1549.** Free admission. Rides have varying costs and run daily 11am–8pm (extended weekend and summer hours)

Cabrillo National Monument ★★★ HISTORIC SITE The drive to this light-house and monument, at the tip of Point Loma, is one San Diego's loveliest, with the road climbing along coastal cliffs and bisecting rows of white tombstones covering 77 acres at Fort Rosecrans National Cemetery. You can glimpse a panorama of San Diego Bay, downtown, and the horizon all the way to Mexico as you near the tip; most visitors immediately head for the viewing platforms to take in the breathtaking views. A statue of Portuguese explorer Juan Rodríguez Cabrillo, who sailed into the bay in1542, dominates the tip of Point Loma at 422 feet above sea level. Other attractions include the restored lighthouse, built in 1855, and visitors' center and gift shop with a wide range of books, games, and souvenirs with San Diego, the US Navy, and national park themes. Free 25-minute videos and slide shows on Cabrillo, tide pools, and sea life are shown on the hour daily from 10am to 4pm at a small theater by the shop. National Park Service rangers lead walks at the monument, and energetic visitors hike the Bay-side Trail, a 3-mile round-trip down the cliff to a lookout over the bay. In the winter (Dec–Mar), the monument serves as an excellent vantage point for watching migrating Pacific gray whales breech. A road just outside the main gate leads west down the cliff to tide pools. *Tip:* Even on a sunny day, temperatures here can be cool, so bring a

Mission Bay & the Beaches Attractions, Hotels & Restaurants

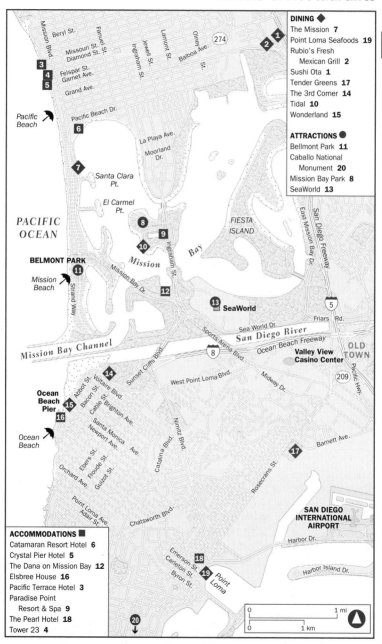

DINING ◆
The Mission **7**
Point Loma Seafoods **19**
Rubio's Fresh
  Mexican Grill **2**
Sushi Ota **1**
Tender Greens **17**
The 3rd Corner **14**
Tidal **10**
Wonderland **15**

ATTRACTIONS ●
Bellmont Park **11**
Caballo National
  Monument **20**
Mission Bay Park **8**
SeaWorld **13**

ACCOMMODATIONS ■
Catamaran Resort Hotel **6**
Crystal Pier Hotel **5**
The Dana on Mission Bay **12**
Elsbree House **16**
Pacific Terrace Hotel **3**
Paradise Point
  Resort & Spa **9**
The Pearl Hotel **18**
Tower 23 **4**

jacket; and pack a lunch—the site has great picnicking spots but no food facilities. Plan on a minimum of 90 minutes here.

1800 Cabrillo Memorial Dr., Point Loma. www.nps.gov/cabr. © **619/557-5450.** Admission $5 per vehicle, $3 for walk-ins (valid for 7 days from purchase). Daily 9am–5pm (last entrance 4:30pm).

Mission Bay Park ★★★ PARK   This 4,200-acre panorama of San Diego at play fills with families and friends most weekends, especially in summer. Thousands of parking spaces disappear quickly and cyclists, skaters, joggers, and strollers stream along scenic trails. Volleyball nets, bocce ball courts, and other toys pop up all over the 90 acres of developed public parks as watercraft zoom about in the bay. Early explorers who termed this area False Bay would surely be astonished. The park opened to the public in 1949, after the Army Corps of Engineers dug channels, dredged tidelands, and shaped the terrain into beaches, coves, and sloping lawns. The park includes a few businesses, SeaWorld, hotels, sportfishing operations, and sports centers. There are several access points from I-5, Sea World Drive, and the beach communities. For information and maps go to www.sandiego.gov/park-and-recreation/parks/regional/missionbay.

SeaWorld San Diego ★ AMUSEMENT PARK   *Editor's Note: There have been many accusations of late that SeaWorld's method of capturing wild marine mammals and keeping them in captivity has led, over the decades, to the untimely deaths of dozens of orcas and dolphins in their custody. Some say that the Parks' policies triggered the orca attacks that caused the deaths of four trainers (at the time of this writing). For more on these charges, you can watch the documentary* Blackfish *(www. seaworldofhurt.com). In response to the documentary, and other charges lobbed against it, SeaWorld has announced it will be expanding the size of its marine enclosures. It's also important to note that SeaWorld has also long been a leader in marine conservation efforts and research. For more on SeaWorld's side of the story, go to seaworld.org/en/conservation-and-research. Whether SeaWorld's efforts are enough, or whether marine mammal shows are inherently unethical, is a question that all visitors to SeaWorld should consider. What follows below is our author's review.*

The parking lots are packed on weekends and in summer, proving this 1964 aquatic theme park is still wildly popular. But it wouldn't be my first choice if I could only pick one expensive outing. These days, 50% of the American public does not want to support orca and dolphin shows, and SeaWorld is feeling the backlash of those opinions. Birch Aquarium (see p. 232). has lots of sea critters to admire (for a lower entrance fee); and young children, frankly, seem happier at LEGOLAND (see p. 261). But SeaWorld has the only thrilling amusement park rides in San Diego, plus splashy animal and marine animal shows—just what some folks want for a fun day (see the SeaWorld website for a list of those).

In addition, SeaWorld offers up simulated marine environments, including an arctic enclosure featuring beluga whales and polar bears, sharks looming overhead in a wrap-around tank, and four penguin species, including the tufted crowned macaroni penguin diving, swimming, and waddling about in an icy enclosure. Colorful clown fish (think Nemo) and bizarre looking scorpion fish swim about in aquariums and tide pools offer hands-on experiences.

Visitors can sign up for various guided tours and interactive offerings. The **Dolphin** and **Beluga Interaction Programs** allow visitors to wade waist-deep with dolphins and beluga whales ($215 per person, not including park admission; participants must be age 10 or older). SeaWorld plays a large role in rescuing and rehabilitating beached

A whale OF A PROBLEM

Animal activists have long opposed to the idea of keeping orcas in tanks and training them to perform in shows. Their protests gained impetus and public support with the 2013 release of the film *Blackfish*, an impassioned documentary about the dangers and consequences of keeping killer whales in captivity. SeaWorld reacted, calling the film "inaccurate and misleading," but that didn't keep park attendance from dropping significantly in 2014. In August 2014, SeaWorld officials announced a plan to double the size of the orca tanks and pledged $10 million in matching funds for killer whale research. Since the park is one of San Diego's largest employers and contributes millions of dollars to the city's coffers, tourism officials and politicians praised the plan, hoping the controversy would dwindle into a bad memory over time.

animals found along the West Coast. Still, there is a troubling aspect to this kind of facility—for another point of view, check out the **Whale and Dolphin Conservation Society** at www.wdcs.org.

SeaWorld also operates **Aquatica by SeaWorld** (2052 Entertainment Circle; aquaticabyseaworld.com; ✆ **800/457-4268**) eight miles south of downtown San Diego in Chula Vista. The park has water slides, a wave pool, lazy river, beach area, and more. It's open daily 10am to 7:30pm in summer, weekends only in winter. Hours and days open change, so check before going. Tickets are $40 adult and kids over 10, $29 children 2 to 9; a two-park pass is available.

500 SeaWorld Dr., Mission Bay. www.seaworld.com. ✆ **800/257-4268** or 619/226-3901. Admission $73 adults, $65 children 3–9, free for children 2 and under; tickets are good for 7 consecutive days of unlimited admission. Hours vary seasonally, but always at least daily 10am–5pm; most weekends and during summer 9am–11pm. Parking $14, $19 RVs.

La Jolla

Century-old palms frame **Ellen Browning Scripps Park ★★★**, named for the generous benefactress who donated many of the buildings and public parks that make La Jolla one of Southern California's loveliest communities. The park edges a rocky coastline from **La Jolla Cove ★★★** south to the **Children's Pool ★★★**, where harbor seals laze in the sun. A sunset walk along the cliff-top path between the two ranks at the top of quintessential San Diego moments. A long block above the park is the Village, an orderly arrangement of streets lined with tasteful boutiques, classy restaurants, and architectural treasures. Several are clustered near the **La Jolla Historical Society** in the 1904 Wisteria Cottage (780 Prospect St.; lajollahistory.org; ✆ **858/459-5335;** Thurs–Sun 2–4pm). Pick up a walking tour map here.

The 1,200-acre **University of California, San Diego (UCSD)** campus, which was established in 1960, covers a mesa north of the village. Nearby is celebrated architect Louis I. Kahn's "Acropolis of Science," the **Salk Institute for Biological Studies ★★★**, 10010 N. Torrey Pines Rd.; ✆ **858-453-4100;** salk.edu, with stark concrete buildings bisected by a silvery water channel running towards the horizon. Free guided tours are available with advance reservations, or you can roam about on your own. At the neighboring **Torrey Pines Gliderport ★★★** (see p. 245), human flyers spread their colorful wings, step off the cliffs above Blacks Beach, and soar with the air currents above the sea. Grab a snack or sandwich from the **Cliffhanger Cafe** beside the launching area and don't even try to hold back your oohs and aahs. And if that isn't high enough, drive into the hills to **Mt. Soledad** (905 La Jolla Scenic Drive South), 822 feet above sea level. Even the distant snow-capped mountains 100 miles away are visible on clear days. The park atop the peak closes at dusk, but evening views are still stunning from viewpoints along the road.

Athenaeum Music & Arts Library ★★ CULTURAL INSTITUTION Founded in 1899, this is 1 of only 16 nonprofit membership libraries in the United States. Year-round, it hosts exceptional art exhibits, intimate concerts (from jazz and classical to more experimental new music), lectures, special events, and classes that are open to the general public. The gracious white Spanish Revival building was designed by William Templeton Johnson for the La Jolla Library in 1921; stepping inside, beneath the rotunda and wood-beamed ceiling, feels like entering a cultural place of worship. Free tours are conducted every third Saturday at 11am.

1008 Wall St. www.ljathenaeum.org. © **858/454-5872.** Gallery and library admission free; various prices for concerts, classes, and lectures. Tues, Thurs–Sat 10am–5:30pm; Wed 10am–8:30pm; closed Sun–Mon.

Birch Aquarium at Scripps ★★ AQUARIUM This fascinating aquarium and museum explores the research taking place at the world-famous Scripps Institution of Oceanography, located right across the street on a bluff overlooking the ocean. Take a moment to watch thousands of silvery sardines swirling in unison around a tall, circular tank before entering the main aquarium with more than 60 marine-life tanks affording close-up views of sea creatures from the Pacific Northwest, the California coast, Mexico's Sea of Cortez, and the tropical seas. Some favorite experiences here include trying to spot the camouflaged sea bass, octopus, leopard sharks, and other creatures in the giant kelp forest; and visiting with the sea stars, anemones, lobsters, crabs, and other critters that hide amid rocks and shells in the hands-on outdoor tide pool (the ocean views from here are spectacular). The museum section is less entrancing, but offers solid exhibits about the Scripps Institution's crucial work in ocean science and conservation. Off-site adventures, such as tide pooling, scouting for grunion runs (p. 239), and whale-watching, are also conducted year-round (call for more details). Give yourself at least 90 minutes here.

2300 Expedition Way. www.aquarium.ucsd.edu. © **858/534-3474.** Admission $17 adults, $13 seniors and children 3–17, free for children 2 and under. Daily 9am–5pm. Free 3-hr. parking.

Museum of Contemporary Art San Diego La Jolla ★★★ ART MUSEUM Combining stunning architecture and a stellar collection of art works produced since 1950, the MCASD is a must-see for anyone even remotely interested in the arts. The collection of more than 4,000 works incorporates varied media and genres, including videos, sculptures, and an impressive collection of Pop Art from the 1960s and 70s. California artists are well represented, as are those working in the U.S.-Mexico border region and in Latin America. Temporary exhibits have focused on everything from art inspired by science fiction to stand-up comedy. Among the many important works here are Nancy Rubins' *The Pleasure Point,* a colorful jumble of actual boats and surfboards assembled in a giant sculpture extending from the museum's ocean-facing exterior. The museum's original home was designed in 1916 by Irving Gill for Ellen Browning Scripps, one of San Diego and La Jolla's most prolific benefactors. Architect Robert Venturi was chosen to direct an expansion and restoration of the Gill design, creating a renewed museum in 1996. Free docent tours are available at 2pm and on

La Jolla Attractions

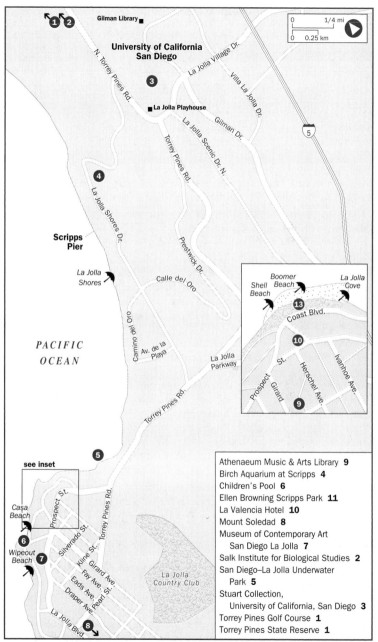

Gilman Library ■

University of California
San Diego

N. Torrey Pines Rd.

La Jolla Village Dr.

Villa La Jolla Dr.

La Jolla Scenic Dr. N.

Gilman Dr.

■ La Jolla Playhouse

Torrey Pines Rd.

5

La Jolla Shores Dr.

Prestwick Dr.

Scripps
Pier

La Jolla
Shores

Calle del Oro

Camino del Oro

Av. de la
Playa

La Jolla
Parkway

PACIFIC
OCEAN

Torrey Pines Rd.

see inset

Casa
Beach

Prospect St.

Torrey Pines Rd.

Wipeout
Beach

Silverado St.

Kline St.

Girard Ave.

Fay Ave.

Eads Ave.

Pearl St.

Draper Ave.

La Jolla
Country Club

La Jolla Blvd.

0   1/4 mi
0   0.25 km

Inset:

Boomer
Beach

La Jolla
Cove

Shell
Beach

Coast Blvd.

Prospect St.

Girard

Herschel Ave.

Ivanhoe Ave.

Legend:

Athenaeum Music & Arts Library **9**
Birch Aquarium at Scripps **4**
Children's Pool **6**
Ellen Browning Scripps Park **11**
La Valencia Hotel **10**
Mount Soledad **8**
Museum of Contemporary Art
    San Diego La Jolla **7**
Salk Institute for Biological Studies **2**
San Diego–La Jolla Underwater
    Park **5**
Stuart Collection,
    University of California, San Diego **3**
Torrey Pines Golf Course **1**
Torrey Pines State Reserve **1**

Sundays. The museum is open on the third Thursday of the month from 5 to 7 pm and admission is free during those hours.

700 Prospect St. www.mcasd.org. © **858/454-3541.** Admission $10 adults; $5 seniors, students 26 and over, and military; free for anyone 25 and under; paid ticket valid for 7 days at all MCASD locations (there are 2 downtown galleries; p. 224). Thurs–Tues 11am–5pm; closed Wed.

Stuart Collection ★ CULTURAL INSTITUTION If you're fond of exceptional public art, do tackle the maze that is the campus of the University of California San Diego (it comprises some 1,200 acres of mesas, canyons, and eucalyptus groves) to see this collection of 18 highly diverse pieces. Among them is Niki de Saint Phalle's *Sun God,* a jubilant 14-foot-high fiberglass bird on a 15-foot concrete base, used by students as the centerpiece of their annual Sun God Festival. Alexis Smith's 560-foot-long slate-tile *Snake Path,* slithers up a hill to the Geisel Library hovering in stacked levels like a glass UFO; Terry Allen's *Trees* spout aphorisms and President Obama's inauguration speech; and Tim Hawkinson's 180-ton granite *Bear* manages to look like a huge, friendly teddy bear. Maps are available at information booths around the campus, and there's visitor parking at lots near the library. Allow at least 2 hours to tour the entire collection, as distances are long between some sights.

University of California, San Diego. stuartcollection.ucsd.edu. © **858/534-2117.** Free admission. From La Jolla, take Torrey Pines Rd. to La Jolla Village Dr., turn right, go 2 blocks to Gilman Dr. and turn left into the campus; in about 1 block an information booth will be visible on the right.

Torrey Pines State Reserve ★★★ PARK/GARDEN The rare Torrey pine tree grows in only two places in the world: Santa Rosa Island, 175 miles northwest of San Diego, and here, at the north end of La Jolla. Even if the twisted, towering, gnarled shape of these awkwardly beautiful trees doesn't lure you to this spot, the equally scarce undeveloped coastal scenery should. This 2,000-acre reserve is one of San Diego's unique treasures, a taste of what Southern California's coast looked like a hundreds of years ago. The reserve encompasses the beach below, as well as a lagoon immediately north, but the focus is the 300-foot-high, water-carved sandstone bluffs providing precarious footing for the trees. In spring, the wildflower show includes blooming bush poppies, Cleveland sage, agave, and yucca. A half-dozen trails, all under 1.5 miles in length, travel from the road to the cliff edge or down to the beach; watch for migrating gray whales in winter and dolphins year-round. Interpretive nature walks are held weekends and holidays at 10am and 2pm, departing from the small visitor center, built in the traditional adobe style of the Hopi Indians. *Note:* No facilities for food or drinks are available in the park. You can bring a picnic lunch, but you have to eat it on the beach; food and drink (other than water) are not allowed in the upper portion of the reserve. You could spend your whole day here, 90 minutes at least.

12600 N. Torrey Pines Rd., btw. La Jolla and Del Mar. www.torreypine.org. © **858/755-2063.** Admission $10 per car; hourly rates available at the North Beach lot ($4 for 1 hr.). Daily 8am–sunset.

Coronado

It's hard to miss San Diego Bay's most noteworthy landmark: the **San Diego–Coronado Bay Bridge ★**. Completed in 1969, this graceful five-lane bridge spans 2¼ miles and links the city and the "island" of Coronado (it's actually a peninsula). Heading to Coronado you can see Mexico, the downtown skyline, the naval station, and Point Loma. When the bridge opened, it put the antiquated commuter ferries out of business, but passenger ferries are available (see "By Water," in the "Getting Around" section on p. 176). Once in Coronado, you can pick up the **Coronado Shuttle** Bus 901 at the Ferry Landing and stops along Orange Avenue. It's free in summer and costs $2.25 in winter.

Hotel del Coronado ★★★ ICON   Built in 1888, this turreted Victorian seaside resort (see p. 195) remains an enduring, endearing national treasure. Whether you're staying here, dining here, or simply touring the grounds, prepare to be enchanted.

1500 Orange Ave., Coronado. www.hoteldel.com. ℂ **800/468-3533** or 619/435-6611. Free admission.

Museum of History and Art ★ MUSEUM   The 1916 neoclassical Spreckels Building claims one entire block and houses a live theater and this small museum's collection of photos and memorabilia recounting the history of this genteel and insular area. In addition, Coronado's considerable military importance is examined, with text and photos of the island's vast US Naval Air Station, which opened in 1917 (the current training ground for the Navy SEALs is along the coast south of the Hotel Del). Guided tours of the Hotel Del begin at the museum on some weekdays at 10:30am and weekends at 2pm ($15); a neighborhood tour departs from the museum on Wednesdays at 10:30am ($10). Call ahead for current information; reservations are required for both.

1100 Orange Ave. www.coronadohistory.org. ℂ **619/435-7242.** Admission $5 adults, $3 seniors, free for active duty military and children under 16. Mon–Fri 10am–6pm; Sat–Sun 10am–5pm.

ESPECIALLY FOR KIDS

Kids rarely run out of things they want to do in San Diego. Sure, they'll beg to visit all the major, pricey attractions. But there are plenty of free options as well. Be sure to check *San Diego Family Magazine* in brochure racks and online at www.sandiegofamily.com (register for free to read it all). The calendar of events and Best of Family Fun sections will give you enough ideas for an endless vacation. Beyond what you'll find there, here are our best suggestions for the young 'uns.

○ **Balboa Park** (p. 214) Street entertainers and clowns around El Prado, especially on weekends, will keep the entire family amused. The **Natural History Museum, Museum of Man, Model Railroad Museum, Air & Space Museum,** and **Reuben H. Fleet Science Center** are options that cater to individual interests. Take a snack break in the shady canopy of the century-old Moreton Bay Fig tree behind the Natural History Museum.

○ The **San Diego Zoo** (p. 221) Start your visit with the double-decker bus tour to figure out where the kids' favorite animals are located. When grumpiness sets it, ride the aerial tram, linger amid flitting birds in one of the aviaries, or pet the sheep and goats at the Children's Zoo.

○ **SeaWorld San Diego** (p. 230) Older kids enjoy the dizzying Wild Arctic ride and terrifying Manta rollercoaster; Shamu's Happy Harbor is a perfect energy release for little ones. Your admission ticket is good for 7 days, so consider a midday break or repeat early morning and late afternoon visits.

○ The **Zoo Safari Park** (p. 264) Ride the Africa Tram early, while animals are active, and don't miss the Cheetah Run held at 3:30pm daily. When energy flags, splash in the Savanna Cool Zone fountains or grab a bite and let kids run wild at the Sambaru Jungle Gym. Bring drinks and snacks for the 30-mile drive from central San Diego.

○ **LEGOLAND California** (p. 261) Impassioned Lego fans should stay at the park's hotel at least one night for complete immersion, or stay nearby for repeat visits. Wander through the cool, dark aquarium to escape the crowds, sun, and noise. Don't try to do the LEGO park and water park on the same day unless time is super-short.

Other Top Kid-Friendly Attractions

○ **Birch Aquarium at Scripps** (p. 232) for the hands-on tide pool.

○ **The New Children's Museum** (p. 224) best for young kids.

○ **Maritime Museum** (p. 224), only if kids are into boats or history

○ **Whale-Watching Tours** (p. 237) thrilling for all, especially in winter.

○ **The Gliderport** (p. 245) will transfix kids as they watch aerial acrobats swoop through the skies of La Jolla.

ORGANIZED TOURS

Water Excursions

Flagship ★★ TOUR   This company (formerly known as San Diego Harbor Excursion) offers daily 1- and 2-hour narrated tours of the bay with two different routes covering the San Diego–Coronado Bridge and Navy shipyards to the south and north to Naval Air Station North Island and Cabrillo National Monument. The boats are usually packed—arrive early to get a good viewing spot. The upper outdoor deck is best for taking in the scenery, but can be either chilly or blazing hot. Two-hour Sunday (and Sat in summer) brunch, and nightly 2½-hour dinner cruises are also available. In winter, whale-watching excursions feature onboard naturalists from the Birch Aquarium.

1050 N. Harbor Dr. www.flagshipsd.com. ℂ **800/442-7847** or 619/234-4111. Harbor tours $23–$28, $2 off for seniors and military, half-price for children 4–12. Dinner cruises start at $70 adults, $42 children; brunch cruise $65 adults, $39 children; whale-watching trips $35–$42 adults, $32–$37 seniors and military, $19–$21 children.

The Gondola Company ★ TOUR   This unique business operates from Loews Coronado Bay Resort, plying the canals and marinas of a nearby luxury waterside community. The gondolas are crafted according to centuries old Venetian designs. Mediterranean music plays while up to five passengers recline with snuggly blankets. The company will even provide antipasti or chocolate-covered strawberries.

Tours with a Twist

If you can't decide between a bus tour or a bay cruise, consider Old Town Trolley Tour's **Sea and Land Adventures** ★★. The 90-minute amphibious vessel tour departs from Seaport Village and motors along the Embarcadero until splashing into San Diego Bay. The craft holds 46 passengers, and the narrated tour covers both the maritime and military history of San Diego. Reservations are required; trips are usually scheduled daily, April through October, and Thursday through Monday the rest of the year. The cost is $34 for adults and $19 for kids 4 to 12. Free for children 3 and under. For info and tickets, visit www.sealtours.com or call ℂ **619/298-8687**.

Another novel way to see the sights is via **GoCar Tours** ★ (2100 Kettner Blvd. in Little Italy; www.gocartours.com; ℂ **800/914-6227**), small, three-wheeled vehicles that putter around town at about 35 mph (56kmph). These two-person open-air minicars are equipped with GPS technology that not only gives directions, but also indicates points of interest and narrates San Diego history. Rates start at $54 for the first hour, and you must be 18 to rent; reserve 24 hours in advance.

503 Grand Caribe Causeway, Coronado. www.gondolacompany.com. ☏ **619/429-6317.** 50-min. cruise $95 per couple, $20 for each additional passenger (up to 6 total), free for children 2 and under. Reservations required. Mon–Fri 3pm–midnight; Sat–Sun 11am–midnight.

Hornblower Cruises ★ TOUR   These 1- or 2-hour narrated tours take passengers through San Diego harbor, highlighting dozens of San Diego landmarks. You'll see the *Star of India,* cruise under the San Diego–Coronado Bridge, and swing by a submarine base and an aircraft carrier or two. Whale-watching trips (mid-Dec to late Mar) are a blast and there's a 2-hour Sunday champagne-brunch cruise and 3-hour dinner/dance cruises nightly.

1066 N. Harbor Dr. www.hornblower.com. ☏ **888/467-6256** or 619/686-8715. Harbor tours from $24 adults, $2 off for seniors and military, half-price for children 4–12. Dinner cruises start at $76; brunch cruise $62; whale-watching trips $39–$44 ($2 off for seniors and military), $18–$20 children.

Bus Tours

Not to be confused with the public transit trolley, the narrated **Old Town Trolley Tours** (www.historictours.com; ☏ **888/910-8687** or 619/298-8687) offer an easy alternative to renting a car or using public transportation. If you're staying several days, it's a convenient way to get an overview of the city and distances between attractions. These vehicles, gussied up like old-time trolleys, do a 30-mile circular route; you can hop off at any one of 11 stops, explore at leisure, and reboard when you please (the trolleys run every half-hour). Stops include Old Town, the Gaslamp Quarter, Coronado, the San Diego Zoo, and Balboa Park. Begin wherever you want, but you must purchase tickets before boarding (most stops have a ticket kiosk, or you can get discounted tickets online). Tickets online cost $35 for adults, $17 for kids 4 to 12, free for children 3 and under for one complete circuit; the route by itself takes about 2 hours. The trolleys operate daily from 9am to 5pm November to February, with extended hours the rest of the year.

Walking Tours

Walkabout International (www.walkabout-int.org; ☏ **619/231-7463**), sponsors more than 100 free walking tours led by volunteers every month, hitting all parts of the county, including the Gaslamp Quarter, La Jolla, and the beaches. **Urban Safaris** (www.walkingtoursofsandiego.com; ☏ **619/944-9255**) provides $10 walking tours with more detailed information on the history and character of various San Diego neighborhoods, including Ocean Beach and Hillcrest on Saturdays. **Where You Want to Be Tours** (www.wheretours.com; ☏ **619/917-6037**) puts a lighthearted touch on its offerings, which include walking, biking, and Segway tours. For your own personal guide, check out the company's "Rent a Local" offering ($220 for 6 people for 3 hours). For those who want to combine socializing and nightlife with a guided outing, both **So Diego Tours** (www.sodiegotours.com; ☏ **888/394-8067** or 619/233-8687) and **Bite San Diego** (www.bitesandiego.com; ☏ **800/979-3700** or 619/634-8476) offer neighborhood walks combining history with bar crawls. Prices start at $45.

Whale-Watching

Whale watching is an eagerly anticipated wintertime activity, when Pacific gray whales pass close by Point Loma on their annual migratory trek. Local whaling in the 1870s greatly reduced their numbers, but federal protection has allowed the species to repopulate; current estimates put the number of grays at about 20,000. When they approach San Diego, the 40- to 50-foot whales are more than three-quarters of the way

THE best OF SAN DIEGO ONLINE

- **www.sandiego.org** is maintained by the San Diego Convention & Visitors Bureau and includes weather data, an events calendar, and a hotel booking engine.
- **www.sandiegomagazine.com** is the online site for *San Diego Magazine*, offering feature stories and dining and events listings.
- **www.sandiegoreader.com**, the site of the free weekly *San Diego Reader*, is a great resource for club and show listings. It also offers discounts for dining and other services, plus opinionated arts, eats, and entertainment critiques.

- **www.signonsandiego.com** is the site for the city's last major daily newspaper, the *U-T San Diego*, offering headline news, and information on restaurants, music, movies, performing arts, and other activities.
- **www.wheresd.com** has a more youthful take on arts, culture, special events, shopping, and dining.
- **www.voiceofsandiego.org** is an excellent online news source that offers information on what's happening in the city politically and culturally.

along their nearly 6,000-mile journey from Alaska to breeding and birthing lagoons in the Pacific and Sea of Cortez, around the southern tip of Baja California. After mating and calving they pass by again, calves in tow, heading back to Alaska. From mid-December to mid-March is the best time to see the migration, and there are several ways to view the procession.

The easiest (and cheapest) way to see the whales is from the cliff tops at **Cabrillo National Monument,** at the tip of Point Loma. If you want to get a closer look, take one of the excursions that locate and follow gray whales, being careful not to disturb their journey. In addition to the boat tour companies mentioned above, several sport-fishing companies (see p. 243) offer winter whale trips. Recently, blue whales and fin whales have been showing up in summer. **San Diego Whale Watch** (www.sdwhale watch.com; © **619/839-0128**) runs year-round 3 hour adults $44, children 2 to 17, military, and seniors $38, no children under 2.

H&M Landing, 2803 Emerson St., Point Loma (www.hmlanding.com; © **619/222-1144**), has 3- and 6-hour trips, starting at $46 for ages 13 and up, $30 for ages 2 to 12.

In La Jolla, the **Birch Aquarium at Scripps** celebrates gray whale season with classes, educational activities, and exhibits, and the outdoor terrace offers another vantage point for spotting the mammals from shore. Birch provides naturalists to accompany the whale watching done by Flagship (see "Water Excursions," above). Call © **858/534-3474,** or go to www.aquarium.ucsd.edu for more information.

OUTDOOR ACTIVITIES

Beaches

San Diego County is blessed with 70 miles of sandy coastline and more than 30 beach communities. When it comes to enjoying the San Diego shores, though, a word (or four actually) to the wise: **May Gray** and **June Gloom.** They're names for a local weather pattern with thick marine layers that can foil sunbathing, especially before noon from mid-May to mid-July. Neither sun nor fog is guaranteed, but you can expect possible gray days with moist, chilly mornings and evenings. The beach weather and sea temperatures are usually best from July through September, with the air and water unpredictably chilly or mild in winter. As can be expected, the beaches are extremely crowded on summer weekends; wise vacationers enjoy the beach far more on week-days. *But remember:* Even when the sun isn't shining you're exposed to harmful UV rays; always wear sunscreen. Another beach precaution worth remembering is the "stingray shuffle," a way to avoid stings by disturbing the sand at water's edge.

Another sting to beware of is the pain you might feel if you're caught drinking alcohol or smoking on any San Diego beach or coastal parks. In 2008, voters approved a **ban on alcohol** at the beach; first offense has a maximum fine of $250. Smoking is also illegal at all city beaches, boardwalks, piers, and parks.

Exploring **tide pools**—potholed, rocky shores that retain ponds of water when the tide's low, providing homes for a plethora of sea creatures—is a time-honored coastal pleasure. You can get a tide chart from many surf and diving shops. Among the best places for tide-pooling are Cabrillo National Monument; Sunset Cliffs in Ocean Beach; and along the rocky coast immediately south of the cove in La Jolla.

Here's a list of central San Diego's most noteworthy beaches listed geographically from south to north. For North County beaches, see chapter 8. All California beaches are open to the public to the mean high-tide line (essentially the hard-packed sand), and you can check **www.sandiego.gov/lifeguards/beaches** for descriptions and water quality. Beach closures due to bacterial contamination are a modern-day fact of life, especially following storms when runoff from city streets makes its way to the ocean—check for posted warnings with county's Beach and Bay Status hot line (www.sdbeachinfo.com; *©* **619/338-2073**). *Note:* All beaches are good for swimming and have public restrooms except as indicated.

IMPERIAL BEACH Imperial Beach is just a half-hour south of downtown San Diego by car or trolley, and only a few minutes from the Mexican border. It's popular with surfers and "I.B." locals, who can be somewhat territorial about "their" beach in summer. There are 3 miles of surf breaks plus a guarded "swimmers only" stretch;

FISHY fun run

The **Grunion Run** ★ is a local tradition—so if someone invites you down to the beach for a late-night fishing expedition, armed only with a sack and flashlight, don't be afraid. Go! Grunion are 5- to 6-inch silvery fish that wriggle out of the water to lay their eggs in the sand. Found only in Southern and Baja California, they make for decent eating, coated in flour and cornmeal, and then fried. April to early June is peak spawning season, but they may only be caught—**by hand**—during the months of March and then June through August; a fishing license is required for those 16 and older. Grunion runs happen twice a month after the highest tides, about 2 to 5 nights after a full or new moon. Anywhere from a few dozen to thousands of grunion can appear during a run. They prefer wide, flat, sandy beaches (such as the Coronado Strand, Mission Beach, and La Jolla Shores); you'll spot more grunion if you go to a less-populated stretch of beach, with a minimum amount of light. For details, go to the little critters' website, www.grunion.pepperdine.edu, or check with the Department of Fish and Game at www.dfg.ca.gov.

check with lifeguards before getting wet, though, since sewage runoff from nearby Mexico can sometimes foul the water.

CORONADO BEACH ★★★   Often named one of the country's best beaches, this long, wide stretch of sand runs along Ocean Boulevard past the Hotel del Coronado and staggeringly pricey mansions. Lovely, wide, and sparkling, it's conducive to strolling, especially in the late afternoon. At the north end, you can watch fighter jets in formation flying from the Naval Air Station, while just south of the Hotel Del, public access ends at the training grounds for the Navy Seals and then begins again at the beautiful, relatively unpopulated **Silver Strand.** Waves are gentle here, and the beach draws many Coronado families—and their dogs, which are allowed off-leash at the most northwesterly end. As in all beach areas, parking is extremely limited. Unless you absolutely love Coronado, choose a more central beach town for your days of sea and sand and check out this beach while touring Coronado's other sights.

OCEAN BEACH ★★   This funky, hippie holdover community has become extremely popular in the past few years despite its reputation as being somewhat seedy and sketchy. The attraction? The sense of an authentic, unpretentious SoCal beach town where families have held on to their beach cottages for generations. At the northern end of Ocean Beach Park, officially known as **Dog Beach,** your pooch can roam freely on the sand. Surfers generally congregate around the **O.B. Pier,** a half-mile-long concrete pier where anglers dangle their lines from the railings and crowds congregate to watch awesome waves. Rip currents can be strong here and sometimes discourage swimmers (check with the lifeguard stations). Facilities include restrooms, showers, picnic tables, volleyball courts, and parking lots—which fill quickly. South of the beach at the end of Sunset Cliffs Boulevard is **Sunset Cliffs Natural Park,** extending 1.5 miles along rough cliffs above the open ocean. Beach access is limited, though local youngsters can't resist jumping from the cliffs into deep coves and surfers find a few spots with powerful waves. Stay away from the cliffs' edge: lifeguard and helicopter rescues are too common here. Naturally, watching the sun set from here is absolutely awesome.

MISSION BAY PARK ★★★   This 4,200-acre aquatic playground contains 27 miles of bayfront, picnic areas, children's playgrounds, and paths for biking, in-line skating, and jogging. There are dozens of access points; one of the most popular is off I-5 at Clairemont Drive. Also accessed from this spot is **Fiesta Island,** where the annual **World Championship Over-the-Line Tournament** is held to raucous enthusiasm in July (see "Calendar of Events, in chapter 6). A 4-mile road loops around the island. Parts of the bay have been subject to closure over the years due to high levels of bacteria, so check for posted warnings.

MISSION BEACH ★★   Anchored by Mission Bay and the **Giant Dipper** roller coaster, Mission Beach is the quintessential party-hearty, anything goes (within reason) beach where bronzed, scantily clad boys and girls leap after volleyballs, lounge languorously in the sand, stroll the boardwalk and generally spend considerable time eyeing each other with interest. The long beach and path extend from the jetty north to Belmont Park and Pacific Beach Drive. Parking can be horrendous, and the police often post signs saying all spots are full by noon on summer weekends. Your best bets are the public lots at Belmont Park or at the south end of West Mission Bay Drive; this street intersects with Mission Boulevard, the centerline of a 2-block-wide isthmus that leads a mile north to Pacific Beach.

PACIFIC BEACH ★★   Pacific Beach shares the boardwalk with Mission Beach. The paved promenade is called **Ocean Front Walk** here, and features a human parade akin to L.A.'s Venice Beach boardwalk (see p. 115). It runs along Ocean Boulevard (just west of Mission Blvd.) past the **Crystal Pier,** where flappers danced at the Crystal Ballroom in the 1920s. The pier is now home to a series of blue and white hotel cottages, but it's still open to the public and a lovely place to stroll above the waves. Surfing is popular year-round here, in marked sections, especially at **Tourmaline Surfing Park,** a half-mile north of the pier, where the sport's old guard gathers and swimmers are prohibited. Other areas are posted for swimmers and the beach is well staffed with lifeguards. You're on your own to find street parking, and plan on hiking 12 blocks or more if you arrive after 10am on summer weekends.

CHILDREN'S POOL ★★   Think clothing-optional Black's Beach is the city's most controversial sun-sea-sand situation? Think again! La Jolla's Children's Pool is currently home to the biggest man-verses-beast struggle since *Moby-Dick.* A sea wall protects this pocket of sand, originally intended as a calm swimming bay for children and a lovely snorkeling and swimming area. Since 1994, when a rock outcrop off the shore was designated as a protected mammal reserve, an ever-expanding harbor seal population has colonized the beach. On an average day you'll spot several dozen lolling in the sun. Some humans have not appreciated losing their favorite beach—and warn of the dangers of allowing abundant shark bait in swimming water—and a heated debate over human vs. seal rights has raged for more than a decade. In 2014, the California Coastal Commission instated a 5-year beach ban prohibiting human access annually from December 15 to May 15 during seal birthing season. Volunteers, with speed dials set to "lifeguard," keep watch to make sure bathers don't interfere with the colony—scofflaws are arrested. The beach is at Coast Boulevard and Jenner Street; there's limited free street parking.

LA JOLLA COVE ★★★   The cove's protected, calm waters—celebrated as the clearest along the coast—attract snorkelers, scuba divers, along with a fair share of families. The stunning setting offers a tiny sandy beach in **Ellen Browning Scripps Park.** The cove's "look but don't touch" policy protects the bright orange Garibaldi, California's state fish, plus octopus and lobster. The unique **Underwater Park** to the northern end of Torrey Pines State Reserve and incorporates kelp forests, artificial reefs, two deep canyons, and tidal pools. Parking is scarce.

LA JOLLA SHORES ★★★   The wide, flat mile of sand might well be the single most popular beach in San Diego, attracting joggers, swimmers, families, kayakers, scuba divers, and beginning body- and board-surfers. It looks like a picture postcard, with fine sand under blue skies, kissed by gentle waves, running north to the pier at the prestigious Scripps Institution of Oceanography. Weekend crowds can be enormous, quickly occupying both the sand and the metered parking spaces in the lot. There are restrooms and showers, as well as picnic areas at grassy, palm-lined Kellogg Park.

BLACK'S BEACH ★   The area's unofficial, illegal nude beach, 2-mile-long Black's lies between La Jolla Shores and Torrey Pines State Beach, at the base of steep, 300-foot-high cliffs. The beach is not easy to reach, but it draws scores with its beauty and good swimming and surfing. There are no restroom facilities and no lifeguard station, though lifeguards are usually present from spring holidays to October. To get here, take North Torrey Pines Road, watch for signs for the Gliderport (where you can park), and clamber down the makeshift path. Cliff rescues occur far too frequently as beachgoers assume they can handle the slippery downhill slope—use caution, wear shoes or sandals with gripping soles, and take your time. To bypass the cliff descent, you can walk to Black's from beaches north (Torrey Pines) or south (La Jolla Shores).

TORREY PINES BEACH ★★★ Past the north end of Black's Beach, at the foot of Torrey Pines State Park, is this fabulous, underused strand, accessed by a pay parking lot at the entrance to the park and a large free lot across the street. Combining a visit to the park with a day at the beach makes for the quintessential San Diego outdoor experience. It's rarely crowded, though you need to be aware of high tide (when most of the sand gets a bath). In almost any weather, it's a great beach for walking. *Note:* At this and any other bluff side beach, never sit at the bottom of the cliffs; they are unstable and could collapse.

Ballooning & Scenic Flights

A peaceful balloon ride reveals sweeping vistas of the Southern California coast, Del Mar and Rancho Santa Fe in North County. Contact **Skysurfer Balloon Company** (www.sandiegohotairballoons.com; ✆ **800/660-6809** or 858/481-6800) and **California Dreamin'** (www.californiadreamin.com; ✆ **800/373-3359** or 951/699-0601). **Barnstorming Adventures** (www.barnstorming.com; ✆ **800/759-5667** or 760/930-0903) offers vintage plane flights from Montgomery Field, 3750 John J. Montgomery Dr., in Kearny Mesa, taking passengers along the coast. Their Air Combat flights with you at the controls (under the guidance of active-duty fighter pilots) offer simulated dogfights; reserve space 1 to 2 weeks in advance.

Biking

With its impeccable weather and varied terrain, San Diego is a preeminent cycling destination. Many major thoroughfares offer bike lanes, and the city has been painting those lanes green and enforcing the "three-foot" state law requiring cars to stay at least 36 inches from cyclists when passing. Download a map of San Diego County's bike lanes and routes at www.511sd.com. The **San Diego County Bicycle Coalition** (www.sdcbc.org; ✆ **858/487-6063**) conducts rides and biking lessons. Bicycle helmets are legally required for those 17 and under.

The paths around Mission Bay are great for leisurely rides; the oceanfront boardwalk between Pacific Beach and Mission Beach can get very crowded, but offers fun people watching. The 16-mile round-trip **Bayshore Bikeway** trail starts at the Ferry Landing Marketplace in Coronado and runs south along the Silver Strand. Traveling old State Route 101 (aka the Pacific Coast Hwy.) from La Jolla north to Oceanside offers terrific coastal views. *Cycling San Diego* by Nelson Copp and Jerry Schad is a valuable resource and available at many local bike shops.

Rental bikes are available downtown at **The Bike Revolution,** 522 Sixth Ave. (www.thebikerevolution.com; ✆ **619/564-4843**) and **San Diego Bike Shop,** 619 C St. (www.sdbikeshop.com; ✆ **619/237-1245**). If you don't feel like huffing and puffing, rent an electric bike in Little Italy at **Ivan Stewart's Electric Bike Center,** 2021 India St. (www.iselectricbikecenter.com; ✆ **619/564-7028**).

In Mission Beach, there's **Cheap Rentals,** 3689 Mission Blvd. (www.cheap-rentals.com; ✆ **800/941-7761** or 858/488-9070), which rents everything from beach cruisers to baby trailers, as well as skates, surfboards, and beach gear. **Mission Beach Surf & Skate,** 704 Ventura Place (✆ **858/488-5050**), has classic beach cruisers and more. In Coronado, **Bikes and Beyond,** conveniently located at the Ferry Landing, 1201 First St. (✆ **619/435-7180**) has beach cruisers, pedal surreys, and skate rentals.

Hike Bike Kayak San Diego, 2246 Av. de la Playa, La Jolla (www.hikebikekayak. com; © **866/425-2925** or 858/551-9510), has a variety of bike tours along La Jolla's coast, around Mission Bay, and down La Jolla's Mount Soledad.

Boating

Sailors yearning to be on the water have a choice of the calm waters of **Mission Bay; San Diego Bay,** with its views of downtown, Coronado, and Point Loma; or the **Pacific Ocean**. You can charter kayaks, cabin cruisers, sailboats, and other water vessels at Mission Bay's **Seaforth Boat Rental** (www.seaforthboatrental.com; © **888/834-2628.** Half- and full-day rates are available. Seaforth has locations at: Mission Bay, 1641 Quivira Rd. (© **619/223-1681**); downtown at the Marriott San Diego Hotel & Marina, 333 W. Harbor Dr. (© **619/239-2628**); and in Coronado at 1715 Strand Way (© **619/437-1514**). **Mission Bay Sportcenter,** 1010 Santa Clara Place (www.mission baysportcenter.com; © **858/488-1004**), is located on an isthmus extending into the bay and rents sailboats, catamarans, kayaks, and powerboats.

If you'd rather just ride along, the **Maritime Museum of San Diego** (www.sdmari time.org; © **619/234-9153**) offers sailing adventures aboard the tall ship the *Californian,* a replica of an 1847 cutter that sailed the coast during the gold rush. One-hour bay cruises are also available most days aboard *Pilot,* the bay's official pilot boat for 82 years. Tickets are $3 plus regular museum admission price.

Sunset champagne cruises on a gorgeous wooden sailing yacht are the lure with **Sail Jada Charters** (www.sailjada.com; © **858/222-9479**). It's also available for whale-watching and private charters. You can pretend you're racing for your country's honor with **Next Level Sailing** (www.nextlevelsailing.com; © **800/644-3454**), which offers bay sails aboard one of two 80-foot International America's Cup Class racing yachts. Whale-watching excursions are offered in winter aboard the 139-foot schooner *America,* a replica of the yacht that brought home what came to be known as the America's Cup in 1851.

Fishing

The sight of 200-pound yellowfin tuna perched on the transom of long-range sportfishing boats at Point Loma's docks send envious anglers into a tizzy—even onlookers who wouldn't dream of baiting a hook are awed by the variety and abundance of fish loaded off San Diego's fleet. Diehard fishermen fly in from the East Coast and even Europe for multi-day and multi-week trips to distant waters, while vacationers line up for half-, and full-day trips to fertile waters off Point Loma and La Jolla. Charter boats depart from Point Loma and Quivira Basin in Mission Bay and provide rods, reels, bait, and helpful crews, and kids are usually given ample special attention. Rates on a large boat average $45 for a half-day trip or $95 for a three-quarter-day trip, or you can spring about $195 for a 20-hour overnight trip. Anglers over 17 need a California fishing license, available from most charter companies. The following outfitters offer short or extended trips: **H&M Landing,** 2803 Emerson St. (www.hmlanding.com; © **619/ 222-1144**); **Point Loma Sportfishing,** 1403 Scott St. (www.pointlomasportfishing. com; © **619/223-1627**); and **Seaforth Sportfishing,** 1717 Quivira Rd. (www.seaforth landing.com; © **619/224-3383**). Check out the **Red Rooster III** for the ultimate in long-range trips costing upwards of $4,000 for 2 weeks, 2801 Emerson St. (www. redrooster3.com; © **619/224-3857**).

Anglers of any age can fish free of charge without a license off any municipal pier in California. There are public fishing piers at Shelter Island, Ocean Beach, Coronado

Ferry Landing, downtown's Embarcadero Marina Park, Crystal Pier in Pacific Beach, and Imperial Beach. For freshwater fishing, San Diego's lakes and rivers are home to bass, channel and bullhead catfish, bluegill, trout, crappie, and sunfish. Most lakes have rental facilities for boats, tackle, and bait; they also provide picnic and (usually) camping areas. A 1-day California State Fishing License costs $14, a 2-day is $22, and a 10-day, nonresident license is $45. For info on lake fishing, call the city's **Lakes Line** at ✆ **619/465-3474.** For more information on fishing in California, contact the **California Department of Fish and Game** (www.dfg.ca.gov; ✆ **858/467-4201**).

Golf

With 90-plus courses, more than 50 of them open to the public, San Diego County has innumerable opportunities to chase little white balls. Duffers intent on sampling the finest private and resort courses spread throughout the county can get a full listing of area courses, including fees, stats, and complete scorecards at www.golfsd.com or www.sandiego.org. When you just want to practice your swing, head to **Stadium Golf Center & Batting Cages,** 2990 Murphy Canyon Rd., in Mission Valley (www.stadium golfcenter.com; ✆ **858/277-6667**). For an enjoyable vacation game, try these convenient, affordable municipal courses.

Balboa Park Municipal Golf Course ★   Everybody has a humble municipal course like this at home, with a bare bones 1920s clubhouse where long-timers take a few more mulligans than they would elsewhere. The fact that it's surrounded by the beauty of Balboa Park, however, makes this 18-hole course (with distractingly nice views of the San Diego skyline), a bit more special than usual. Nonresident greens fees are $40 weekdays, $50 weekends. Reserve at least a week in advance. **Tobey's 19th Hole,** the clubhouse's simple cafe, offers splendid views from its deck and cheap, diner-esque meals—and beer and cocktails so the loser can buy a round.

2600 Golf Course Dr. (off Pershing Dr. or 26th St. in the southeast corner of the park), San Diego. www.sandiego.gov/golf. ✆ **619/570-1234** (automated reservation system), 619/235-1184 (info), or 619/239-1660 (pro shop).

Coronado Municipal Golf Course ★   Opened in 1957, this course is easily accessed if you're staying in central San Diego and offers stunning views of San Diego Bay and downtown—sure to distract your competition. It's an 18-hole, par-72 course with a coffee shop, pro shop, and driving range. Half of the daily tee times are awarded via a day-of-play lottery (6–8:59am); reserve the rest at ✆ 619/435-3122 up to 2 days out, or ✆ **619/435-3121** 3 to 14 days prior. Greens fees are $35 weekdays, $40 weekends for 18 holes.

2000 Visalia Row, Coronado. www.golfcoronado.com. ✆ **619/435-3121.**

Torrey Pines Golf Course ★★★   Golf fans who never miss a televised tournament can't resist these two gorgeous municipal 18-hole championship courses. Even the pros and tournament commentators gush about the postcard-perfect setting on a rugged bluff above the ocean during the annual Farmers Insurance Open, and millions of viewers added the course to their bucket list after 2008 U.S. Open. Tee times are taken 8 to 90 days in advance by automated telephone system ($43 booking fee). Greens fees on the south course are $183 weekdays, $229 weekends; the north course is $100 weekdays and $125 weekends. *Tip:* Single golfers stand a good chance of getting on the course if they turn up and get on the waiting list for a threesome.

11480 Torrey Pines Rd., La Jolla. www.sandiego.gov/torreypines. ✆ **877/581-7171.**

paddling WITH THE FISHES

With no experience and a little arm strength, you can enjoy one of San Diego's best marine adventures—and it's not at any theme park. Explore the protected waters of La Jolla, from its legendary cove to its seven sea caves, in a kayak. You can go solo or in a tandem kayak, self-guided, or on a tour, and it's almost guaranteed that you'll spot frolicking seals or California's neon-bright state fish, the garibaldi. In summer, you may spy harmless leopard sharks circling beneath you; in winter you can head out for whale watching. For rentals or tours, check in with **La Jolla Kayak,** 2199 Avenida de la Playa (www.lajollakayak.com; ✆ **858/459-1114**).

Hang Gliding & Paragliding

Adrenalin junkies can't resist the **Torrey Pines Gliderport ★★★**, 2800 Torrey Pines Scenic Dr., La Jolla (www.flytorrey.com; ✆ **858/452-9858**), one of the world's top spots for nonmotorized flight since 1928. Set on a 300-foot windy cliff top above Black's Beach, it draws legions of hang-gliding and paragliding enthusiasts, as well as hobbyists with radio-control aircraft. A 20- to 25-minute tandem flight with instructor costs $175 for paragliding and $225 for hang gliding (no age limit; $10 discount for paying cash). The difference between the two sports? Hang gliders are suspended from a fixed wing, while paragliders are secured to a parachute-like nylon wing. Rental gear and classes are available. The Gliderport is open daily from 9am to sunset.

Scuba Diving & Snorkeling

Timid leopard sharks with tiny teeth swarm just off La Jolla Shores in August and September, attracting hordes of divers and snorkelers happily swimming amid a relatively harmless version of the villain in *Jaws*. In the spring, lucky divers hit the water during the few days when thousands of squid rise to the sea's surface to spawn, releasing clouds of white eggs. San Diego's nutrient rich waters nourish all sorts of sea life year round, giving divers and snorkelers underwater views far different than in clear tropical waters. Snorkelers are happiest at La Jolla Cove, spotting orange Garibaldi, crabs, fluttering white anemones, and yellow sea stars in clear, calm waters. Divers prefer the golden kelp forests sheltering sea bass, scorpion fish, rockfish, and eels off La Jolla and Point Loma. Boat, shore, wall, night, and wreck dives are all possible with local outfitters, including **Scuba San Diego** (www.scubasandiego.com; ✆ **619/260-1880**), and **OEX Dive & Kayak Centers** (www.oexcalifornia.com) with locations in La Jolla, 2243 Av. de la Playa (✆ **858/454-6195**), Point Loma, 5060 N Harbor Dr. (✆ **619/224-4241**). The **San Diego Oceans Foundation** (www.sdoceans.org; ✆ **619/523-1903**) is a nonprofit devoted to the stewardship of local marine waters; the website features good info about the diving scene.

Surfing

Hanging 10—or at least trying—is a San Diego rite-of-passage, and there are plenty of ways to learn. I've enjoyed single-day and weekend classes with **Surf Diva,** 2160 Av. de la Playa (www.surfdiva.com; ✆ **858/454-8273**) at La Jolla Shores. The instructors are great fun and able to get even the shakiest folks balancing on a board, thanks to the individual attention they offer each surfer wannabe. Plus, their shop is packed with irresistible surf-style clothing sure to impress the folks back home. If you'd rather stick close to downtown, **San Diego Surfing School** (www.sandiegosurfingschool.com; ✆ **858/205-7683**) holds classes in Ocean Beach and Pacific Beach. Both

What's SUP

Wonder how those bodies past the surf stay upright? They're practicing the latest popular water sport, stand-up paddle boarding (SUP). It looks hard, but is actually far easier than surfing as the boards are wider and flatter than surfboards, making balance a cinch. If you can go from a kneeling to standing position without wobbling, you're halfway there. Most first-timers are stroking through the water after one lesson, comfortable enough to look for dolphin on the horizon. Surf Diva and Mission Bay Aquatic Center mentioned offer SUP lessons.

companies offer group and individual classes. Already a surfer? Rent gear at **La Jolla Surf Systems,** 2132 Av. de la Playa, La Jolla Shores (www.lajollasurfsystems.com; ✆ **858/456-2777**); **Pacific Beach Surf Shop,** 4150 Mission Blvd. (www.pbsurfshop.com; ✆ **858/373-1138**); and **Ocean Beach Surf & Skate,** 4940 Newport Ave. (www.obsurfandskate.com ✆ **619/225-0674**); and in Coronado at **Emerald City: The Boarding Source,** 1118 Orange Ave. (www.emeraldcitysurf.com; ✆ **619/435-6677**). For surf reports, check out www.surfingsandiego.com or www.surfline.com.

SHOPPING
Downtown, the Gaslamp Quarter & Little Italy

In Downtown and the Gaslamp Quarter, high rents have led to the influx of deep-pocketed chains and brand names, but a few local stores remain. For hip clothing and gifts, check out **Dolcetti Boutique,** 635 5th Ave. (✆ **619/501-1559**). **Kita Ceramics & Glassware,** 517 Fourth Ave. (www.kitaceramicsglass.com; ✆ **619/239-2600**), stocks fine Japanese pottery and colorful Italian glass products. **Chuck Jones Gallery,** 232 Fifth Ave. (www.chuckjones.com; ✆ **619/294-9880**) features animation cels by Dr. Seuss and Jones, creator of Bugs Bunny and others. There's high-end art at **White Box Contemporary,** 1040 Seventh Ave. (www.whiteboxcontemporary.com; ✆ **619/531-8996**). **Industry Showroom,** 345 Sixth Ave. (www.industryshowroom.com; ✆ **619/701-2162**) features art and fashion plus podcast and photo studios in a DIY collective environment.

In Little Italy, **Pecoff Gallery,** 1825 India St. (www.pecoff.com; ✆ **619/231-1991**) features the artist's ocean- and San Diego-themed work. Fir Street Cottages shops include **Vitreum,** 619 W. Fir St. (www.vitreum-us.com; ✆ **619/237-9810**), an artfully Zen shop with home décor items and jewelry. **Nelson Photo,** 1909 India St., (www.nelsonphotosupplies.com; ✆ **619/234-6621**) is my go-to source for camera gear and repairs. They also host photo classes.

The Headquarters at Seaport District ★★ Several chic shops and restaurants have opened in Downtown's restored 1939 Spanish Colonial Old Police Headquarters beside Seaport Village. Highlights include **Pizzeria Mozza** from top chefs Mario Batali, Joseph Bastianich, and Nancy Silverton, **Lolo** boutique with clothing from L.A. and local designers, and Simply Local featuring jewelry, candies, and clothing from local producers and artists. 789 W. Harbor Dr. www.theheadquarters.com. ✆ **619/235-4014.**

Seaport Village ★ Shops displaying toys, hammocks, kites, books, and candy plus four sit-down restaurants and a variety of sidewalk eateries draw tourists to this bayside complex. Daily 10am to 10pm; restaurants have extended hours. 849 W. Harbor Dr. www.seaportvillage.com. ✆ **619/235-4014.**

Hillcrest & Uptown

Compact Hillcrest, the hub of San Diego's gay and lesbian community, has shopping for hip fashion, chic housewares, used books, vintage clothing, and memorabilia. The greatest concentration of boutiques is clustered around University and Fifth avenues. For provocative gifts, step into wacky **Babette Schwartz,** 421 University Ave. (www. babette.com; ✆ **619/220-7048**), a pop-culture emporium. **Village Hat Shop,** 3821 Fourth Ave. (www.villagehatshop.com; ✆ **619/683-5533**); displays stylish modern and vintage hats. **Buffalo Exchange,** 3862 Fifth Ave. (www.buffaloexchange.com; ✆ **619/298-4411**) is a long-time favorite for vintage clothing. University Heights and North Park contain trendy, independent clothing boutiques such as **Mimi & Red,** 3032 University Ave. (www.mimiandred.com; ✆ **619/298-7933**). **Pigment,** 3801 30th St. (www.shop pigment.com; ✆ **619/501-6318**), offers everything from pet accessories to home decor, and **Vintage Religion,** 3821 32nd St. (www.vintagereligion.com; ✆ **619/280-8408**), sells jewelry, apparel, and collectibles inspired by global religions and cultures.

Old Town & Mission Valley

Some of **Old Town State Historic Park**'s historic structures house shops with a general-store theme carrying gourmet treats, Mexican crafts, and the obligatory San Diego–emblazoned souvenirs. **Fiesta de Reyes,** 2754 Calhoun St. (www.fiestadereyes. com; ✆ **619/297-3100**) features 10 specialty shops and three restaurants. Just outside the park, the shops at **Bazaar del Mundo,** 4133 Taylor St. (www.bazaardelmundo. com; ✆ **619/296-3161**), feature high-quality Mexican and Latin American folk art, accessories, and clothing. Old Town's best spot for Mexican collectibles is **Miranda's Courtyard,** 2548 Congress St. (✆ **619/296-6611**). For Native American art and jewelry, breeze into **Four Winds Trading,** 2448 San Diego Ave. (www.4windsarts.com; ✆ **619/692-0466**).

Mission Bay & the Beaches

The beach communities offer plenty of surf shops, beach gear, and casual garb. In Mission Beach, the best women's swimwear is at **Pilar's,** 3790 Mission Blvd. (www. pilarsbeachwear.com; ✆ **858/488-3056**). **Liquid Foundation Surf Shop,** 3731 Mission Blvd. (www.liquidfoundationsurfshop.com; ✆ **858/488-3260**), specializes in board shorts for guys. **Chillers Showroom,** 4667 Cass St. (www.chillersshowroom. com; ✆ **858/274-3112**), has his and hers clothing and accessories. The best shopping in Pacific Beach is on Garnet Avenue. **The Fabulous Rag Boutique**, 8219 Garnet Ave., (www.facebook.com/thefabulousrag; ✆ **858/270-1993**) suits its name with trendy women's clothing. **Play It Again Sports**, 1401 Garnet Ave., (www.playitagain sportssd.com; ✆ **858/490-0222**), is a dependable source for new and used bikes, boards, and other play gear.

Newport Avenue is the heart of Ocean Beach's shopping district, with several women's clothing boutiques and shops selling posters, incense, herbs, and all manner of hippie gear. **The Black,** 5017 Newport Ave., (theblackoceanbeach.com; ✆ **619/222-5498**) sets the tone for OB's laid-back reputation with its collection of black-light posters, lava lamps, and smoking accessories. **South Coast Surf Shop,** 5023 Newport Ave., (www.southcoast.com; ✆ **619/223-7017**), opened in 1974 and is a favorite for custom boards and gear. A women's offshoot, **Wahines,** 5037 Newport Ave., (✆ **619/223-8808**), sells irresistible beachwear and accessories.

La Jolla

Shopping is a major pastime in La Jolla, with conservative, costly clothing, jewelry, fine art and objets d'art boutiques lining Prospect Street and Girard Avenues. **Laura Gambucci,** 7629 Girard Ave., Suite C3 (© 858/551-0214), bucks the staid trend with contemporary apparel for women; find a sexy local line of bathing suits (for her and him) at **Sauvage,** 1025 Prospect St. (www.sauvagewear.com; © 858/729-0015). **Blondtone Jewelry Studio,** 925 Prospect St. (www.blondstone.com; © 858/456-1994), has locally made jewelry that incorporates seashells and tumbled sea-glass. **Emilia Castillo,** 1273 Prospect St. (www.emiliacastillolajolla.com; © 858/551-9600), features one-of-a-kind jewelry and home decor from a silversmith based in Taxco, Mexico.

There are also more than 20 art galleries in La Jolla village, including **Quint Contemporary Art,** 7547 Girard Ave. (www.quintgallery.com; © 858/454-3409), and **Scott White Contemporary Art,** 7655 Girard Ave. (www.scottwhiteart.com; © 858/255-8574). Serene, museum-like **Tasende Gallery,** 820 Prospect St. (www.tasendegallery.com; © 858/454-3691), has sculptural work; **Joseph Bellows Gallery,** 7661 Girard Ave. (www.josephbellows.com; © 858/456-5620), exhibits vintage and contemporary photography.

Art of a more natural sort is on display at **Adelaide's,** 7766 Girard Ave. (www.adelaides.com; © 858/454-0146), my choice as San Diego's finest flower shop. Should you need a housewarming or thank-you gift, flowers from Adelaide's will make a big impression.

Coronado

The best of Coronado's limited shopping opportunities line Orange Avenue, where you'll find home-decor and clothing boutiques and gift shops. **Seaside Papery,** 1162 Orange Ave. (www.seasidepapery.com; © 619/435-5565) carries artful cards and stationery; **Island Surf,** 1009 Orange Ave. (www.islandsurfcoronado.com; © 619/435-1527) sells sunglasses, sandals, beach clothes and rents surfboards, stand up paddleboards, and wet suits. Off the avenue, find one-of-a kind clothing, jewelry, and accessories at **Zazen,** 1110 First Ave. (© 619/435-4780. Ferries from downtown arrive at Ferry Landing Marketplace 1201 First St. (www.coronadoferrylandingshops.com; © 619/435-8895) with its turreted red rooftops with jaunty blue flags fluttering in the wind. Amid the souvenir shops **Bikes and Beyond** (www.bikes-and-beyond.com; © 619/435-7180) rents bikes and surreys. There's also a farmers' market every Tuesday.

SHOPPING A TO Z

Antiques & Collectibles

India Street Antiques ★★ ANTIQUES   You might not want to lug a stained glass window or marble fireplace mantle home, but you'll still enjoy wandering amid gorgeous solid wood armoires, dining tables and escritoires made by true craftsmen. Smaller items include gorgeous English pottery, Belgian glass, and cut glass doorknobs. 2361 India St., Little Italy. www.indiastreetantiques.com. © 619/231-3004.

Newport Avenue Antique Center & Coffee House ★ ANTIQUES   Once a five-and-dime store with a little bit of everything, this 18,000 square-foot warehouse is the centerpiece of Ocean Beach's 2-block Antique District on Newport Avenue. It too, covers the gamut from vintage jewelry to cartoon character lunchboxes and '50s memorabilia. Other district shops specialize in textiles, mid-century furnishings, gardening accouterments, and collector-quality antiques. 4864 Newport Ave., Ocean Beach. www.antiquesinsandiego.com. ✆ **619/222-8686.**

Art & Crafts

A powerhouse in the local art world, **La Jolla's** Prospect Street and Girard Avenue have more galleries than any other San Diego neighborhood. Some show only photography or a single artist's works; there's plenty of interesting browsing. **Little Italy's** emerging art scene includes a few small galleries open by appointment; check www. littleitalysd.com/shop/art-galleries-supplies for a list. During North Park's **Ray at Night** (www.northparkarts.org) artists, fashionistas, and sightseers wander through galleries and boutiques while live bands play and food trucks dispense goodies the second Saturday of each month at 6pm. At Balboa Park's **Spanish Village Art Center,** 1770 Village Place (spanishvillageart.com; ✆ **619/233-9050**) more than 200 artists display and/or create art and hold classes and art camps.

Kettner Arts ★ ART   Check out the art at this member-supported collection of studios and galleries, one of Little Italy's first art complexes. The artists are happy to chat with browsers and classes in knitting, painting, digital photography, and other arts are available. 1772 Kettner Blvd., Little Italy. www.kettnerarts.com ✆ **619/269-6900.**

Taboo Studio ★★★ ART   This impressive gallery exhibits the wearable art from jewelry designers from throughout the United States. 1615½ W. Lewis St., Mission Hills. www.taboostudio.com. ✆ **619/692-0099.**

Books

Barnes & Noble ★★   Bookworms will find most everything they need at this massive store, from children's books to cookbooks to all the newest fiction. 3150 Rosencrans Place, San Diego. www.barnesandnoble.com. ✆ **619/225-0465.**

Bay Books ★★★   A superb collection of international magazines hints at breadth of offerings at this long-standing independent shop whose faithful customers appreciate meeting Newt Gingrich, "Sully" Sullenberger, and other thought-provoking authors. 1029 Orange Ave., Coronado. www.baybookscoronado.com. ✆ **619/435-0070.**

Controversial Bookstore ★   Serious students of metaphysics, spirituality, witchcraft, and healing find a welcoming home in this '60s era holdout with an incredible collection of crystals, charms, candles, potions, and—of yes—books on top of books. 3063 University Ave., North Park. www.controversialbookstore.com. ✆ **619/296-1560.**

D.G. Wills Books ★★   Literary heavy hitters frequent this rather dark and musty headquarters for the La Jolla Cultural Society, where Allen Ginsburg, Christopher Hitchens and other luminaries have held forth amid shelves stuffed with new and used scholarly tomes. 7461 Girard Ave., La Jolla. www.dgwillsbooks.com. ✆ **858/456-1800.**

Warwick's ★★★   When Hilary Clinton, Khaled Hosseini, and John Sanford put out new books, they're sure to show up at this family-owned independent bookstore. Warwick's is also just about the last fine stationery store in town, where we picky writers gather stashes of favorite pens and notebooks. 7812 Girard Ave., La Jolla. www.warwicks. com. ✆ **858/454-0347.**

Food & Drink

Ocean Beach People's Organic Food Market ★★★ FOOD   This organic food co-op opened in 1971 as a worker's collective. It's now housed in an environmentally responsible "green" building and remains an excellent high-quality organic, vegetarian market carrying natural foods, remedies, personal care products, and books. A deli dispenses healthy, delicious soups, salads, sandwiches, and baked goods 4765 Voltaire St. Ocean Beach. obpeoplesfood.coop. ☏ **619/224-1387.**

Venissimo Cheese ★★★ FOOD   Knowledgeable cheese mongers lure customers with samplings of Italian truffle-flecked Sottocenere, Spanish Capricho Cabra and other exotics, including enough varieties of Brie alone to boggle the palate. 789 W. Harbor Dr., Downtown. ☏ **619/358-9081;** Flower Hill Promenade in Del Mar, 2650 Via de la Valle, Del Mar. ☏ **858/847-9616.**

The Wine Bank ★★★   Attend one of this cramped shop's weekly wine tastings on Friday and Saturday evenings ($20, reservations required) and you'll sample vintages from some of the more than a dozen countries represented on neat shelves covering two stories. Other spirits are well represented as well—they even have Casa Dragones, a silky, silvery tequila costing nearly $300 per liter. 363 Fifth Ave. Downtown. www.sdwinebank.com. ☏ **619/234-7487.**

Music

Off the Record ★   Browse through the new and used CDs and vinyl in this tiny shop and you'll find reminders of every music genre you ever enjoyed, no matter how obscure or trendy. 2912 University Ave., North Park. www.offtherecordmusic.com. ☏ **619/298-4755.**

Record City ★   *USA Today* named this browser's delight one of the "10 best record stores in the USA" for good reason. You can find just about any favorite among the used vinyls and CDs, be it vintage blues or early hip-hop. The album covers may not be in the best condition, but the records are and the prices are amazingly low. There's a great collection of CDs, posters, and DVDs too. 3757 Sixth Ave., Hillcrest. www.record cityonline.com. ☏ **619/291-5313.**

Travel Accessories

Index Urban ★   Travelers who bemoaned the closure of John's Fifth Avenue luggage shop are happy to find this excellent replacement carrying high-end luggage, backpacks and accessories. Best of all, they also handle luggage repair. 3833 Fourth Ave., Hillcrest. www.johnsluggage.com. ☏ **619/255-5755.**

Traveler's Depot ★★   Around since 1983, this family-run shop offers travel books and maps, plus a great array of accessories, backpacks, and luggage. 1655 Garnet Ave., Pacific Beach. www.travelersdepot.com. ☏ **858/483-1421.**

Malls

Fashion Valley Center ★★   Upscale brands including Jimmy Choo, Coach, and Henri Bendel draw shoppers to this Mission Valley mall anchored by Bloomingdale's, Nordstrom, Macy's, and Penny's. The Apple and Microsoft stores are always packed, as are the restaurants, food court, and 18-screen movie complex. Shopping hours Monday to Saturday 10am to 9pm, Sunday 11am to 7pm. 7007 Friars Rd. www.simon.com/mall/fashion-valley. ☏ **619/688-9113.**

Horton Plaza ★   Covering 6½ downtown city blocks, the multilevel shopping center has more than 130 stores including Macy's and Nordstrom. The Lyceum Theatre, home to the San Diego Repertory Theatre, p. 252), is located at street level; a

14-screen cinema anchors the top level beside a lineup of food outlets. Shopping hours Monday to Friday 10am to 9pm, Saturday 10am to 8pm, Sunday 11am to 6pm. 324 Horton Plaza. www.westfield.com/hortonplaza. ✆ **619/239-8180.**

Mission Valley Center★ Geared toward budget-minded shoppers, this sprawling mall contains Nordstrom Rack, Loehmann's, specialty stores, a 20-screen movie complex, food court and restaurants. Strip malls with chain specialty stores and restaurants line the streets around the center. Shopping hours Monday to Saturday 10am to 9pm, Sunday 11am to 6pm. 1640 Camino del Rio N. www.westfield.com/missionvalley. ✆ **619/296-6375.**

University Towne Center (UTC) ★★ After a $180-million makeover, UTC now has seating areas with fire pits, a dog park, playground, fitness center, new restaurants, and public Wi-Fi. The indoor food court surrounding an ice-skating rink offers ethnic fast food. Shopping hours Monday to Saturday 10am to 9pm, Sunday 11am to 7pm. 4545 La Jolla Village Dr. www.westfield.com/utc. ✆ **858/546-8858.**

ENTERTAINMENT & NIGHTLIFE

San Diego's nightlife options grow more robust each year as older neighborhoods are re-gentrified and entrepreneurs tap into the demand for top-notch entertainment. Vibrant, award-winning theaters, fun outdoor concert venues, and a staggering number of clubs, bars, and lounges have lifted San Diego's reputation as more than a sunny day beach town.

For a rundown of the week's performances, gallery openings, and other events, check *San Diego CityBeat* (www.sdcitybeat.com), the *San Diego Reader* (www. sandiegoreader.com), and the *U-T San Diego* entertainment section, "Night and Day." (www.utsandiego.com).

Getting Tickets

Deeply discounted same-day and advance tickets to theater, music, and dance events are available at the **ARTS TIX** booth in Horton Plaza Park, at Broadway and Third Avenue (www.sdartstix.com; ✆ **858/381-5595**) The Horton Plaza kiosk doubles as a Ticketmaster outlet (www.ticketmaster.com; ✆ **800/745-3000**), selling seats to concerts throughout California.

The Performing Arts

THEATER

San Diego's premier theater companies have produced scores of Broadway-bound plays, including Jersey Boys, The Who's Tommy, and The Full Monty, and nearly every community has at least one small theater company. Those doing notable work include **Cygnet Theatre** (www.cygnettheatre.com; ✆ **619/337-1525**), **Lamb's Players Theater** (www.lambsplayers.org; ✆ **619/437-6000**), **North Coast Repertory Theatre** (www.northcoastrep.org; ✆ **858/481-1055**), and **Moxie Theatre** (www.moxie theatre.com; ✆ **858/598-7620**). **Broadway San Diego** (www.broadwaysd.com; ✆ **619/ 564-3000**) presents touring musicals at the Civic Theatre downtown. The **Spreckels Theatre,** 121 Broadway (www.spreckels.net; ✆ **619/235-950**), and **Copley Symphony Hall,** 750 B St. (www.sandiegosymphony.org; ✆ **619/235-0804**), are wonderful old vaudeville houses located downtown, used by touring acts throughout the year.

Diversionary Theatre ★ Focusing on LGBT themes, this 104-seat theater in University Heights benefits from the surrounding neighborhoods, the epicenter of the gay community. There are several trendy bars and restaurants nearby, making it a good choice for a night out. 4545 Park Blvd., University Heights. www.diversionary.org. ☏ **619/220-0097.**

La Jolla Playhouse ★★★ If you only have time for one play during your stay, go for this stellar powerhouse or the Old Globe. Located on the campus of UCSD (University of California San Diego), the Playhouse was founded in 1947 by Gregory Peck, Dorothy McGuire, and Mel Ferrer and received a 1993 Tony Award for outstanding regional theater. The calendar always includes takes on classics and Broadway-bound blockbusters, including the rock musical *The Who's Tommy* and *How to Succeed in Business Without Really Trying.* 2910 La Jolla Village Dr., La Jolla. www.lajollaplayhouse.org. ☏ **858/550-1010.**

The Old Globe ★★★ The Tony Award–winning Globe in Balboa Park has consistently entertained theatergoers for more than 70 years. Originally constructed for the 1935–36 exposition as a replica of England's Elizabethan Globe Theater, the complex has been rebuilt and expanded several times over subsequent decades and now includes three stages. The first plays presented here were called *Streamlined Shakespeare,* 40-minute condensations of the bard's most popular plays. The Shakespeare festival continues during the summer in the Globe's outdoor theater, with a far more authentic tone. The Globe attracts first-class actors and has produced Broadway-bound plays including *The Full Monty,* along with several world premiers. Combine a play with dinner at the park's The Prado restaurant for a memorable evening. Balboa Park. www.theoldglobe.org. ☏ **619/234-5623.**

San Diego Repertory Theatre ★★ Acting as a "cultural town hall," the Rep hosts nearly daily events, exhibits, and shows along with plays and musicals at the Lyceum Theatre in Horton Plaza. The Rep has a strong multicultural, bi-national bent presenting works by playwrights from Mexico, along with hosting an annual African-American Kuumba Fest and Jewish Arts Festival. 79 Broadway Circle, in Horton Plaza, Downtown. www.sdrep.org. ☏ **619/544-1000.**

CLASSICAL MUSIC

La Jolla Music Society ★★ This cultural organization presents 40-plus annual shows featuring a wide range of international artists including Yo-Yo-Ma and Itzhak Perlman. The main season runs from October through May with performances at venues around town and the **SummerFest,** a 3-week series of concerts and artist encounters, is held in August. Box office: 7946 Ivanhoe Ave., Stuite 103, La Jolla. www.ljms.org. ☏ **858/459-3728.**

San Diego Symphony ★ The symphony's season runs October through May at Copley Symphony Hall, a baroque jewel dating from 1929. The popular **Summer Pops** series, with programs devoted to rock, Broadway, and Tchaikovsky, is held from July to early September on the Embarcadero. 750 B St., Downtown. www.sandiegosymphony.org. ☏ **619/235-0804.**

OPERA

San Diego Opera ★ Though once one of San Diego's most successful arts organizations, San Diego Opera came very close to folding in 2014, due to financial difficulties and alleged mismanagement. Last-minute fundraising success plus cost-cutting measures, including the firing of the opera's handsomely paid general director, saved the 2015 season—the opera's 50th. Civic Theatre, 1200 Third Ave., Downtown. www.sdopera.com. © **619/533-7000.**

DANCE

Dance Place at Liberty Station (2650 Truxtun Rd., Point Loma), provides studio, performance, and educational space for several of San Diego's leading companies, including **San Diego Ballet** (www.sandiegoballet.org; © **619/294-7378**), **Malashock Dance** (www.malashockdance.org; © **619/260-1622**), and **Jean Isaacs San Diego Dance Theater** (www.sandiegodancetheater.org; © **619/225-1803**).

California Ballet (www.californiaballet.org; © **858/560-5676**) produces four shows annually around town. **City Ballet** (www.cityballet.org; © **858/272-8663**) performs at the Spreckels Theatre Downtown. Both companies present *The Nutcracker* during the holidays. The socially conscious modern dance troupe **Eveoke Dance Theatre,** 2811 University Ave., North Park (www.eveoke.org; © **619/238-1153**), performs and offers an eclectic range of dance classes.

MIXED USE VENUES

The **Birch North Park Theatre,** 2891 University Ave. (www.birchnorthparktheatre. net; © **619/239-8836**), a restored 1928 vaudeville and movie house, reopened in its latest incarnation in 2014 as a concert hall hosting varied musical acts along with other performances. Downtown's **Balboa Theatre,** 868 Fourth Ave. (www.sandiegotheatres. org; © **619/570-1100**), was built in 1924, completely restored in 2008, and hosts a wide range of music, dance, theater performances, and films with highlights including solo presentations from Jane Lynch and David Sedaris.

THE CLUB & MUSIC SCENE: LIVE MUSIC
Small & Medium-Size Venues

The Belly Up Tavern ★★★ The always-popular granddaddy live music club in an old Quonset hut in Solana Beach, a 30-minute drive from downtown, hosts A-List musicians in all genres. 143 S. Cedros Ave., Solana Beach. www.bellyup.com. © **858/481-8140.**

The Casbah ★ Still the best semi-underground venue for new local and national indie rock bands after 25 years, the Casbah has only 200 seats so get there early! 2501 Kettner Blvd., at Laurel St., Little Italy. www.casbahmusic.com. © **619/232-4355.**

House of Blues ★★ The HOB, with its New Orleans meets Mexico voodoo vibe could never be called boring. Add underground stages, 1,000 screaming fans and bands covering everything from blues to hip hop and you've got a smokin' night. 1055 Fifth Ave., Downtown. www.hob.com/sandiego. © **619/299-2583.**

Humphrey's ★★★ Locals eagerly await each summer's concert schedule (mid-April to Oct) at this 1,400-seat outdoor venue hosting rock, blues, jazz, and comedy headliners. No ticket? Find a friend with a boat and float in San Diego Bay beside the stage. The indoor lounge, **Humphrey's Backstage,** also has music nightly. 2241 Shelter Island Dr., Point Loma. www.humphreysconcerts.com. © **619/224-3577.**

Large Venues

Valley View Casino Center (formerly known as the San Diego Sports Arena), 3500 Sports Arena Blvd. (www.valleyviewcasinocenter.com; © **619/224-4171**), has hosted all the big names since 1976, despite its lousy acoustics. Newer venues now draw the top acts, but the arena's 15,000 to 18,000 seats still draw screaming fans.

The acoustics are far better at the 4,000-seat **Open Air Theatre** (www.as.sdsu.edu; ☎ 619/594-6947), on the San Diego State University campus, northeast of downtown, and many big-name performers prefer the more intimate setting and college vibe. Also at SDSU, **Viejas Arena** (same contact info) has equally superb acoustics in an indoor, 12,000-seat facility. Both these venues are on the San Diego Trolley Green Line.

Sleep Train Amphitheatre, 2050 Entertainment Circle, Chula Vista, near the Mexican border, (www.livenation.com; ☎ 619/671-3500) overwhelms the senses with its 20,000-seat capacity (10,000 in festival seating in a grassy outfield) and superb acoustics, and draws the best of the best talent. Sadly, it's about 20 miles south of downtown, traffic's horrendous, and there's no public transportation. Savvy concertgoers group together and splurge on limos.

COMEDY CLUBS

The American Comedy Co. ★ Access to top-notch touring comedians keeps this 200-seat underground speakeasy full; come for dinner to get comfortable seats at a table. There's a two-drink minimum on top of tickets. 818 Sixth Ave., Gaslamp Quarter. www.americancomedyco.com. ☎ 619/795-3858.

The Comedy Store ★ Up-and-coming and a few star L.A. comedians enjoy hanging out in San Diego and performing in this old-timer. It's also the best place for locals to tune-up their acts. There's no food and a two-drink minimum. 916 Pearl St., La Jolla. lajolla.thecomedystore.com. ☎ 858/454-9176.

Lips ★★ Camp and raunchy fun has fans roaring at this all-ages restaurant/drag club, where the aptly named Bitchy Bingo keeps 'em laughing on Wednesdays and the gospel brunch is far from preachy. Late shows are ages 21 and over only, and most parents are only comfortable bringing kiddies too young to get the joke. 3036 El Cajon Blvd., North Park. www.lipssd.com. ☎ 619/295-7900.

National Comedy Theatre ★★ Families chuckle together as improv champs battle for the most laughs while performing audience suggestions. There's no drink or age minimum. 3717 India St., Mission Hills. www.nationalcomedy.com. ☎ 619/295-4999.

BARS, COCKTAIL LOUNGES & DANCE CLUBS
Downtown & Little Italy

Downtown rocks most nights of the week, thanks to its proximity to the convention center and San Diego's liveliest clubs. Cover charges range from about $10 to $20 on weekends, and dress codes shun tank tops, sports jerseys, tennis shoes, and the like.

Altitude Sky Lounge ★★ A stellar 22-story view of PETCO Park and the Gaslamp's hectic streets from a hotel rooftop, with a casual dress code, fire pits, and unpretentious vibe attracts a mixed-age crowd. 660 K St, Gaslamp Quarter. www.sandiego gaslamphotel.com/nightlife/altitude. ☎ 619/696-0234.

Craft & Commerce ★★★ The interior gives a nod to old-fashioned libraries with stacks of books. Deep thoughts appearing on mirrors, counters and walls hint at the seriousness paid to the short list of classy cocktails and longer list of fine whisky, rye, and scotch. 675 W. Beech, Little Italy. www.craft-commerce.com. ☎ 619/269-2202.

Noble Experiment ★★★ Text ahead for one of only 35 seats, amid crystal chandeliers, a wall covered with shiny gold skulls, and mixologists creating serious cocktails to suit your whims. 777 G St., East Village. www.nobleexperimentsd.com. ☎ 619/888-4713 (texts only accepted, to keep the crowds young).

Tipsy Crow ★★ A three-story nightlife compound hosting concerts, comedy, DJs, and corner bar, this popular spot, in a Gaslamp historic building, draws raves from fans who enjoy the lounge-style rooftop nest and the Underground space for dancing or comedy nights. 770 Fifth Ave. (at F St.), Gaslamp Quarter. www.thetipsycrow.com. ℰ **619/338-9300.**

Top of the Hyatt ★★★ The views from this penthouse bar on the 40th floor of downtown's tallest hotel draw a classy, more subdued crowd—unless there's a big convention or concert in town and attendees let their hair down. It's a martinis up kind of place with table and couch seating and a menu of light fare including a charcuterie plate. 1 Market Pl., Downtown. ℰ **619/232-1234.**

Waterfront Bar & Grill ★★★ Long before Little Italy became a metrosexual hangout, this much-loved dive catered to 1930's workers at a nearby aerospace factory. These days it draws a more stylish crowd, with a few holdouts at the bar. Spicy bloody Marys and huevos rancheros draw Sunday brunchers; expect a line if you arrive after 9pm. 2044 Kettner Blvd., Little Italy. www.waterfrontbarandgrill.com. ℰ **619/232-9656.**

Elsewhere in San Diego

Blind Lady Ale House ★ San Diego's craft beers get top billing (at least two dozen on tap) at this neighborhood bar/pizzeria with old beer cans lining one wall of the long, industrial-style room and a friendly, laid-back clientele. 43416 Adams Ave., Normal Heights. www.blindladyalehouse.com. ℰ **619/255-2491.**

Pacific Shores ★ There are no beers on tap or cutesy cocktails at Pac Shores, where old-timers coexist with hipsters floating through for inexpensive, generous cocktails. Take care with the booze, however, as the black lights and paintings of mermaids and bubbles could make you woozy. 4927 Newport Ave., Ocean Beach. ℰ **619/223-7549.**

The PB Shore Club ★ Ocean views and breezes though open windows keep things cool at this SoCal classic smack beside the boardwalk. It's packed, loud, and filled with hopeful singles plus a large contingent of active and retired Navy personnel (the bar supports all sorts of Vet programs) downing Vodka Red Bull slushies and lobster tacos 4343 Ocean Blvd., Pacific Beach. www.pbshoreclub.com. ℰ **858/272-7873.**

Starlite ★★ A pioneer in the stylish bar trend, this high-concept restaurant/lounge has won architectural awards and rave reviews for its burgers and Moscow Mules in curvy copper mugs. 3175 India St., Middletown. www.starlitesandiego.com. ℰ **619/358-9766.**

GAY & LESBIAN NIGHTLIFE

San Diego has become a very gay-friendly destination, with politicians, military personnel and police officers happily partaking in the annual **Pride Parade, Rally, and Festival** (see p. 178), one of the country's biggest LGBT events. Hillcrest is the heart of the community; it has a number of queer bars and clubs and tons of lively restaurants. Check out the action online at www.gaylesbiantimes.com.

Bourbon Street Bar & Grill ★★ With nights devoted to karaoke, open mic, wet underwear, women's night (Sunday), plus half-off happy hour (til 9pm), DJs, and various spaces (including a patio) and you've got a mini-New Orleans where straight and gay play. 4612 Park Blvd., University Heights. www.bourbonstreetsd.com. ℰ **619/291-4043.**

The Brass Rail ★ It's been through several reincarnations, but Hillcrest's iconic gay bar remains a rowdy, sexy, inviting hangout with relatively cheap drinks and various theme nights (80s-style Manic Mondays are the current favorite). 3796 Fifth Ave., Hillcrest. www.thebrassrailsd.com. ℰ **619/298-2233.**

EVENING BAY cruises

Unless you're prone to seasickness—and the water's usually calm—at least one sunset cruise on **San Diego** Bay is a must. The San Diego skyline takes on a soft golden glow as the sun slowly sets, then glitters like a Christmas tree after dark. **Flagship** (1050 N. Harbor Dr. at Broadway Pier, Downtown; www.flagshipsd. com; ℂ **619/234-4111**) offers nightly dinner cruise packages; brunch and prime rib dinner cruises are both offered on Sundays. For an additional fee you can guarantee yourself a private table with window, plus a bottle of champagne, wine, or cider. A DJ plays dance music during the 2½-hour outing on a luxury yacht. **Hornblower Cruises** (1800 N. Harbor Dr. at Grape St. Pier; www. hornblower.com; ℂ **619/686-8700**) runs dinner cruises on the 151-foot antique-style yacht *Lord Hornblower*. With three decks and separate salons there's plenty of room for guests to wander. A lively DJ encourages everyone to dance after dinner and announces every birthday, anniversary, and honeymoon guests are celebrating. The company also offers Sunday Brunch and lobster dinner cruises. Both companies also run daytime whale watching and bay cruises.

Redwing ★ Whether you're gay, goth, a bear, or a misfit you'll feel welcome at this casual dive where the drinks are cheap and the staff friendly. The burgers are great, too. 4012 30th St., North Park. www.richssandiego.com. ℂ **619/281-8700.**

Rich's ★ Dance your heart and feet out in two cavernous rooms with separate DJs and swift bartenders. Thursday Lez Night is jammed. Closed Monday and Tuesday. 1051 University Ave., Hillcrest. www.richssandiego.com. ℂ **619/295-2195.**

CASINOS

Several San Diego County American tribes operate casinos in east and north San Diego County. Most operate free shuttle buses from central San Diego.

Valley View Casino, 16300 Nyemii Pass Rd., Valley Center (www.valleyviewcasino. com; ℂ **760/291-5500**), has a hotel, gaming floor and popular all-you-can-eat lobster buffet.

Viejas Casino, 5000 Willows Rd., Alpine (www.viejas.com; ℂ **800/847-6537** or 619/445-5400) presents live music in its 700-seat showroom and has an outlet center, hotel all other legal gaming options.

Barona Resort & Casino, 1932 Wildcat Canyon Rd., Lakeside (www.barona.com; ℂ **888/722-7662** or 619/443-2300) has an award-winning 18-hole golf course along with a hotel, spa, and plenty of gaming.

Harrah's Resort, 777 Harrah's Resort Southern California Way, Valley Center, (www.harrahsresortsoutherncalifornia.com; ℂ **760/751-3100**) is popular.

Sycuan Resort & Casino, 5469 Casino Way, Dehesa (www.sycuan.com; ℂ **800/279-2826** or 619/445-6002) features an eclectic array of musical performances from Larry Gatlin to Sheila E. in its 450-seat theater along with gaming, a 1,200-seat bingo palace and the nearby Sycuan Golf Resort with a hotel and 54 holes of golf.

Spectator Sports

BASEBALL & SOFTBALL The **San Diego Padres** (sandiego.padres.mlb.com; ✆ **877/374-2784**) play April through September at downtown's much-lauded **PETCO Park** (100 Park Blvd.; ✆ **619/795-5000**) overlooking San Diego Bay. The playing field is framed by historic buildings used for offices and private boxes and the Park at the Park, a grassy area with views of the park open to the public. The park is on the San Diego Trolley's Green Line and there are several pay parking lots nearby.

The racy, offbeat **World Championship Over-the-Line Tournament** is held in Mission Bay on the second and third weekends of July.

BOATING The **San Diego Crew Classic** at Mission Bay in April (www.crew classic.org; ✆ **619/225-0300**) draws rowing teams from across the United States.

FOOTBALL Despite demands for a new stadium, the **San Diego Chargers** (www. chargers.com; ✆ **800/745-3000**) continue to play at **Qualcomm Stadium** ("the Q"), 9449 Friars Rd., Mission Valley, on the San Diego Trolley's Green Line and close to several freeways.

GOLF The **Farmers Insurance Open** (www.farmersinsuranceopen.com; ✆ **858/ 535-4500** or 858/886-4653) takes place in February at Torrey Pines Golf Course (11480 Torrey Pines Park, La Jolla; ✆ **858/ 581-7171**).

HORSE RACING & EQUESTRIAN EVENTS Live thoroughbred racing takes place at the **Del Mar Racetrack** (2260 Jimmy Durante Blvd., Del Mar; www.dmtc. com; ✆ **858/755-1141**) from mid-July to early September. Paid parking at the track and free shuttle from the Solana Beach train station.

The **San Diego Polo Club** (14555 El Camino Real, Del Mar. www.sandiegopolo. com; ✆ **858/481-9217**), has Sunday matches from June to October (with a summer break mid-July to mid-Aug).

SOCCER The San Diego **Sockers** (www.sdsockers.com; ✆ **866/799-4625**) play at the Valley View Casino Center from November to February.

SIDE TRIPS FROM SAN DIEGO

by Maribeth Mellin

8

San Diego County sprawls over more than 4,500 square miles and is nearly as large as the entire state of Connecticut. I think of many parts of the county as overnight or weekend getaways, since I'd rather enjoy my destination than spend hours driving to and fro. If pressured, I'd have to say the North County Coast is my favorite area. The coastline's long stretches of golden sand provide multiple options for leisurely beach days, while shops and restaurants reflect the characters of small beach towns. There's more rugged adventure in the East County's mountains and the stark Anza-Borrego desert, especially beautiful when cacti burst into bloom in Spring. Each area can be covered in a day trip; start out early and drive in a leisurely fashion, stopping at lookout points, produce stands, and parks along the way.

NORTH COUNTY BEACH TOWNS

The string of picturesque beach towns that dot coastal San Diego County from Del Mar to Oceanside make great day-trip destinations for sun worshipers and surfers. They're also extremely popular bases for vacationers seeking proximity to attractions without big city hustle. Some of San Diego's finest resorts are located in North County, including ritzy hideaways where celebs and politicos vacation, knowing their privacy is guaranteed. Outstanding restaurants are another draw. I've included some of the finest, along with a few exceptional moderately-priced picks. Amtrak and Coaster trains run along one of the coast's loveliest routes between I-5 and the beach; don't ever cross the tracks without looking both ways.

Essentials

GETTING THERE **Del Mar** is only 18 miles north of downtown San Diego, **Carlsbad** about 33 miles, and **Oceanside** approximately 36 miles. If you're driving, follow I-5 North; Del Mar, Solana Beach, Encinitas, Carlsbad, and Oceanside all have freeway exits. The other choice by car is the scenic coast road, known as Camino del Mar, "PCH" (Pacific Coast Hwy.), Old Highway 101, and County Highway S21. *Tip:* Parking is scarce in most of these towns. Look for available spots a couple of blocks inland, over the train tracks. From San Diego, the **Coaster** (www.transit.511sd.com; ✆ **800/262-7837**) commuter train provides service to Solana Beach, Encinitas, Carlsbad, and Oceanside; and **Amtrak** (www.amtrak.com; ✆ **800/872-7245**) stops in Solana Beach and Oceanside.

VISITOR INFORMATION   The **Del Mar Village Association**, www.delmarmain street.com; ✆ **858/735-3650** has an informative website. The **Solana Beach Visitors Center** is near the train station at 103 N. Cedros (www.solanabeachchamber.com; ✆ **858/350-6006**). The **Encinitas Visitors Center** is at 859 Second St. (corner of H St.) in downtown Encinitas (www.gonorthcounty.com; ✆ **760/753-6041**); the **Encinitas 101 Mainstreet Association** also maintains a handy site at www.encinitas101. com. The **Carlsbad Visitor Information Center,** 400 Carlsbad Village Dr. (in the old Santa Fe Depot; www.visitcarlsbad.com; ✆ **800/227-5722** or 760/434-6093), has a very informative and helpful staff. **Oceanside,** the northernmost coastal town in San Diego County, has a **California Welcome Center,** 928 N. Coast Hwy. (www.visit oceanside.org; ✆ **800/350-7873** or 760/721-1101).

Del Mar ★★

Tasteful, genteel, and manicured, with only 4,500 inhabitants in a 2-square-mile municipality, Del Mar is one of the most upscale communities in the greater San Diego area. It's usually relatively sedate, but in summer the town swells as visitors flock in for the thoroughbred horseracing season and the San Diego County Fair. The history and popularity of Del Mar are linked to the **Del Mar Racetrack & Fairgrounds** at 2260 Jimmy Durante Blvd. In 1933, actor/crooner Bing Crosby enlisted Hollywood friends including Lucille Ball, Desi Arnaz, and Bob Hope to develop the **Del Mar Thoroughbred Club.** Soon the good times were off and running and they haven't stopped since. Racing season runs mid-July through early September; in 2014 a second season was added for the month of November. The expansive complex also hosts the **San Diego County Fair** (www.sdfair.com; ✆ **858/755-1161** or 858/793-5555) from early June to early July.

Two excellent beaches flank Del Mar: **Torrey Pines State Beach** and **Del Mar State Beach.** Both are immensely popular and have designated areas for swimming and surfing. **Seagrove Park,** the town green, sits above the state beach on 15th Street; just below is the sand. There are free concerts at adjacent **Powerhouse Park** during the summer. **Del Mar Plaza,** 1555 Camino del Mar (www.delmarplaza.com), at the north end of town, is an open-air shopping center with fountains, sculptures, and several good restaurants and shops. Shops and restaurants along Camino Del Mar (part of the coast highway) are housed in pristine Tudor and Victorian buildings and tend to be upscale. On the beach, **Poseidon del Mar Restaurant,** 1670 Coast Blvd. (www.poseidon restaurant.com; ✆ **858/755-9345**), is good for California cuisine and fabulous sunsets.

WHERE TO DINE

Addison ★★★ FRENCH   San Diego County's only AAA Five-Diamond dining establishment is grandly European in style, with huge fireplaces, plush draperies, carved stone columns, and wrought-iron fixtures. There's even a private banquet space that resembles a great room in a Spanish castle. Chef William Bradley incorporates the best local and seasonal ingredients in multi-course contemporary French tasting menus. There's also a jaw-dropping wine list that's more like a book. Dress to impress. 5200 Grand Del Mar Way. www.addisondelmar.com. ✆ **858/314-1900.** Reservations recommended. 3-course menu $90; 4-course menu $98; 7-course menu $140; 10-course menu $225. Tues–Thurs 6–9pm; Fri–Sat 5:30–9:30pm.

Market Restaurant + Bar ★★★ CALIFORNIAN   Native San Diegan Carl Schroeder specializes in regional San Diego cuisine, showcasing the best ingredients from the area's top farms, ranches, and fishmongers in this casual yet classy spot near the racetrack. The menu is printed daily, depending on what he finds at the produce stands (though the killer blue cheese soufflé is always present); the weekly and cocktail lists are no less quality-obsessed. This is truly fine dining in a relaxed atmosphere.

3702 Via de la Valle (at El Camino Real), Del Mar. www.marketdelmar.com. ✆ **858/523-0007.** Reservations recommended. Main courses $25–$35. Daily 5:30–10pm. Free valet parking.

WHERE TO STAY
Expensive

The Grand Del Mar ★★★   Resembling a Tuscan villa tucked in the Del Mar highlands far from the hoi poloi, this resort boasts a Las Vegas-like opulence. Paying homage to the Spanish Revival creations of architect Addison Mizner, the resort features Mediterranean-style courtyards, a chapel, sublime spa, and a Tom Fazio-designed golf course. Rooms are palatial, with furnishings in rich golds and browns and blissful creature comforts. The signature restaurant, **Addison** one of San Diego's most refined. The name is no idle boast; this is one grand hotel.

5300 Grand Del Mar Court, Del Mar. www.thegranddelmar.com. ✆ **855/314-2030** or 858/314-2000. 249 units. From $445 double; from $795 suites. Valet parking $25; free self-parking. **Amenities:** 4 restaurants; 5 bars; live entertainment; kids' activity center; concierge; 18-hole championship golf course; equestrian center; Jacuzzi; 4 swimming pools; room service; spa; 2 tennis courts; free transportation (14-mile radius); free Wi-Fi.

L'Auberge Del Mar Resort & Spa ★★   Sporting a French beach-château look, this classy property has a stand-alone spa and lavish pool area with lattice deck and fire pit lounge. Beach cottage style rooms have fireplaces and shelves stocked with coffee-table books and decorative seashells. Many have balconies or patios. The beach is a 3-minute walk away. The signature **Kitchen 1540** is one of the town's fanciest eatery.

1540 Camino del Mar (at 15th St.), Del Mar. www.laubergedelmar.com. ✆ **800/245-9757** or 858/259-1515. 120 units. From $350 double; from $600 suite. Valet parking $25. **Amenities:** Restaurant; 2 bars; concierge; nearby health club; Jacuzzi; 2 pools; room service; full-service spa; 2 tennis courts; free Wi-Fi.

Moderate

Les Artistes ★★   Take a 1940s motel, put it in the hands of an artistic owner, and you get a clever Indo-Latino mash-up, with rooms named for artists (the Diego Rivera feels like a warm Mexican painting come to life) and lush gardens with a koi pond. Upstairs rooms have partial ocean views; downstairs rooms have tiny private garden decks. Les Artistes is very popular with European travelers.

944 Camino del Mar. www.lesartistesinn.com. ✆ **858/755-4646.** 12 units. $105–$250 double. Free parking. **Amenities:** Free Wi-Fi.

Solana Beach, Encinitas & Carlsbad ★★★

North of Del Mar about a 45-minute drive from downtown San Diego, the pretty communities of Solana Beach, Encinitas, and Carlsbad provide many reasons to linger and spend a few nights: good swimming and surfing beaches, small-town atmosphere, an abundance of charming shops, and a seasonal display of the region's most beautiful flowers. It's also the location of kid-centric **LEGOLAND** theme park.

The hub of activity for **Solana Beach** is South Cedros Avenue, 1 block east of and parallel to Pacific Coast Highway. The **Cedros Design District** (www.cedrosavenue. com) is the setting for many of San Diego's best furniture and home-design shops, antiques stores, art dealers, and boutiques. You'll also find the **Belly Up Tavern,** one of San Diego's most appealing concert venues (p. 253). In **Encinitas,** everyone flocks to **Moonlight Beach** for good reason—it offers plenty of facilities, including free parking, free Wi-Fi, a children's playground, volleyball nets, restrooms, showers, picnic tables, and fire rings. The beach entrance is at the end of B Street (at Encinitas Blvd.). Just south of the beach, exotic-looking domes rise above the **Self-Realization Fellowship Retreat and Hermitage** (www.yogananda-srf.org; © **323/225-2471**) founded in 1920 by Indian guru Paramahansa Yogananda. Visitors are welcome to tour the serene meditation gardens with fern-shaded paths and koi streams above Swami's Beach. Enter the gardens at 215 W. K St.; they are open Tuesday through Saturday 9am to 5pm, and Sundays 11am to 5pm. Admission is free.

Carlsbad has evolved into a major tourism destination, thanks in part to its location roughly midway between downtown San Diego and Disneyland. Hotels and restaurants of all levels are abundant, the beaches are long, safe, and gorgeous, and the town has a safe, family-friendly feel. Locals queue at the **Carlsbad Mineral Water Spa,** 2802 Carlsbad Blvd. (www.carlsbadmineralspa.com; © **760/434-1887**), an ornate European-style building where outdoor stations refill multi-gallon jugs with "Most Healthful Water." It's sold by the bottle as well, and you can step inside for mineral baths and body treatments. **Carlsbad State Beach** (aka Tamarack Surf Beach) parallels downtown and has a wide concrete walkway perfect for walking, jogging, and in-line skating even at night (thanks to good lighting). About 4 miles south of town is **South Carlsbad State Beach** (www.parks.ca.gov; © **760/438-3143**), with almost 3 miles of cobblestone-strewn sand. A state-run campground at the north end is immensely popular year-round. Carlsbad and its neighbor Encinitas make up a noted commercial flower-growing region. The most colorful display can be seen each spring (Mar through early May) at the **Flower Fields at Carlsbad Ranch,** 5704 Paseo del Norte (www.theflowerfields.com; © **760/431-0352**), just east of I-5 on Palomar Airport Road.

LEGOLAND California ★ The ultimate monument to the world's most famous plastic building block, this 128-acre theme park is located just east of downtown Carlsbad and 34 miles north of downtown San Diego. We'll be blunt: LEGOLAND is geared toward children ages 2 to 12, and there's just enough of a thrill-ride component to amuse preteens, but teenagers find it a snooze. That being said, there are more than 50 rides, shows, and attractions, including hands-on interactive displays. **Star Wars Miniland** re-creates scenes from the beloved film series, while in the Egyptian-themed **Land of Adventure,** the signature ride takes you on a search for stolen treasure and tests your laser-shooting skills. **Pirate Shores** features buccaneer-themed, water-based attractions—all designed to get you good and wet; and the **Wild Woods** miniature golf course plays through more than 40 LEGO forest animals. Just outside the LEGOLAND gates—**Sea Life Aquarium,** focuses on the creatures (not LEGO facsimiles) found in regional waters. Separate admission is required; discounted two-park tickets are available. The 5½-acre **LEGOLAND Water Park** is where kids can splash down water slides, float along a lazy river, or wade at a sandy beach; ticket upgrades including the Water Park are $15. An on-site LEGOLAND resort hotel completes the picture for the truly obsessed.

1 Legoland Dr. www.legoland.com, www.visitsealife.com. ℭ **877/534-6526** or 760/918-5346. LEGOLAND $78 ages 13 and up, $68 children 3–12, free for children 2 and under; Sea Life $20 adults, $15 seniors and children 3–12; discounted 1- or 2-day park-hopper tickets available. June daily 10am–6 or 8pm; July–Aug daily 10am–8pm; off season Thurs–Mon 10am–5 or 6pm. Parking $12. Closed Tues–Wed Sept–May, but open daily during winter and spring holiday periods. Water Park closed Nov–Mar, weekends only early Sept–Oct and May.

WHERE TO DINE

Always crowded, **Fidel's Little Mexico** ★ is reliable for tasty Mexican food and kickin' margaritas; it's in Solana Beach at 749 Genevieve St. (www.fidelslittlemexico. com; ℭ **858/755-5292**). **Claire's on Cedros** ★★, 246 N. Cedros Ave. (www.claires oncedros.com; ℭ **858/259-8597**), is another Solana Beach crowd pleaser, serving breakfast and lunch. Encinitas hangouts include and casual **Swami's Cafe** ★, 1163 S. Coast Hwy. 101 (ℭ **760/944-0612**), for sandwiches, wraps, and smoothies. Chocoholics should not miss Venezuelan **Chuao Chocolatier** ★★, in the Lumberyard mall, 937 S. Coast Hwy. 101, Suite C-109 (www.chuaochocolatier.com; ℭ **888/635-1444** or 760/635-1444).

WHERE TO STAY
Expensive
Park Hyatt Aviara Resort ★★★   High standards plus Vivace, an exceptional signature restaurant, an award-winning spa, Arnold Palmer–designed golf course, even a surf concierge who can give lessons, keep international celebs and escapists returning. In 2014, a VeraVia (veraviafit.com) wellness and weight-loss spa opened at the resort (under separate management). Despite its pedigree, the hotel is blissfully comfortable and accommodating, no matter your status.

7100 Aviara Resort Dr., Carlsbad. www.parkaviara.hyatt.com. ℭ **760/448-1234** or 855/ 924-9288. 329 units. From $300 double; from $400 suite. Valet parking $30. **Amenities:** 4 restaurants; 2 bars; golf course; Jacuzzi; 2 outdoor pools; room service; spa; tennis courts; free Wi-Fi.

West Inn & Suites ★★★   This family-owned, family-oriented property charms with its friendly service, thoughtful touches, and plentiful freebies. It's my top option whether traveling with kids . . . or not. The rooms are carpeted and have heavy drapes, keeping noise down; suites have a separate area with a sofa bed and TV. There's a courtesy shuttle (within a 5-mile radius, including LEGOLAND), free breakfast, a library stocked with games and books, and cookies and milk at night.

4970 Avenida Encinas, Carlsbad. www.westinnandsuites.com. ℭ **866/431-9378** or 760/448-4500. 86 units. $160–$200. Rates include full breakfast. Free parking. Pets accepted. **Amenities:** 2 restaurants; 2 bars; concierge; dog park; exercise room; Jacuzzi; outdoor pool; room service; free Wi-Fi.

Oceanside

Located at the edge of Camp Pendleton, a huge Marine base offering a stretch of undeveloped land between San Diego and Orange counties, Oceanside is another good base for exploring north and south. Its four miles of beaches, the West Coast's longest wooden pier, and downtown attractions are all within easy walking distance of the train station. Though it's long been considered a blue-collar military and surf town, there's a welcoming, Middle America feel and a strong sense of community. The city's **harbor** has a Cape Cod–themed shopping village with a faux rustic charm; the marina bustles with pleasure craft, fishing boat charters, and sightseeing excursions. A string of beaches starts here and runs south to the border of Carlsbad. Oceanside's world-famous surfing spots also attract competitions, including the **World Bodysurfing Championships** and **Longboard Surf** contest both held in August. The **California**

Surf Museum ★ at 312 Pier View Way (www.surfmuseum.org; ✆ **760/721-6876**) has an extensive collection of surfboards, photos documenting surfing's early days, and other relics that chronicle the development of the sport. It's open daily from 10am to 4pm (Thurs until 8pm); admission is $5 adults, $3 seniors, students and military, and ages 11 and under are free. The museum is free to all on Tuesdays. The **Oceanside Museum of Art** ★, 704 Pier View Way (www.oma-online.org; ✆ **760/435-3720**), presents contemporary artwork by both regional and international artists; past exhibits have included everything from pop surrealism to quilts. It's open Tuesday through Saturday 10am to 4pm, Sunday 1 to 4pm; admission is $8 adults, $5 seniors, free for students and military. Free admission the first Sunday of every month. If you can visit only one mission while in California, make it Oceanside's **Mission San Luis Rey de Francia** ★, 4050 Mission Ave. (www.sanluisrey.org; ✆ **760/757-3651**), known as the "King of the Missions." It's the largest of California's 21 missions, with an impressive church, exhibits, and grounds; admission is $5 for adults; $4 seniors and children ages 6 to 18; free for kids 5 and under and for active-duty military. Hours are Monday through Friday 9:30am to 5pm, and weekends 10am to 5pm.

Livening up the dining scene is **333 Pacific** ★★, 333 N. Pacific St. (www.cohn restaurants.com; ✆ **760/433-3333**), a spendy steak and seafood spot with a deep vodka selection and ocean views. Hipster sushi is available at **Harney Sushi** ★, 301 Mission Ave. (www.harneysushi.com; ✆ **760/967-1820**), with a cool design, mood lighting, and DJs adding some grooves to go along with the rolls. At the end of the long pier you'll find the 1950s-style diner **Ruby's** (www.rubys.com; ✆ **760/433-7829**). This place can get crazy busy, but it's a great spot for burgers and fountain drinks, especially in the Tiki-inspired upstairs dining room and patio. Get a side helping of history with your burger and fries at the original **101 Cafe,** 631 S. Coast Hwy. (www.101cafe.net; ✆ **760/722-5220**). This humble diner dates from the earliest days of the old coast highway, the only route between Los Angeles and San Diego until 1953 brought the interstate. Slow food specialist **Flying Pig Pub & Kitchen** ★★, 626 S. Tremont St. (www.flyingpigpubkithen.com; ✆ **760/453-2940**), serves rustic American cuisine.

Book early for a summertime stay at the **Wyndham Oceanside Pier Resort** ★★ 333 N. Myers St. (www.wyndhamvacationresorts.com; ✆ **800/251-8736** or 760/901-1200). The privately owned one- and two-bedroom suites at this property feature lots of amenities, look out over the pier, and have kitchens and sleeper sofas—and they book up fast. Beware of studio rooms with no view and train tracks for a neighbor. The moderately priced **Holiday Inn Oceanside Marina** ★, 1401 Carmelo Dr. (www.holiday inn.com; ✆ **888/465-4329** or 760/231-7000), is clean and contemporary. For a seaside home away from home, check in with **Beachfront Only Vacation Rentals** (www. beachfrontonly.com; ✆ **760/453-2467**).

EASTERN SAN DIEGO COUNTY

The vast inland regions of San Diego encompass several cities, suburban communities, and state parks. A few are popular for day trips as well as overnight stays. The East County highlights include: **Escondido,** home to the **San Diego Zoo Safari Park;** the small mountain town of **Julian;** and the town of **Borrego Springs** in the **Anza-Borrego Desert.**

Essentials

GETTING THERE   To reach Escondido, 30 miles northeast of downtown, and Palomar Mountain, 67 miles northeast of downtown, drive north on Hwy. 15. You can make the trip northeast east to Julian on Highway 78 or I-8 to Highway 79; to reach Borrego Springs follow 79 North to Julian, then east on Highway 78.

VISITOR INFORMATION   For information on **Escondido** check www.downtown escondido.com. The **Julian Chamber of Commerce,** 2129 Main St. (www.julianca. com; *✆* **760/765-1857**), is open daily from 10am to 4pm. The **Borrego Springs Chamber of Commerce,** 786 Palm Canyon Dr. (www.borregospringschamber.com; *✆* **800/559-5524** or 760/767-5555), is open Monday through Saturday, 9am to 5pm.

Escondido

35 miles NE of San Diego

Best known as the home of the **San Diego Zoo Safari Park** (see below), Escondido is a city of 138,000, surrounded by citrus and avocado groves (neighboring Fallbrook is known as the "avocado capital of the world"). With few good hotels or restaurants it's not yet an overnight destination, but plans are in the works for a major hotel.

San Diego Zoo Safari Park ★★★ ZOO   Thirty miles north of San Diego, outside of Escondido, this "zoo of the future" transports visitors to the African plains and other faraway landscapes. It's a magnificent park covering 1,800 acres in the dry, stark countryside, where many of the animals roam freely in vast enclosures, allowing giraffes to interact with antelopes, much as they would in Africa. Getting here is a trek—it takes nearly an hour to cover the 35 miles from downtown San Diego—so plan to spend much of the day. Think twice in summer, however, as it can be blazing hot. Sunhats, sunscreen, and comfortable walking shoes are necessities year round. Arrive the moment the park opens (9am) to skip waiting in line for **Africa Tram Safari** (included with admission), aboard an open-air, soft-wheeled tram. The 2½-mile circuit, which takes about 30 minutes, brings guests close to giraffes, water buffalos, zebras, and dozens of other species roaming as if in the Serengeti.

Active, energetic types find plenty to do here, from hiking to the **Elephant Overlook** and **Lion Camp,** to flying above the African and Asian enclosures on the **Flightline** zipline ($75, minimum age 8), to climbing rope bridges and aerial tightropes in the **Jungle Ropes Safari** ($55, minimum age 7). Combo tickets for activities are available. The commercial hub of the park is **Nairobi Village,** with souvenir stores and several spots for mediocre dining, but even here animal exhibits are interesting, including the **nursery area,** a **petting station,** the **lowland gorillas,** and the **African Aviary.** There's an amphitheater for bird shows, and other animal encounters are scheduled throughout the park; **Cheetah Run** is a particular highlight, with the world's fastest land mammal chasing after a mechanical lure. New in 2014, the **Tiger Trail** passes through a simulated Sumatran environment containing orangutans, rhinos, elephants, and majestic Sumatran tigers who prowl about and swim in a deep pool. There are a variety of up-close safaris (some are seasonal with varying age requirements); prices start at $105, and reservations are required (*✆* 619/718-3000).

15500 San Pasqual Valley Rd., Escondido. www.sandiegozoo.org. *✆* **760/747-8702.** Admission $46 adults, $36 children 3–11, free for children 2 and under and active-duty military; discounted 2-day passes can be used for both the zoo and Zoo Safari Park; children 11 and under are free in Oct Daily 9am–4pm (grounds close at 5pm); extended hours during summer and Festival of Lights (2 weekends in Dec). Parking $10, RV $15. Take I-15 to Via Rancho Pkwy. follow signs for about 3 miles.

Stone Brewing World Bistro & Gardens ★★★ INTERNATIONAL   A gem with a super-cool, Asian-influenced modern design, this is the creation of one of San Diego's most famous microbreweries. Beer aficionados travel here to tour the brewery, sample more than 30 draft beers, plus a huge bottle list, from an international roster of craft brewers, dine on international cuisine ranging from chicken *tikka masala* to duck tacos, to mac 'n' beer cheese, and take a strolls through the gardens, pint in hand.

1999 Citracado Pkwy. www.stoneworldbistro.com. *℃* **760/294-7866.** Reservations recommended for weekends. Main courses $11–$19 lunch, $15–$33 dinner. Sun–Thurs 11am–11pm; Fri–Sat 11am–midnight (kitchen closes nightly at 10pm).

Julian

60 miles NE of San Diego; 31 miles W of Anza-Borrego Desert State Park

Radiating the aura of the Old West, Julian offers an abundance of early California history, quaint Victorian streets, fresh air, and friendly people. It's most popular in autumn, when apple orchards produce plenty of fruit for the town's locally famous apple pies. Rest assured, apple pies are baking around town year-round. But autumn is perfect; the air is crisp and bracing. Julian gets dusted (sometimes buried) by snow during the winter; spring prods patches of daffodils into bloom.

The best way to experience Julian is on foot. Two or three blocks of Main Street offer plenty of diversions for an afternoon or longer. The **Julian Drug Store & Miner's Diner,** 2130 Main St. (*℃* 760/765-3753), is an old-style soda fountain serves sparkling sarsaparilla, burgers, and sandwiches. Built in 1886, the brick structure is one of the many well-preserved buildings in town on the National Historic Register; it's jam-packed with local memorabilia. The **Eagle and High Peak Mine,** built around 1870, at the end of C Street (*℃* 760/765-0036), offers an educational look at the town's one-time economic mainstay. At the **Smith Ranch,** 2353 Ethelwyn Lane (www.pioneerways.com; *℃* 760/765-2288), you can ride on a narrow-gauge railroad, explore a gold mine (then pan for gold), and get an immersion in the old-time ways.

Within 10 miles of Julian are numerous hiking trails that traverse rolling meadows, high chaparral, and oak and pine forests. The 26,000-acre **Cuyamaca Rancho State Park,** along Highway 79 between Julian and I-8 has creeks and wildflower-enhanced meadows, and more than 100 miles of trails for hikers, bikers, and horseback riders. For a map and further information about park status, stop in at the **park headquarters** (www.parks.ca.gov; *℃* 916/653-6995), or check in with the **Cuyamaca Rancho State Park Interpretive Association** (www.cuyamacasp.org; *℃* 619/756-5354). Eight miles south of Julian (and not part of the state park), **Lake Cuyamaca** has a tiny community at the 4,600-foot elevation that centers on lake activities—primarily boating and fishing for trout (stocked year-round), bass, catfish, bluegill, and sturgeon.

WHERE TO DINE

Before you leave, you must try Julian's apple pies. You'll need to sample them all to judge whether the best pies come from **Mom's Pie House** ★, 2119 Main St. (www.momspiesjulian.com; *℃* 760/765-2472); the **Julian Pie Company** ★, 2225 Main St. (www.julianpie.com; *℃* 760/765-2449); **Apple Alley Bakery** ★, a nook on Main Street between Washington and B streets (*℃* 760/765-2532); or the **Julian Café & Bakery** ★, 2112 Main St. (*℃* 760/765-2712). A number of **roadside fruit stands and orchards** dot the Julian hills; during autumn they're open all day, every day; in the off-season, some might open only on weekends or close entirely. Depending on the season, most stands sell apples, pears, peaches, cider, jams, jellies, and other homemade foodstuffs. Ask San Diegans who regularly make excursions to Julian, and they'll concur: No trip would be complete without stopping for a loaf (or three) of bread from **Dudley's Bakery,** 30218 Hwy. 78, Santa Ysabel (www.dudleysbakery.com; *℃* 760/765-0488). Loaves are stacked high, and folks are often lined up at the counter clamoring for the nearly 20 varieties of bread baked fresh daily since 1963.

Dudley's is open Thursday through Sunday from 9am to 5pm, and on Monday from 9am to 1pm.

WHERE TO STAY

The **Julian Bed & Breakfast Guild** (www.julianbnbguild.com; ℃ **760/765-1555**) has about 10 members and is a terrific resource for locating accommodations that suit your taste. **Pine Hills Lodge,** 2960 La Posada Way (www.pinehillslodge.com; ℃ **760/765-1100**), is a rustic getaway about 2 miles from town that serves a Sunday.

Orchard Hill Country Inn ★★★ This AAA Four-Diamond inn is the most upscale lodging in Julian—a surprisingly posh, two-story Craftsman lodge and 12 cottages on a hill overlooking the town.

2502 Washington St., at Second St. www.orchardhill.com. ℃ **800/716-7242** or 760/765-1700. 22 units. $195–$275 double; from $295 for cottages. 2-night minimum stay some weekends. Rates include breakfast and afternoon hors d'oeuvres. **Amenities:** Restaurant; bar; bikes.

ANZA-BORREGO DESERT STATE PARK ★★★

90 miles NE of San Diego; 31 miles E of Julian

The sweeping 650,000-acre Anza-Borrego Desert State Park lies mostly within San Diego County (in fact it makes up more than 20% of the county). A sense of timelessness pervades this landscape—the desert is home to fossils and rocks dating from 540 million years ago; human beings arrived about 12,000 years ago. The terrain ranges in elevation from 15 to 6,100 feet above sea level. It incorporates dry lakebeds, sandstone canyons, granite mountains, palm groves fed by year-round springs, and more than 600 kinds of desert plants. After the winter rains, thousands of wildflowers burst into bloom, transforming the desert into a brilliant palette of pink, lavender, red, orange, and yellow. When planning a trip here, keep in mind that temperatures rise to as high as 125°F (52°C) in July and August. Winter days are very comfortable, with temps averaging 70°F (21°C) December through January, but nighttime temps can drop to freezing. Hypothermia is as big a killer out here as the heat.

In **Borrego Springs,** a town completely surrounded by the state park, Palm Canyon Drive is the main drag. Christmas Circle surrounds a grassy park at the entry to town; the "mall" is just west and contains many of the town's businesses. The architecturally striking **Anza-Borrego Desert State Park Visitor Center** (www.parks.ca.gov; ℃ **760/767-5311**) lies 2 miles west of Borrego Springs; it's cut into the side of a hill and is totally invisible from the road. In addition

> ### Desert Blooms in Anza-Borrego
>
> The natural beauty of the Anza-Borrego Desert State Park is enhanced by the almost magical appearance of **desert wildflowers ★★** in the spring: blazing star, wild heliotrope, prickly poppy, Spanish needles, scarlet bugler, desert lily (the holy grail for aficionados), and more. The full bloom is only for 2 to 6 weeks—usually from late February through March, depending on winter rainfall. The park provides a **wildflower hotline** (℃ **760/767-4684**). Or check www.parks.ca.gov for the latest information.

TIJUANA: GOING south of the border

Vibrant, chaotic, colorful, and confounding, Tijuana ("Tee-wanna") fluctuates in popularity with travelers. On the one hand, its border-Mexican character is utterly fascinating; on the other, it can be intimidating. The city has some fabulous restaurants and a burgeoning art and music scene, and it's the entry point for a chain of beach towns along a coastline reminiscent of Big Sur. If all that sounds interesting, follow these tips:

Take a Tour Tijuana is 17 miles south of downtown San Diego. You can walk or drive through the Mexican border into Tijuana, but it's a lot easier for first-timers to go with **Five Star Tours** (www.sdsuntours.com; ℂ **619/ 232-5040**), which runs bus tours to Tijuana and down the coast. Returning through the U.S. border can be time-consuming. Waits of 2 hours or more are common.

Legalities You must have a valid **passport** or passport card to return through the U.S. border. A driver's license or other ID won't work.

Information See the site of the Tijuana Convention & Visitors Bureau (www.seetijuana.com). If you run into problems in Tijuana, get English-speaking tourist assistance by dialing ℂ **078;** it operates 24/7. Mexico's "911" is ℂ **066.**

Helpful Tips The city does not take time for an afternoon siesta; you'll always find shops and restaurants open, as well as people in the streets. Most streets are safe for walking; observe the same precautions you would in any large city. Most people who deal with the traveling public speak English, often very well.

Currency The Mexican currency is the peso, but you can easily visit Tijuana without changing money; dollars are accepted just about everywhere. Visa and MasterCard are accepted in many places, but never assume they will be; ask before dining or purchasing.

to a small museum with interactive exhibits, it supplies information, maps, and audiovisual presentations. s, contact the **Borrego Springs Chamber of Commerce,** 786 Palm Canyon Dr. (www.borregospringschamber.com; ℂ **800/559-5524** or 760/767-5555); it's open Monday through Saturday, 9am to 5pm.

PLANNING YOUR TRIP

G reat vacations begin with solid pre-trip research. This chapter contains practical information to help with that preparation; more specific details about navigating and finding local resources are in the "Essentials" section of both the Los Angeles and San Diego chapters.

WHEN TO GO

9

Tourism peaks during **summer,** when coastal hotels fill to capacity, restaurant reservations are scarce, and top attractions are packed with visitors and locals off from work or school. Summer can be stifling in the inland valleys, but the beach communities almost always remain comfortable. Moderate temperatures, fewer crowds, and lower hotel rates make travel to Southern California most pleasurable from early **autumn** to late **spring.** What rain the region gets generally falls between November and April and is practically unheard-of between May and November. Even in January—usually the wettest month—daytime temperatures reach into the mid-60s Fahrenheit (high teens Celsius) and sometimes higher.

So you can sunbathe throughout the year, but only die-hards and wet-suited surfers venture into the ocean in winter, when water temps hover around 50° to 55°F (10°–13°C). The water is warmest in summer and fall, usually about 65° to 70°F (18°–21°C), but even then the Pacific can be too chilly for many.

Contrary to the popular notion that Southern California has no seasons, the region has its own unique seasons. "May Gray" and "June Gloom" often shrouds the coast in fog—generated by inland heat meeting cooler coastal temperatures—until about noon and again by sunset. Less predictable are "the Santa Anas": hot, dry, winds that blow in from the desert a couple of times a year, usually in mid-autumn. The desiccating winds invariably bring warm temperatures, clear skies, and optimal surfing conditions, but can also cause disastrous wildfires.

Los Angeles' Average Temperatures

	JAN	FEB	MAR	APR	MAY	JUNE	JULY	AUG	SEPT	OCT	NOV	DEC
TEMP (°F)	66/48	68/50	69/51	71/54	73/57	77/60	82/63	84/64	82/63	78/59	73/53	68/50
TEMP (°C)	19/9	20/10	21/11	22/12	23/14	25/16	28/17	29/18	28/17	26/15	23/12	20/10

San Diego's Average Temperatures

	JAN	FEB	MAR	APR	MAY	JUNE	JULY	AUG	SEPT	OCT	NOV	DEC
TEMP (°F)	65/48	66/50	66/52	68/55	69/58	72/61	76/65	77/66	77/65	74/60	71/53	66/49
TEMP (°C)	18/8	18/10	18/11	20/12	20/14	22/16	24/18	25/18	25/18	23/15	21/11	18/9

GETTING AROUND

By Car

Los Angeles and San Diego are big, sprawling cities, and neither have public transportation systems that come near to the reach of Eastern cities, so driving is still usually the most efficient way to get around. (See individual city chapters for advice.) One thing to keep in mind is that California drivers tend to fall apart when it rains, especially during the first rain after few dry days, because oil builds up on the roads and rain turns them into giant Slip 'N Slides. Vehicles careening out of control during these rare wet spells keep the Highway Patrol and local news channels very busy. For up-to-the-minute traffic info, call ℂ **511** or visit quickmap.dot.ca.gov.

If you somehow end up stranded on a Los Angeles freeway, the **Freeway Service Patrol** (www.metro.net/projects/fsp) may be able to help. Drivers with the free service can jump-start a dead battery, refill your radiator, change a flat tire, or provide a gallon of gasoline; they can also tow you to a safe location off the freeway. Similar service is provided during commute hours in San Diego, Orange, Riverside and San Bernardino counties. Call ℂ **511** to request aid.

Note on driving to Mexico: If you plan to drive to Mexico, check with your insurance company at home to verify exactly the limits of your policy. Even if your insurance covers areas south of the border, you should plan to purchase Mexican car insurance because of the two countries' different liability standards. Baja California Norte, just south of San Diego, requires insurance with a minimum of $143,000 liability; Baja California Sur requires more than $335,000 liability. Mexican car insurance is available from various agencies (visible to drivers heading into Mexico) on the U.S. side of the border, or online from agencies such as Baja Bound (www.bajabound.com) or Lewis and Lewis (www.mexicanautoinsurance.com).

CAR RENTALS

Cars rented from most major agencies on the U.S. side are not allowed to cross the border into Mexico. Two San Diego-area rental firms permitting border crossings are **International Car Rental** (www.intlcarrentals.com; ℂ **619/428-5100**), which provides shuttle service to its San Ysidro office (near the last U.S. exit off I-5 and I-805) from the San Diego airport, and **Sun Diego Van & Car Rental** (www.sundiegocarrental.com; ℂ **866/704-8267**), which has an office near the airport.

DRIVING RULES

California has a **seat-belt law** for both drivers and passengers, so buckle up before you venture out. State law requires drivers to use **hands-free cell phone** technology (drivers age 17 and under cannot use a cell phone at all); **text messaging** while driving is also illegal. The first-offense fine for both is $20, but additional penalties could more than triple the fee. **Smoking in a car with a child** age 17 and under is punishable by a $100 fine; an officer cannot pull you over for this, but can tack it onto another infraction. You may **turn right at a red light after stopping** unless a sign says otherwise; likewise, you can turn left on a red light from a one-way street onto another one-way street after coming to a full stop. **Pedestrians have the right of way** at all times, not just in crosswalks, so stop for pedestrians who have stepped off the curb.

Penalties in California for **drunk driving** are among the toughest in the country, including immediate suspension of licenses for those whose blood alcohol concentration is over .08%. Speed limits on freeways, particularly Highway 8 through San Diego's Mission Valley, are aggressively enforced after dark, partly to catch intoxicated drivers. Random checkpoints set up on main beach arteries to catch drunk drivers are also not uncommon.

GASOLINE

You'll find gas stations everywhere, and almost all accept credit cards; many accept cards at the pump even after the station has closed. At press time, gasoline (also known as gas, but never petrol), cost about $4 per gallon in Los Angeles and San Diego. Taxes are included in the price on the pump. One U.S. gallon equals 3.8 liters or .85 imperial gallons.

PARKING

Parking rules are aggressively enforced in Los Angeles and San Diego, with substantial fines ($60 and up) and towing possible. Street-parking rules are color-coded by painted curbs, as follows:

o **Red curb:** No stopping at any time.
o **Blue curbs:** Parking for people with disabilities—note the fine for parking without a disabled placard or license plate is $363 in Los Angeles, $450 in San Diego (out-of-state disabled plates are okay).
o **White curb:** Passenger loading zone; time limit is 3 minutes (10 minutes in front of a hotel).
o **Yellow curb:** Commercial loading zone—trucks and commercial vehicles only between 6am and 6pm Monday through Saturday; other vehicles may stop for 3 minutes to unload passengers (from 6pm–6am and all day Sunday, anyone can park in a yellow curb zone unless a sign indicates a 24-hour zone).
o **Green curb:** Short-term parking, usually 15 or 30 minutes as posted.
o **Unpainted curbs:** Subject to parking rules on signs or meters.

By Bus

Los Angeles and San Diego have extensive local and regional bus networks; see "Essentials" for each chapter. For travel to other cities, see "Getting There," earlier in this chapter.

By Train

In addition to its national routes, **Amtrak** (www.amtrak.com; ✆ **800/872-7245;** 001/215-856-7953 outside the U.S.) travels several Pacific Coast routes, including the *Coast Starlight* between Seattle and Los Angeles, a scenic 34-hour journey with 26 California stops, starting at $115 for one seat to $574 for a "roomette" with bunk beds for two. The *Pacific Surfliner* connects San Diego with San Luis Obispo, stopping in L.A., Santa Barbara, and 30 other destinations. Sample one-way fares: L.A.-San Diego (2¾ hours), $37; L.A.-Santa Barbara (2½ hours), $31; San Diego-Santa Barbara (5½ hours), $42.

[Fast FACTS]

ATMs/Banks San Diego (p. 176).

Business Hours Banks are open weekdays from 9am to 4pm or later, and sometimes Saturday morning. Stores in shopping malls tend to operate from 10 or 11am until about 9pm weekdays and until 6pm weekends, and are open on secondary holidays.

Customs Every visitor 21 years of age or older may bring in, free of duty, the following: (1) 1 U.S. quart of alcohol; (2) 200 cigarettes, 50 cigars (but not from Cuba), or 3 pounds of smoking tobacco; and (3) $100 worth of gifts. Various items are forbidden; check the complete list at www.cbp. gov/travel/international-visitors/kbyg/prohibited-restricted. International visitors may carry in or out up to $10,000 in U.S. or foreign currency; larger sums must be declared to U.S. Customs. For details regarding U.S. Customs and Border Protection, consult your nearest U.S. embassy or consulate, or U.S. Customs (www.cbp.gov).

Disabled Travelers Organizations that offer a vast range of resources and assistance to travelers with disabilities include **MossRehab** (www.mossresourcenet.org; ℰ **800/225-5667**), the **American Foundation for the Blind** (www.afb.org; ℰ **800/232-5463**), and the **Society for Accessible Travel & Hospitality** (www.

sath.org; ℰ **212/447-7284**). **Access-Able Travel Source** (www.access-able.com) offers a comprehensive database of destination-specific access information and links to resources.

Air Ambulance Card (ℰ **877/424-7633** or 205/297-0060; www.air ambulancecard.com) will fly you home to the hospital of your choice if you need medical assistance while traveling; plans start at $195 per year.

Many travel agencies offer customized tours and itineraries for travelers with disabilities. Among them are **Flying Wheels Travel** (www.flyingwheelstravel. com; ℰ **877/451-5006** or 507/451-5005) and **Accessible Journeys** (www.disability travel.com; ℰ **800/846-4537** or 610/521-0339).

Doctors & Dentists See "Fast Facts" in Los Angeles (p. 31) and San Diego (p. 176).

Drinking Laws The legal age for purchase and consumption of alcoholic beverages in California is 21. **Proof of age is a necessity**—it's requested at bars, nightclubs, and restaurants, even from those well into their 30s and 40s. Beer, wine, and hard liquor are sold daily from 6am to 2am and are available in most markets.

Do not carry open containers of alcohol in your car or at any public area not zoned for alcohol

consumption—the police can fine you on the spot. **Alcohol is forbidden at all city beaches, boardwalks, and coastal parks.**

Electricity Like Canada, the United States uses 110 to 120 volts AC (60 cycles), compared to 220 to 240 volts AC (50 cycles) in most of Europe, Australia, and New Zealand. Most low-voltage electronics such as laptops and cellphone chargers will do fine with 110 volt--check with the manufacturer to be sure. Downward converters that change 220 to 240 volts to 110 to 120 volts are difficult to find in the United States, so bring one with you. Small adaptors change a European-style prong to fit a North American flat one- or three-prong outlet. Convertors and adaptors can be hard to find, so bring them with you.

Embassies & Consulates All embassies are in the nation's capital, Washington, D.C. Check www. embassy.org/embassies for your nation's location or call information in Washington, D.C. (ℰ **202/555-1212**) See "Fast Facts" in Los Angeles (p. 32) and San Diego (p. 176) for information on Consulates.

Emergencies Call ℰ **911** for fire, police, and ambulance.

Health Tap water is safe to drink but many travelers prefer bottled water. Fish and shellfish should be

271

cooked, though sushi, sashimi, ceviche, and seafood cocktails are safe to be eaten raw in reputable restaurants. Check with your insurance company before traveling to see it your policy covers medical and hospital services. Contact the **International Association for Medical Assistance to Travellers** (www.iamat.org; ℂ **716/754-4883** or 416/652-0137 in Canada) for tips on travel and health concerns, and for lists of local doctors. See "Fast Facts" in Los Angeles (p. 32) for information on local doctors, dentists, and hospitals.

Holidays Banks, city services, schools, and some offices are typically closed for federal holidays including: New Year's Day, January 1); Martin Luther King Day (third Monday in Jan.), Washington's Birthday (third Monday in Feb.); Memorial Day (last Mon. in May) Independence Day, July 4; Labor Day (first Mon. in Sept.; Columbus Day second Mon. in Oct.; Veterans Day (Nov. 11); Thanksgiving Day, (fourth Thurs. in Nov.); Christmas Day, December 25

Insurance For information on traveler's insurance, trip cancellation insurance, and medical insurance while traveling, please visit www.frommers.com/planning.

Internet & Wi-Fi More and more hotels, resorts, airports, cafes, and retailers are going Wi-Fi (wireless fidelity), becoming

"hotspots" that offer free high-speed Wi-Fi access or charge a small fee for usage. To find other public Wi-Fi hotspots, check www.jiwire.com; its Hotspot Finder holds the world's largest directory of public wireless hotspots. If you don't have a computer with you, try www.cybercaptive.com or www.cybercafe.com to hunt for publicly accessed computers. Many **public libraries** have computers available.

Legal Aid While driving, if you are pulled over for a minor infraction (such as speeding), never attempt to pay the fine directly to a police officer; this could be construed as attempted bribery, a serious crime. Once arrested, a person can make one telephone call to a party of his or her choice. International visitors should call their embassy or consulate.

LGBT Travel See "Fast Facts" in Los Angeles (p. 32) and San Diego (p. 177).

Mail At press time, domestic postage rates were 32¢ for a postcard and 45¢ for a letter. For international mail, a first-class letter of up to 1 ounce costs $1.05 (85¢ to Canada); a first-class postcard costs the same as a letter. For more information, go to www.usps.com and click on "Calculate Postage." Always include zip codes when mailing items in the U.S. If you don't know your zip code, visit www.usps.com/zip4.

Mobile Phones You may be able to use your cellphone if it is compatible. Take a look at your wireless company's coverage on its website before heading out. If you need to stay in touch at a destination where you know your phone won't work, **rent** a phone that does from **InTouch USA** (www.intouchglobal.com; ℂ **800/872-7626** or 703/222-7161). InTouch offers 99¢ rates for incoming and outgoing calls. If you're not from the U.S., you'll be appalled at the poor reach of the **GSM (Global System for Mobile Communications) wireless network,** which is used by much of the rest of the world. Your phone will probably work in most major U.S. cities; it definitely won't work in many rural areas. To see where GSM phones work in the U.S., check out www.t-mobile.com/coverage. And you may or may not be able to send SMS (text messaging) home.

If you have Web access while traveling, consider a broadband-based telephone service (in technical terms, **Voice-over Internet Protocol,** or **VoIP**) such as **Skype** (www.skype.com) or **Vonage** (www.vonage.com), which allow you to make free international calls from your laptop. Neither service requires the people you're calling to also have that service (though there are fees if they do not). Check the websites for details. **WhatsApp** is an app for iPhone, BlackBerry, Android, Windows Phone, and Nokia, free for the first year then 99 cents per year and Viber is a free app for iPhone and Android. You can use them to text people internationally for free (over WiFi), and Viber allows international calls over WiFi.

Money & Costs Frommer's lists prices in local currency. The currency conversions quoted here were correct at press time. However, rates fluctuate; before departing, consult a currency exchange website such as www.xe.com and www.oanda.com/currency/converter to check up-to-the-minute rates. It's always advisable to bring money in a variety of forms on a vacation: a mix of cash, credit cards, or a prepaid debit card. Traveler's checks are rarely used, and not all banks exchange currency. You should also exchange enough petty cash to cover airport incidentals, tipping, and transportation to your hotel before you leave home, or withdraw money upon arrival at an airport ATM.

Packing Evenings can be cooler and damper than many visitors anticipate. Be prepared with a light coat or sweater. Dress is casual nearly everywhere except at the fanciest restaurants and resorts.

Pharmacies See "Fast Facts" in San Diego (p. 177).

Safety See "Fast Facts" in San Diego (p. 177).

Senior Travel Nearly every attraction offers a senior discount; age requirements vary. Public transportation and movie theaters also have reduced rates. Don't be shy about asking for discounts, but always carry identification, such as a driver's license, that shows your date of birth.

Smoking Smoking is prohibited all indoor public places, including hotels, and some outdoor places In 1998, California enacted legislation prohibiting smoking in all restaurants and bars, except those with outdoor seating—and some places don't allow smoking anywhere around the premises. *Be forewarned:* Fines start at $100.

Taxes The United States has no value-added tax (VAT) or other indirect tax at the national level. Every state, county, and city may levy its own local tax on all purchases, including hotel and restaurant checks and airline tickets. These taxes will not appear on price tags. In Southern California, sales tax in restaurants and shops is 8%. Hotel taxes range between 10½% and 15%.

Tipping Tips are a very important part of many workers' income, and gratuities are the standard way of showing appreciation for services provided. (Tipping is certainly not compulsory if the service is poor.) In hotels, tip **bellhops** at least $1 per bag ($2–$3 if you have a lot of luggage) and tip the **chamber staff** $1 to $2 per day (more if you've left a disaster area for him or her to clean up). Tip the **doorman** or **concierge** only if he or she has provided you with some specific service (for example, calling a cab for you or obtaining difficult-to-get theater tickets). Tip the **valet-parking attendant** at least $1 every time you get your car.

In restaurants, bars, and nightclubs, tip **service staff and bartenders** 15% to 20% of the check, tip **checkroom attendants** $1 per garment, and tip **valet-parking attendants** at least $1 per vehicle.

THE VALUE OF THE DOLLAR VS. OTHER POPULAR CURRENCIES

US$	Aus$	Can$	Euro €	NZ$	UK £
$1	A$.1.09	C$1.09	1.29€	NZ$1.21	.63£

As for other service personnel, tip **cabdrivers** 15% of the fare; tip **skycaps** at airports at least $1 per bag ($2–$3 if you have a lot of luggage); and tip **hairdressers** and **barbers** 15% to 20%.

Toilets   You won't find public toilets or "restrooms" on the streets in most cities, but they can be found in hotel lobbies, bars, restaurants, museums, department stores, train and bus stations, and service stations. Large hotels and fast-food restaurants are often the best bet for clean facilities. Restaurants and bars in resorts or heavily visited areas may reserve their restrooms for patrons.

Index

See also Accommodations and
Restaurant indexes, below.

General Index

A

The Abbey (Los Angeles), 136
Abbot Kinney Boulevard (Los
Angeles), 122
A Bug's Land (Disney California
Adventure), 144–145
Accommodations. *See also*
Accommodations Index
Del Mar, 260
Disneyland, 146–148
Julian, 266
Laguna Beach, 157
Long Beach, 152–153
Los Angeles, 2, 32–56
Newport Beach, 156
North County, 262
Oceanside, 263
San Clemente, 158
San Diego, 5, 179–196
Santa Barbara, 169–170
Santa Catalina, 163–164
Adamson House (Los Angeles),
114
Adventureland (Disneyland), 143
Aero Theatre (Los Angeles), 132
Ahmanson Theatre (Los Angeles),
129–130
Air tours, Los Angeles, 114
Air travel
Anaheim, 140
Los Angeles, 18
San Diego, 172–173
Akbar (Los Angeles), 138
American Cinematheque (Los
Angeles), 132
The American Comedy Co. (San
Diego), 254
American Indian Arts Marketplace
(Los Angeles), 31
America Tropical Interpretive
Center (Los Angeles), 109
Amoeba Music (Los Angeles), 126
Amtrak, 270
Los Angeles, 19, 29
San Diego, 173
Santa Barbara, 165
Angelino Heights (Los Angeles),
96
Annenberg Community Beach
House (Los Angeles), 79
Annenberg Space for
Photography (Los Angeles), 83
Anza-Borrego Desert State Park,
266–267
Aquarium of the Pacific (Long
Beach), 151–152
Aquatica by SeaWorld (San
Diego), 231
ArcLight Cinemas (Los Angeles),
133

Arroyo Burro Beach County Park
(Santa Barbara), 168
Arroyo Terrace (Los Angeles), 105
Athenaeum Music & Arts Library
(San Diego), 232
Autry National Center of the
American West (Los Angeles),
91
Avalon (Santa Catalina), 161
The Avalon Hollywood, 133
Avila Adobe (Los Angeles), 109

B

The Baked Potato (Los Angeles),
134–135
Balboa Island, 156
Balboa Park (San Diego), 14,
214–223, 235
Balboa Park Municipal Golf
Course (San Diego), 244
Balboa Pavilion & Fun Zone (San
Diego), 155
Balboa Peninsula, 155
Balboa Theatre (San Diego), 253
Ballooning and scenic flights, San
Diego, 242
Banning House Lodge (Santa
Catalina), 163
Barnes & Noble (Los Angeles),
125
Barnes & Noble (San Diego), 249
Baseball, 138, 257
Basketball, Los Angeles, 138
Bay Books (San Diego), 249
Bayshore Bikeway (San Diego),
242
Beaches
Los Angeles, 114–115
North County, 258, 259, 261
San Diego, 238–242
Santa Barbara, 168
Santa Catalina, 163
Belmont Park (San Diego), 228
Bergamot Station (Los Angeles),
125
Beverly Boulevard (Los Angeles),
120
The Beverly Center (Los Angeles),
123
Beverly Hills. *See* L.A.'s Westside
& Beverly Hills
Biking
Los Angeles, 114, 117
San Diego, 242–243
Santa Barbara, 165
Birch Aquarium at Scripps (San
Diego), 232, 238
Birch North Park Theatre (San
Diego), 253
Black's Beach (San Diego), 241–
242
The Boardwalk (Knott's Berry
Farm), 150
Boating and sailing. *See also*
Kayaking
Los Angeles, 118–119
San Diego, 243, 257
Santa Barbara, 169

Bolsa Chica Ecological Reserve
(Huntington Beach), 155
Book Soup (Los Angeles), 125
Botanical Building and Lily Pond
(San Diego), 216
Boyle Heights (Los Angeles),
107–108
The Bradbury Building (Los
Angeles), 9, 96
Brickyard Pub (Los Angeles),
136–137
Brinkerhoff Avenue (Santa
Barbara), 169
Buena Vista Street (Disney
California Adventure), 145
Bungalow Heaven (Los Angeles),
105
Buses and shuttles
Los Angeles, 19, 20–21, 28
San Diego, 173–175
Bus and van tours, 113, 237

C

Cabrillo National Monument (San
Diego), 16, 228, 230, 238
Cafe-Club Fais Do-Do (Los
Angeles), 135
Calendar of events
Los Angeles, 29–31
San Diego, 178–179
California African American
Museum (Los Angeles), 96
California Science Center (Los
Angeles), 98
California Surf Museum
(Oceanside), 262–263
Camera Obscura (Los Angeles),
79, 82
Camp Snoopy (Knott's Berry
Farm), 150
Capitol Records Building (Los
Angeles), 91
Carlsbad, 258, 260–262
Cars Land (Disney California
Adventure), 145
Car travel and rentals, 269–270
Los Angeles, 19, 26–27
San Diego, 173, 175
Casinos, San Diego County, 256
Catalina Island JazzTrax Festival,
31
Catalina Island Museum, 162
Cathedral of Our Lady of the
Angels (Los Angeles), 98
Cellphones, 272
Central Library (San Diego), 223
Charles F. Lummis House (El
Alisal) and Garden (Los
Angeles), 98–99
Chase Palm Park (Santa Barbara),
166
Children's Pool (San Diego), 241
Chinatown, Los Angeles, 108–109
Chinese New Year (Los Angeles),
29, 109
Chino Farms (San Diego), 197
Christmas, Los Angeles, 31

Accommodations— San Diego & environs

Restaurants— Los Angeles & environs

Restaurants— San Diego & environs